Smith and Roberson's Business Law
Twelfth Edition

Richard A. Mann

Professor of Business Law

The University of North Carolina at Chapel Hill

Member of the North Carolina Bar

Barry S. Roberts

Professor of Business Law

The University of North Carolina at Chapel Hill

Member of the North Carolina and Pennsylvania Bars

Prepared by

Peter T. Kahn

University of Minnesota, Twin Cities

THOMSON

SOUTH-WESTERN

WEST

Australia · Canada · Mexico · Singapore · Spain · United Kingdom · United States

THOMSON

SOUTH-WESTERN

WEST

Study Guide for Smith and Roberson's Business Law, Twelfth Edition

Richard A. Mann and Barry S. Roberts

VP/Team Director:
Mike Roche

Sr. Acquisitions Editor:
Rob Dewey

Developmental Editor:
Bob Sandman

Marketing Manager:
Nicole Moore

Sr. Production Editor:
Deanna Quinn

Manufacturing Coordinator:
Rhonda Utley

Media Technology Editor:
Vicky True

Media Developmental Editor:
Peggy Buskey

Media Production Editor:
Mark Sears

Printer:
Phoenix Color – BTP

ISBN: 0-324-15854-8

CONTENTS

PURPOSE OF THE STUDY GUIDE

PURPOSE OF THE STUDY GUIDE

Students in college business law courses are often studying law for the first time. As with other demanding, challenging areas of study, law uses a specialized vocabulary to convey complicated theories, concepts and principles. Such semantic and conceptual complexity poses difficulties. Acquiring a working understanding of the American legal system and its related fields of specific study is not an easy task.

For legal knowledge, presented in text materials and classroom lectures, to have value, students must apply their learning to everyday life experiences. Clearly, the purpose of introductory law courses is not to train or prepare students to become legal experts qualified to handle legal matters with the same degree of precision and expertise as an attorney. The realistic goals of "first-exposure" courses in law are limited to presenting the law, its terminology and basic principles, in a manner that enables students to: understand the legal system they are part of; apply the terms and concepts they learn to their own lives; consider law as a future career; and know how to effectively seek professional legal assistance when the need arises.

This *Study Guide* was written with these goals in mind. Used properly, the *Study Guide* will prove to be an invaluable learning tool in conjunction with textual readings and classroom instruction.

HOW TO USE THE STUDY GUIDE

By keeping pace with in-class lectures and text reading assignments with related *Study Guide* chapters, students will receive the most beneficial use of the *Study Guide*. Completing *Study Guide* assignments topically concurrent with classroom instruction and text material will aid students in comprehending the text as well as provide a useful frame of reference for organizing class notes. *Study Guide* assignments also help in exam review and preparation.

The *Study Guide* format is designed with assignments keyed to each test chapter. Answers for *Study Guide* questions are included at the end of the *Guide*.

Each *Study Guide* chapter opens with a brief review of the textbook materials upon which the chapter is based. These introductory SCOPE NOTES explain the major theme of a chapter, how it relates to the preceding material, and how it is connected to subsequent chapters. Following the introductory comments, EDUCATIONAL OBJECTIVES focus student attention on important concepts and doctrines to remember from the chapter, which can prove useful in exam preparation.

The next section of the *Guide* is a CHAPTER OUTLINE. Its purpose is not to supplant careful reading of the text, but to assist in reading and studying the text by summarizing and highlighting major concepts of each chapter. The CHAPTER OUTLINE is followed by a series of objective questions intended to enhance student mastery of textual and classroom material. TRUE-FALSE questions have been written to facilitate understanding important legal doctrines and principles. To gain the most benefit from the TRUE-FALSE items, refrain from over-analyzing or reading too much into the questions. Thoughts, interpretations or assumptions that are not in the question itself should not be addressed. To challenge your understanding of the legal principles from which the TRUE-FALSE questions are drawn, rephrase false statements to become true and vice-versa.

MATCHING EXERCISES are the next category of questions. These items introduce terms and phrases that are vital to understanding various legal doctrines. The third set of objective exercises is MULTIPLE CHOICE items. They are designed to enhance comprehension of the important constructs underlying the relationship among the various doctrines and principles studied.

Individual *Study Guide* chapters close with CASE ANALYSIS problems. They are written to help students apply academic principles to factual situations. After conceptualizing the problem developed in the facts, students should identify the pertinent legal issues. Recalling relevant text and classroom material, reach a solution to the problem supported by sound, coherent reasoning. It is important to read the facts slowly and carefully while working through the short answer essay items. This is the only way to precisely define the nature of the dispute, its relevant legal issues, and reach a proper decision. This will help to achieve a real understanding of the legal concepts and issues discussed in the text.

After completing the *Study Guide* chapter, check your answers with the ANSWER KEY at the end of the *Guide*. Failure to understand why some answers are incorrect makes our study effort frustrating and fruitless.

The fifty-three text chapters are divided into ten separate Study Units. The *Study Guide* chapters comprising a single Study Unit close with RESEARCH QUESTIONS drawn from the material for that Unit. These QUESTIONS follow: Part One–The Legal Environment of Business, Chapters 1-8; Part Two–Contracts, Chapters 9-18; Part Three–Agency, Chapters 19-20; Part Four–Sales, Chapters 21-25; Part Five–Negotiable Instruments, Chapters 26-30; Part Six–Unincorporated Business Associations, Chapters 31-33, Part Seven–Corporations, Chapters 34-37; Part Eight–Debtor and Creditor Relations, Chapters 38-39, Part Nine–Regulation of Business, Chapters 40-48; and Part Ten–Property, Chapters 49-53. The RESEARCH QUESTIONS are designed to challenge our understanding of the basic principles, doctrines and concepts examined in the text by asking us to apply our knowledge to broader, contemporary social issues and problems.

HOW TO STUDY LAW:
TEST, CLASS AND EXAMS

HOW TO STUDY LAW: TEXT, CLASS AND EXAMS

In response to the often asked question, "How should I study for a course of this nature?" the authors would like to offer several suggestions. First, be at ease with confusion. Since law is a difficult field of study, it is rare that a single reading of the text or attending class without taking notes will lead to understanding the material sufficient to handle exams adequately. Usually, the first reading of the text and noteless class attendance results in total confusion. What do these strange, seemingly foreign terms mean? How do these entangled, complicated legal principles and doctrines fit together? DON'T BECOME DISCOURAGED! Practicing attorneys and legal educators rarely grasp all the ramifications of a particular court decision, legislative enactment or administrative ruling after an initial reading. It is only after many readings of the rule in question, prolonged study, review and discussion with colleagues that the fog of analytic confusion begins to lift. Be cautioned, however, that this short-term apparent comprehension may in many cases, give way to long-term mystification as the future implications, meanings and interpretations of the principle in question become clouded with speculation and uncertainty following social and political changes.

WRESTLING WITH THE TEXT

Review the Preface, Table of Contents and Introduction. This provides an overall perspective on the course and the approach to the material taken by the authors. Noting the organization of the text and determining how the chapters relate to one another enables students to see how text material relates to classroom discussion. The text chapters contain both narrative (definitional) and case (illustrative) material. The cases, since they apply the legal principles discussed in the preceding material, should be read after the narrative portion to reduce confusion and enhance understanding of the terms and doctrines developed in the chapter.

WRESTLING WITH EXAMS

Proper preparation for tests is crucial. Do not fall behind in text reading or class attendance. Keep up with text and lecture material. Concentrate on preparing for an exam over an extended period rather than attempting to cover the material just before the exam. Law is a complex, complicated area of study. Last minute cramming might trigger a sense of panic, lowering our concentration and detracting from effective studying. Outlining, underlining and note-taking are all effective study techniques. Taking complete class notes and participating in class discussion are also effective learning tools. They help to maintain attention and concentration, as well as indicate the material that the instructor considers most important–a clue to the content of an upcoming exam. Remember that most of the students in the class, and in some situations the instructor as well, may be just as confused about certain topics as you. Actively participating in class discussion will help to overcome this confusion.

Once an exam has begun, budget time carefully. Avoid spending too much time on a single question. Before answering an objective question (true-false, multiple choice, matching, etc.), make sure that its content is fully understood. Do not misread or overread a question. Read it slowly and carefully. Do not read into the question unstated interpretative information. Focus exclusively on the doctrine, principle or term addressed in the question.

For essay questions, several readings may be required. It might prove useful to diagram the facts. Make sure an answer addresses the significant legal issues and quotes relevant legal doctrines for its solution. Be sure to develop the reasons for an answer. Don't make the exam grader read your mind. Explain answers with full, pertinent information. For some questions, there might not be single correct answer but several possibly correct answers depending on how the item is analyzed. In those cases, a successful answer will depend more on the approaches taken in analyzing the issues and facts involved, and relating them to appropriate concepts, doctrines, and principles, than on arriving at a single, specific conclusion.

These suggestions are offered to assist understanding the material studied in your law course. Hopefully, they will make learning about the American legal system and its workings easier and more enjoyable. Happy reading in your journey through law.

Assistant Professor Peter T. Kahn, J.D.
Professor Dennis R. Hower, J.D.

Chapter 1

INTRODUCTION TO LAW

SCOPE NOTE

As modern life has become increasingly crowded, complicated, and subject to fast-paced change, our everyday affairs have become more subject to legal scrutiny and regulation. Our daily activities carry profound legal implications. It is therefore important to gain a working understanding of this all-pervasive influencing force in our lives: the American legal system. Chapter One introduces basic terminology, concepts and principles relevant to the nature, origin, and growth of our system of laws. Through understanding the foundations of our legal identities (rights/duties), we will have a useful frame of reference when studying the specific areas of legal inquiry contained in the subsequent chapters. What is law? What is the legal reasoning process? What are the sources of law? These and other fundamental topics are the focus of discussion in Chapter One.

EDUCATIONAL OBJECTIVES

1. Define law and discuss the importance of the phrase, "a society governed by a system of laws."

2. Enumerate the functions of and purposes served by law.

3. Discuss the "legal analysis" process.

4. Explain the interrelationships among law, morality, and justice.

5. Differentiate among the various classifications of law.

6. Identify the law-making bodies within the American legal system.

7. Develop the importance of stare decisis in the formation of common law.

8. Trace the historical origins of America's system of laws.

9. Evaluate the significance of the movement towards uniform, codified laws in various arenas of legal regulation.

10. Define and explain the significance of equity.

CHAPTER OUTLINE

I. Nature of Law
    A. Definition of Law–"a rule of civil conduct prescribed by the supreme power in a state, commanding what is right, and prohibiting what is wrong"
    B. Functions of Law–the primary function is to maintain stability in the social, political and economic system while at the same time permitting change
    C. Legal Sanctions–the means by which the law enforces the decisions of the courts
    D. Law and Morals–are NOT the same. Law and ethics are similar but they differ because rules of law have sanctions; rules of ethics do not
    E. Law and Justice–without law there can be no justice, but law is no guarantee of justice

II. Classification of Law
    A. Substantive and Procedural Law–substantive laws create, define, and regulate legal rights and obligations; procedural law sets the rules for enforcing the rights that exist by substantive law
    B. Public and Private Law–public law consists of constitutional, administrative, and criminal law; private law includes civil and business law
    C. Civil and Criminal Law–civil law defines duties that, if violated, constitute a wrong against the party injured by the violation; criminal law establishes duties that, if violated, constitute a wrong against the whole community

III. Sources of Law
    A. Constitutional Law–is established by the U.S. Constitution and the individual state constitutions
    B. Judicial Law–is established by Federal and State courts
        1. Common Law–also called case law (judge-made decisions)
        2. Equity–a supplementary court system to courts of law (common law) with its own remedies when no adequate remedy is available at common law
        3. Restatements of Law–the authoritative statement of the common law of the United States
    C. Legislative Law–is established by Federal and State enactments (statutes)
        1. Treaties–agreements between or among independent nations
        2. Executive Orders–laws issued by the President or by governors of the states

    D. Administrative Law–rules and regulations created by Federal, State and local administrative agencies

IV. Legal Analysis–the method of analyzing and briefing Federal and State judicial decisions

TRUE–FALSE: Circle true or false.

T   F   1. In order to survive, a civilized society must have an efficient and stable legal system.

T   F   2. Civil law is concerned with a wrong against an injured party while criminal law is concerned with a wrong against the whole community.

T   F   3. Stare decisis is a doctrine based on present court decisions following previous ones, and it should never be overturned.

T   F   4. A "maxim" is a general legal principle formulated over the years by courts of equity.

T   F   5. The source of American law superior to all other sources within a state is the state statutes.

T   F   6. The government has the burden of proving a defendant guilty of a crime beyond a reasonable doubt.

T   F   7. The source of American law to which all other sources are subordinate is a President's executive order.

T   F   8. The person who sues in a lawsuit is called the plaintiff, the person being sued is the defendant.

T   F   9. The Uniform Commercial Code was prepared and developed to make the law governing commercial transactions uniform within the various jurisdictions of Minnesota.

T   F   10. Legal sanctions are the means by which the law enforces the decisions of the courts.

T   F   11. Statutory law results from the independent decisions of the state and federal courts.

T   F   12. An authoritative statement of the common law of the United States can be found in the Restatements of Law.

KEY TERMS–MATCHING EXERCISE: Select the term that best completes each statement below.

1. Federal Trade Commission	7. Injunction	14. Equity
2. Federal statutes	8. Maxims	15. Stare decisis
3. Uniform Commercial Code	9. Money damages	16. Uniform Probate Code
4. Crime	10. U.S. Constitution	17. Administrative law
5. Substantive law	11. Tort law	18. Executive order
6. Procedural law	12. Restatements of Law	19. Rescission
	13. Legal sanctions	20. Treaty

_____ 1. A public wrong committed against society or the state.

_____ 2. The law that establishes rules for enforcing rights.

_____ 3. The remedy obtainable from a court of law for a civil lawsuit.

_____ 4. A guiding principle whereby a court follows previous decisions in deciding the present case before it.

_____ 5. A system of judicial relief that developed because of a lack of a proper remedy from the common law system.

_____ 6. One type of remedy available only in a court of equity requiring a party to refrain from doing a specific act.

_____ 7. The means by which the law enforces judgments.

_____ 8. The supreme law of the land.

_____ 9. The law that governs commercial transactions in most states.

_____ 10. The law that defines, creates, and regulates legal rights and duties.

_____ 11. An agreement between or among independent nations.

_____ 12. General legal principles formulated by equity courts.

_____ 13. Legislative laws passed by the Federal government.

_____ 14. A governor of a state may issue this source of law.

_____ 15. A remedy in equity in which a party is allowed to invalidate a contract.

MULTIPLE CHOICE: Select the alternative that best completes each statement below.

_____ 1. Equitable remedies include (a) specific performance (b) rescission (c) reformation (d) all of the above.

_____ 2. Federal Court decisions are not found in which of the following? (a) Federal Reporter (b) Lawyers Edition (c) Federal Supplement (d) North Western Reporter.

_____ 3. Of the following, the one with present authority over commercial transactions is the (a) Uniform Commercial Code (b) Uniform Sales Act (c) Uniform Bills of Lading Act (d) Bulk Sales Act.

_____ 4. Which of the following is most accurate? (a) All states have adopted the Uniform Commercial Code (b) The majority of states have adopted the Uniform Commercial Code (c) Only one state has not adopted the entire Uniform Commercial Code (d) All the statements are false.

_____ 5. An example of a legal sanction for a criminal conviction is (a) a fine (b) capital punishment (c) imprisonment (d) all of the above.

_____ 6. The branch of public law that deals with regulatory functions of the government as performed and supervised by public officials or commissions is (a) judicial law (b) legislative law (c) administrative law (d) none of the above.

_____ 7. Which of the following is not a "maxim" of equity? (a) Equity will not suffer a wrong to be without a remedy. (b) He who comes into equity must come with clean hands. (c) He who seeks equity must do equity. (d) Equity favors a forfeiture.

_____ 8. Law can best be classified into categories as (a) procedural or substantive (b) public or private (c) civil or criminal (d) all of the above.

_____ 9. That law that deals with the rights and powers of the government is (a) private law (b) public law (c) administrative law (d) tort law.

_____ 10. A source of law in our American legal system includes (a) the Federal Constitution (b) court decisions (c) municipal ordinances (d) all of the above.

_____ 11. Torts and contracts are examples of (a) private law (b) public law (c) criminal law (d) all of the above.

_____ 12. A remedy in equity in which a party to a contract is required to perform her obligations according to the contract is (a) an injunction (b) specific performance (c) reformation (d) rescission.

_____ 13. Public law consists of (a) administrative law (b) constitutional law (c) criminal law (d) all of the above.

CASE PROBLEMS–SHORT ESSAY ANSWERS:
Read each case problem carefully. When appropriate, answer by stating a Decision for the case and by explaining the rationale–Rule of Law–relied upon to support your decision.

1. Sarah is in her first year of law school. The teaching method used at the school is the "case method" in which the students read and analyze the reports of court decisions or "cases." One such case is *Brown v. Board of Education of Topeka*, 347 U.S. 686, 74 S. Ct. 686 (1954). Explain to Sarah how to find this case in a law library.

   Decision: _____

   _____

   Rule of Law: _____

   _____

2. Harold signs a contract to buy Maude's home. Although he has the funds, Harold breaches the contract. Maude sues, asking for the remedy of specific performance. Harold demands a jury trial. Is he entitled to one? Explain.

   Decision: _____

   _____

   Rule of Law: _____

   _____

3. Nathanial Horn was walking along the street when he was arrested and booked for arson. At his trial, the state brought evidence showing that Horn was indeed in the immediate area when the fire purportedly began. Has the state proven its case against Horn?

   Decision: _____

   _____

   Rule of Law: _____

   _____

4. Anita wins a civil suit against Baker for damages of $10,000. Two questions: Would this case be an example of an "action at law" or a "suit in equity"? Could Anita have a right to a jury trial?

Decision: _____

_____

Rule of Law: _____

_____

5. John Powers, one of the best-known swimmers in America, was walking near a river one day when he saw Mollie drowning. John, who was wearing a brand new shirt, didn't feel like getting wet. Would the State have a criminal action against John for not attempting to rescue Mollie? Explain.

Decision: _____

_____

Rule of Law: _____

_____

Chapter 2

BUSINESS ETHICS AND THE SOCIAL RESPONSIBILITY OF BUSINESS

SCOPE NOTE

This chapter focuses on the important areas of business ethics and its responsibilities to society. Ethical problems in business concerning the relationship of employers to employees, of business to its customers and its owners, of competing business to each other, and between business and society are identified. Various ethical theories are described and discussed. The chapter also examines ethical standards in business and concludes by explaining the ethical responsibilities of business.

EDUCATIONAL OBJECTIVES

1. Define and explain ethics and its subset–business ethics.

2. Explain the differences between law and ethics.

3. Identify, compare and contrast the various ethical theories.

4. Understand and explain the application of ethical theories to the world of business.

5. Explain and discuss Lawrence Kohlberg's stages of moral development.

6. Identify and explain the ethical responsibilities of business.

CHAPTER OUTLINE

I. Law versus Ethics–law and morality are not the same

II. Ethical Theories
   A. Ethical Fundamentalism–is a theory in which individuals look to a central authority or set of rules to guide them in ethical decision making
   B. Ethical Relativism–is a doctrine asserting that actions must be judged by what individuals feel is right or wrong for themselves
   C. Utilitarianism–is a doctrine that assesses good and evil in terms of the consequences of actions
   D. Deontology–the followers of this theory believe that actions cannot be measured simply by their results but must be judged by the means and motives as well
   E. Social Ethics Theories–assert that special obligations arise from the social nature of human beings
   F. Other Theories–several other ethical theories, including intuitionism, are mentioned

III. Ethical Standards in Business
   A. Choosing an Ethical System–these ethical theories provide insight into ethical decision making and help us formulate issues and resolve moral dilemmas
   B. Corporations as Moral Agents–the issue of whether or not corporations can or should be held morally accountable for their actions is debated

IV. Ethical Responsibilities of Business
   A. Regulation of Business–the American economic system of capitalism has failed to accomplish its objective of efficient resource allocation, and it cannot be relied on to achieve all of the social and public policy objectives required by a pluralistic democracy. Increased governmental intervention has been necessary to preserve the competitive process in our economic system and to achieve social goals extrinsic to the efficient allocation of resources
   B. Corporate Governance–the 5,000 largest U.S. corporations currently produce over half of the nation's gross national product. The economic power of these corporations is controlled by a handful of individuals. Therefore, many observers insist that corporations should have a responsibility to undertake projects that benefit society
   C. Arguments Against Social Responsibility
      1. Profitability–businesses are established to permit people to engage in profit making, not social activities
      2. Unfairness–whenever corporations stray from their designated role of profit maker, they take unfair advantage of company employees and shareholders
      3. Accountability–corporations are private institutions that are subject to a lower standard of accountability than are public ones

      4. Expertise–corporations may not possess a talent for recognizing or managing so-
cially useful activities
  D. Arguments in Favor of Social Responsibility
      1. The Social Contract–corporations, just like other members of society, owe a moral
debt to contribute to the overall well-being of society
      2. Less Government Regulation–the more responsibly corporations act, the less the
government must regulate them. For example, if companies use more reasonable and
voluntary methods of pollution control, then government will be less likely to legis-
late more regulations
      3. Long-Run Profits–when corporations are involved in social causes and problems, it
improves the corporation's image and makes good business sense; consumers support corporations with good images and avoid those with bad images

TRUE–FALSE: Circle true or false.

T   F   1. Ethics can be distinguished from a religious approach to morality because it uses reason and not revelation.

T   F   2. Like the law, ethics has a central authority, like courts, that establishes univer-sally agreed upon standards.

T   F   3. Law, ethics and morality are one and the same.

T   F   4. If a course of action is legal, it can be relied upon as an infallible guide to moral behavior.

T   F   5. The two ethical theories, ethical relativism and situational ethics, are substan-tially the same.

T   F   6. A small group of corporate officers control a vast amount of our nation's wealth and power.

T   F   7. The primary responsibility of business is to make a reasonable profit on its investment by producing a quality product at a reasonable price.

T   F   8. An indispensable component for repeat customers is the services and policies of a company that creates good will.

T   F   9. A major criticism of the theory of utilitarianism is that it ignores justice.

T   F   10. Under ethical fundamentalism, it would be ethical to compel a few people (e.g., convicts) to undergo fatal medical tests in order to develop cures for the rest of the nation.

T   F   11. Strict utilitarianism and absolutism are identical ethical codes.

T   F   12. The social ethics theory proposed by John Rawls is called social egalitarianism.

KEY TERMS–MATCHING EXERCISE: Select the term that best completes each statement below.

1. Ethical relativism	8. Experience	15. Corporation
2. Act utilitarianism	9. Adam Smith	16. Economic motivation
3. Ethics	10. Absolutism	17. Imprisonment
4. John Rawls	11. Robert Nozick	18. Intuitionism
5. Ethical fundamentalism	12. Karl Marx	19. Education
6. A priori	13. Distributive justice	20. Immanuel Kant
7. Deontology	14. Rule utilitarianism	

_____ 1. The study of what is right or good for human beings.

_____ 2. Reasoning that is based on theory rather than experimentation and that draws conclusions from cause to effect.

_____ 3. Another name for ethical fundamentalism.

_____ 4. An ethical doctrine that holds that actions must be judged by what individuals feel is right or wrong for themselves.

_____ 5. A form of business organization that is an artificial entity created by the State.

_____ 6. Ethical fundamentalists could make use of the writings of this man.

_____ 7. The ethical theory that seeks to analyze the type of society that people would establish if they could not determine in advance which members would be talented, rich, healthy or ambitious.

_____ 8. The philosopher who stresses that the most important duty society owes its members is liberty.

_____ 9. The philosopher who professes the theory that one should not do anything that he or she would not have everyone do in a similar situation.

_____ 10. This ethical theory holds that actions cannot be measured simply by their results but must be judged by the means and motives as well.

_____ 11. This ethical theory holds that rational people possess inherent powers to assess the correctness of actions.

_____ 12. Lawrence Kohlberg noted that people progress through stages of moral development according to two major variables: one is age, name the other.

_____ 13. The author of *The Wealth of Nations* who explains and justifies the economic system of capitalism.

_____ 14. A form of utilitarianism that assesses each separate act according to whether it maximizes pleasure over pain.

_____ 15. One of Adam Smith's six "institutions" that combined to establish our capitalistic system.

MULTIPLE CHOICE: Select the alternative that best completes each statement below.

_____ 1. Ethics (a) is a rational systematic attempt to determine the rules that should govern human conduct. (b) is an attempt to discover the values worth pursuing in life (c) concerns itself with human conduct that is done knowingly and willingly (d) all of the above.

_____ 2. Regulation of business may occur by (a) self-regulation (b) the "invisible hand" of competition (c) the government (d) all of the above.

_____ 3. The principal arguments opposing business involvement in socially responsible activities include (a) accountability (b) profitability (c) expertise (d) all of the above.

_____ 4. Immanuel Kant's philosophy (a) is premised on man's rationality (b) stems from a direct pronouncement from God (c) is the essential belief that universal revealed truths are derived from a central moral authority (d) is none of the above.

_____ 5. Our criminal laws apply the reasoning of the following ethical theory (a) ethical fundamentalism (b) deontology (c) ethical relativism (d) utilitarianism.

_____ 6. Libertarians (a) stress justice as the most important obligation owed by society to its members (b) require that the wealth of a nation be distributed to all its citizens (c) stress market outcomes as the basis for distributing society's rewards (d) all of the above.

_____ 7. The one ethical system subscribed to by all present-day philosophers is (a) egalitarianism (b) libertarianism (c) intuitionism (d) none of the above.

_____ 8. Immanuel Kant's "categorical imperative" theory (a) is one of the deontological theories (b) rejects notions of the end justifying the means (c) is a variation of the Golden Rule (d) all of the above.

_____ 9. According to Lawrence Kohlberg's conventional level stage of moral development, the motivation for people to conform their behavior to meet group expectations is (a) affection (b) loyalty (c) trust (d) all of the above.

_____ 10. To preserve the competitive process of our nation's economic system and to achieve desired social goals, the government has (a) regulated monopolies (b) protected specific groups (labor and agriculture) from failures in the marketplace (c) corrected imperfections in the market system (d) all of the above.

_____ 11. The ethical theory that holds that before evaluating a person's decision or act it must be viewed from the perspective of a person in the actor's shoes is (a) ethical relativism (b) deontology (c) situational ethics (d) utilitarianism.

_____ 12. The following is not one of Adam Smith's six "institutions" that established industrial capitalism (a) private property (b) increased government intervention (c) free enterprise (d) competition.

_____ 13. Ethical fundamentalists who look to a central authority or set of rules to guide their ethical decisions may be followers of the (a) writings of Karl Marx (b) Bible (c) Koran (d) all of the above.

CASE PROBLEMS–SHORT ESSAY ANSWERS: Read each case problem carefully. When appropriate, answer by stating a Decision for the case and by explaining the rationale–Rule of Law–relied upon to support your decision.

1. Whenever they are together, Andy and Barney argue about what constitutes ethical conduct. Andy's position is that whatever is legal is also ethical. If you are Barney, how would you respond to Andy by differentiating between law and ethics?

   Decision: _____

   _____

   Rule of Law: _____

   _____

2. America's Jerry Falwell and Iran's former Ayatullah Khomeini have been identified as ethical fundamentalists. Explain this ethical theory. From what source would each man derive his position as a proponent of absolutism? List two criticisms of this ethical doctrine.

   Decision: _____

   _____

   Rule of Law: _____

   _____

3. The Boston Strangler was a widely publicized serial killer. Identify and explain the ethical theory our criminal laws would apply in determining the innocence or guilt of this man.

    Decision: _____

    _____

    Rule of Law: _____

    _____

4. Psychologist Lawrence Kohlberg proposed that all people progress through stages of moral development according to two major variables: age and education. Explain Kohlberg's three stages of moral development and his conclusions drawn from this research.

    Decision: _____

    _____

    Rule of Law: _____

    _____

5. You have been hired as a consultant by a major business corporation to improve the socially responsible activities of the corporation within its local community. List some of the activities you might recommend to make this improvement.

    Decision: _____

    _____

    Rule of Law: _____

    _____

Chapter 3

LEGAL PROCESS

SCOPE NOTE

Over the past decades, increased demands have been placed on our legal system to solve a multitude of previously nonexistent societal and individual problems. Courts, informal dispute settling processes, and administrative bodies have been called upon not only to resolve such conflicts, but to carve out new directions in social, political and economic policy. As individuals and groups continue to make greater use of the legal process, knowledge of its operational dynamics becomes vital. Chapter Three introduces students to the principles and practices of the part of the American legal system responsible for dispute-settling courts. How does a particular dispute move through the American civil law trial process? What are the rights/duties of parties to litigation? These and other concerns are focused upon in the context of our two basic court systems, State and Federal, as well as from the perspective of the overriding concern for fairness (due process) in these dispute-settling arenas. Of major concern is understanding how courts apply legal principles to the facts of a controversy in performing a conflict-resolving function.

EDUCATIONAL OBJECTIVES

1. Outline the organization and the types of cases heard by State and Federal courts.

2. Chart the passage of a case through the judicial process, from the pleadings stage through an appeal of an adverse judgment.

3. Define and identify the basic elements of jurisdiction.

4. Develop the importance of venue.

5. Explain conflict of law problems from both a State and Federal court perspective.

6. Discuss the importance of arbitration as a court substitute for resolving conflict.

CHAPTER OUTLINE

I. The Court System
   A. The Federal Courts
      1. District courts–the trial courts in the Federal system
      2. Courts of Appeals–the Federal courts that primarily hear appeals from Federal district courts and administrative agencies
      3. The Supreme Court–the nation's highest court consisting of nine justices whose principal function is to review decisions of the Federal Courts of Appeals and the highest State courts
      4. Special courts–include the U.S. Claims Court, the Tax Court, the U.S. Bankruptcy Courts, and the U.S. Court of Appeals for the Federal Circuit
   B. State Courts
      1. Inferior trial courts–decide the least serious criminal and civil cases; small claims courts decide only civil cases involving a limited amount of money
      2. Trial courts–State trial courts of general jurisdiction over civil and criminal cases
      3. Special courts–include probate and family courts
      4. Appellate courts–include the highest court of each state whose decisions are usually final

II. Jurisdiction
   A. Subject Matter Jurisdiction–the authority of a particular court to adjudicate a controversy of a particular kind
      1. Federal Jurisdiction
         a. Exclusive Federal jurisdiction–Federal courts have exclusive jurisdiction over federal criminal cases, admiralty, bankruptcy, antitrust, patent, trademark, and copyright cases
         b. Concurrent Federal jurisdiction–cases that may be heard by either State or Federal courts; it is either federal question jurisdiction or diversity jurisdiction
      2. State Jurisdiction
         a. Exclusive State jurisdiction–jurisdiction over all other cases
         b. Choice of law in State courts–a court in one state may be the proper forum for a case even though the relevant events occurred in another state
      3. Stare decisis in the dual court system–only decisions of the U.S. Supreme Court are binding on all other courts, Federal or State
   B. Jurisdiction Over the Parties–jurisdiction over the parties involved in the dispute
      1. In personam jurisdiction–jurisdiction of the court over the parties to a lawsuit
      2. In rem jurisdiction–jurisdiction over property
      3. Attachment jurisdiction–quasi in rem jurisdiction over property
      4. Venue–the location where a lawsuit should be brought

III. Civil Dispute Resolution
   A. Civil Procedure
      1. The pleadings–the purpose of pleadings is to establish the issues of fact and law presented and disputed
         a. Complaint and summons–a claim and demand for relief followed by service requiring a specific response
         b. Responses to complaint–the options available in response to a complaint and summons
      2. Pretrial procedure–each party has the right to obtain evidence from the other party by discovery
         a. Judgment on pleadings–a request for a judge's ruling on the merits of the demand for relief
         b. Discovery–the process of obtaining information or evidence from the other party
         c. Pretrial conference–the procedure to define the scope of the dispute and promote settlement
         d. Summary judgment–a request for a judge's ruling for disposition of the dispute without trial
      3. Trial–the proceeding to determine the outcome of a case with or without a jury
         a. Jury selection–the process of impaneling a jury
         b. Conduct of trial–the trial procedure
         c. Jury instructions–the directions given by the judge to the jury covering the rules of law that apply to the dispute
         d. Verdict–the decision rendered by the jury
         e. Motions challenging the verdict–the options available to the unsuccessful party for a new trial
      4. Appeal–the purpose is to determine whether the trial court committed prejudicial error
      5. Enforcement–the process to collect a judgment
   B. Alternative Dispute Resolution
      1. Arbitration–the disputing parties select a third person who renders a binding decision
         a. Types of arbitration–the two basic types are consensual arbitration and compulsory arbitration
         b. Procedure–the arbitration procedure
         c. International arbitration–the procedure for resolving international disputes
         d. Court-annexed arbitration–the procedure adopted by Federal and State courts in civil cases with limited damages
      2. Conciliation–methods of resolving disputes by use of a conciliator
      3. Mediation–a third party (the mediator) selected by the disputants helps them reach a resolution
      4. Mini-trial–occurs when both disputants are corporations
      5. Summary jury trial–a mock trial where the dispute is presented to an advisory jury
      6. Negotiation–the consensual bargaining process between the parties to reach a settlement without third party participation

TRUE–FALSE: Circle true or false.

T   F   1.   Venue is the power and authority of a court to hear and decide a case.

T   F   2.   A court may not render a binding decision unless it has jurisdiction over the dispute and over the parties to that dispute.

T   F   3.   The only court expressly created by the Federal Constitution is the U.S. Supreme Court.

T   F   4.   The decisions of a State Supreme Court are always final.

T   F   5.   The purpose of discovery is to enable each party to be informed of the evidence so there will be no surprises at the trial.

T   F   6.   A decision of the U.S. Supreme Court on Federal questions is binding on all other courts, Federal or State.

T   F   7.   In arbitration, the decision of the arbitrator is generally binding on the parties involved in the dispute.

T   F   8.   Generally speaking, appellate courts hear the same witnesses' testimony as the trial court.

T   F   9.   The United States has a dual court system: separate State and Federal courts.

T   F   10. The examination or questioning of potential jurors in the jury selection process is called voir dire.

T   F   11. The membership of the U.S. Supreme Court consists of nine justices.

T   F   12. Disputes involving public employees, such as police officers or fire fighters, may require compulsory arbitration as stated in the U.S. Constitution.

KEY TERMS–MATCHING EXERCISE: Select the term that best completes each statement below.

1. Pleadings	6. Appellate jurisdiction	11. Depositions
2. Writ of certiorari	7. Original jurisdiction	12. Counterclaim
3. Mediator	8. Complaint	13. Jurisdiction
4. Discovery	9. Summons	14. Instructions
5. Venue	10. Arbitration	15. Verdict

16. Conciliator   18. Mediation   20. Interrogatories

17. Award   19. Judgment

_____ 1. The type of jurisdiction the U.S. Supreme Court has in cases coming from Federal Courts of Appeals.

_____ 2. The place (county) where the lawsuit should be filed or has to be tried.

_____ 3. The "charges" given by the judge for the purpose of aiding the jury in reaching its decision.

_____ 4. The jury's decision.

_____ 5. The use of a neutral person selected by the disputing parties to decide the dispute.

_____ 6. Pretrial testimony under oath taken out of court that may be used at the trial.

_____ 7. The document that contains the claims of the plaintiff which, when filed, commences a civil lawsuit.

_____ 8. The pretrial procedure by which each party has the right to obtain evidence, or information that might lead to evidence, from the other party.

_____ 9. A method of appealing a case to the U.S. Supreme Court.

_____ 10. The power or authority a court must have to hear and decide a case.

_____ 11. A claim by the defendant in a civil lawsuit that she has been damaged and claims compensation (money).

_____ 12. Written questions submitted to the opposing party in a civil lawsuit requiring written answers made under oath but before the trial.

_____ 13. A person who proposes possible solutions to disputing parties that are not binding.

_____ 14. The decision of an arbitrator.

_____ 15. Notice to a defendant that a civil lawsuit has been brought against the defendant.

MULTIPLE CHOICE: Select the alternative that best completes each statement below.

_____ 1. Diversity of citizenship exists when (a) the plaintiff and defendant are citizens of different states (b) a foreign country brings an action against U.S. citizens (c) a dispute is between U.S. citizens and citizens of a foreign country (d) all of the above.

_____ 2. The trial court in the Federal court system is the (a) Federal district court (b) Court of Appeals (c) U.S. Supreme Court (d) Court of Claims.

_____ 3. A motion made by the losing party in a civil action to the judge after the jury's verdict is a (a) directed verdict (b) judgment (c) judgment n.o.v (d) writ of execution.

_____ 4. The majority of appellate cases that reach the U.S. Supreme Court come from (a) a State court declaring a Federal statute invalid (b) a State court declaring a treaty invalid (c) all appeals reach the U.S. Supreme Court (d) a writ of certiorari.

_____ 5. _____ is not one of the grounds for judicial review of an arbitration award. (a) arbitrator's decision issued more than three months after the arbitration proceedings ended (b) corruption or fraud in the arbitration process (c) arbitrator exceeding designated authority (d) none of the above

_____ 6. The inferior State court that generally hears civil cases involving a limited amount of money is the (a) district court (b) circuit court (c) small claims court (d) none of the above.

_____ 7. Under its appellate jurisdiction, the U.S. Supreme Court (a) must hear and decide every case appealed to the court (b) hears all cases appealed to the court by writ of certiorari (c) hears only those cases in which a State court declares a Federal statute invalid (d) none of the above.

_____ 8. The special Federal court that hears claims against the Federal government is the (a)Tax Court (b) U.S. Court of Federal Claims (c) Customs Court (d) none of the above.

_____ 9. In order for a court to proceed with a lawsuit, it must have jurisdiction over the (a) plaintiff (b) defendant (c) subject matter of the case (d) all of the above.

_____ 10. In a civil lawsuit, the defendant's answer to the plaintiff's complaint may contain (a) admissions or denials (b) affirmative defenses (c) counterclaims (d) all of the above.

_____ 11. The Federal courts have exclusive jurisdiction over cases involving (a) patents (b) bankruptcy (c) copyrights (d) all of the above.

_____ 12. The purpose of this type of jurisdiction is to resolve conflicting claims to property (a) attachment jurisdiction (b) in personam jurisdiction (c) in rem jurisdiction (d) none of the above.

_____ 13. Alternative dispute resolutions include (a) arbitration (b) conciliation (c) mediation (d) all of the above.

CASE PROBLEMS–SHORT ESSAY ANSWERS: Read each case problem carefully. When appropriate, answer by stating a Decision for the case and by explaining the rationale–Rule of Law–relied upon to support your decision.

1. In a civil action, Mary Swift sues James Swanson in a State district court for negligently damaging her property. Mary wins, and James appeals to the State Supreme Court. The Supreme Court reverses and remands the decision of the district court. What does remand mean and, according to the rules of civil procedure, what happens to this case? Explain.

   Decision: _____

   _____

   Rule of Law: _____

   _____

2. A labor management dispute occurs in the Ajax Corporation. Neither side wants to go through an expensive and lengthy civil lawsuit, and both sides want a binding resolution of their problem. What type of alternative dispute resolution would you recommend to the parties? Explain.

   Decision: _____

   _____

   Rule of Law: _____

   _____

3. A Georgia Supreme Court decision in a civil law paternity suit favors the defendant–the man alleged to be the father. If a case involving the same facts was brought before a Texas court, would the Texas court be obligated to follow the Georgia decision under the "stare decisis" doctrine? Explain.

   Decision: _____

   _____

   Rule of Law: _____

   _____

4. While on vacation in Colorado, Amy Bums negligently struck Malcolm Morris with her ski, causing Malcolm to lose his sight in one eye. Amy is a resident of (or domiciled in) the State of Minnesota, and Malcolm lives in Colorado. Can this case be heard in Federal district court? Explain.

Decision: _____

_____

Rule of Law: _____

_____

5. Karla Johnson, a resident of Iowa, appeals a case to the Eighth Circuit Court of Appeals and wins. If a case involving the same facts was brought on appeal to the Fourth Circuit Court of Appeals, must that circuit court follow the decision of the Eighth Circuit? Explain.

Decision: _____

_____

Rule of Law: _____

_____

Chapter 4

CONSTITUTIONAL LAW

SCOPE NOTES

The founding fathers of the American government feared powerful, centralized, and unitary government. They were committed to a political philosophy that stressed "limited government." The Federal Constitution, as the blueprint for governing authority, embodies the principles of limited government in its separation of powers, checks and balances, federalism, and other structural restrictions. Chapter Four examines the purpose and functions of the fundamental law of American society: the Federal Constitution.

EDUCATIONAL OBJECTIVES

1. Discuss policy underlying concepts of constitutional law.

2. Identify fundamental doctrines characterizing the U.S. Constitution.

3. Outline major powers held by the Federal and State governments.

4. Explain the limits the U.S Constitution places on the Federal government and the states.

CHAPTER OUTLINE

I. Basic Principles of Constitutional Law
   A. Federalism–means that governing power is divided between the Federal government and the states
   B. Federal Supremacy and Preemption–all law in the United States is subject to the U.S. Constitution, which is the supreme law of the land

C. Judicial Review–the process by which the courts examine governmental actions to determine whether they conform to the U.S. Constitution

D. Separation of Powers–our Constitution establishes three distinct and independent branches of government: executive, legislative, and judicial

E. State Action–includes any actions of the Federal and state governments that are protected by the U.S. Constitution and its amendments

II. Powers of Government

A. Federal Commerce Power–the Constitution gives Congress the power to regulate commerce with other nations and among the states

B. State Regulation of Commerce–the commerce clause of the Constitution also restricts the States' power to regulate activities if the result obstructs interstate commerce

1. Regulations–the U.S. Supreme Court decides the extent of permissible state regulation affecting interstate commerce

2. Taxation–the commerce clause, in conjunction with the import-export clause, also limits the power of the states to tax

C. Federal Fiscal Powers–including the power to tax, to spend, to borrow and coin money, and the power of eminent domain

1. Taxation–the Constitution grants Congress broad powers to tax with three major limitations

2. Spending power–an important way the Federal government regulates the economy

3. Borrowing and coining money–enables the Federal government to establish a national banking system: the Federal Reserve System

4. Eminent domain–the government's power to take private property for public use

III. Limitations on Government

A. Contract Clause–this clause of the Constitution restricts states from retroactively modifying public charters and private contracts

B. First Amendment–the protection of free speech with some limits

1. Corporate political speech–is indispensable to the discovery and spread of political truth

2. Commercial speech–is the expression related to the economic interests of the speaker and its audience, e.g., advertisements of a product or service

3. Defamation–a tort consisting of a false communication that injures a person's reputation

C. Due Process–the Fifth and Fourteenth Amendments prohibit the Federal and State governments from depriving any person of life, liberty, or property without due process of law

1. Substantive due process–involves a court's determination of whether a particular governmental action is compatible with individual liberties

2. Procedural due process–pertains to the governmental decision-making process that results in depriving a person of life, liberty, or property

D. Equal Protection–the guarantee of equal protection requires that similarly situated persons be treated similarly by governmental actions

1. Rational relationship test–a standard of review used by the Supreme Court to determine whether governmental action satisfies the equal protection guarantee
2. Strict scrutiny test– another standard of review
3. Intermediate test–a third standard of review

TRUE–FALSE: Circle true or false.

T F 1. Public law is concerned with the rights and powers of government and its relation to individuals or groups.

T F 2. The Constitution of the United States was adopted in Washington, D.C. on August 1, 1776.

T F 3. The Federal commerce clause grants virtually complete power to the individual states to regulate the economy and business.

T F 4. The Federal government regulates the nation's economy by its power to spend money.

T F 5. The U.S. Supreme Court ruled that the contract clause of the Federal Constitution precludes the states from exercising eminent domain or their police powers.

T F 6. The judicial branch of the U.S. government has the power to enforce the law.

T F 7. Defamation is a crime that injures a person's reputation.

T F 8. The first ten amendments to the U.S. Constitution are known as the Federalist Papers.

T F 9. An example of a concurrent governmental power is police power.

T F 10. An example of the Federal government's fiscal powers is the prosecution of crimes that violate Federal law.

T F 11. The legislative branch of the U.S. government has the power to make law.

T F 12. Judicial review is a function of the President of the United States.

KEY TERMS–MATCHING EXERCISES: Select the term that best completes each statement below.

1. Administrative law	9. Procedural due process	15. First Amendment
2. *Marbury v. Madison*	10. Equal Protection clause	16. Tenth Amendment
3. *McCulloch v. Maryland*	11. Veto power	17. President
4. Bill of Rights		18. Fifth Amendment
5. Import-export clause	12. Federal Commerce Clause	19. Constitutional law
6. Eminent domain	13. Federal fiscal powers	20. Thirteenth Amendment
7. Defamation	14. Judicial review	
8. Chief Justice		

_____ 1. The landmark Supreme Court decision that verified the supremacy of the Constitution over every other source of law.

_____ 2. The power of the government to take private property for public use.

_____ 3. The clause of the U.S. Constitution that grants complete power to Congress to regulate the economy.

_____ 4. The Federal power that allows the Federal government to tax, spend, borrow, and coin money.

_____ 5.   A tort that consists of a communication that injures a person's reputation.

_____ 6. The right to a fair hearing (trial) before the government can deprive a person of life, liberty or property.

_____ 7. The procedure by which a President can reject legislation passed by Congress.

_____ 8. The Amendment to the Constitution that protects the right of free speech.

_____ 9. A type of public law other than constitutional or criminal law.

_____ 10. The guarantee that requires that similarly situated persons be treated the same by governmental actions.

_____ 11. The first ten Amendments to the U.S. Constitution.

_____ 12. The Amendment that abolished slavery.

_____ 13. The person who has the power to veto legislation.

_____ 14. The fundamental law that created the levels of government in the United States.

_____ 15. The process by which courts determine whether governmental actions conform to the U.S. Constitution.

MULTIPLE CHOICE: Select the alternative that best completes each statement below.

_____ 1. The source of law that is the "supreme law of the land" is (a) U.S. Supreme Court decisions (b) Federal statutes (c) the U.S. Constitution (d) none of the above.

_____ 2. The final arbiter of the constitutionality of any law in the U.S. is (a) the U.S. Constitution (b) Congress (c) the President (d) the U.S. Supreme Court.

_____ 3. The doctrine that divides the U.S. government into three branches–executive, legislative, and judicial–is the (a) separation of powers principle (b) Bill of Rights (c) Judicial Review (d) Federalist doctrine.

_____ 4. Public law consists of all of the following except (a) criminal law (b) tort law (c) constitutional law (d) administrative law.

_____ 5. Basic principles of the U.S. Constitution include (a) separation of powers (b) federalism (c) federal supremacy (d) all of the above.

_____ 6. Federalism means that (a) the U.S. Constitution is the supreme law (b) the federal government and the states divide the governing power (c) judicial review is constitutional (d) all of the above.

_____ 7. The standard the U.S. Supreme Court uses in determining whether legislation satisfies the equal protection guarantee is the (a) strict scrutiny test (b) rational relationship test (c) both a and b above (d) none of the above.

_____ 8. The equal protection guarantee (a) applies when governmental action involves classification of people (b) requires that persons similarly situated be treated similarly by the government (c) is included in the Fourteenth Amendment to the Constitution (d) all of the above.

_____ 9. Federal fiscal powers do not include the power (a) to pay debts of the federal government (b) of eminent domain (c) to allow the states to levy duties on exports (d) all of the above.

_____ 10. Procedural due process considers "property" to include (a) real property (b) personal property (c) social security payments and food stamps (d) all of the above.

_____ 11. The branch of the U.S. government that has the power to veto bills enacted by Congress is the (a) executive branch (b) legislative branch (c) judicial branch (d) none of the above.

_____ 12. The branch of the U.S. government that has the power to reject executive appointments is the (a) executive branch (b) legislative branch (c) judicial branch (d) none of the above.

_____ 13. The "one person, one vote" rule decided by the U.S. Supreme Court is an example of the Court's use of the (a) rational relationship test (b) due process test (c) intermediate test (d) strict scrutiny test.

CASE PROBLEMS–SHORT ESSAY ANSWERS: Read each case problem carefully. When appropriate, answer by stating a Decision for the case and by explaining the rationale–Rule of Law–relied upon to support your decision.

1. (Optional) Explain the reason President Richard Nixon's claim of executive privilege was denied by the U.S. Supreme Court, resulting in the requirement that certain presidential tapes be produced and ultimately in President Nixon's resignation. [See *United States v. Nixon*, 418 U.S. 683 (1974).] (NOTE: Outside research is necessary to answer this question.)

   Decision: _____

   _____

   Rule of Law: _____

   _____

2. The State of Minnesota places an import tax on all foreign cars arriving at its international port, the city of Duluth. The Datsun Company of Japan refuses to pay the state tax. If a lawsuit between these parties commences, who would prevail? Explain.

   Decision: _____

   _____

   Rule of Law: _____

   _____

3. Mai Thai Fong has immigrated to the United States. She asks you to explain the separation of powers doctrine, one of the fundamental principles upon which our government is based. What would be your response?

   Decision: _____

   _____

   Rule of Law: _____

   _____

4. The powers of the Federal government are superior to any and all of our fifty states. Yet each state has its own constitution and sovereignty over its own courts and citizens. Which Amendment to the U.S. Constitution expressly grants this right of sovereignty to the states?

   Decision: _____

   _____

   Rule of Law: _____

   _____

5. Explain the strict scrutiny test used by the U.S. Supreme Court in its decision in the *Brown v. Board of Education of Topeka* case concerning the equal protection guarantee of the Fourteenth Amendment.

   Decision: _____

   _____

   Rule of Law: _____

   _____

Chapter 5

ADMINISTRATIVE LAW

SCOPE NOTE

This chapter discusses administrative agencies, sometimes referred to as the "fourth branch of government." In the complex, crowded urban society that constitutes present-day America, many complicated socioeconomic problems arise that demand attention and expertise beyond the capacity of traditional lawmakers, courts and legislatures. Chapter Five includes a discussion of the growth of administrative law as the primary responder to such complex problems. How administrative agencies function is examined. Students should remember that the federal agencies focused upon reflect the types of activities engaged in by similar lawmakers in their own states and towns.

EDUCATIONAL OBJECTIVES

1. Discuss policy underlying concepts of administrative law.

2. Explain the operation of administrative agencies.

3. List activities pursued by administrative lawmakers.

4. Distinguish among significant federal administrative lawmakers.

5. Identify the limits imposed on administrative agencies.

CHAPTER OUTLINE

I. Operation of Administrative Agencies–most of these agencies perform three basic functions.
   A. Rulemaking–is the process by which an administrative agency enacts or promulgates rules of law

1. Legislative rules–are called regulations and are issued by the agency
2. Interpretative rules–are statements by the agency that explain how the agency construes its governing statute
3. Procedural rules–establish rules of conduct for practice before the agency and describe its method of operation

B. Enforcement–agencies determine whether their rules have been violated
C. Adjudication–an agency may use informal or formal methods to resolve disputes; the formal method is called adjudication

II. Limits on Administrative Agencies
   A. Judicial Review–acts as a control or check by a court on a particular rule or order of an administrative agency
      1. General requirements–the parties must have standing and must have exhausted their administrative remedies
      2. Questions of law–during a review, applicable law, constitutional provisions, and agency authority are determined by a court
      3. Questions of fact–the three standards used by courts are the arbitrary and capricious test, the substantial evidence test, and the unwarranted by the facts test
   B. Legislative Control–is exercised over administrative agencies through budget control or even by completely eliminating the agency
   C. Control by Executive Branch–is exercised by the President's power to appoint and remove the chief administrator of the agency
   D. Disclosure of Information–requires agencies to disclose information about their actions
      1. Freedom of Information Act–gives the public access to most records in the files of Federal administrative agencies
      2. Government in the Sunshine Act–requires meetings of many Federal agencies to be open to the public

TRUE–FALSE: Circle true or false.

T   F   1. An enabling statute is passed by Congress to create a federal agency.

T   F   2. The scope of administrative law has diminished dramatically in the past 50 years.

T   F   3. The rules created by administrative agencies are called statutes.

T   F   4. The President can abolish federal administrative agencies of the executive branch with the approval of Congress.

T   F   5. A jury will decide a controversy brought to an administrative hearing.

T   F   6. All administrative agencies receive their authority from the judicial branch of the federal government.

T F 7. When a decision of a controversy is made by an administrative agency, that decision usually may be appealed to the appropriate state or federal court.

T F 8. The adjudication of a controversy between an individual and one of the federal administrative agencies is presided over by an administrative law judge.

T F 9. In the adjudication of a controversy between an individual and a federal administrative agency, the agency serves as both prosecutor and decision maker.

T F 10. State administrative agencies play a very limited role in our society today.

T F 11. Federal administrative agencies are classified as either independent or executive agencies.

T F 12. Once Congress has created a federal administrative agency, it cannot terminate the agency.

KEY TERMS–MATCHING EXERCISE: Select the term that best completes each statement below.

1. Administrative law

2. Judgment

3. Administrative process

4. Order

5. Executive control

6. Rulemaking

7. Administrative agency

8. Chief Justice

9. "Fourth branch of government"

10. Legislative control

11. Procedural rules

12. Legislative rules

13. Interpretive rules

14. Judicial review

15. Enabling statute

16. First Amendment

17. President

18. Constitutional law

19. Administrative law judge

20. Adjudication

_____ 1. The entire set of activities in which administrative agencies engage while carrying out their functions.

_____ 2. The process by which an administrative agency enacts rules of law.

_____ 3. These rules are also called regulations.

_____ 4. Rules that explain how an administrative agency construes its governing statute.

_____ 5. The party who acts as prosecutor of an administrative hearing.

_____ 6. Another name for administrative agencies.

_____ 7. Rules that establish proper conduct for practice before an administrative agency.

_____ 8. The law that creates an administrative agency.

_____ 9. Public law that governs the powers and procedures of administrative agencies.

_____ 10. When Congress amends an enabling statute it exercises this control.

_____ 11. The name for the final disposition of an adjudication.

_____ 12. The formal procedure by which an administrative agency resolves a case.

_____ 13. The person who has the power to appoint and remove the chief administrator of an agency.

_____ 14. The person who presides over an administrative agency hearing.

_____ 15. The process by which courts determine whether governmental actions conform to the U.S. Constitution.

MULTIPLE CHOICE: Select the alternative that best completes each statement below.

_____ 1. Federal administrative agencies are not responsible for (a) taxation (b) elections (c) workers' compensation (d) all of the above.

_____ 2. Federal administrative agencies are responsible for (a) national security (b) commerce (c) labor relations (d) all of the above.

_____ 3. Basic functions performed by administrative agencies include (a) making rules (b) making statutes (c) presiding over administrative hearings (d) all of the above.

_____ 4. Public law consists of all of the following except (a) criminal law (b) tort law (c) constitutional law (d) administrative law.

_____ 5. Administrative agencies (a) create more legal rules than Congress (b) adjudicate more controversies than our state and federal courts (c) have increased in number tremendously in the past 50 years (d) all of the above.

_____ 6. Administrative agencies do not (a) make rules and regulations (b) create statutes (c) enforce the agency's rules (d) adjudicate controversies.

_____ 7. In essence, an adjudication is (a) a civil trial (b) a criminal trial (c) an administrative trial (d) none of the above.

_____ 8. Administrative agencies are (a) governmental entities (b) controlled by the legislative branch of government (c) called boards or commissions (d) all of the above.

_____ 9. Activities of the numerous administrative agencies are referred to as the (a) legislative process (b) judicial process (c) administrative process (d) none of the above.

_____ 10. If Congress amends the enabling statute, the administrative agency's authority may be (a) increased (b) modified (c) decreased (d) all of the above.

_____ 11. The branch of the U.S. government that has the power to impound money appropriated to an agency by Congress is the (a) executive branch (b) legislative branch (c) judicial branch (d) none of the above.

_____ 12. The branch of the U.S. government that has the power to confirm high-level appointments to administrative agencies is the (a) executive branch (b) legislative branch (c) judicial branch (d) none of the above.

_____ 13. In a judicial review of an order of an administrative agency, the court (a) decides questions of law (b) interprets statutory provisions (c) determines the meaning of terms (d) all of the above.

CASE PROBLEMS–SHORT ESSAY ANSWERS: Read each case problem carefully. When appropriate, answer by stating a Decision for the case and by explaining the rationale–Rule of Law–relied upon to support your decision.

1. Mary has been denied benefits under her state's Medical Assistance program. She has appealed the denial to the state's Department of Health. A hearing before an administrative law judge is being scheduled. Mary requests a jury trial for this administrative hearing. Is she entitled to a jury trial? Explain.

   Decision: _____

   _____

   Rule of Law: _____

   _____

2. The increase in the number of federal, state and local administrative agencies in our country has been astounding. William and Howard are arguing the merits of this proliferation and specifically, the need for uniformity and consistency in running these agencies since, in the past, rules of evidence varied from agency to agency. Name and explain the law enacted by Congress that helped to resolve this concern.

   Decision: _____

   _____

Rule of Law: _____

_____

3. As in question #2, William and Howard are continuing their discussion of administrative agencies. Howard tells William there are three sources of law that control the formation of an agency and the issuance of valid legislative regulations by the agency. Name the three and explain each one.

Decision: _____

_____

Rule of Law: _____

_____

4. Formal rulemaking procedures for administrative agencies require that the agency must hold a formal hearing resembling a trial in civil court. The agency must base the rule it creates on the record of the trial-like hearing. If the rule is challenged in court as part of the judicial review process, the factual determination by the court must abide by the standard called the "substantial evidence test." Explain this test.

Decision: _____

_____

Rule of Law: _____

_____

5. The Clean Air Act authorizes the Environmental Protection Agency (EPA) to issue regulations banning fuel additives that pollute the air and endanger the public health. When the EPA, using informal rulemaking procedures, banned lead additives to gasoline, the manufacturers of the additives challenged the regulations. Although the EPA could only establish the relationship between lead, in general, and health hazards, the federal court held the EPA did not need rigorous proof of cause and effect. Where regulations deal with health hazards, courts defer to the agency's judgment so long as it is based on more than wild guesses. What standard of review of factual determinations was used in this case? Explain.

Decision: _____

_____

Rule of Law: _____

_____

Chapter 6

CRIMINAL LAW

SCOPE NOTE

The preceding materials have examined the American legal system from the perspective of civil law, usually involving disputes between private individuals. This chapter undertakes a different approach. That aspect of the American legal process that addresses disruptions of the public interest and society at large–criminal law–is discussed. The significant concepts and doctrines of both substantive and procedural criminal law are developed.

EDUCATIONAL OBJECTIVES

1. Evaluate various policy assumptions underlying American criminal law.

2. Distinguish tort law from criminal law.

3. Differentiate civil from criminal procedures.

4. Identify sources of criminal law.

5. Explain major classifications of criminal law.

6. Discuss the essential elements of a crime.

7. Outline prosecutorial burden of proof requisites for various specific crimes.

8. Discuss white-collar crimes and crimes against business.

9. Explain common defenses to criminal charges.

10. Discuss criminal procedure.

CHAPTER OUTLINE

I. Nature of Crimes
   A. Essential Elements–of a crime consists of two elements: the wrongful or overt act and criminal intent
   B. Classification–of crimes range from the most serious–a felony–to a misdemeanor
   C. Vicarious Liability–is liability imposed upon one person for the acts of another person
   D. Liability of the Corporation–historically, corporations were not held criminally liable; today, corporations can be liable and punished by a fine

II. White-Collar Crime
   A. Computer Crime–includes the use of a computer to steal money or services, or to tamper with information
   B. Racketeer Influenced and Corrupt Organizations Act–its purpose is to stop the infiltration of organized crime into legitimate business

III. Crimes Against Business
   A. Larceny–is the trespassory taking and carrying away of personal property of another with the intent to deprive the victim permanently of the goods
   B. Embezzlement–is the fraudulent conversion of another's property by one who was in lawful possession of it
   C. False Pretenses–is a crime enacted to close a loophole in the requirements of larceny
   D. Robbery–is a larceny in which the property is forcibly taken from the victim
   E. Burglary–according to modem law, is an entry into a building with the intent to commit a felony
   F. Extortion and Bribery–extortion is blackmail, while bribery is the offer of money or property to a public official to influence a decision by the official
   G. Forgery–is the falsification of a document with the intent to defraud another person
   H. Bad Checks–is knowingly writing a check with insufficient funds in the account to cover the check

IV. Defenses to Crimes
   A. Defense of Person or Property–individuals may use reasonable force to protect their property
   B. Duress–is a valid defense to criminal conduct other than murder
   C. Mistake of Fact–an honest and reasonable mistake of fact will justify the defendant's conduct
   D. Entrapment–arises when a law officer induces a person to commit a crime when that person would not have done so otherwise

V. Criminal Procedure
   A. Steps in Criminal Prosecution–a basic overview of the procedures in a criminal prosecution is presented
   B. Fourth Amendment–protects individuals against unreasonable searches and seizures
   C. Fifth Amendment–protects persons against self-incrimination, double jeopardy, and being charged with a capital crime except by grand jury indictment

    D. Sixth Amendment–provides the accused with a speedy and public jury trial and the right to counsel for her defense

TRUE–FALSE: Circle true or false.

T   F   1. The standard by which the government has to prove the defendant guilty of a crime is "guilt by a preponderance of the evidence."

T   F   2. The same act (conduct) may constitute both a tort and a crime.

T   F   3. The distinction between the crimes of larceny and false pretenses is that in the latter, possession of the personal property is voluntarily transferred to the thief.

T   F   4. All jurisdictions (states), except Nevada, have passed legislation making it a crime to issue bad checks.

T   F   5. A criminal defense that arises when an official induces a person to commit a crime is duress.

T   F   6. A "bench trial" is a case tried by a judge without a jury.

T   F   7. In order to obtain a search warrant, the judge or magistrate issuing the warrant must believe that probable cause exists that the search will reveal evidence of a crime.

T   F   8. Civil law is private law; criminal law is public law.

T   F   9. Computer crime is an example of one type of white-collar crime.

T   F   10. Extortion and bribery are identical crimes.

T   F   11. Federal crimes are exclusively covered by statutory law.

T   F   12. Today, a corporation cannot be found guilty of a crime because it cannot be imprisoned.

KEY TERMS–MATCHING EXERCISE: Select the term that best completes each statement below.

1. White-collar crime	5. Murder	9. Due process
2. Search warrant	6. Racketeering	10. Equal protection
3. Nondeadly force	7. Defamation	11. Actus reus
4. True bill	8. Deadly force	12. Mens rea

13. Felony   16. Durham test   19. Duress

14. Ordinance   17. Arraignment   20. Information

15. Misdemeanor   18. Entrapment

_____

_____ 1. A pattern of criminal conduct that is defined as the commission of two or more predicate acts within a period of ten years.

_____ 2. The crime for which duress is not a valid defense.

_____ 3. The criminal intent required for a crime to exist.

_____ 4. The type or classification of crime punishable by death or imprisonment.

_____ 5. The type of nonviolent crime involving deceit or breach of trust.

_____ 6. The right to a fair hearing (trial) before the government can deprive a person of life, liberty or property.

_____ 7. The wrongful act that is a necessary element of a crime.

_____ 8. A crime punishable by fine or imprisonment in a local jail.

_____ 9. The kind of force that is generally never reasonable to use to protect property.

_____ 10. A grand jury's decision to indict the defendant in a criminal case.

_____ 11. The formal accusation of a crime brought by a county prosecutor.

_____ 12. The hearing at which the accused is informed of the charge against him and a plea is entered.

_____ 13. A document that allows a legal search of a person's home.

_____ 14. A criminal defense when a law officer induces a person to commit a crime that the person would not have committed otherwise.

_____ 15. A criminal defense in which a person is threatened with serious bodily harm unless the person participates in committing a crime.

MULTIPLE CHOICE: Select the alternative that best completes each statement below.

_____ 1. The amendment to the U.S. Constitution that prohibits double jeopardy in criminal cases is the (a) Eighth Amendment (b) Sixth Amendment (c) Fourth Amendment (d) Fifth Amendment.

_____ 2. Robbery differs from larceny in that the stolen property may be taken (a) directly from the victim (b) by force (c) by the threat of deadly force (d) all of the above.

_____ 3. The purpose of the exclusionary rule is to (a) deter all police activity (b) hinder the search for the truth in the case (c) protect individual liberty (d) none of the above.

_____ 4. The privilege against self-incrimination as guaranteed by the Fifth Amendment protects the accused from being forced to (a) testify against himself (b) stand in a "line up" for identification purposes (c) provide a handwriting sample (d) take a blood test.

_____ 5. A search warrant is not necessary (a) to search a person's luggage (b) when voluntary consent to search is given (c) to search a person's home (d) all of the above.

_____ 6. The accused in a serious criminal case (a) is not always entitled to a jury trial (b) if found guilty, may request a new trial (c) if acquitted must allow the State the right to appeal the acquittal to a higher court (d) must be proven guilty by a preponderance of the evidence.

_____ 7. Punishment for criminal conduct does not include (a) fines (b) imprisonment (c) a lawsuit for money damages (d) the death penalty.

_____ 8. Under our legal system (a) a defendant's guilt is presumed (b) the defendant must testify in her own defense (c) the burden of proof of innocence or guilt is on the defendant (d) none of the above.

_____ 9. The amendment of the U.S. Constitution that protects individuals from unreasonable searches and seizures is the (a) First Amendment (b) Second Amendment (c) Fourth Amendment (d) Fifth Amendment.

_____ 10. The U.S. Supreme Court has ruled that juries deciding criminal cases (a) may consist of twelve jurors (b) may consist of six jurors (c) need not reach unanimous verdicts in all State court cases (d) all of the above.

_____ 11. The membership of a grand jury consists of not more than (a) six persons (b) twelve persons (c) twenty-three persons (d) none of the above.

_____ 12. Criminal liability imposed upon one person for the criminal acts of another person is (a) computer crime (b) racketeering (c) voluntary manslaughter (d) vicarious liability.

_____ 13. The amendment of the U.S. Constitution that provides for the assistance of counsel (an attorney) for the person accused of a crime is the (a) Fourth Amendment (b) Fifth Amendment (c) Sixth Amendment (d) Eighth Amendment.

CASE PROBLEMS–SHORT ESSAY ANSWERS: Read each case problem carefully. When appropriate, answer by stating a Decision for the case and by explaining the rationale–Rule of Law–relied upon to support your decision.

1. Allen Johnson, an undercover FBI agent, convinces Melvin Howard, an industrialist whose company is in financial trouble, to participate in the purchase and resale of narcotics. If Melvin is arrested, what defense would you recommend for him? Explain.

    Decision: _____

    _____

    Rule of Law: _____

    _____

2. Carol Olson is convicted by a six-member jury of the crime of embezzlement from the bank where she is employed. Carol appeals her conviction on the grounds she was wrongfully deprived of a jury of twelve persons in violation of her Constitutional rights. What result? Explain.

    Decision: _____

    _____

    Rule of Law: _____

    _____

3. Karla Johnson is arrested for first degree murder in her home through the use of an arrest warrant, together with an "information" of the charge at the time of arrest. What other method could be used to initiate prosecution of Karla for this crime? Explain.

    Decision: _____

    _____

    Rule of Law: _____

    _____

4. Thelma and Louise decide to rob a bank. They spend two days planning every detail they believe will be necessary to execute their plan successfully. Then they change their minds. Have Thelma and Louise committed a crime? Explain.

    Decision: _____

    _____

    Rule of Law: _____

    _____

5. In a famous Supreme Court case, *Gideon v. Wainwright*, 372 U.S. 335, 9 L. Ed. 799 (1963), the defendant, Gideon, charged with the commission of a felony, was unable to afford a lawyer for his defense, and the trial court denied his request to appoint a lawyer for him. Gideon was found guilty, and he was imprisoned. On appeal, the U.S. Supreme Court reversed the conviction and ordered his release. On what grounds did the Court make its decision?

Decision: _____

_____

Rule of Law: _____

_____

Chapter 7

INTENTIONAL TORTS

SCOPE NOTE

Causing harm to people and property, apart from possible criminal implications, can often result in the injured party (victim) having a right of civil recovery against the wrongdoer. Torts is that area of the law that concerns injury-causing conduct and compensation to a victim. The vocabulary and principles of private, civil wrongs stemming from breaches of legal duties to act without danger to others, is focused on in Chapters Seven and Eight. Because tort law is essentially an exercise in loss-shifting (the recovering victim transfers to the injury-causer the financial liability for the loss suffered through the injury), our attention will be directed towards those types of acts that trigger the loss-shifting mechanism: deliberate, intentional harm to others, discussed in Chapter Seven; careless conduct resulting in, accidental harm and the concept of "strict liability," both focused on in Chapter Eight.

Chapter Seven introduces the terminology and basic concepts of intentional torts. What acts constitute the deliberate injuring of another person or their property? What excuses or justifications for such conduct are recognized that absolve the actor from liability? These and other concerns are addressed in relation to the overriding purpose of tort law–compensation to the injured party.

EDUCATIONAL OBJECTIVES

1. Be familiar with the range of conflicts brought to tort law for resolution.

2. Differentiate among the various legal/equitable remedies available to a tort victim.

3. Identify and distinguish among the various acts recognized as intentional harm to business, property or persons.

4. Discuss the plaintiff's burden of proof in the context of intentional torts.

5. Enumerate the various valid defenses and their respective required elements associated with an intentional tort theory of recovery.

CHAPTER OUTLINE

I. Intent–the term denotes either that the person desires to cause the consequences of his act or that he believes that those consequences are substantially certain to result from his act

II. Harm to the Person
    A. Battery–an intentional infliction of harmful or offensive bodily contact
    B. Assault–intentional conduct toward another person that puts him in fear of immediate bodily harm
    C. False Imprisonment–or false arrest, is the intentional confining of a person against her will
    D. Infliction of Emotional Distress–atrocious, intolerable conduct beyond all bounds of decency

III. Harm to the Right of Dignity
    A. Defamation–false communication that injures a person's reputation
        1. Elements of defamation–include libel and slander (written and spoken defamation).
        2. Defenses to defamation–truth and privilege are defenses to defamation
    B. Invasion of Privacy–consists of four distinct torts
        1. Appropriation–of a person's name or likeness
        2. Intrusion–unreasonable and offensive interference with the solitude or seclusion of another
        3. Public disclosure of private facts–offensive publicity of private information
        4. False light–unreasonable and untruthful publicity that places another in a false light that is highly offensive
        5. Defenses–absolute, conditional, and constitutional privilege are defenses to invasion of privacy
    C. Misuse of Legal Procedure–consists of three torts: malicious prosecution, wrongful civil proceedings, and abuse of process

IV. Harm to Property
    A. Real Property–land and anything attached to it such as buildings, trees, and minerals
        1. Trespass–entering on, remaining on, and failing to leave land in possession of another
        2. Nuisance–a non-trespassory invasion of another's interest in the private use and enjoyment of land
    B. Personal Property–is any property other than an interest in land
        1. Trespass–an intentional taking or unauthorized use of another's personal property
        2. Conversion–an intentional exercise of dominion or control over another's property that justly requires the payment of full value for the property

V. Harm to Economic Interests
  A. Interference with Contractual Relations–subjects a person to liability for the monetary loss that results
  B. Disparagement–publication of false statements about the title or quality of another's property or products
  C. Fraudulent Misrepresentation–a false representation of fact, opinion, or law to induce another to act or to refrain from action

VI. Defenses to Intentional Torts
  A. Consent–willingness that an act shall occur that negates the wrongfulness of the act
  B. Privilege–includes conditional and absolute privileges

TRUE–FALSE: Circle true or false.

T   F   1. A tort is a private wrong generally resulting in personal injury or in property damage or destruction.

T   F   2. Battery is the threat of bodily harm by the tortfeasor.

T   F   3. An example of the tort of emotional distress is rude and abusive language.

T   F   4. An obvious defense to the tort of trespass is that the trespasser was mistakenly unaware of the trespassing.

T   F   5. Any force by an owner, including deadly force, can be used to prevent a trespass across the owner's property.

T   F   6. One defense to the commission of an intentional tort is the plaintiff's consent to the defendant's conduct.

T   F   7. If the accused in a criminal case is found not guilty, that person can sue the public prosecutor for malicious prosecution.

T   F   8. Like other subject matter areas of the law such as contracts, tort law is static, i.e., it never changes.

T   F   9. Truth is the only complete defense to a lawsuit for defamation.

T   F   10. The privilege of self-defense to prevent harm to oneself may exist whether or not danger actually exists.

T   F   11. Tort law is primarily based upon common law.

T   F   12. The law protects the rights of the possessor of real property to its exclusive use and quiet enjoyment.

KEY TERMS–MATCHING EXERCISE: Select the term that best completes each statement below.

1. Tort	8. False imprisonment	15. Defamation
2. Slander	9. Malicious prosecution	16. Intrusion
3. Battery	10. Conditional privilege	17. Appropriation
4. Assault	11. Absolute privilege	18. False light
5. Disparagement	12. Nuisance	19. Libel
6. Chattel	13. Conversion	20. Exemplary
7. Privilege	14. Duress	

_____ 1. The kind of conduct that furthers an important social interest and creates immunity from tort liability.

_____ 2. A wrongful act causing personal injury or property damage or destruction.

_____ 3. A threat to do immediate bodily harm.

_____ 4. Intentionally confining a person against her will within fixed boundaries and without an available alternative exit.

_____ 5. An unjust commencement of a criminal proceeding without probable cause and for an improper purpose.

_____ 6. Like the defense of truth, this type of privilege protects the defendant from liability for defamation regardless of motive or intent.

_____ 7. Another name for personal property.

_____ 8. A non-trespassory invasion of another's interest in the use and enjoyment of land.

_____ 9. Interference with another's right of control of personal property as to require full payment for the property.

_____ 10. False statements intended to cast doubt upon the quality of another's products.

_____ 11. Another name for punitive damages.

_____ 12. The type of defamatory communication that is written.

_____ 13. The use of a plaintiff's name or photograph for the benefit of a defendant.

_____ 14. The type of invasion of privacy that is an unreasonable and highly offensive interference with the solitude of another.

_____ 15. The type of defamatory communication that is oral.

MULTIPLE CHOICE: Select the alternative that best completes each statement below.

_____ 1. Which of the following are responsible for their intentional torts? (a) adults (b) minors (c) incompetent persons (d) all of the above

_____ 2. The tort of defamation includes (a) libel and slander (b) assault and battery (c) trespass and public nuisance (d) all of the above.

_____ 3. A person may commit the tort of trespass (a) on land (b) beneath the ground (c) above the surface of the land (d) all of the above.

_____ 4. Concerning chattels, the measure of damages (a) for the tort of trespass is the amount of damage for the actual harm to the value of the chattel (b) for the tort of conversion is the full value of the chattel (c) for both trespass and conversion is the amount of damages for the loss of possession of the chattel (d) only a and b above.

_____ 5. An example of a tort that is not intentional is (a) defamation (b) negligence (c) invasion of privacy (d) emotional distress.

_____ 6. The tort of invasion of privacy does not include (a) the appropriation of a person's name (b) the unreasonable publication of private facts (c) trespassing on another's property (d) entering of another's home uninvited.

_____ 7. Interference with the performance of a contract by another may be (a) by the use of physical force (b) by threats (c) by an offer of higher pay for the performer (d) all of the above.

_____ 8. Consent to conduct, resulting in damage to the consenter's property but no liability, is valid if made by (a) an adult (b) a minor (c) an incompetent (d) an intoxicated person.

_____ 9. The privilege of self-defense exists (a) as an absolute privilege (b) provided the defendant reasonably believed that it was necessary (c) only in cases in which actual danger to the defender occurs (d) all of the above.

_____ 10. A fraudulent misrepresentation that induces another to enter a written agreement could involve a lawsuit within the law of (a) torts (b) contracts (c) both torts and contracts (d) none of the above.

_____ 11. The type of invasion of privacy that imposes liability for false publicity that places another in a position that is highly offensive is (a) intrusion (b) appropriation (c) false light (d) all of the above.

_____ 12. Privilege is a defense to intentional torts and it includes (a) defense of property (b) defense of other persons (c) self-defense (d) all of the above.

_____ 13. Intentional interference with property rights includes the torts of (a) trespass to real or personal property (b) conversion (c) nuisance (d) all of the above.

CASE PROBLEMS–SHORT ESSAY ANSWERS: Read each case problem carefully. When appropriate, answer by stating a Decision for the case and by explaining the rationale–Rule of Law–relied upon to support your decision.

1. While playing ice hockey, A knocks B down and continues to slam B's head against the ice. B's right eye is injured, and B sues. A argues that everyone knows hockey is a "violent" sport and that B's consent to play the game discharges any liability of A to B. Has a tort been committed? Explain.

   Decision: _____

   _____

   Rule of Law: _____

   _____

2. A says to B, "I'm going to beat you up." There is no way B can avoid the fight. A starts the fight. B grabs a rock and smashes A's head with it. A is seriously injured. What kind of tort liability, if any, would B have in this case? Explain.

   Decision: _____

   _____

   Rule of Law: _____

   _____

3. A newspaper prints a photograph of A with a caption stating that A has been accused of rape. In fact, the newspaper printed a photograph of the wrong person. Have the torts of defamation and invasion of privacy both been committed? Explain.

Decision: _____

_____

Rule of Law: _____

_____

4. A says to B that C has a venereal disease. A's statement is not true. C learns of A's comment and sues. What tort has been committed? Explain.

Decision: _____

_____

Rule of Law: _____

_____

5. As a practical joke, A calls B on the phone and tells B that B's child has been hit by a car and is in the hospital. B sues A. Who wins? Explain.

Decision: _____

_____

Rule of Law: _____

_____

Chapter 8

NEGLIGENCE AND STRICT LIABILITY

SCOPE NOTE

The basic elements associated with recovery to the victim of careless conduct (negligence) or ultra-hazardous behavior (strict liability) are the focus of attention in Chapter Eight. What is negligence? How does the law determine whether an accident was unavoidable (no victim recovery) or avoidable (negligence)? What types of behavior fall within the strict liability category? These and other issues developed in Chapter Eight close out our discussion of tort law.

EDUCATIONAL OBJECTIVES

1. Define and discuss the basic elements of negligence.

2. Distinguish among the various sources of duty of care.

3. Develop the meaning and significance of the res ipsa loquitur doctrine vis-a-vis the burden of proof of the victim/plaintiff.

4. Define and explain the importance of proximate causation.

5. Differentiate among the various defenses to a complaint of negligence.

6. Enumerate the types of harm falling under strict liability.

7. Develop the defenses that can be successfully asserted in response to a strict liability complaint.

CHAPTER OUTLINE

I. Negligence
   A. Breach of Duty of Care
      1. Reasonable person standard–the degree of care that a reasonable person would exercise in a given situation
         a. Children–a child's conduct must conform to that of a child of like age, intelligence and experience
         b. Physical disability–a disabled person's conduct must conform to that of a reasonable person under like disability
         c. Mental deficiency–a mentally deficient person is held to the reasonable person standard
         d. Superior skill or knowledge–professionals must exercise the care and skill of members in good standing within their profession
         e. Emergencies–the standard is still the reasonable person but under emergency circumstances
         f. Violation of statute–the reasonable person standard of conduct may be established by statute
      2. Duty to act–generally, no one is required to aid another in peril
      3. Duties of possessors of land
         a. Duty to trespassers–generally, none
         b. Duty to licensees–the possessor of land owes a higher duty of care to licensees than to trespassers
         c. Duty to invitees–duty to exercise reasonable care to protect invitees against dangerous conditions
      4. Res ipsa loquitur–a rule that permits the jury to infer both negligent conduct and causation from the mere occurrence of certain types of events
   B. Proximate Cause
      1. Causation in fact–the defendant's conduct was the actual cause of the injury
      2. Limitations on causation in fact
         a. Unforeseeable consequences–may negate the defendant's liability for negligence
         b. Superseding cause–an intervening act that relieves the defendant's liability to the plaintiff
   C. Injury–the defendant's negligence must have caused harm or injury
   D. Defenses to Negligence
      1. Contributory negligence–both parties contribute to the negligence that causes the harm; damages cannot be recovered
      2. Comparative negligence–damages are apportioned between the parties in proportion to their degree of negligence
      3. Assumption of risk–a plaintiff who voluntarily and knowingly assumes the risk of harm arising from the negligence of the defendant cannot recover for such harm

II. Strict Liability
  A. Activities Giving Rise to Strict Liability
     1. Abnormally dangerous activities–for harm resulting from such activities, strict liability is imposed
     2. Keeping of animals
        a. Trespassing animals–owners are generally strictly liable for harm caused by trespass of their animals
        b. Nontrespassing animals–keepers of wild animals are strictly liable for damage they cause, whether or not they are trespassing
     3. Products liability–a form of strict liability upon manufacturers and merchants who sell goods in a defective condition
  B. Defenses to Strict Liability
     1. Contributory negligence–is not a defense to strict liability
     2. Comparative negligence–some states apply this doctrine to products liability cases
     3. Assumption of risk–is a defense to an action based upon strict liability

TRUE–FALSE: Circle true or false.

T   F   1. The basis of liability for negligence is the failure to exercise reasonable care for the safety of other persons or their property.

T   F   2. Generally, the burden of proof in a civil action for negligence is on the plaintiff.

T   F   3. A physically disabled person and a mentally deficient person are held to the standard of conduct of a reasonable person with like disabilities or deficiencies.

T   F   4. Manufacturers and merchants who sell defective goods that are unreasonably dangerous to a consumer are strictly liable regardless of due care.

T   F   5. Keepers (owners) of dangerous and domestic animals are strictly liable for the injuries the animals cause only if the keeper is aware that the animals are dangerous.

T   F   6. Keepers of domestic animals are only liable for the injuries caused by their animal to other people.

T   F   7. Strict liability refers to a defendant's absolute liability without regard to negligence or intent on the part of the tortfeasor (defendant).

T   F   8. No one is under an affirmative duty to aid another who is in danger under any circumstances.

T   F   9. It is possible for a person to be injured by another without the latter having any liability.

T   F   10. Landowners who know that trespassers are crossing their property owe no duty to warn the trespassers of any hazards that exist on the land.

T   F   11. Parents are liable for all torts committed by their minor children.

T   F   12. The reasonable person standard means that a reasonable person is always careful, prudent and never negligent.

KEY TERMS–MATCHING EXERCISE: Select the term that best completes each statement below.

1. Res ipsa loquitur	8. Contributory negligence	14. But for rule
2. Reasonable person		15. Proximate cause
3. Strict liability	9. Products liability	16. Last clear chance
4. Licensee	10. Assumption of risk	17. Conversion
5. Trespasser	11. Comparative negligence	18. Substantial factor test
6. Negligence	12. Act of God	19. Superseding cause
7. Public invitee	13. Modified	20. Business visitor

_____ 1. Conduct that falls below the standard established by law for protection of others against unreasonable risk of harm.

_____ 2. Type of comparative negligence that denies any recovery to a tort plaintiff whose self-carelessness is equal to or greater than the defendant's negligence.

_____ 3. The doctrine that apportions damages between parties in proportion to the degree (percentage) of fault.

_____ 4. A person privileged to enter upon land only with the consent of the lawful possessor.

_____ 5. The rule that means "the thing speaks for itself".

_____ 6. A widely applied test for causation in fact.

_____ 7. A standard of conduct involving the duty of care and imposed by law.

_____ 8. A business invitee such as a plumber who enters a home for the purpose of making repairs.

_____ 9. A common law defense available in a few states in negligence cases in which the plaintiff and defendant are both at fault and neither can recover damages.

_____ 10. A person who enters on the land of another without permission.

_____ 11. A person who enters a municipal pool to swim.

_____ 12. An intervening event that may relieve the defendant of liability.

_____ 13. Another name for absolute liability or liability without fault.

_____ 14. A valid defense to a charge of negligence that prohibits the plaintiff's recovery because of plaintiff's consent to encounter a known danger.

_____ 15. A form of strict liability imposed on manufacturers who sell defective goods.

MULTIPLE CHOICE: Select the alternative that best completes each statement below.

_____ 1. Which of the following is not a defense to strict liability? (a) contributory negligence (b) comparative negligence (c) assumption of risk (d) all of the above.

_____ 2. The possessor of land owes no duty of care to (a) invitees (b) licensees (c) business visitors (d) an adult trespasser.

_____ 3. Domestic animals that are generally considered safe to mankind include (a) cats and dogs (b) horses and sheep (c) cattle (d) all of the above.

_____ 4. Under the ALI's Restatement of Torts #3, (a) any type of assumption of risk is completely eliminated as a recognized defense (b) implied assumption of risk is treated as a form of contributory negligence (c) express assumption of risk is recognized only if based on a written contract (d) none of the above.

_____ 5. Which of the following is not a defense to a charge of negligence? (a) assumption of risk (b) contributory negligence (c) proximate cause (d) comparative negligence

_____ 6. The reasonable person standard (a) is what a judge or jury determines that a reasonable person would have done in specific circumstances (b) requires a child who drives a boat or car to be held to the standard of care of a child of like age, intelligence and experience under the same circumstances (c) does not hold insane persons responsible for their negligent acts (d) all of the above.

_____ 7. Which of the following professional or skilled persons would not be required to exercise special care and skill normally possessed by those practicing their professions or trade? (a) doctors and attorneys (b) teachers and professors (c) carpenters and electricians (d) architects and engineers.

_____ 8. The duty of affirmative action is not imposed on a defendant to aid or protect the plaintiff if the parties are (a) parent and child (b) employer and employee (c) best friends and neighbors (d) innkeeper and guest.

_____ 9. Strict liability will be imposed regardless of intent or negligence for (a) crop dusting that kills other life (b) faulty merchandise that results in injury (c) the use of dynamite in populated areas (d) all of the above.

_____ 10. If the plaintiff is aware of the dangerous or negligent conduct of the defendant and ignores it and is subsequently injured, the plaintiff cannot recover damages due to the doctrine of (a) contributory negligence (b) comparative negligence (c) assumption of risk (d) last clear chance.

_____ 11. A parent is responsible for the torts of her minor children if the parent (a) authorizes the tort (b) ratifies the tort (c) does not properly control her child's behavior (d) all of the above.

_____ 12. The possessor of land owes a duty of care to (a) licensees (b) public invitees (c) business visitors (d) all of the above.

_____ 13. Which of the following is not a factor that imposes limitations on the causal connection between the defendant's negligence and the plaintiff's injury? (a) foreseeable events (b) superseding causes (c) unforeseeable consequences (d) none of the above.

CASE PROBLEMS–SHORT ESSAY ANSWERS:
Read each case problem carefully. When appropriate, answer by stating a Decision for the case and by explaining the rationale–Rule of Law–relied upon to support your decision.

1. While flying her airplane and performing various stunts, Joelene Brady loses control of the plane and crashes into Sarah Johnson's home. Sarah sues. Joelene claims it was an unintentional accident. Who wins? Explain.

    Decision: _____

    _____

    Rule of Law: _____

    _____

2. Mark Benson is taking care of five-year-old Kathy Walsh while Kathy's mother is in the hospital. Kathy wanders from the house onto a nearby railroad track. Mark sees her on the track and a train is approaching. To avoid liability, must Mark make an attempt to rescue Kathy at the risk of his own life? Explain.

Decision: _____

_____

Rule of Law: _____

_____

3. While crossing a street, Abner and Baker meet in the middle of the street, have an argument, and begin fighting. Abner knocks Baker down, causing him to strike his head on the pavement and rendering him unconscious. Abner walks away. Carol unavoidably runs over the unconscious Baker with her car, seriously injuring him. Was the intervening force (Carol's car striking Baker) a superseding cause that relieves Abner of liability? Explain.

Decision: _____

_____

Rule of Law: _____

_____

4. In a state that has a comparative negligence statute, a jury determines that the plaintiff, Susan, has sustained damages of $50,000 and that the percentages of fault of the parties to the case, Susan and the defendant, Michael, are: plaintiff–10% negligent; defendant–90% negligent. What would be Susan's judgment award in damages in this case?

Decision: _____

_____

Rule of Law: _____

_____

5. The Swanberg Soup Company has shipped cases of its soup that are contaminated with botulism food poisoning to its retailers. Matthew purchases a can of the soup, eats some of it, and becomes very sick. Explain the type of liability the company has to Matthew in this case.

Decision: _____

_____

Rule of Law: _____

_____

LEGAL ENVIRONMENT OF BUSINESS RESEARCH QUESTIONS:

Drawing upon information contained in the text, as well as outside sources, discuss the following questions:

1. Common law does not impose a legal duty on persons to assist endangered strangers. Some states have enacted "Good Samaritan" Statutes eliminating this common law rule and creating a legal duty, under certain circumstances, to assist strangers facing danger. Has your state enacted such a statute? What are the advantages/disadvantages associated with laws creating such a legal duty of assistance?

2. Some jurists and social commentators have pointed out the necessity for calling a Constitutional Convention to address various amendments to the Constitution, including equal rights, right to life, balanced budget, anti-flag desecration, and right to die. Should such a Convention be called? What would be gained by such action and at what cost?

Chapter 9

INTRODUCTION TO CONTRACTS

SCOPE NOTE

Contracts is an area of law that touches nearly all other branches of business law. Understanding contract law provides a useful foundation for learning and applying principles associated with other specific fields of business law. Chapter Nine focuses on basic concepts of contract law, the various types of binding agreements recognized by courts and important introductory terminology. This knowledge provides a crucial frame of reference for the successful study of the principles and vocabulary that comprise the specific areas of contract law that will occupy our further inquiry into the arena of binding agreements.

EDUCATIONAL OBJECTIVES

1. Discuss the importance of contracts in business.

2. Identify present day controlling sources of contract law.

3. Define what is meant by "contract."

4. Differentiate the various classifications of contracts based on such factors as extent of performance, validity, method of creation and type of use.

5. Enumerate the particular elements that make up a contract.

6. List examples of contracts that you have entered into during recent weeks.

CHAPTER OUTLINE

I. Development of the Law of Contracts
  A. Common Law–contracts are primarily governed by state common law
  B. The Uniform Commercial Code–governs all sales contracts concerning personal property
  C. Types of Contracts Outside the Code– general contract law governs these contracts

II. Definition of a Contract–a contract is a set of promises that the courts will enforce

III. Requirements of a Contract–the four basic requirements of a contract are mutual assent, consideration, legality of object, and capacity

IV. Classification of Contracts
  A. Express and Implied Contracts–contracts created either by express language or by conduct of the parties
  B. Unilateral and Bilateral Contracts–contracts created by a promise for an act or by an exchange of promises
  C. Valid, Void, Voidable, and Unenforceable Contracts–contracts classified according to their enforceability
  D. Executed and Executory Contracts–contracts that are completed or unperformed
  E. Formal and Informal Contracts–contracts based upon a particular form or those that are not dependent upon formality for their validity

V. Promissory Estoppel–under this doctrine, some noncontractual promises are enforceable in order to avoid injustice

VI. Quasi Contracts–are implied in law contracts

TRUE–FALSE: Circle true or false.

T F 1. Contract law could be referred to as the law of enforceable promises.

T F 2. A source of law upon which much of contract law is based is state common law.

T F 3. The Uniform Commercial Code (U.C.C.) is the sole source of contract law in the United States today.

T F 4. According to the U.C.C., all contracts are promises and all promises are contracts.

T F 5. A bilateral contract results from the exchange of one promise for another.

T F 6. When it is not clear whether a unilateral or bilateral contract has been formed, a unilateral contract will be presumed by the courts.

T   F   7. Both the defrauded and fraudulent parties to a contract may declare the contract void.

T   F   8. A void contract may be enforceable.

T   F   9. To be executed, a contract must be fully performed by all parties.

T   F   10. A quasi contract may be considered an obligation imposed by law and based upon equitable principles.

T   F   11. In a bilateral contract there are two promisors and two promisees.

T   F   12. Only written contracts, not oral ones, are binding and enforceable.

KEY TERMS–MATCHING EXERCISE: Select the term that best completes each statement below.

---

1. Common Law	8. Forbearance	15. Goods
2. Uniform Commercial Code	9. Quasi	16. Promisor
3. Voidable	10. Promissory estoppel	17. Formal
4. Bilateral	11. Void	18. Breach
5. Implied	12. Unilateral	19. Informal
6. Executory	13. Executed	20. Promisee
7. Recognizances	14. Fraudulent	

_____   1. The U.C.C. term for movable, tangible personal property.

_____   2. An enforceable contract formed by conduct.

_____   3. A contract created by a promise for a performance.

_____   4. The primary source of contract law.

_____   5. A contract that either may be avoided or enforced.

_____   6. Formal acknowledgments of indebtedness made in court.

_____   7. A promise not to do an act.

_____   8. A contract in which there are one or more unperformed promises.

_____ 9. A contract imposed by law where there has been no expressed assent.

_____ 10. The source of contract law governing the sale of personal property.

_____ 11. The failure to properly perform a contract.

_____ 12. The person who makes a promise.

_____ 13. The person to whom the promise is made.

_____ 14. A contract created by an exchange of promises.

_____ 15. Simple contracts that do not depend upon formality for their legal validity.

MULTIPLE CHOICE: Select the alternative that best completes each statement below.

_____ 1. The U.C.C. modifies contract law and applies to a type of contract involving (a) the transfer of title to goods from seller to buyer for a price (b) employment contracts (c) contracts for the sale of patents and copyrights (d) all of the above.

_____ 2. Contracts may be (a) oral (b) written (c) implied from the parties' conduct (d) all of the above.

_____ 3. An example of a formal contract is (a) a promise under seal (b) a negotiable instrument (c) a recognizance (d) all of the above.

_____ 4. A says to B, "If you paint my garage, I will pay you one hundred dollars." B paints the garage. This creates a (a) bilateral contract (b) unilateral contract (c) void contract (d) all of the above.

_____ 5. A contract induced by fraud is (a) void (b) express (c) voidable (d) unenforceable.

_____ 6. An essential element of all contracts is (a) manifestation of mutual assent (b) consideration (c) legality of the object (d) all of the above.

_____ 7. The party entitled to elect to avoid a contract induced by fraud is called (a) a minor. (b) the defrauded part y (c) the fraudulent party (d) none of the above.

_____ 8. The law of contracts is also basic to which of the following fields of law? (a) agency (b) commercial paper (c) sales of personal property (d) all of the above.

_____ 9. An authoritative reference book that gives an orderly presentation of the law of contracts is the (a) Reporter (b) American Law Institute (c) Restatement (d) none of the above.

_____ 10. The only state that has not adopted all sections of the U.C.C. is (a) Minnesota (b) Georgia (c) Louisiana (d) Arizona.

_____ 11. General contract law governs all of the following except (a) sales of personal property (b) sales of real property (c) insurance contracts (d) service contracts.

_____ 12. A contract that fails to satisfy the requirements of the Statute of Frauds is classified as (a) valid (b) unenforceable (c) void (d) voidable.

_____ 13. An oral or written contract in which all the terms have been definitely stated and agreed upon by the parties is an (a) informal contract (b) implied contract (c) express contract (d) none of the above.

CASE PROBLEMS–SHORT ESSAY ANSWERS: Read each case problem carefully. When appropriate, answer by stating a Decision for the case and by explaining the rationale–Rule of Law–relied upon to support your decision.

1. When Sara became ill, Mary performed housekeeping services for Sara without any agreement that Mary be paid. Sara requested the services, and Mary expected to be paid. Sara died. In a lawsuit seeking compensation for Mary, the court ruled a contract existed. What kind of contract is it? Explain.

   Decision:_____

   _____

   Rule of Law:_____

   _____

2. Julie plans a summer trip to Europe. Her best friend, Karen, has been accepted to medical school in the fall. Karen says, "Julie, while on your trip, if you buy a microscope for me, I will give you $100.00." Julie buys the microscope in Europe and returns home. Does a contract exist? Explain.

   Decision:_____

   _____

   Rule of Law:_____

   _____

3. Barry says to Arnold, "I will sell you my motorcycle for $400." Arnold replies, "O.K." Neither party used the word promise in their negotiation. Was a bilateral contract created? Explain.

Decision:_____

_____

Rule of Law:_____

_____

4. Michael lied to Joyce about important terms of their contract. On the basis of Michael's statement, Joyce agreed to the terms and signed the contract. How would such a contract be classified? Explain.

Decision:_____

_____

Rule of Law:_____

_____

5. An employee of Harold's Hardware and Appliances Store delivers a TV set to Mary Martin mistakenly believing she had ordered it. Would the hardware store be entitled to the return of the set? Explain the legal concept of contract law involved in this case.

Decision:_____

_____

Rule of Law:_____

_____

Chapter 10

MUTUAL ASSENT

SCOPE NOTE

An agreement (meeting of the minds) is the basis for a contract. All contracts must be agreements, but all agreements are not contracts. The first and most important area of contract study is how the parties to a contract reached an agreement. Meeting of the minds, as a primary factor in creating a legally valid and enforceable agreement, concerns the process by which the parties come to an understanding of the crucial terms that embody an agreement.

EDUCATIONAL OBJECTIVES

1. Identify the acts that together form an agreement.

2. Discuss the various requirements for a valid offer and acceptance.

3. Discuss the types of conduct of the parties and events that bring the life of an offer to an end.

4. Enumerate the significance of silence at the agreement formation stage.

CHAPTER OUTLINE

I. Offer
   A. Essentials of an Offer
      1. Communication–mutual assent to form a contract requires that the offeree must have knowledge of the offer that was made by the offeror to the offeree.
      2. Intent–to have legal effect, an offeror must manifest an intent to enter into a contract
         a. Preliminary negotiations–are not valid offers that can create a contract
         b. Advertisements–a merchant invites customers to make offers to buy goods

        c. Auction sales–the auctioneer does not make offers to sell but invites offers to buy

     3. Definiteness–the terms of a contract must be reasonably certain

        a. Open terms–the Code provides standards by which omitted terms may be determined

        b. Output and requirements contracts–are enforceable agreements under the Code when based upon the good faith of the parties

  B. Duration of Offers

     1. Lapse of time–if no time is stated in the offer, an offer will terminate after a reasonable time

     2. Revocation–an offer may be revoked any time before it is accepted

        a. Option contracts–the offeror is bound to hold open an offer for a specified time

        b. Firm offers under the Code–are those made by a merchant in writing and signed

        c. Statutory irrevocability–certain offers are irrevocable by statute

        d. Irrevocable offers of unilateral contracts–the Restatement holds that once performance begins, the offeror is obligated not to revoke the offer for a reasonable time

        e. Promissory estoppel–a noncontractual promise may be enforced to avoid an injustice

     3. Rejection–a refusal of the offer terminates it

     4. Counteroffer–is a counterproposal that also terminates the original offer

     5. Death or incompetency–of either party terminates the offer

     6. Destruction of subject matter–of an offer terminates the offer

     7. Subsequent illegality–discharges the obligations of both parties under the contract

II. Acceptance

  A. Communication of Acceptance

     1. General rule–in all bilateral contracts, acceptance must be communicated to the offeror; in unilateral contracts, notice of acceptance to the offeror may not be required

     2. Silence as acceptance–generally, silence or inaction is not an acceptance of the offer

     3. Effective moment–a contract is formed when the last act necessary to its formation is done

        a. Stipulated provisions in the offer–of the means of acceptance must be followed

        b. Authorized means–the means of communication expressly authorized by the offeror

        c. Unauthorized means–if the medium of communication used by the offeree is unauthorized, it still may be effective if it is received in a timely manner

        d. Acceptance following a prior rejection–must be received by the offeror prior to the receipt of the rejection

  B. Variant Acceptances

     1. Common law–an acceptance must be positive and unequivocal; it must be the mirror image of the offer

     2. Code–because of the realities of modern business practices, the Code modifies the common law

TRUE–FALSE: Circle true or false.

T   F   1. One of the essentials of a contract is the agreement between two or more parties.

T   F   2. Parties usually manifest their mutual assent by means of an offer and an acceptance.

T   F   3. An auction sale is a binding offer to sell the property being auctioned.

T   F   4. It is essential to the contractual relationship that the offeree have knowledge of the offer.

T   F   5. After rejecting an offer, the offeree no longer has the power to bind the parties by accepting.

T   F   6. Illegality subsequent to the formation of a contract will discharge the contractual obligations of the parties.

T   F   7. The acceptance of an offer can create a contract only if the offer was communicated to a specifically named offeree.

T   F   8. As a general rule, silence on the part of a person to whom an offer is made is considered an acceptance of the offer.

T   F   9. After an offer has expired, there can be no acceptance of it.

T   F   10. An authorized means of communicating an acceptance is the method stated by the offeror in the offer or, if none is stated, it is the method used by the offeror.

T   F   11. Retail prices listed by merchants on items in a clothing or appliance store are not considered offers made by the merchants that a customer may accept.

T   F   12. The incompetency of either the offeror or the offeree ordinarily terminates an offer.

KEY TERMS–MATCHING EXERCISE: Select the term that best completes each statement below.

1. Offeree	6. Revocation	11. Counteroffer
2. Offeror	7. Alternative	12. Good faith
3. Option	8. Firm offer	13. Auctioneer
4. Mirror image rule	9. Inverted unilateral contract	14. Silence
5. Definiteness	10. Jest	15. Acceptance

16. Output contract   18. Unilateral contract   20. Forbearance

17. Invitation   19. Merchant

_____ 1. An overt act by the offeree that manifests assent to the terms of the offer.

_____ 2. An act by the offeree that will terminate the offer yet indicates a willingness to contract.

_____ 3. Inaction by the offeree that may result in an acceptance under special circumstances.

_____ 4. The person who makes the offer in a contractual dealing.

_____ 5. A circumstance where one may lack the required intent to form a contract.

_____ 6. The person to whom an offer is made.

_____ 7. This term is defined as "honesty in fact in the conduct or the transaction concerned."

_____ 8. A contract in which the offeror is bound to keep open an offer for a specified time.

_____ 9. A contract created by an act for a promise.

_____ 10. No acceptance of a contract exists under common law because similar terms of agreement, contained in printed forms used by both buyers and sellers, are not present.

_____ 11. An agreement of a buyer to purchase the entire production of a seller's factory.

_____ 12. The person who is bound to keep a written offer to buy or sell goods open for up to three months.

_____ 13. The promise to refrain from doing an act.

_____ 14. The withdrawal of an offer that occurs before the offer is accepted.

_____ 15. A contract created by a promise exchanged for an act.

MULTIPLE CHOICE: Select the alternative that best completes each statement below.

_____ 1. The terms of an offer may be accepted by (a) spoken words (b) a letter (c) a telegram (d) all of the above.

_____ 2. An offer may terminate by (a) revocation (b) rejection (c) death of either party (d) all of the above.

_____ 3. A definite contractual proposal requesting a forbearance and made by one person to another is (a) an offer (b) an invitation (c) an acceptance. (d) a quasi contract.

_____ 4. To create a contract, an offer must (a) be definite and certain (b) be communicated to the offeree (c) have contractual intent (d) all of the above.

_____ 5. When the auctioneer brings the hammer down on the bidding, the result is (a) a withdrawal (b) an offer (c) a manifestation (d) a contract.

_____ 6. If the offeror has the power to terminate the offer before acceptance, the offeror has (a) rejection power (b) the power to lapse (c) irrevocable options (d) the power of revocation.

_____ 7. The manifestation of an unwillingness to accept an offer is called a (a) revocation (b) rejection (c) withdrawal (d) counteroffer.

_____ 8. An offer (a) may be a promise for a promise (b) must manifest intent to create a contract.(c) that consists of a statement indicating a willingness to offer is not itself a binding offer (d) all of the above.

_____ 9. The following is generally effective upon being sent (dispatched): (a) an offer (b) an acceptance (c) a rejection (d) a revocation.

_____ 10. The standard the law applies to determine if a manifestation of mutual assent has occurred by the words or acts of the parties is (a) an objective standard (b) a subjective standard (c) a relative standard (d) none of the above.

_____ 11. An offer (a) may be a promise for an act (b) may be in the form of an act for a promise (c) requires an offeror and an offeree (d) all of the above.

_____ 12. Lapse of time of an offer (a) may terminate the offer (b) will terminate the offer after a reasonable period of time if no time for termination is stated (c) may be for one day if perishable goods are involved (d) all of the above.

_____ 13. A counteroffer (a) has no effect on the original offer (b) indicates a total rejection of the original offer (c) operates like a rejection (d) none of the above.

CASE PROBLEMS–SHORT ESSAY ANSWERS: Read each case problem carefully. When appropriate, answer by stating a Decision for the case and by explaining the rationale–Rule of Law–relied upon to support your decision.

1. Sam sent a telegram to Jerome offering Jerome the exclusive rights to a certain line of goods. Sam requested a reply by telegram. Jerome sent a registered letter to Sam saying he accepts. Sam refused to comply, and Jerome brings suit. Who prevails? Explain.

Decision: _____

_____

Rule of Law: _____

_____

2. A mailed a box of candy to B, stating that if B wanted to keep the candy, it would cost $5. B never requested the candy. B keeps the candy but refuses to pay. What result?

Decision: _____

_____

Rule of Law: _____

_____

3. A pays B $1,000 for a one-year option to buy five acres of land. Ten months later the value of the land has doubled, and B suddenly dies. B's executor refuses to honor the option, alleging B's death as a termination of the offer. Who prevails? Explain.

Decision: _____

_____

Rule of Law: _____

_____

4. William, whose child is trapped in his burning house, screams hysterically that he will pay $100,000 to anyone who will save the child. Sharon, a bystander, hears William and, at the risk of her life, rescues the child. Was William's statement an offer? Explain.

Decision: _____

_____

Rule of Law: _____

_____

5. Suppose that A mailed B a letter stating, "I wish I could find someone to buy my cattle for $10,000." B knows that $10,000 is a reasonable price. Therefore, B mails a letter to A stating, "I will buy your cattle for $10,000." Does a contract exist? Explain.

Decision: _____

_____

Rule of Law: _____

_____

Chapter 11

CONDUCT INVALIDATING ASSENT

SCOPE NOTE

This chapter focuses upon factors that distinguish an enforceable contract from a voidable or unenforceable contract due to unfairness/inequality in the manner in which the parties reached their agreement. Contracts that seem, on the face, to be valid because essential formation elements are apparently present may, however, be voidable as a result of "contaminations" (misconduct of the parties) in the negotiation (agreement formation) process. What are the "wrongful acts" or misdeeds that remove "reality of consent" from the meeting of the minds process? What remedies are available to contracting parties when "reality of consent" is absent?

EDUCATIONAL OBJECTIVES

1. Define and identify the essential elements of fraud and discuss the consequences of fraud.

2. Differentiate fraud from innocent misrepresentation and discuss the significance of the latter.

3. Define and identify examples of and discuss the differences between duress and undue influence.

4. Distinguish between and discuss the significance of unilateral and bilateral mistakes.

5. Identify situations where a contracting party faces a duty of disclosure and the consequences of failing to meet that duty.

71

CHAPTER OUTLINE

I.   Duress–the law will not enforce any contract induced by improper physical force or improper threats
   A. Physical Compulsion–a type of duress using actual physical force
   B. Improper Threats–include economic and social coercion to compel a person to enter a contract

II. Undue Influence–is taking unfair advantage of a person by reason of a dominant position based upon a confidential relationship

III. Fraud–the following are the two types of fraud:
   A. Fraud in the Execution–a misrepresentation that deceives the defrauded person as to the nature of the contract
   B. Fraud in the Inducement–an intentional misrepresentation of a material fact on which the defrauded person enters the contract in reliance upon the misrepresentation; five requisite elements of fraud in the inducement are:
      1. False representation
      2. Fact
      3. Materiality
      4. Knowledge of falsity and intention to deceive
      5. Justifiable reliance

IV. Nonfraudulent Misrepresentation–a majority of courts permit a rescission of a contract for negligent or innocent misrepresentation if all of the remaining elements of fraud are present

V.   Mistake–an understanding or belief that is not in accord with facts
   A. Mutual Mistake–occurs when both parties are mistaken as to the same facts
   B. Unilateral Mistake–occurs when only one party is mistaken
   C. Assumption of Risk of Mistake–will not allow a party to avoid the contract
   D. Effect of Fault upon Mistake–generally does not allow a party who fails to read a contract to avoid it; a party is held to what she signs
   E. Mistake in Meaning of Terms–generally, there is no mutual assent if both parties in good faith attach different meanings to the terms of their agreement

TRUE–FALSE: Circle true or false.

T   F   1. When undue influence is the issue in a legally challenged contract, the law presumes that advantage was taken by the dominant party.

T   F   2. Sellers are allowed some leeway to puff their goods to the public.

T   F   3. Forcing a person to create a contract against the person's will is called fraud.

T   F   4. All fraudulent contracts are void.

T   F   5. Generally, when a person signs a contract without reading it, the person is bound by its terms.

T   F   6. Duress is always either a tort or a crime.

T   F   7. An example of duress is a threat to sue another for civil damages.

T   F   8. Most courts today allow a rescission of a contract even if the false misrepresentation of a material fact that induces the plaintiff to enter the contract is innocently done.

T   F   9. If there is a mutual mistake between the parties concerning a material fact, the contract may be avoided.

T   F   10. If a contracting party makes a mistake as to the value of the subject matter, the court will rescind the contract.

T   F   11. To establish fraud, the misrepresentation must be known by the fraudulent party to be false and must be made with an intent to deceive.

T   F   12. As a general rule, silence alone does not constitute fraud.

KEY TERMS–MATCHING EXERCISE: Select the term that best completes each statement below.

1. Materiality	8. Mistakes of law	15. Ward
2. Rescission	9. Fiduciary	16. Damages
3. Mistake	10. Duress	17. Unilateral mistake
4. Concealment	11. Scienter	18. Valid
5. Undue influence	12. Mutual	19. Fraudulent person
6. Defrauded person	13. Voidable	20. Silence
7. Opinion	14. Void	

_____ 1. Conduct in which a parent, through unfair persuasion, induces a child to enter a contract.

_____ 2. A statement by a seller that a car is the best "deal" in town.

_____ 3. An element of fraud of sufficient substance to induce reliance in another to enter a contract.

_____ 4. A belief that is not in accord with the facts.

_____ 5. The kind of mistake in which both parties are mistaken.

_____ 6. The Restatement treats some of these beliefs the same as mistakes of fact.

_____ 7. The remedy that returns the parties to the status quo by canceling the contract.

_____ 8. The person who is often unduly influenced by a guardian.

_____ 9. One who is in a relationship of trust and confidence with another.

_____ 10. The classification of a contract induced by improper threats or undue influence.

_____ 11. The classification of a contract induced by actual physical force.

_____ 12. The element of fraud that consists of knowledge of the falsity of the intentional misrepresentation.

_____ 13. The innocent person upon whom fraud is committed.

_____ 14. The use of improper physical coercion to create a contract.

_____ 15. The person who commits fraud.

MULTIPLE CHOICE: Select the alternative that best completes each statement below.

_____ 1. When the courts decide that one should not be held to a contract that was not entered into voluntarily, they are speaking of (a) a mistake of the facts (b) a mistake of the law (c) duress (d) none of the above.

_____ 2. A creditor could threaten to (a) sue a debtor in civil court (b) criminally prosecute he debtor (c) do both of the above (d) do both but be guilty of duress in each instance.

_____ 3. A contract obtained by fraud in the inducement is generally (a) void (b) voidable (c) enforceable (d) none of the above.

_____ 4. A contract obtained by fraud in the execution is generally (a) void (b) voidable (c) mutually enforceable (d) none of the above.

_____ 5. A necessary element for fraud is a false representation concerning (a) a material fact (b) an opinion (c) a prediction (d) none of the above.

_____ 6. Generally, when a person gives an opinion that later proves to be erroneous, the person is liable for (a) fraud (b) duress (c) undue influence (d) none of the above.

_____ 7. A seller is obligated to disclose to a buyer (a) all defects concerning the subject matter (b) latent defects concerning the subject matter (c) defects that would be discovered by an ordinary examination (d) none of the above.

_____ 8. The denial of knowledge of a fact that one knows to exist can form the basis for (a) mistake (b) fraud (c) conversion (d) all of the above.

_____ 9. The required elements for fraud in the inducement are (a) a false representation of a material fact (b) a false representation made with knowledge of its falsity and intent to deceive (c) a false misrepresentation that is justifiably relied upon (d) all of the above.

_____ 10. An erroneous understanding or an inaccurate belief that, if acted upon, may produce an unfortunate result for the acting party is (a) fraud (b) duress (c) undue influence (d) a mistake.

_____ 11. Courts will grant relief from (a) duress (b) fraud (c) undue influence (d) all of the above.

_____ 12. An example of a confidential relationship in which one party could unfairly persuade another to create a contract is (a) an attorney and client (b) a physician and patient (c) a trustee and beneficiary (d) all of the above.

_____ 13. A voidable contract is created when (a) one person unduly influences another (b) an agent breaches her fiduciary duty to her principal (c) there has been a mutual mistake of a material fact (d) all of the above.

CASE PROBLEMS–SHORT ESSAY ANSWERS: Read each case problem carefully. When appropriate, answer by stating a Decision for the case and by explaining the rationale–Rule of Law–relied upon to support your decision.

1. Abner, who is negotiating the sale of his business to Betty, informs Betty that his business made a $10,000 profit during the last year. Betty tells Abner she will let him know of her decision to buy in one week. During this week, but before Betty gives her decision, Abner finds a mistake in the books that shows that he made only a $5,000 profit last year. Betty accepts Abner's offer. Betty now wants to rescind for misrepresentation concerning last year's profit. Can Betty rescind? Explain.

Decision: _____

_____

Rule of Law: _____

_____

2. X points a gun at Y and orders Y to sign a written contract or be shot. X knows the gun is not loaded; Y does not. Later, Y repudiates the contract, and X claims the contract exists because the gun was empty. Does a contract exist? Explain.

    Decision: _____

    _____

    Rule of Law: _____

    _____

3. Barney signs a document without reading it. Later he discovers the document is a written contract. Since no fraud was involved, Barney claims he had no knowledge that he was signing a contract and therefore lacked contractual intent. Does a contract exist? Explain.

    Decision: _____

    _____

    Rule of Law: _____

    _____

4. Seller, in good faith, informs buyer that the stock of a certain corporation will probably be listed on the New York Stock Exchange within two weeks. Buyer, relying on this statement, buys the stock. Can buyer rescind when it is discovered the statement was incorrect? Can buyer sue for damages?

    Decision: _____

    _____

    Rule of Law: _____

    _____

5. Seller offers to sell buyer 1,000 bushels of potatoes growing on seller's farm. Buyer accepts the offer. The potatoes were destroyed by a flood three hours before the contract was signed. Neither buyer nor seller knew of the flood. Can the buyer recover from the seller, if the seller fails to deliver the potatoes? Explain.

    Decision: _____

    _____

    Rule of Law: _____

    _____

Chapter 12

CONSIDERATION

SCOPE NOTE

Parties bargaining for an exchange of items of value is a central factor in the creation of a contract. Understanding the function and purpose of consideration in the formation of valid, enforceable agreements is crucial. What is legally sufficient consideration? How do courts address the issue of adequacy of consideration? How do "moral consideration" and legal consideration differ? These and other issues associated with consideration are developed in this chapter.

EDUCATIONAL OBJECTIVES

1. Define and explain the central position occupied by consideration in the formation of a contract.

2. Enumerate the types of acts/promises that constitute legally sufficient consideration.

3. Distinguish between the various tests used to determine legally sufficient consideration.

4. Discuss the meaning and importance of forbearance in the context of consideration.

5. Clarify the doctrine of consideration in debtor-creditor agreements.

6. Point out situations and related rationale where binding agreements exist even without consideration.

CHAPTER OUTLINE

I. Legal Sufficiency
    A. Adequacy–legal sufficiency has nothing to do with adequacy of consideration
    B. Unilateral Contracts–a promise for an act or a forbearance to act
    C. Bilateral Contracts–a promise for a promise
    D. Illusory Promises–are statements that are in the form of a promise but impose no obligation on the maker of the statements
        1. Output and requirements contracts–an agreement to sell the entire production of a seller or to purchase all the materials of a particular kind that the purchaser needs
        2. Exclusive dealing contracts–a manufacturer grants an exclusive right to a distributor to sell her goods in a designated area
        3. Conditional promises–a contract does not exist until a specific happening or non-happening of an uncertain event occurs
    E. Preexisting Obligation–such a duty is not consideration
        1. Modification of a preexisting contract–must be supported by mutual consideration according to common law, but the Code modifies that law
        2. Substituted contracts–such contracts are valid and discharge the original contract
        3. Settlement of a liquidated debt–is not legally sufficient and thus is not consideration
        4. Settlement of an unliquidated debt–acceptance of the lesser amount discharges the debt but see the position of the Restatement

II. Bargained for Exchange
    A. Past Consideration–is no consideration and unenforceable
    B. Third Parties–may be consideration if the promisor requests the benefit be given to a third person

III. Contracts Without Consideration
    A. Promises to Perform Prior Unenforceable Obligations
        1. Promise to pay debt barred by the Statute of Limitations–an action to enforce a debt must be initiated within a set time period after the debt was due
        2. Promise to pay debt discharged in bankruptcy–another exception to the requirement of consideration if allowed by the Bankruptcy Act
        3. Voidable promises–another promise that is enforceable without new consideration is a new promise to perform a voidable obligation that has not previously been avoided
        4. Moral obligation–under the common law, a promise made to satisfy a preexisting moral obligation lacks consideration and is unenforceable
    B. Promissory Estoppel–if detrimental reliance on a noncontractual promise occurs, the promisor is prohibited from denying the promise
    C. Promises Made Under Seal–a formal or solemn promise executed under seal
    D. Promises Made Enforceable by Statute
        1. Contract modifications–the Code has abandoned the common law rule requiring that a modification of an existing contract be supported by consideration in order to be valid
        2. Renunciation–a written and signed waiver that can discharge a contract without consideration

3. Irrevocable offers–a written offer signed by a merchant to keep open the offer to buy or sell goods is not revocable for lack of consideration during the time stated that it is open, not to exceed three months, or if no time is stated, for a reasonable time

TRUE–FALSE: Circle true or false.

T F 1. Consideration is basically whatever is given in exchange for a promise.

T F 2. The central idea behind consideration is that the contracting parties have entered into a bargained exchange with one another.

T F 3. Valid consideration may exist even though the promises of both parties to a contract are not legally sufficient.

T F 4. Legal sufficiency is equivalent to adequacy of consideration.

T F 5. A legal detriment to you may be nothing more than attending a college, at the request of another, that you might not have attended otherwise.

T F 6. Past consideration is not valid consideration, therefore, no contract exists.

T F 7. An exchange of the offeror's promise for the offeree's forbearance is consideration.

T F 8. A new promise of an obligor to perform a preexisting contractual duty is a legal detriment.

T F 9. Promises to purchase as much of an item as one may want or desire are generally upheld.

T F 10. If, before maturity of a debt, the creditor accepts from the debtor a lesser sum offered in full satisfaction, the entire debt will be canceled.

T F 11. Under the Uniform Commercial Code, a contract for the sale of goods can be effectively modified by the parties without new consideration so long as the modification was intended and in good faith.

T F 12. Under common law, a promise made to satisfy a preexisting moral obligation does constitute valid consideration.

KEY TERMS–MATCHING EXERCISE: Select the term that best completes each statement below.

1. Disputed debt
2. New promise
3. Charitable subscriptions
4. Legal sufficiency
5. Illusory promise
6. Requirements contract
7. Legal detriment

8. Legal benefit
9. Firm offer
10. A promise to satisfy a moral obligation
11. Output contract
12. Promissory estoppel
13. Undisputed debt
14. Contracts under seal

15. Consideration
16. Statute of Limitations
17. Bankruptcy
18. Renunciation
19. Statute of Frauds
20. Past consideration

_____ 1. A debt that is certain as to the monetary amount.

_____ 2. One way in which the Statute of Limitations time period may be extended.

_____ 3. Although technically a gift, courts generally rule such promises are binding.

_____ 4. The result when a promisee takes definite and substantial action in reliance on the promisor's promise.

_____ 5. Doing something you are under no prior legal obligation to do.

_____ 6. The test for consideration that is not dependent on the adequacy of the consideration.

_____ 7. A promise that is so indefinite that no obligation is imposed on the promisor.

_____ 8. An agreement that affords sellers an assured market for all their goods.

_____ 9. An agreement to purchase all the materials of a particular kind that the purchaser needs.

_____ 10. A promise to pay the previous debts of an elderly parent is an example of this unenforceable promise under common law.

_____ 11. A contested obligation to pay a sum certain in money.

_____ 12. The reason that a promise made on account of something that the promisee has already done is unenforceable.

_____ 13. Laws that provide a prescribed period of time in which actions to enforce payment of debts must be initiated after the debts become due.

_____ 14. The Uniform Commercial Code has specifically eliminated the use of these contracts for the sale of goods.

_____ 15. A procedure whereby a claim in a breach of contract case can be discharged without consideration by a written waiver signed and delivered by the aggrieved party.

MULTIPLE CHOICE: Select the alternative that best completes each statement below.

_____ 1. Consideration for a promise may be defined as (a) an act other than a promise (b) a forbearance (c) the creation, modification or destruction of a legal relation (d) all of the above.

_____ 2. The receipt by the promisor of that which the promisor had no prior legal right to receive is a (a) legal benefit (b) legal detriment (c) contract (d) gift.

_____ 3. An event, the happening of which qualifies the duty of performance of a promise, is called a (a) consideration (b) condition (c) gratuitous promise (d) none of the above.

_____ 4. The contract created when a promise is exchanged for an act or a forbearance to act is a (a) bilateral contract (b) void contract (c) gratuitous contract (d) unilateral contract.

_____ 5. The person to whom a promise is made is called the (a) offeree (b) promisor (c) promisee (d) donee.

_____ 6. Where the amount of the debt to be paid has not been agreed upon by the parties, there is (a) an exclusive dealing (b) an undisputed debt (c) a disputed debt (d) none of the above.

_____ 7. A promise made to perform a preexisting public or contractual obligation is generally (a) binding (b) a contract. (c) unenforceable (d) none of the above.

_____ 8. According to the U.C.C., a binding promise that requires no consideration is (a) an agreement made in good faith modifying a contract for the sale of goods (b) a written offer to buy or sell goods by a merchant during the time the offer is open (c) a written waiver, signed and delivered by the aggrieved party, of a claim due to an alleged breach of contract (d) all of the above.

_____ 9. A promise that the promisor should reasonably expect to induce action or forbearance by the promisee may be binding under the doctrine of (a) gratuitous contracts (b) waiver (c) promissory estoppel (d) none of the above.

_____ 10. An exception to the requirement of consideration is (a) a new promise by a debtor to pay a debt dismissed by the Statute of Limitations (b) a promise to pay a debt discharged in bankruptcy (c) a promise under seal in some states (d) all of the above.

_____ 11. In a bilateral contract (a) the parties to the contract exchange promises (b) each party is both a promisor and a promisee (c) mutuality of obligation exists (d) all of the above.

_____ 12. Contracts under seal (a) require consideration to be binding in all states (b) are recognized as binding without consideration in all states (c) are required by the Uniform Commercial Code to contain seals in all contracts for the sale of goods (d) none of the above.

_____ 13. A promise to give a person a present on the person's birthday (a) is a contract (b) is a condition (c) lacks consideration (d) none of the above.

CASE PROBLEMS–SHORT ESSAY ANSWERS: Read each case problem carefully. When appropriate, answer by stating a Decision for the case and by explaining the rationale–Rule of Law–relied upon to support your decision.

1. In early 1993, Mrs. Good signed a pledge to the All Heart Fund for the sum of $25,000. Later, she was hardpressed for money and wished to rescind. As attorney for the fund, what could you argue?

   Decision: _____

   _____

   Rule of Law: _____

   _____

2. Samantha fixed Ray's car and tendered a bill of $75.00. Ray, in good faith, disputed the debt and returned $60.00 by check to Samantha stating on the check, "payment in full." Samantha cashed the check and months later sued for the $15.00. What results?

   Decision: _____

   _____

   Rule of Law: _____

   _____

3. Amy sells a piano to Betty for $1,000. The next day, Betty asks Amy to guarantee (warrant) the condition of the piano, and Amy agrees. How would this case be decided by the U.C.C.? Explain.

   Decision: _____

   _____

   Rule of Law: _____

   _____

4. If Mary saves the life of Bill's son, and one week later Bill, in a moment of gratitude, tells Mary he will pay her $5,000 for her heroism, can Mary demand the $5,000 in a court of law? Explain.

   Decision: _____

   _____

   Rule of Law: _____

   _____

5. William's uncle, Ben, promises William that if he does not drink or smoke until he is 30, Ben will pay William $10,000. William fulfills his part of the agreement. Ben refuses to pay. What right does William have?

   Decision: _____

   _____

   Rule of Law: _____

   _____

Chapter 13

ILLEGAL BARGAINS

SCOPE NOTE

A valid, binding agreement must contain acts and promises that are legal. Illegal acts and promises generally make an agreement void. Validity of subject matter, as an essential element of a contract, is discussed in this chapter in terms of the types of restricted/unlawful acts and promises that invalidate an agreement, as well as the remedial consequences of such illegality.

EDUCATIONAL OBJECTIVES

1. Define and give examples of "invalid subject matter."

2. Enumerate different classes of illegal agreements.

3. Discuss the relationship between illegality and divisible contracts.

4. Describe how types of illegality influence the availability of remedies.

5. Give examples of how illegality of bargain varies among states.

CHAPTER OUTLINE

I. Violations of Statutes
   A. Licensing Statutes–may be regulatory to protect the public from unqualified persons or merely for the purpose of raising revenue
   B. Gambling Statutes–are generally not enforceable with some exceptions such as state regulated and operated lotteries
   C. Usury Statutes–laws that establish a maximum rate of permissible interest on contract loans

    D. Sunday Statutes–some states have blue laws that prohibit certain types of commercial activity on Sundays

II. Violations of Public Policy
    A. Common Law Restraint of Trade–made such contracts illegal
        1. Sale of a business–today if restraints covering territory and time are reasonable, they are allowed
        2. Employment contracts–contracts not to compete may be allowed if reasonable and necessary
    B. Exculpatory Clauses–a clause that excuses one party from liability for his or her tortious conduct is usually unenforceable
    C. Unconscionable Contracts–the Code and Restatement may deny enforcement to such contracts
    D. Tortious Conduct–a promise to commit a tort is unenforceable on public policy grounds

III. Effect of Illegality
    A. General Rule: Unenforceability–if an agreement is illegal neither party can successfully sue and recover
    B. Exceptions
        1. Party withdrawing before performance–can recover
        2. Party protected by statute–can recover
        3. Party not equally at fault–can recover
        4. Excusable ignorance–can recover
        5. Partial illegality–provides two possibilities: either the contract is wholly unenforceable or only the illegal part of the contract will be unenforceable

TRUE–FALSE: Circle true or false.

T   F   1. The term "illegal bargain" is directly equivalent to "illegal contract."

T   F   2. A bargain is "illegal" when its formation or performance is criminal or tortious or opposed to public policy.

T   F   3. One who has practiced a trade in violation of a regulatory statute will normally be able to collect a fee for services.

T   F   4. A revenue measure seeks to protect the public against the incompetent or unqualified practitioner.

T   F   5. Normally, the courts have refused to recognize the enforcement of a gambling contract.

T   F   6. At common law, a valid contract could be made on Sunday.

T   F   7. A "usury law" will protect the borrower by providing for a minimum interest rate.

T   F   8. All states have legislation pertaining to gambling or wagering.

T   F   9. Managers must sign employment contracts prohibiting them from competing with their current employers for the rest of their lives.

T   F   10. In all cases, the entire contract is void if any part of it is illegal.

T   F   11. The Code and the Restatement define the word unconscionable as "exceeding that which is reasonable or customary."

T   F   12. Statutes that prohibit commercial activity on Sunday are Blue Laws.

KEY TERMS–MATCHING EXERCISE: Select the term that best completes each statement below.

1. Revenue license	8. "Blue sky law"	14. Blue Laws
2. Lotteries	9. Exculpatory clause	15. Unconscionable
3. Injunction	10. An agreement (covenant) not to compete	16. Reasonable
4. Time-price differential		17. Forbearance
5. "Public policy"	11. Regulatory license	18. Criminal conduct
6. Usury law	12. Licensing statute	19. Employment contracts
7. Adhesion contract	13. Unenforceable	20. Garnishment

_____ 1. A contract term that excuses one party from liability for that person's own negligence.

_____ 2. A typical restraint that usually accompanies the sale of a business.

_____ 3. A standard form contract in which one party offers the other party a contract on a "take-it-or-leave-it" basis.

_____ 4. A statute that historically protected a borrower of money from excessive interest charges on the loan.

_____ 5. A statute that prohibits the sale of unregistered securities.

_____ 6. A law commonly applied to the professions of law, medicine and dentistry.

_____ 7. A form of gambling that, if permitted at all, is usually state regulated and operated.

_____ 8. Statutes that prohibit certain types of commercial activity on Sunday.

_____ 9. The rationale used by a court that may allow a statute to reach beyond its stated bounds.

_____ 10. A contract of sale, the terms of which are unscrupulous, unprincipled or unjust.

_____ 11. A license designed for the protection of the public against unqualified persons.

_____ 12. The type of restraint of trade that is enforceable.

_____ 13. A court order prohibiting an employee from competing with her former employer in a described area for a given time.

_____ 14. The agreement managers are often required to sign restraining them from competing with their employers during the time of their employment.

_____ 15. A license regarded as a taxing measure.

MULTIPLE CHOICE: Select the alternative that best completes each statement below.

_____ 1. "Blue Laws" are state statutes that (a) follow the common law rule that a valid contract can be made on Sunday (b) prohibit certain types of commercial activity on Sunday (c) prohibit acts of "necessity" or "charity" from being performed on Sunday (d) none of the above.

_____ 2. A common example of a licensing statute would be one (a) prohibiting larceny (b) prohibiting forgery (c) requiring professional people to register (d) all of the above.

_____ 3. A statute that requires the licensing of plumbers but does not establish standards of competence would be a (a) revenue statute (b) criminal statute (c) regulatory statute (d) usury statute.

_____ 4. A scheme for the distribution of property by chance among persons who have paid or agreed to pay a valuable consideration for the chance is a (a) usury loan (b) gambling statute (c) lottery (d) all of the above.

_____ 5. A statute establishing a maximum rate of permissible interest is a (a) Sunday statute (b) gambling statute (c) usury law (d) revenue statute.

_____ 6. To find a transaction usurious, the courts have traditionally required the following factor(s): (a) a loan or forbearance (b) money that is repayable absolutely (c) an interest charge exacted in excess of the interest rate allowed by law (d) all of the above.

_____ 7. Common examples of professions to which licensing statutes apply would be (a) brokers (b) accountants (c) dentists (d) all of the above.

_____ 8. The usual method by which an employer seeks to enforce a covenant not to compete by a former employee is (a) specific performance (b) rescission of the employment contract (c) an injunction (d) none of the above.

_____ 9. If a seller takes unfair advantage of a buyer in an unequal bargaining position and extorts an exorbitant price for the purchased goods, the contract is (a) a gambling contract (b) a usury contract (c) an exculpatory contract (d) an unconscionable contract.

_____ 10. The typical restraint of trade could occur in a situation such as a (a) sale of a business, including the good will (b) sale of merchandise (c) sale of a covenant (d) none of the above.

_____ 11. The classification of an agreement to commit a tort is (a) valid (b) voidable (c) unenforceable (d) none of the above.

_____ 12. Generally, when an agreement is illegal (a) neither party can win a lawsuit against the other for breach (b) neither party can recover damages for any services rendered (c) the court will leave the parties where it finds them (d) all of the above.

_____ 13. The type of reasonable restraint on the seller of a business that a court will enforce is a restraint that covers (a) time (b) territory (c) both time and territory (d) none of the above.

CASE PROBLEMS–SHORT ESSAY ANSWERS: Read each case problem carefully. When appropriate, answer by stating a Decision for the case and by explaining the rationale–Rule of Law–relied upon to support your decision.

1. The maximum rate of annual interest in state Z is 8%. The legal rate is 6%. If A loans B $1,000 and the parties agree that B is to pay $72.00 as interest each year ($6.00 per month), is the contract usurious? Explain.

Decision: _____

_____

Rule of Law: _____

_____

2. Adam had Barbara, a plumber, install a shower in Adam's home. When Adam learned Barbara wasn't licensed, he declined to pay. The pertinent statute has the payment of $10.00 as its only requirement for a plumber's license. Barbara sues. Decide and discuss.

Decision: _____

_____

Rule of Law: _____

_____

3. After searching three weeks for an apartment to rent, Abby finds one suitable for her family. Daniel, the landlord, adds to the lease agreement Abby must sign if she wants the apartment, a clause stating that he will not be liable for any negligence he might commit while the apartment is rented. Is this clause enforceable? Explain.

Decision: _____

_____

Rule of Law: _____

_____

4. A sold a barbershop to C. The contract called for A not to enter the barber business in the county for a period of five years. Two years later, A opened a barbershop across town from C and C sued. Decide and discuss.

Decision: _____

_____

Rule of Law: _____

_____

5. A contracts with B whereby B is to kill C for $50,000. Although B could be criminally prosecuted for this act, B wanted the contract with A enforced. What result?

Decision: _____

_____

Rule of Law: _____

_____

Chapter 14

CONTRACTUAL CAPACITY

SCOPE NOTE

Another basic requirement of a valid, enforceable contract is capacity–the ability of a party to make a binding agreement. Various groups of people are deemed to lack such ability, either completely or partially. Who are these persons and what tests are applied to determine when someone possesses or lacks contractual capacity? This is the focus of Chapter 14.

EDUCATIONAL OBJECTIVES

1. Distinguish between classes of persons considered totally incompetent and those who are only partially limited relevant to contractual capacity.

2. Discuss the rationale for excusing certain persons from contractual obligations that they have entered.

3. Identify minimal obligations ("necessaries") to which incapacitated parties are held.

4. Understand the significance of and restrictions on affirmance/disaffirmance.

5. Clarify the consequences of false representations of capacity as they relate to disaffirmance.

CHAPTER OUTLINE

I. Minors–A person who is not of legal age
   A. Liability on Contracts–general rule: minor's contracts are voidable at the minor's option
      1. Disaffirmance–the right of a minor to avoid a contract through words or conduct
      2. Ratification–is binding on the minor but only if it occurs after the minor reaches legal age

B. Liability for Necessaries–a minor is liable for the reasonable value of necessaries actually delivered to the minor

C. Liability for Misrepresentation of Age–the majority of states still allow the minor to disaffirm the contract

D. Liability for Tort Connected With Contract–generally minors are liable for their torts but if the tort is so connected to a contract that a court must enforce both the tort action and the contract, the minor in such cases is not liable for the tort

II. Incompetent Persons–persons who lack mental capacity
   A. Person Under Guardianship–such a person's contracts are void, not voidable
   B. Mental Illness or Defect–allows the person to make voidable contracts

III. Intoxicated Persons–as a general rule, an inebriated person makes voidable contracts

TRUE–FALSE: Circle true or false.

T   F   1. All persons have the legal capacity to make a valid contract.

T   F   2. Today, almost without exception, a minor's contract is valid once made.

T   F   3. It is conceivable that a court would rule school instruction, such as a college education, a necessary.

T   F   4. A minor has no power to ratify a contract while still a minor.

T   F   5. A minor may not disaffirm a contract after becoming an adult.

T   F   6. Under the U.C.C., personal property conveyed by a minor to a buyer and subsequently reconveyed by that buyer to a third person, e.g., a bona fide purchaser for value, can be recovered by the minor.

T   F   7. In contract law in the majority of the states, when age is misrepresented by a minor, the minor will be bound to the contract.

T   F   8. A mentally incompetent person cannot avoid a contract for necessaries actually furnished to that person.

T   F   9. As a general rule, if intoxication is voluntary, the intoxicated party may not avoid a contract.

T   F   10. An incompetent person's voidable contracts may not be ratified or disaffirmed even if the person becomes competent.

T   F   11. Ratification of a contract by a minor must be express to be legally binding.

T   F   12. Generally, minors are not liable for their torts.

KEY TERMS–MATCHING EXERCISE: Select the term that best completes each statement below.

---

1. Torts
2. Disaffirmance
3. Ratification
4. "Emancipated" minors
5. Luxury items
6. Case law
7. Necessaries

8. Intoxicated persons
9. Misrepresentation of age
10. Persons under guardianship
11. Minor
12. Quasi contract
13. Capacity

14. Express
15. Restitution
16. Void
17. Adult
18. Contract
19. Voidable
20. Guardian

_____ 1. Persons whose property is supervised by court order and whose contracts are void.

_____ 2. Persons who are unable to understand the nature and effect of their acts or unable to act reasonably.

_____ 3. The return of property or the equivalent of what has been received.

_____ 4. The theory under which incompetent persons and minors are held contractually liable.

_____ 5. Acts for which minors have always been held liable as a general rule.

_____ 6. An act by a minor that is not allowed until majority age when a contract involves the conveyance of land.

_____ 7. An act that binds the minor to the contract only upon reaching majority age.

_____ 8. Minors who are basically on their own, free from parental control.

_____ 9. The kind of fraud today for which some courts are denying disaffirmance by minors.

_____ 10. Those things regarded as necessary to maintain oneself in a particular station of life.

_____ 11. Items of personal property, such as boats and TV sets, that are not considered necessities of life.

_____ 12. The classification of most contracts made by minors.

_____ 13. An infant who has not attained legal age.

_____ 14. A person appointed by a court to manage the property of an incompetent individual.

_____ 15. The classification of a contract made by a person who is under guardianship by court order.

MULTIPLE CHOICE: Select the alternative that best completes each statement below.

_____ 1. An item considered a necessary is (a) lodging (b) medicine (c) a textbook (d) all of the above.

_____ 2. Cameras, tape recorders, and the like are usually classified as (a) luxury items (b) necessaries (c) professional items (d) none of the above.

_____ 3. A minor may choose to approve a contract after becoming an adult by (a) disaffirmance (b) ratification (c) a loan (d) none of the above.

_____ 4. Under proper circumstances, which of the following would most likely be a necessary? (a) new boat (b) TV set (c) class ring (d) new suit.

_____ 5. Which of the following persons does not have limited contractual capacity? (a) minors (b) eccentric persons (c) incompetent persons (d) intoxicated persons.

_____ 6. Ratification (a) makes the contract valid and binding from the beginning (b) is final and cannot be withdrawn (c) must validate the entire contract (d) all of the above.

_____ 7. By the majority view, a minor who wishes to disaffirm an executed contract for the sale of a chattel must (a) pay for it (b) simply return it (c) return and pay for the use of it (d) return it in the same condition as it was received.

_____ 8. Based upon the principle of quasi contract, which of the following persons are liable for necessaries? (a) minors (b) incompetent persons (c) intoxicated persons (d) all of the above.

_____ 9. Generally, minors are liable for the tort of (a) libel (b) negligence (c) assault and battery (d) all of the above.

_____ 10. Ratification of a contract by an incompetent person can (a) be done at anytime (b) be done when sane (c) be done only while insane (d) never be done.

_____ 11. An incompetent person may (a) be a person who is mentally ill (b) be a person who has a mental defect (c) ratify or disaffirm contracts when the person becomes competent (d) all of the above.

_____ 12. An intoxicated person (a) has contractual capacity (b) makes void contracts like a minor (c) makes voidable contracts like an incompetent person (d) none of the above.

_____ 13. Ratification of a minor's contract may be (a) implied (b) express (c) created by continued use of the property (d) all of the above.

CASE PROBLEMS–SHORT ESSAY ANSWERS: Read each case problem carefully. When appropriate, answer by stating a Decision for the case and by explaining the rationale–Rule of Law–relied upon to support your decision.

1. Mary is a minor. Mary looks like she is over eighteen (majority age) and tells Bob that she is twenty years old. Mary buys a motorcycle from Bob for $300. After using the motorcycle in a race over the weekend, Mary returns it to Bob and demands he return her money on the basis that she is, in fact, a minor. What result? Explain.

    Decision: _____

    _____

    Rule of Law: _____

    _____

2. Your friend's brother is unstable. He has been judged incompetent and a court has ordered a guardian appointed for him. He goes out and orders $2,000 worth of blue jeans. The merchant wants to complete the sale. How would you advise your friend? Explain.

    Decision: _____

    _____

    Rule of Law: _____

    _____

3. Charlie, at age 20, in a state where one is still a minor at 20, signs a contract to buy a new Corvette. He keeps it until he is 24, when it finally falls apart. Charlie wishes to disaffirm the contract. Can he? Explain.

    Decision: _____

    _____

    Rule of Law: _____

    _____

4. A is intoxicated. For months B has tried to buy A's Picasso painting, but each time A has refused to sell. B again makes the offer, and A, in his inebriated condition, accepts. When A becomes sober and learns of the contract, A refuses to sell. B sues. What result?

    Decision: _____

    _____

    Rule of Law: _____

    _____

5. Howard, a minor, has just moved into an apartment and is preparing to enter the freshman class at the University. A sales person convinces Howard to sign a contract for the purchase of cooking utensils, e.g., pots and pans. The contract reads that the purchaser (Howard) agrees the utensils are necessaries. Howard wants to disaffirm the contract. How would you advise him? Explain.

Decision: _____

_____

Rule of Law: _____

_____

Chapter 15

CONTRACTS IN WRITING

SCOPE NOTE

Most oral contracts are fully enforceable regardless of their form. Some agreements, however, because of the perceived importance of their subject matter, must be written and signed to be enforceable. This chapter focuses on the Statute of Frauds and specific provisions of the U.C.C. that dictate those agreements that must be in writing and signed for enforcement. Parties to an otherwise valid, oral agreement that "falls within the Statute of Frauds" will most likely encounter a court refusal to enforce it. Parties entering oral agreements that fall "outside the Statute of Frauds" need not worry about lack of enforcement due to the absence of a writing, yet they should recognize the advisability of reducing their agreement to a written form to avoid conflict and confusion over the terms, conditions, and interpretations of their contract. The requirements for and exceptions to the Parol Evidence Rule are discussed.

EDUCATIONAL OBJECTIVES

1. Enumerate classes of contracts that must be written and signed to be enforced.

2. Describe the type and extent of writing required to comply with the provisions of the Statute of Frauds.

3. Identify exceptions to the general rule that contracts "within the Statute of Frauds" must be in writing and signed to be enforced.

4. Discuss those agreements that, although not required, should nevertheless be in writing.

5. Define and discuss the Parol Evidence Rule.

6. Distinguish the terms parol, parol evidence, and the Parol Evidence Rule.

7. Enumerate exceptions to the Parol Evidence Rule.

8. Explain the significance and effect of primary and secondary rules of contract interpretation.

CHAPTER OUTLINE

I. Statute of Frauds
    A. Contracts Within the Statute of Frauds–include certain oral contracts only
        1. Suretyship provision–a promise by a surety to a creditor to perform the duties of the debtor
            a. Original promise–made by a promisor to become primarily liable is not within the Statute of Frauds
            b. Main purpose doctrine–an exception to the suretyship provision
            c. Promise made to debtor–is not within the Statute
        2. Executor-administrator provision–a promise to pay personally the debts of the decedent is within the Statute
        3. Marriage provision–a promise made in consideration of marriage is within the Statute
        4. Land contract provision–a promise to transfer "any interest in land" is within the Statute
        5. One year provision–all contracts that cannot possibly be fully performed within one year are within the Statute
            a. The possibility test–can the contract possibly be performed within one year
            b. Computation of time–the year runs from the time the agreement is made
            c. Full performance by one party–makes the promise of the other party enforceable
        6. Sales of goods–the Code provides that a contract for the sale of goods over $500 is not enforceable unless in writing
            a. Admission–the Code enforces an oral contract for the sale of goods against a party who admits a contract was made
            b. Specially manufactured goods–the Code enforces an oral contract for such goods that were made for the buyer and the seller has substantially begun their manufacture
            c. Delivery or payment and acceptance–under the Code they validate the contract only for the goods that have been accepted or for which payment has been accepted
        7. Modification or rescission of contracts within the Statute of Frauds–an oral contract modifying an existing contract is unenforceable if the resulting contract is within the Statute, but an oral rescission of a written contract may be effective
    B. Compliance With the Statute of Frauds–even though a contract is within the Statute it will be enforced if there is a sufficient writing or memorandum that complies with the requirements of the Statute of Frauds
        1. General contracts provisions–the writing must specify the parties, the subject matter, the terms, and it must be signed by the party to be charged or her agent
        2. Sale of goods–the Code provisions are more liberal

C. Effect of Noncompliance–the oral contracts are unenforceable
1. Full performance–if all promises of an oral contract have been performed, the Statute no longer applies
2. Restitution–may be recovered by a party who acted in reliance upon the contract even though it was unenforceable because of the Statute
3. Promissory estoppel–a number of courts have used this doctrine to avoid the writing requirement of the Statute

II. Parol Evidence Rule
A. The Rule–a written contract that contains the complete agreement of the parties may not be modified in any way with the use of parol (oral or written) evidence
B. Situations to Which the Rule Does Not Apply–eight exceptions are listed
C. Supplemental Evidence–may be used to explain a written contract

III. Interpretation of Contracts–the determination of the meaning to be given to the written language of a contract is outside the scope of the Parol Evidence Rule; twelve rules that aid interpretation are listed

TRUE–FALSE: Circle true or false.

T   F   1. Except as provided by Statute, an oral contract is just as valid and enforceable as a written one.

T   F   2. Contracts of a type or class governed by the Statute of Frauds are said to be "within" the Statute.

T   F   3. The Statute of Frauds is rendered inapplicable when the "main purpose doctrine" is available.

T   F   4. If an executor promises to pay the decedent's debt out of the executor's own pocket, it is unenforceable unless in writing and signed.

T   F   5. Only the "party to be charged," or the "party's agent," must have signed the written contract or memo in order to make it legally binding.

T   F   6. If they are to be enforced, all oral contracts must be in writing according to the Statute of Frauds.

T   F   7. Courts do not regard promises made by a surety to a debtor as being within the Statute of Frauds.

T   F   8. Mutual promises to marry do not have to be in writing according to the Statute of Frauds.

T   F   9. An oral contract to care for a handicapped person while that person attends college for the next four years is not enforceable.

T　F　10. Parol evidence consists of oral evidence only.

T　F　11. An executed (completely performed) oral contract is no longer within the Statute of Frauds.

T　F　12. The theory of the Parol Evidence Rule is that the parties will voluntarily and intentionally state in a written contract the terms to which they have agreed.

KEY TERMS–MATCHING EXERCISE: Select the term that best completes each statement below.

1. Unenforceable
2. Parol evidence
3. "Main purpose"
4. Goods
5. "Original promise"
6. Voidable
7. Parol

8. Void
9. "Collateral promise"
10. Statute of Frauds
11. "Party to be charged"
12. Securities
13. Parol Evidence Rule
14. Estoppel

15. Enforceable
16. Promisee
17. Executor
18. Administrator
19. Surety
20. Uniform Commercial Code

_____ 1. The name given a promise to pay the debt of another if the debtor fails to pay.

_____ 2. Another name for the defendant, i.e., the person who must sign a written contract according to the Statute of Frauds.

_____ 3. Another name for stocks and bonds.

_____ 4. The term that means speech or words.

_____ 5. Any evidence consisting of words, spoken or written, that is not contained in a written contract.

_____ 6. The classification of an oral contract that is to last the lifetime of another.

_____ 7. The doctrine that is an exception to the section of the Statute of Frauds that deals with promises to answer for the debt of another.

_____ 8. Oral or written words of any prior agreement will not be permitted to vary, change, alter, or modify the terms of a written contract.

_____ 9. Another name for tangible (movable) personal property as defined by the U.C.C.

_____ 10. The classification of an oral contract that is in noncompliance with the Statute of Frauds.

_____ 11. The source of law that governs the enforceability of contracts for the sale of goods.

_____ 12. The law that requires certain types of contracts to be in a particular form to be enforceable.

_____ 13. The name for a person who promises a creditor to perform the obligations of a third person.

_____ 14. The kind of promise made by a promisor who agrees to become primarily liable for its performance.

_____ 15. The person named in a valid will to administer the estate of the decedent.

MULTIPLE CHOICE: Select the alternative that best completes each statement below.

_____ 1. The Statute of Frauds requires all contracts that cannot be performed within one year to be in writing. The year runs from the time the (a) performance is to begin (b) contract is made (c) contract is breached (d) none of the above.

_____ 2. The signature of the "party to be charged" (a) must be handwritten (b) must be at the bottom of the last page of the contract (c) may be typewritten or printed (d) none of the above.

_____ 3. The U.C.C. allows an oral contract for the sale of goods to be enforced if (a) the party defending against the contract admits it (b) the goods are to be specially manufactured (c) part payment has been made and accepted (d) all of the above.

_____ 4. The basic difference between the "main purpose doctrine" and the "leading object rule" is (a) one of fundamental law (b) a slight variance in technique (c) nothing–they are the same (d) none of the above.

_____ 5. Which of the following are within the Statute of Frauds? A man promises a woman (a) an allowance to marry him (b) to convey land to her if they marry (c) to share his estate with her brother if she will marry him (d) all of the above.

_____ 6. Which of the following is personal property? (a) growing crops (b) land (c) buildings (d) easements.

_____ 7. The Parol Evidence Rule does not apply to a contract (a) that is partly oral and partly written (b) with a typographical error (c) that has ambiguous terms (d) all of the above.

_____ 8. If you orally contracted for the sale of goods, at what price would you become concerned with the requirements of the Statute of Frauds? (a) $5,000 (b) $500 (c) $50,000 (d) $450.

_____ 9. The person appointed by the court to administer the estate of a decedent who died without a will is the (a) administrator (b) executor (c) executrix (d) none of the above.

_____ 10. The Parol Evidence Rule does not apply to a defense to a contract of (a) fraud (b) duress (c) undue influence (d) all of the above.

_____ 11. The kind of promise in which the promisor is not the person who is primarily liable is (a) an original promise (b) a collateral promise (c) an objective promise (d) none of the above.

_____ 12. The reason a court may deem it inequitable for the Statute of Frauds to apply after reliance by the purchaser in a land sales contract is (a) hardship (b) the "part performance doctrine" (c) the "main purpose doctrine" (d) none of the above.

_____ 13. The Parol Evidence Rule does not apply if the written contract (a) is illegal (b) contains a clerical error (c) is subsequently and mutually rescinded (d) all of the above.

CASE PROBLEMS–SHORT ESSAY ANSWERS: Read each case problem carefully. When appropriate, answer by stating a Decision for the case and by explaining the rationale–Rule of Law–relied upon to support your decision.

1. A and B have a valid written contract. A telephones B and they mutually agree to rescind the contract. In a lawsuit between A and B, can B prevent A from introducing this oral evidence? Explain.

   Decision: _____

   _____

   Rule of Law: _____

   _____

2. A and B agree in a written memo to the sale of "some things." The writing doesn't specify the quantity of the items to be sold. Could this writing be enforced in court? Explain.

   Decision: _____

   _____

Rule of Law: _____

_____

3. A, a carpenter, and B, a homeowner, make an oral contract whereby B is to give A a certain tract of land in return for A's building an addition to B's house. Is this contract enforceable by A upon completion of the construction? Explain.

Decision: _____

_____

Rule of Law: _____

_____

4. A is the only person who can use widgets. A places an oral order with XYZ Company to make 10,000 widgets at $2.00 each. Later, A refuses to accept the widgets and alleges the Uniform Commercial Code Statute of Frauds as a defense to the suit for breach of contract. Who prevails?

Decision: _____

_____

Rule of Law: _____

_____

5. After an oral contract for the sale of a tract of land has been made, Allen writes a letter to Bernard, repeating that he will sell the land to Bernard, and Allen signs the letter. Bernard refuses to buy, and Allen sues. Bernard asserts the Statute of Frauds. Decide.

Decision: _____

_____

Rule of Law: _____

_____

Chapter 16

THIRD PARTIES TO CONTRACTS

SCOPE NOTE

As a general rule, only the original contracting parties have rights to enforce an agreement or seek damages for its breach. In some cases, however, persons not original parties to an agreement may have enforceable rights under it. Additionally, original parties to a contract might wish to transfer to others the right to receive performance or the duty to perform contained in the original agreement. Chapter 16 addresses the type of contractual relations that create non-original-party enforceable rights and duties under a contract from the perspective of third-party beneficiary contracts as well as assignment and delegation.

EDUCATIONAL OBJECTIVES

1. Define and discuss the significance of assignment/delegation.

2. Identify classes of rights and duties that cannot be assigned or delegated.

3. Explain rules of priority controlling multiple assignment situations.

4. Differentiate important characteristics and relative advantages/disadvantages among assignment, delegation and novation.

5. Distinguish assignment/delegation from third-party beneficiary contracts.

6. Discuss differences between creditor, donee and incidental beneficiaries.

CHAPTER OUTLINE

I.   Assignment of Rights
   A. Law Governing Assignments–is primarily common law but with a few Code modifications
   B. Requirements of an Assignment–no special words are necessary to create an assignment and consideration is not required for an effective assignment
      1. Revocability of assignments–if a contract exists between the assignor and the assignee, the assignor cannot revoke the assignment without the assent of the assignee
      2. Partial assignments–a transfer of part of the contractual rights to one or more assignees
   C. Rights That Are Assignable–as a general rule, most contract rights are assignable
   D. Rights That Are Not Assignable–are those to protect the obligor or the public
      1. Assignments that materially increase the duty, risk, or burden–are not assignable
      2. Assignments of personal rights–those of a highly personal nature are not assignable
      3. Express prohibition against assignment–is handled differently by the Code than by common law
      4. Assignments prohibited by law–regulate the assignment of certain contract rights
   E. Rights of the Assignee
      1. Obtains rights of assignor–but no new rights
      2. Notice–to the obligor of an assignment is not required
   F. Implied Warranties of Assignor–to the assignee are listed
   G. Express Warranties of Assignor–assignor is bound by any express warranties he makes to assignee
   H. Successive Assignments of the Same Right–the majority rule is that the first assignee in point of time prevails over subsequent assignees

II. Delegation of Duties
   A. Delegable Duties–contract duties are generally delegable but exceptions are listed
   B. Duties of the Parties–a delegatee becomes liable for performance only if she assents to perform the delegated duties; however, a delegation still leaves the delegator bound to perform
III. Third-Party Beneficiary Contracts
   A. Intended Beneficiary–there are two types
      1. Donee beneficiary–is the case in which the third party receives the benefit as a gift
      2. Creditor beneficiary–is the case in which the third party is a creditor who receives the benefit to satisfy a debt
      3. Rights of intended beneficiary–are those that can be enforced
      4. Vesting of rights–states vary considerably as to when vesting takes place
   B. Incidental Beneficiary–is not an intended beneficiary and has no enforceable rights under the contract

TRUE–FALSE: Circle true or false.

T   F   1. An effective assignment terminates the assignor's rights arising from a contract.

T   F   2. A delegation of duties is the voluntary transfer of contract rights to a third party.

T F 3. To be valid, an assignment must be in writing.

T F 4. Just as rights are assignable, so are duties.

T F 5. Rights and duties of a highly personal nature cannot be assigned or delegated.

T F 6. A valid assignment requires that notice be given to the obligor.

T F 7. Assignments of future wages are governed by statutes that sometimes prohibit them.

T F 8. The assignee of a contract claim has rights superior to those of the assignor.

T F 9. An assignee will lose the rights against the debtor if the latter pays the assignor without notice of the assignment.

T F 10. Unlike an assignment or a novation, a delegation of duties and an assumption of the delegated duties leaves the delegator and the delegatee liable for proper performance of the original contractual duties.

T F 11. In a third-party beneficiary life insurance contract, the donee beneficiary has the right to sue and recover from the promisor (insurance company) but not from the promisee (insured).

T F 12. In a third-party beneficiary contract, the creditor beneficiary may sue either or both the original promisor and the promisee.

KEY TERMS–MATCHING EXERCISE: Select the term that best completes each statement below.

1. Creditor beneficiary

2. Incidental beneficiary

3. Personal rights

4. Delegation

5. Delectus personae

6. Partial assignment

7. Subsequent assignee

8. Assignor

9. Donee beneficiary

10. Third-party beneficiary contract

11. Novation

12. An assignee in good faith who gives value

13. Intended beneficiary

14. Implied warranty

15. Successive assignments

16. Obligor

17. Payment of money

18. Delegatee

19. Consideration

20. Assignee

_____ 1. A method of discharging a contract in which a third party becomes bound upon a promise to the obligee.

_____ 2. An assignment of parts of a claim to different assignees.

_____ 3. A third party designated by the two parties of a contract to receive benefits and rights from the performance of the contract.

_____ 4. An assignment of the same right to different persons.

_____ 5. A second assignee who may collect an account before the first assignee in time and keep it.

_____ 6. An intended beneficiary of a contract who receives the benefit of the contract as a gift.

_____ 7. The guarantee which the assignor who receives value makes to the assignee.

_____ 8. A contract in which a party promises to render a performance to a third person.

_____ 9. A third party who obtains possible benefits but no rights under the contract.

_____ 10. The transfer of contract duties to a third person.

_____ 11. The person who makes an assignment.

_____ 12. A requirement for a valid contract but not for an effective assignment.

_____ 13. The most common contract right that may be assigned.

_____ 14. An example of a contract right that is not assignable.

_____ 15. The person to whom a contract duty is transferred.

MULTIPLE CHOICE: Select the alternative that best completes each statement below.

_____ 1. Contract rights are not assignable if they (a) materially increase the risk upon the obligor (b) transfer personal contract rights (c) are prohibited by Statute (d) all of the above.

_____ 2. The following is not assignable (a) an option contract (b) a wage assignment (c) a partial assignment (d) an automobile liability policy.

_____ 3. Contracts (a) create rights and duties for the contract parties (b) create rights that are often assignable (c) establish contract duties that are not assignable but generally can be delegated (d) all of the above.

_____ 4. If the delegator desires to be discharged from a duty, the delegator will have to seek which of the following from the obligee? (a) payment (b) a novation (c) another obligee (d) none of the above

_____ 5. In a suit by the assignee against a debtor (obligor), the debtor may plead (a) fraud (b) failure of consideration (c) duress (d) all of the above.

_____ 6. A third party who benefits from the performance of a contract even though it was not the intention of the parties to the contract is (a) a creditor beneficiary (b) a donee beneficiary (c) an incidental beneficiary (d) none of the above.

_____ 7. An example of a third-party donee beneficiary contract is (a) a life insurance policy (b) a fire insurance policy (c) an assumption of a mortgage in a real estate purchase (d) none of the above.

_____ 8. Courts enforce contracts for the benefit of all of the following except (a) incidental beneficiaries (b) donee beneficiaries (c) creditor beneficiaries (d) none of the above.

_____ 9. According to the majority rule in the United States involving successive assignments of the same rights, which of the following prevails? The first assignee (a) to give notice (b) in point of time (c) to reassign (d) none of the above.

_____ 10. A subsequent assignee in good faith who gives value may prevail over the prior assignee when the subsequent assignee obtains (a) payment or satisfaction of the obligor's duty (b) a judgment against the obligor (c) a new contract with the obligor (d) all of the above.

_____ 11. The person to whom an assignment is made is (a) an assignor (b) an assignee (c) an obligor (d) a delegatee.

_____ 12. When a valid delegation and an assumption of the delegated duties have been made (a) only the delegator is liable for performance of the contractual duty (b) only the delegatee is liable for performance of the duty (c) both delegator and delegatee are liable (d) none of the above.

_____ 13. A delegation will not be permitted if (a) it is prohibited by Statute (b) it is prohibited by public policy (c) the duties delegated are personal (d) all of the above.

CASE PROBLEMS–SHORT ESSAY ANSWERS: Read each case problem carefully. When appropriate, answer by stating a Decision for the case and by explaining the rationale–Rule of Law–relied upon to support your decision.

1. Unknown to Y, X took out a life insurance policy naming Y, her best friend, as the beneficiary. X died and the company attempted to deny Y recovery. What result?

    Decision: _____

    _____

    Rule of Law: _____

    _____

2. For service to be done by A, B promises to purchase and deliver a new motorcycle to A. A completes the work. B refuses to buy and deliver the motorcycle. C, the exclusive motorcycle dealer (who would obviously benefit), brings suit against B. What result?

    Decision: _____

    _____

    Rule of Law: _____

    _____

3. A buys an appliance from company X on credit. A then assigns the right to the credit purchase to B. The company says that it will not honor the assignment. B sues. What result?

    Decision: _____

    _____

    Rule of Law: _____

    _____

4. E agrees to construct a swimming pool for X. E then delegates the duties to Y Swimming Pool Company. X refuses to allow Y Company to do the work. Y and E bring suit against X. What result?

    Decision: _____

    _____

    Rule of Law: _____

    _____

5. X, being an unscrupulous fellow, assigns the right to future wages first to Y and then to T. T gives notice to the employer first. Both T and Y seek to obtain the wages. Who prevails?

Decision: _____

_____

Rule of Law: _____

_____

Chapter 17

PERFORMANCE, BREACH, AND DISCHARGE

SCOPE NOTE

The cycle of the existence of a contract–formation, operation, termination–is completed in this chapter. The events, developments, and conduct that relieve parties of their contractual obligations are discussed. Also addressed is the impact the presence of conditions has on performance under the terms of the agreement.

EDUCATIONAL OBJECTIVES

1. Identify the requirements for adequate performance through payment of money.

2. Differentiate between "substantial performance" and "partial performance" both in terms of required elements and remedial options.

3. Discuss the methods and significance of termination of contracts by agreement of the parties.

4. Explain the circumstances under which termination occurs through operation of law.

5. Develop the doctrinal importance of Frustration of Purpose and Commercial Impracticability.

6. Define and discuss the significance of anticipatory repudiation.

7. Outline the problems associated with personal satisfaction as a performance evaluator.

8. Discuss the effect of impossibility of performance on contractual obligations.

9. Enumerate types of contractual conditions and their influence on the duties of parties under the agreement.

CHAPTER OUTLINE

I. Conditions–a condition is an event whose happening or non-happening affects a duty of performance under a contract
   A. Express Condition–these are explicitly set forth in language
      1. Satisfaction of a contracting party–a contracting party is not obligated to pay unless satisfied
      2. Satisfaction of a third party–a contract may provide that performance be approved by a third party
   B. Implied-in-fact Conditions–are understood by the parties to be part of the agreement even though they are not stated in express language
   C. Implied-in-law Conditions–are imposed by law in order to accomplish a just and fair result
   D. Concurrent Conditions–are performances by two promisors that are to take place at the same time
   E. Conditions Precedent–an event that must occur before performance under a contract is due
   F. Conditions Subsequent–is an operative event that terminates an existing duty

II. Discharge by Performance–the most frequent method of discharging a contract duty

III. Discharge by Breach–the unexcused failure of a party to perform his promise
   A. Material Breach–is an unjustifiable failure to perform substantially the duties promised in a contract
      1. Prevention of performance–if one party interferes with the performance of another, constituting a breach, the other party is discharged from her contract duties
      2. Perfect tender rule–the Code provides that any deviation from the promised performance in a sales contract constitutes a material breach of the contract
   B. Substantial Performance–essential but not complete performance
   C. Anticipatory Repudiation–if a party repudiates the contract in advance, the courts treat this as a breach
   D. Material Alteration of Written Contract–to be a discharge, a party must fraudulently and materially alter the written contract

IV. Discharge by Agreement of the Parties
   A. Mutual Rescission–an agreement between the parties to terminate their contract duties
   B. Substituted Contract–the parties agree to rescind their original contract and enter into a new one
   C. Accord and Satisfaction–an agreement of a promisee in a contract to accept a stated performance in satisfaction of an existing contractual duty
   D. Novation–a substituted contract involving three parties

V. Discharge by Operation of Law
   A. Impossibility–subjective impossibility does not discharge the contractual duty but objective impossibility may
      1. Destruction of subject matter–without the fault of the promisor is excusable impossibility
      2. Subsequent illegality–if a legal contract becomes illegal because of subsequently enacted law, the duty of performance is discharged
      3. Frustration of purpose–a doctrine under which a contract is discharged if supervening circumstances make impossible the fulfillment of the purpose of the contract
      4. Commercial impracticability–may excuse nonperformance according to the Restatement and the Code
   B. Bankruptcy–discharges a contractual duty of a debtor
   C. Statute of Limitations–does not discharge the duty but does bar the creditor's remedy

TRUE–FALSE: Circle true or false.

T   F   1. Discharge of a contract refers to the termination of the duties created upon the formation of the contract.

T   F   2. A condition is an event that may limit the obligation to perform a contract.

T   F   3. There is no difference between the breach of a promise and the failure, or nonhappening, of a condition; they are the same.

T   F   4. "Provided that" is a phrase connoting an implied condition often found in a contract.

T   F   5. The standard of satisfaction in matters involving personal taste is that of the reasonable person.

T   F   6. A condition precedent is an event that precedes the creation of a duty of immediate performance under a contract.

T   F   7. Once the parties to a contract agree to an accord, the contract is discharged.

T   F   8. A mutual rescission is a contract to modify an existing contract without terminating it.

T   F   9. Less than exact performance does not fully discharge a party to a contract.

T   F   10. Bankruptcy and the Statute of Limitations are methods of discharging a contract by operation of law.

T   F   11. A material breach of a contract discharges the aggrieved party from any further duty under the contract.

T   F   12. Breach of contract is the unexcused failure of a party to perform her promise.

KEY TERMS–MATCHING EXERCISE: Select the term that best completes each statement below.

---

1. Novation

2. Material alteration

3. Bankruptcy

4. Concurrent conditions

5. Nonmaterial breach

6. Condition precedent

7. Perfect tender rule

8. Prevention of performance

9. Anticipatory repudiation

10. Statute of Frauds

11. Statute of Limitations

12. Illegality

13. Mutual rescission

14. Satisfaction

15. Accord

16. Aggrieved person

17. Material breach

18. Prohibition Statute

19. Frustration of purpose doctrine

20. Tender

_____ 1. The position of the Code that any deviation from the promised performance in a sales contract constitutes a material breach of the contract.

_____ 2. An announcement prior to the date performance is due that a party will not perform.

_____ 3. The statute that does not discharge a contract but only acts to bar a creditor's right to bring an action.

_____ 4. An agreement between the parties to terminate their respective duties under the contract.

_____ 5. An acceptable different performance that replaces the original contractual obligation.

_____ 6. An agreement that involves three parties whereby one is a substitute promisee.

_____ 7. An act that may result in a discharge of the entire contract because of the unauthorized relevant changes by a party to the contract.

_____ 8. The discharge of a contract by operation of law available to a debtor.

_____ 9. The kind of conditions in which the contract promisors' proposed reciprocal and agreed performances are to take place at the same time.

_____ 10. A procedure in which one party substantially interferes with the other's performance of a contract and that acts as a discharge.

_____ 11. A name for the injured party who has a right to sue for breach of contract.

_____ 12. One example of a supervening illegality.

_____ 13. The kind of breach that does not discharge a contract but allows a plaintiff to recover damages.

_____ 14. An executory accord does not discharge a contract until this performance is completed.

_____ 15. The term for an attempted performance by a party who is ready, willing, and able to perform.

MULTIPLE CHOICE: Select the alternative that best completes each statement below.

_____ 1. An agreement between the parties to a contract to cancel their original contract and enter a new contract is a (a) substitution (b) novation (c) release (d) none of the above.

_____ 2. Where no one is able to perform the contract for reasons beyond the control of the parties, the contract is discharged due to (a) a mistake (b) impossibility (c) fraud (d) a concurrent obligation.

_____ 3. A material breach of contract (a) gives the aggrieved party a cause of action (b) excuses nonperformance by the aggrieved party (c) discharges the aggrieved party from any further duty to perform (d) all of the above.

_____ 4. The running of the Statute of Limitations on a contract between a creditor and debtor (a) discharges the debt (b) acts as an accord (c) bars the creditor's remedy (d) all of the above.

_____ 5. Which of the following may cause a binding promise to cease to be binding? (a) performance of the parties (b) a discharge by operation of law (c) a breach by one of the parties (d) all of the above

_____ 6. A condition may be (a) express (b) implied-in-fact (c) implied-in-law (d) all of the above.

_____ 7. The expressions "on condition that" and "as soon as" are often part of (a) implied conditions (b) subsequent statements (c) express conditions (d) concurrent conditions.

_____ 8. An event that terminates the existing contractual duty of immediate performance is a (a) condition subsequent. (b) condition precedent (c) concurrent condition (d) none of the above.

_____ 9. Accord and satisfaction is a method of discharging a contract by (a) operation of law (b) agreement of the parties (c) breach of the contract (d) none of the above.

_____ 10. An agreement between the parties to a contract to terminate their respective contractual duties is a (a) mutual rescission (b) material alteration (c) novation (d) none of the above.

_____ 11. The most frequent method of discharging a contractual duty is a discharge by (a) breach (b) performance (c) operation of law (d) impossibility.

_____ 12. Which of the following is not a method of discharging contractual duties by agreement of the parties? (a) novation (b) substitution (c) bankruptcy (d) rescission.

_____ 13. Which of the following is not a method of discharging contractual duties by operation of law? (a) objective impossibility (b) bankruptcy (c) the statute of limitations (d) all of the above.

CASE PROBLEMS–SHORT ESSAY ANSWERS: Read each case problem carefully. When appropriate, answer by stating a Decision for the case and by explaining the rationale–Rule of Law–relied upon to support your decision.

1. A rents a room from B to watch the Duke of Earle ride by in a parade. B knows this is the reason. The Duke is assassinated by revolutionaries before the parade. B sues for the rent. What result?

   Decision: _____

   _____

   Rule of Law: _____

   _____

2. Farmer A agrees to pay dentist B $500 to put braces on his son's teeth. Once the dental work is finished and instead of paying the money, A and B agree that A will butcher a cow and deliver the meat to B. The meat is delivered. Is the contract discharged? Explain.

   Decision: _____

   _____

   Rule of Law: _____

   _____

3. X has purchased a bicycle from Y and now owes Y $150. X, Y and Z agree that Z will pay the debt, and X will be discharged. If Z refuses to pay the money, can Y sue Z? Explain.

   Decision: _____

   _____

Rule of Law: _____

_____

4. X employs Y to work for one year beginning March I and on February 28, Y refuses to begin the job. X doesn't really care and agrees. Then X hires Z. X decides in May to sue Y for damages. What result?

Decision: _____

_____

Rule of Law: _____

_____

5. B contracts in writing to sell a car to A for $1,500. Nothing is written about time of delivery or payment. A demands the delivery of the car before payment as A needs the car now but won't be able to pay for it until later. B refuses and A sues. What result?

Decision: _____

_____

Rule of Law: _____

_____

Chapter 18

CONTRACT REMEDIES

SCOPE NOTE

Adequate performance by both parties to a contract discharges their duties. In cases where performance is inadequate–"defective"–a breach has occurred. What forms of relief both at law and in equity are available to injured parties when they are faced with performance falling short of the terms of the agreement? How do these remedies differ? When will the nonbreaching party be forced to make an election between mutually exclusive remedies?

EDUCATIONAL OBJECTIVES

1. Distinguish the various types of damages.

2. Discuss the importance of liquidated damages.

3. Enumerate the types of relief available from a court of equity and when they apply.

4. Identify the various formulas used to compute damages.

5. Explain the role and meaning of the Mitigation of Damages doctrine.

CHAPTER OUTLINE

I. Interests Protected by Contract Remedies–include expectation, reliance, and restitution interests

II. Monetary Damages
   A. Compensatory Damages–the right to these damages for breach of contract is always available to the injured party

1. Loss of value–the difference between the value of the promised performance and the value of the actual performance
2. Incidental damages–the costs that arise directly out of the breach
3. Consequential damages–the lost profits and injury to person or property resulting from defective performance
4. Expenses saved–the cost or loss the injured party avoids by not having to perform

B. Nominal Damages–a small amount of damages fixed without regard to the amount of loss
C. Reliance Damages–foreseeable loss caused by reliance upon the contract
D. Damages for Misrepresentation
1. Fraud–a party induced by fraud to enter a contract may recover general damages in a tort action
2. Nonfraudulent misrepresentation–if the misrepresentation is neither fraudulent nor negligent, out-of-pocket damages are allowed by the Restatement

E. Punitive Damages–damages awarded in cases involving willful, wanton, or malicious conduct
F. Liquidated Damages–a provision in a contract by which the parties agree in advance to the damages to be paid in event of breach
G. Limitations on Damages–limitations of foreseeability, certainty and mitigation have been imposed upon monetary damages
1. Foreseeability of damages–the breaching party is not liable for loss that was not foreseeable at the time the contract was made
2. Certainty of damages–an injured party can recover for only reasonably certain damages
3. Mitigation of damages–the injured party cannot recover damages for loss that he could have avoided by reasonable effort and without undue risk, burden or humiliation

III. Remedies in Equity
A. Specific Performance–an equity court decree that compels the defaulting party to perform her contractual duties
B. Injunctions–formal court order commanding a person to refrain from doing something

IV. Restitution
A. Party Injured by Breach–is entitled to restitution (a return of the consideration that was given)
B. Party in Default–is entitled to restitution for any benefit she has given in excess of the loss she has caused by her breach
C. Statute of Frauds–if the Statute applies, the party acting in reliance on the contract is entitled to restitution to the benefits conferred on the other party
D. Voidable Contracts–in such contracts, the party who rescinds is entitled to restitution for any benefit conferred on the other party

V. Limitations on Remedies
    A. Election of Remedies–a choice does not necessarily prevent a person from seeking a second remedy unless the remedies are inconsistent and the other party materially changes her position in reliance
    B. Loss of Power of Avoidance
        1. Affirmance–of a contract will not allow the party who affirms to later avoid the contract
        2. Delay–may cause the loss of the power of avoidance
        3. Rights of third parties–the intervening rights of third parties may limit the power of avoidance and the accompanying right to restitution

TRUE–FALSE: Circle true or false.

T   F   1. A breach of contract means a failure to perform a contract promise.

T   F   2. The injured party can always seek and obtain money damages from the wrongdoer for breach of contract.

T   F   3. The purpose of allowing damages for breach of contract is to put the injured party in as good a position as the wrongdoer.

T   F   4. A party with the power of avoidance has no time limit for rescinding a contract.

T   F   5. After learning that the goods sold to the buyer are unfit, the buyer may continue to use the goods and then sue the seller for greater damages.

T   F   6. An example of nominal damages would be a $100,000 recovery for personal injury that one suffers as a result of a traffic mishap.

T   F   7. The remedy of specific performance will generally be granted for breach of a contract for personal services.

T   F   8. Punitive damages are always recoverable for breach of contract.

T   F   9. For breach of contract, the injured party may recover consequential damages for lost profits.

T   F   10. Liquidated damages must bear a reasonable relationship to the actual or probable damage suffered for breach of a contract.

T   F   11. The purpose of restitution is to restore the injured party to the position she was in before the contract was made.

T   F   12. An injunction is the equitable remedy that compels the performance of a contract according to its terms.

KEY TERMS–MATCHING EXERCISE: Select the term that best completes each statement below.

1. Court of law

2. Penalty

3. Uniform Commercial Code

4. Money damages

5. Fraud

6. Uniqueness

7. Specific performance

8. Special damages

9. Nominal damages

10. Injunction

11. Punitive damages

12. Equity court

13. Mitigation

14. Restitution

15. Liquidated damages

16. Out-of-pocket damages

17. Reliance damages

18. Reformation

19. Benefit-of-the-bargain rule

20. Compensatory damages

_____ 1. The usual judgment for breach of contract.

_____ 2. A recovery of $ 1.00 and costs.

_____ 3. A remedy by a court of law looking to deter wrongful conduct.

_____ 4. A provision in the contract calling for payment of money in the event of breach of the contract.

_____ 5. When breach occurs, the plaintiff is required to lessen damages if possible.

_____ 6. A return of the consideration, or its value, to the aggrieved party.

_____ 7. The source of law that allows a defrauded party the right to rescind the contract and recover damages for breach of a contract for the sale of goods.

_____ 8. The court that grants the remedies of specific performance and reformation.

_____ 9. The characteristic of real property that allows the equity court to always grant the remedy of specific performance for breach of a sales contract.

_____ 10. The method the court uses to enforce a contract for an employee's exclusive personal services where damages for a breach are inadequate.

_____ 11. Breach of contract remedy giving non-breaching parties the monetary value of the anticipated contractual benefit reduced by any savings that result from the injured party being discharged from his performance under the contract.

_____ 12. A remedy that results in placing the injured party in as good a position as she would have been in had the contract not been made.

_____ 13. The damages the injured party may recover that are equal to the difference between the value of what she has received and the value of what she was given for it.

_____ 14. An unreasonable sum of money included as a provision of a contract that is to be paid in the event of a breach of the contract.

_____ 15. An equitable remedy whereby the court corrects a written contract to make it conform to the true agreement of the parties.

MULTIPLE CHOICE: Select the alternative that best completes each statement below.

_____ 1. A remedy for breach of contract that represents the actual dollar loss to the plaintiff is (a) specific performance (b) compensatory damages (c) restitution (d) punitive damages.

_____ 2. A court order conveying the title to a parcel of land from the seller to the buyer in compliance with their contractual agreement is (a) restitution (b) punitive damages (c) specific performance (d) none of the above.

_____ 3. Ordering a reconveyance of land would be (a) restitution (b) specific performance (c) punitive damages (d) compensatory damages.

_____ 4. _Hadley v. Baxendale_ involved an issue of (a) nominal damages (b) foreseeability of injury (loss) (c) an intentional tort (d) punitive damages.

_____ 5. Unreasonable payment for nonperformance as expressed in the contract is deemed (a) a penalty (b) liquidated damages (c) punitive damages (d) all of the above.

_____ 6. A reasonable payment for nonperformance as expressed in a contract is deemed (a) a penalty (b) liquidated damages (c) punitive damages (d) all of the above.

_____ 7. Damages that arise directly out of the breach of contract are called (a) nominal damages (b) consequential damages (c) incidental damages (d) reliance damages.

_____ 8. A liquidated damages clause that becomes a penalty because it is excessive is (a) enforceable at a reasonable rate (b) unenforceable (c) enforceable (d) reasonable.

_____ 9. Specific performance will be granted by an equity court when the case involves (a) a contract for personal services (b) a performance by a concert pianist (c) a unique item of property (d) none of the above.

_____ 10. Remedies that are mutually exclusive or inconsistent require an election of remedies. Which of the following would require the election? (a) specific performance and restitution (b) restitution and total damages (c) specific performance and compensation for incidental damages (d) only a and b above.

_____ 11. A contract can be avoided due to (a) lack of capacity (b) fraud (c) duress (d) all of the above.

_____ 12. A party who has the right and power to avoid a contract may lose that power because (a) she affirms the contract (b) she unreasonably delays in disaffirming the contract (c) rights of third parties intervene (d) all of the above.

_____ 13. The remedies of specific performance and injunction (a) will not be granted where there is an adequate remedy at law (b) are remedies at law (c) will be granted if the contract is created by fraud or duress (d) none of the above.

CASE PROBLEMS–SHORT ESSAY ANSWERS: Read each case problem carefully. When appropriate, answer by stating a Decision for the case and by explaining the rational–Rule of Law–relied upon to support your decision.

1. Suppose that you own a legal gambling hall and the roulette wheel breaks down. You desperately need this machine in operation to continue business. In order to have the wheel fixed, you deliver it to Ace Repairs, hoping that they will rush it back to you. Ace takes weeks to repair the wheel. Is there any legal remedy you might pursue?

   Decision: _____

   _____

   Rule of Law: _____

   _____

2. Suppose X, a lawyer, tells A, the trusting client, that the deal X has been working on for A is all set and that all A need do is give X $5,000. As it turns out, X knowingly defrauded A. Can A get more than $5,000 damages? Explain.

   Decision: _____

   _____

   Rule of Law: _____

   _____

3. A and B have a contract whereby if one party breaches the contract, the other is entitled to $2,000. B breaches in the most minor of ways. Can A enforce the clause for the $2,000? Explain.

   Decision: _____

   _____

Rule of Law: _____

_____

4. A and B have a contract whereby A is to manufacture 5,000 lawnmowers for B. After 500 are built, B repudiates the contract. A pays no attention and continues to build. A then sues B. What result?

Decision: _____

_____

Rule of Law: _____

_____

5. A offers to sell B an antique car, a one-of-a-kind rare gem. After the written contract is made, A decides not to sell. Can B force A to part with the car? Explain.

Decision: _____

_____

Rule of Law: _____

_____

CONTRACT UNIT RESEARCH QUESTIONS: Drawing upon information contained in the text, as well as outside sources, discuss the following questions:

1. Identify five examples of oral or written contracts you have made in the past month.

2. Using either a landlord-tenant lease (contract); an insurance contract, e.g., life or car insurance; a sales contract; or a service contract, e.g., work you performed for another person, explain how the document fulfills the requirements of a valid contract and explain the terms of the agreement.

Chapter 19

RELATIONSHIP OF PRINCIPAL AND AGENT

SCOPE NOTE

If all commercial transactions had to be conducted directly between primary parties, business would progress at a snail's pace. The marketplace process would be cumbersome. To facilitate the flow of commerce, representatives are appointed to act on behalf of others, within a defined scope of authority, negotiating and finalizing business agreements. Chapter 19 introduces the area of law–agency–which regulates the relationship of one person (agent) acting on behalf of another (principal). The nature and function of the agency relationship, how it is created, its basic concepts and terminology, the legal identities of its originating parties, and how their rights and duties differ from other legal relationships (employment and independent contractors) are focused upon.

EDUCATIONAL OBJECTIVES

1. Define and discuss the benefits derived from an agency relationship.

2. Identify the methods for creating a valid agency relationship.

3. Explain the qualifications necessary for a principal or agent.

4. Know the source and significance of the duties/liabilities owed by agents and principals to one another.

5. Understand the tort liability of principals and agents.

6. List and explain the various ways of ending an agency relationship.

CHAPTER OUTLINE

I. Nature of Agency–relationship between principal and agent who, as intermediary, is authorized to act for principal with third persons; agent negotiates contract terms and binds the principal
   A. Scope of Agency Purposes–whatever activity persons may accomplish personally may be done through an agent
   B. Other Legal Relations–agency contrasted to employment relationship: employer controls physical conduct of employee
      1. Independent contractor–contract with another to do a particular job, not subject to control of the other

II. Creation of Agency–consensual relationship formed by contract or agreement; may be without consideration (gratuitous agency)
   A. Formalities–none required; contract may be express or implied; Statute of Frauds regulations apply
   B. Capacity–similar to contractual capacity; minors and incompetents not under guardianship may act as agents–contract may be avoidable between principal and agent, but contract between principal and third party is valid

III. Duties of Agent to Principal–primarily determined by contract terms or imposed by law, liability of agents for losses caused by breach of duties
   A. Duty of Obedience–act only as authorized, obey all reasonable, legal, ethical instructions and directions
   B. Duty of Diligence–act with reasonable care/skill in performing work
   C. Duty to Inform–use reasonable efforts to provide relevant, accurate information to principal; notice to agent is notice to principal
   D. Duty to Account–maintain, provide true/complete accounts of money, property received, expended on principal's behalf; keep principal's property separate
   E. Fiduciary Duty–utmost loyalty and good faith
      1. Conflicts of interest–act solely in interest of principal, not own interest or in interest of another; not represent principal in any transaction in which agent has a personal interest; not act on behalf of adverse parties to a transaction without principal's consent
      2. Duty not to compete–not compete with principal nor act on behalf of a competitor
      3. Confidential information–not use/disclose confidential information, unique business methods, trade secrets, business plans, customer lists obtained in course of agency for own benefit or contrary to interest of principal; may reveal confidential information relating to principal's criminal behavior
      4. Duty to account for financial benefits–account for any financial benefit, bribes, kickbacks, gifts, secret profits, received as direct result of transactions conducted on behalf of principal
      5. Principal's remedies–breach of duty triggers agent discharge, avoiding transaction; tort/contract recovery against agent or restitution; agent's loss of right to compensation

IV. Duties of Principal to Agent–agent's rights against principal resulting in duties principal owes to agent
   A. Contractual Duties–compensation, reimbursement, indemnification
      1. Compensation–agent right unless agency gratuitous; duty to pay reasonable value of authorized services performed when no definite sum stated; loss of right to compensation triggered by breaching duties of obedience, loyalty, or proper performance on contract
      2. Reimbursement–pay back authorized payments made by agent
      3. Indemnification–pay agent for losses incurred while acting as directed
   B. Tort Duties–disclose actually/implied known risks involved in agency; provide reasonably safe conditions and warn of unreasonable risks

V. Termination of Agency–occurs on withdrawal of principal's consent; agent's actual authority ends; no compensation for services thereafter; termination occurs through acts of parties or by operation of law
   A. Acts of Parties–occurs by provisions of contract, by subsequent acts of either or both parties
      1. Lapse of time–agent's authority ends at expiration of stated or reasonable period of time
      2. Fulfillment of purpose–agent's authority ends when stated act performed/purpose accomplished
      3. Mutual agreement of parties–contractual relationship created/ended by mutual agreement
      4. Revocation of authority–act of principal to end agent's authority; occurs at any time; triggers recovery of damages against principal if breach of contract
      5. Renunciation by agent–agent ends relationship by notice to principal; damages recovery against agent triggered by unjustified renunciation prior to expiration of stated time if breach of contract
   B. Operation of Law–agency ended by an event occurring
      1. Bankruptcy–filing petition in bankruptcy ends debtor's agency relationships
      2. Death–principal's/agent's death ends agency
      3. Subsequent incapacity of parties–happens after agency created; terminates agent's authority and agency
      4. Change in business conditions–notice or knowledge of change in value of subject matter or change in business conditions
      5. Loss or destruction of subject matter–when agent's authority relates to a specific subject matter that becomes lost or destroyed
      6. Loss of qualification of principal or agent–not obtaining or loss of regulatory license
      7. Disloyalty of agent–without principal's knowledge, agent acquires interests adverse to principal's or breaches duty of loyalty
      8. Subsequent change of law–occurs after agency is created, making performance on contract illegal
      9. Outbreak of war–if makes agency parties enemies

C. Irrevocable Agencies–agency coupled with an interest of agent (agent has a security interest in subject matter), agency not revocable; agency not ended by principal's death, incapacity unless contract specifically so provides

TRUE–FALSE: Circle true or false.

T   F   1. Most forms of business associations, including partnerships, sole proprietorships, and corporations, are based on the general principles of agency law.

T   F   2. An agent who is a minor can only make voidable contracts on behalf of an adult, competent principal.

T   F   3. A person having interests adverse to that of another is generally not permitted to act as an agent for that other person.

T   F   4. Employers are generally not responsible for the torts of independent contractors committed during the course of employment.

T   F   5. The law of agency is mainly controlled by the U.C.C.

T   F   6. A fiduciary duty is one that arises out of a position of trust and confidence between persons.

T   F   7. Agents employed to sell may not become purchasers for themselves.

T   F   8. When a principal wrongfully revokes an agent's authority, the agent may recover money damages for breach of contract.

T   F   9. When an agency agreement does not mention an amount of compensation for the agent, the principal is under no obligation to pay for the agent's services.

T   F   10. The power of the principal to terminate an agency is unlimited.

T   F   11. When conducting business on behalf of a principal, an agent is usually a party to the contract entered into with the third person.

T   F   12. Agency relationships terminate when the subject of the agency (goods to be sold by an agent) are destroyed through no one's fault.

KEY TERMS–MATCHING EXERCISE: Select the term that best completes each statement below.

---

1. Diligence	8. Infants	15. Account
2. Master	9. Gratuitous agent	16. Indemnification
3. Disloyalty	10. Independent contractor	17. Confidential
4. Rescission	11. Servant	18. Bankruptcy
5. Renunciation	12. Revocation	19. Power of attorney
6. Principal	13. Compensation	20. Reimbursement
7. Agency	14. Fiduciary	

_____ 1. A legal relationship under which an individual acts as the business representative of another person.

_____ 2. Persons who authorize others to act on their behalf.

_____ 3. One acting on behalf of another under an agency relationship created without consideration.

_____ 4. An agent's duty to perform work with reasonable care and skill.

_____ 5. Agent's duty to keep accurate records regarding conduct on behalf of the principal and supply such records to the principal.

_____ 6. A person who contracts to act for another but is not controlled by that other person in the performance of authorized acts.

_____ 7. A right lost by an agent who breaches a fiduciary duty.

_____ 8. Acts by an agent that are adverse to the principal's interest.

_____ 9. The withdrawal of the agent's authority by the principal to act on the latter's behalf.

_____ 10. Notice to the principal given by the agent that the agent wishes to discontinue the agency.

_____ 11. Principal's duty to pay an agent for authorized expenses paid out of the agent's own pocket.

_____ 12. Principal's duty to pay an agent for losses suffered by the latter while acting in an authorized manner.

_____ 13. A form of agency under which the agent acts as an attorney for the principal.

_____ 14. Information that, if disclosed, causes harm to the principal's business.

_____ 15. Federal court proceedings granting judicial relief to financially troubled debtors.

MULTIPLE CHOICE: Select the alternative that best completes each statement below.

_____ 1. Agency relationships are generally created by (a) operation of law (b) statute (c) contract (d) equitable estoppel.

_____ 2. Examples of information that agents are duty bound to communicate to their principals include (a) insolvency of debtors and customers of the principal (b) change of marital status of a creditor of the principal (c) change in credit rating of independent contractors (d) pending tax increases on property owned by the agent.

_____ 3. In most situations (a) agency contracts must be sealed and notarized to be valid (b) no specific formalities are required for valid agency contracts (c) agency contracts must be written to be enforceable (d) agency contracts must be witnessed to be valid.

_____ 4. An agent's right to compensation ends when the (a) loyalty duty has been breached by the agent (b) agent has been arrested for committing a felony (c) agency contract contains provisions in violation of state law (d) all of the above.

_____ 5. Factors examined in distinguishing an employment from an independent contractor relationship do not include (a) method of payment (b) adoption of the Uniform Independent Contractor Code (c) length of time (d) who supplies equipment, materials and other necessities.

_____ 6. An agency is terminated by (a) mutual agreement of the parties (b) fulfillment of the agency's purpose (c) insanity, death or bankruptcy of either principal or agent (d) all of the above.

_____ 7. Which of the following are duties owed a principal by the agent? (a) to act with reasonable care (b) to act only as authorized (c) to inform the principal of all relevant information (d) all of the above.

_____ 8. Which of the following is not a duty an agent owes to the principal? (a) ratification (b) diligence (c) loyalty (d) accounting.

_____ 9. Under the Restatement, the two main elements to an agency relationship are by the principal and by the agent (a) accord/satisfaction (b) authorization/consent (c) indemnification/compensation (d) receivership/allocation.

_____ 10. When the parties to an agency or the agency contract do not specify how long the agency relationship is to last, it expires (a) automatically at the end of 90 days (b) no later than two weeks after the contract is signed (c) at the end of a reasonable length of time (d) none of the above.

_____ 11. Tort duties owed by an employer–principal to an employee–agent include (a) insuring that work settings are hazard free (b) liability for intentional torts of employees (c) warning employees of any risks associated with the job (d) none of the above.

_____ 12. Duties owed by a principal to an agent that are contractual in nature include (a) obedience (b) accounting (c) indemnification (d) all of the above.

_____ 13. Principal Paul and Agent Abel enter an agreement whereby Abel agrees to sell, for a fee, Paul's pickle packing plants. Shortly after reaching their agreement, Paul, having inhaled excessive amounts of pickling vapor, is adjudicated mentally incompetent and Abel is confined to a hospital with a severe case of shingles. Their relationship (a) ceases through subsequent incapacity (b) continues unaffected by these tragedies (c) terminates through changed business conditions (d) ends due to changes in law.

CASE PROBLEMS–SHORT ESSAY ANSWERS: Read each case problem carefully. When appropriate, answer by stating a Decision for the case and by explaining the rationale–Rule of Law–relied upon to support your decision.

1. A promises to personally try a lawsuit for B but instead asks a fellow attorney and friend to do it because A doesn't have enough time. May A do this? Explain.

   Decision: _____

   _____

   Rule of Law: _____

   _____

2. P instructs A to buy stock in XYZ corporation. A, instead, sells his own XYZ stock to P at the market price without disclosing this fact to P. Can P rescind this transaction? Explain.

   Decision: _____

   _____

   Rule of Law: _____

   _____

3. A hires B to sell A's home. The market price is $50,000. B finds a buyer for $51,500 and tells A the house sold for $50,000. Can B keep the $1,500 profit on the sale? Explain.

Decision: _____

_____

Rule of Law: _____

_____

4. P authorizes A to sell one of P's valuable paintings. A sells the painting to C at a price exceptionally favorable to P. C wants another of P's paintings and is willing to pay "any price." Can A sell it to C?

Decision: _____

_____

Rule of Law: _____

_____

5. English businessperson Throckmorton contracts with Argentine businessperson Domine-quez to represent Throckmorton in various business dealings in Argentina. What effect on this contract would a flare-up of British-Argentine hostilities over the Balkin Islands have? Explain.

Decision: _____

_____

Rule of Law: _____

_____

Chapter 20

RELATIONSHIP WITH THIRD PARTIES

SCOPE NOTE

Our discussion of agency law concludes by examining the rights/duties of the originating parties to the agency relationship as against third persons. Contract, criminal and tort foundations for such liability are focused upon. Attention is given to those situations where the agent is acting both with and without the principal's authority. Also discussed in this chapter are circumstances that trigger third-party liability to the principal and the agent.

EDUCATIONAL OBJECTIVES

1. Define and explain the nature of the principal's contractual liability to third persons.

2. Distinguish between actual and apparent authority of an agent.

3. Discuss when an agent may delegate authority to another and the effect of such delegation.

4. Explain how terminating the agency relationship and ratification affect the principal's and agent's contractual liability.

5. Understand the principal's direct and vicarious tort liability to third persons stemming from the authorized or unauthorized acts of the agent.

6. Know the basis for holding the principal criminally liable to third persons.

7. Distinguish between the situations when an agent is personally liable to third persons based on terms of warranty of authority, competence and existence of the principal, and disclosure of representative status.

8. Explain the breadth of an agent's liability for the torts committed during the agency.

CHAPTER OUTLINE

I. Relationship of Principal and Third Persons–principal's potential contract, tort liability against third parties; third party recovery rights against principal

   A. Contract Liability–agent changes legal status of principal by binding principal through actual or apparent authority; depends upon whether principal is disclosed (existence and identity known), partially disclosed (known existence but not identity), or undisclosed (existence/identity unknown)

      1. Types of authority–actual (given by actual consent) or apparent (given by acts or conduct of principal)

         a. Actual express authority–principal's spoken/written words communicated to agent

         b. Actual implied authority–principal's words/conduct creating impression of agency, based on custom, trade usage of business

         c. Apparent authority–principal's words/conduct creating agency expectation in third persons with reasonable reliance

      2. Delegation of authority–agents authorized to appoint or select other persons (subagents) to perform or assist in performing their duties; subagent's acts bind principal

      3. Effect of termination of agency–ending agency ends actual authority; notice of termination to third persons not required if agency ends by death, incapacity, bankruptcy, or impossibility of performance; apparent authority continues until third party has actual knowledge or receives actual notice if third party had prior credit dealings with agent, agent has begun dealings with third party with principal's knowledge

         a. Actual notice–knowledge actually, expressly communicated

         b. Constructive notice–knowledge imputed by law (publication in a newspaper of general circulation in area where agency is regularly carried on)

      4. Ratification–principal's affirmance of agent's prior unauthorized act binds principal and third party as if agent had been authorized

         a. Requirements of ratification–principal's intent to ratify entire act or contract with knowledge of all material facts; demonstrated by express language or implied from conduct

         b. Effect of ratification–same as initial authority; rights, duties and remedies of principal and third party same as if agent had originally possessed due authority

      5. Rules of contractual liability–relations between principal and third party

         a. Disclosed and partially disclosed principal and third party contractually bound if agent acts within actual or apparent authority

         b. Undisclosed principal and third party contractually bound if agent acts within actual authority unless existence fraudulently concealed

         c. Principal not contractually bound to third party if agent acts without authority unless principal ratifies contract

   B. Tort Liability of Principal–arises directly/indirectly (vicariously) from agent's authorized or unauthorized acts

      1. Direct liability of principal–for damages resulting from directing agent to commit tort or failing to exercise care in employing competent agents (negligence)

         a. Authorized acts of agent–principal authorizes agent to commit tort against another's property or person; liable for injury or loss sustained

      b. Unauthorized acts of agent–principal's liability for negligent or reckless conduct in hiring, instructing, supervising, or controlling employee or other agent

  2. Vicarious liability of principal for unauthorized acts of agent–indirect legal responsibility for another's act depends on whether agent an employee; principal liable for unauthorized tort committed by employee in course of employment; principal not liable for tort committed by independent contractor

      a. *Respondeat Superior*–"let the superior respond"; liability without fault based on rationale that person who carries out business activities through employees or agents, not independent contractors, should be liable for their torts committed while carrying out business purposes

C. Criminal Liability of Principal–applies to agent's authorized criminal acts if directed, participated in, or approved by principal

II. Relationship of Agent and Third Persons–by assisting principal in carrying out orders, agent acquires rights against third parties but incurs no liabilities; exceptions to this rule (agent is liable) include:

A. Contract Liability of Agent

  1. Disclosed principals–agent acting on behalf of disclosed principal, not normally a party to contract made with third person, incurs no contractual liability to either party

      a. Unauthorized contracts–agent exceeding actual or apparent authority releases principal from contract; agent liable to third party for damages if agent expressly or impliedly warranted has authority; principal liable if ratifies contract; agent not liable if third party knew agent was unauthorized

      b. Agent assumes liability–agent agrees to become liable on contract between principal and third party by making contract in own name, by co-making contract with principal, or by guaranteeing contract

  2. Partially disclosed principal–agent liable on contract regardless of authorized/unauthorized status; agent authorized to make contract binds agent and partially disclosed principal

  3. Undisclosed principal–agent personally liable on contract unless third person, after discovering existence and identity of principal, elects to hold principal liable on contract

  4. Nonexistent or incompetent principal–person, acting as agent for a principal, where agent and third party know principal is nonexistent or incompetent, make agent personally liable on contract

B. Tort Liability of Agent–personal liability for torts that injure third persons, whether or not acts authorized, whether or not principal also liable

C. Rights of Agent Against Third Person–usually no right of action against third person for breach of contract in disclosed principal situation since agent not contracting party

TRUE–FALSE: Circle true or false.

T   F   1. An agent can bind the principal to a contract with apparent authority.

T   F   2. Apparent authority is the same as express authority.

T   F   3. A principal may never be held criminally accountable for the acts of an agent.

T   F   4. Authority to make contracts for a principal is usually inferred from the agent's authority to conduct business for the principal.

T   F   5. Subagents, appointed with authority from the principal, are agents of both the principal and the agent.

T   F   6. An agent for a disclosed principal is a party to the contract made on behalf of the principal and is liable to the third person with whom the contract is made.

T   F   7. For the doctrine of respondeat superior to take effect, the agent must be acting within the normal scope of employment.

T   F   8. The principal may be liable for an agent's contracts but not for the agent's torts.

T   F   9. Ratification by a principal of an agent's unauthorized acts may occur only through express language of the principal.

T   F   10. When conduct of the parties terminates an agency, the agent's apparent authority continues with respect to some third persons until actual notice of the termination is given to them.

T   F   11. Situations of apparent authority apply to cases of both disclosed and undisclosed principals.

T   F   12. Ratification cannot occur in settings where the principal is undisclosed.

KEY TERMS–MATCHING EXERCISE: Select the term that best completes each statement below.

1. Apparent authority	8. Ratification	15. Partially disclosed
2. Vicarious	9. Delegation	16. Disclosed
3. Privity of contract	10. Contract liability	17. Actual notice
4. Actual	11. Respondeat superior	18. Constructive notice
5. Authority	12. Frolic of his/her own	19. Implied
6. Allocation	13. Undisclosed	20. Subagent
7. Express	14. Independent contractors	

_____ 1. Persons who are not employees of the parties for whom services are performed.

_____ 2. Spoken or written authority communicated by the principal to the agent.

_____ 3. Transferring to another the right or power to perform some act.

_____ 4. An agency in which a third party deals with the agent knowing only the existence but not the identity of the principal.

_____ 5. The type of liability a principal incurs when an agent commits an unauthorized negligent act while in the scope of employment.

_____ 6. The doctrine that makes a principal liable for the agent's torts.

_____ 7. The principal's confirmation or adoption of an agent's unauthorized act.

_____ 8. The kind of agency in which a third person believes there is no agency relationship.

_____ 9. A basic type of authority that is based on the consent shown by the principal to the agent.

_____ 10. The power of an agent to change the legal status of a principal.

_____ 11. Type of authority arising out of the principal's behavior that creates in another's mind the reasonable, justified belief that the agent has actual authority.

_____ 12. Authority arising from the statements or behavior the principal demonstrates to the agent.

_____ 13. A principal whose existence and identity are known by the party.

_____ 14. Persons acting on behalf of an agent.

_____ 15. Express statement to a third party of the termination of an agency relationship.

MULTIPLE CHOICE: Select the alternative that best completes each statement below.

_____ 1. A valid ratification (a) may stem from unauthorized acts of an agent regardless of whether the principal existed at the time of the acts (b) cannot be revoked once made (c) relates back only to the time of disclosure of the principal (d) none of the above.

_____ 2. Normally the principal is not liable for contracts created by an agent's acts that are (a) unauthorized (b) expressly authorized (c) actually authorized (d) implicitly authorized.

_____ 3. Principals adjudged liable for their agents' torts have rights of (a) equitable contribution (b) injunctive relief (c) indemnification (d) condemnation against the agents.

_____ 4. An agent is liable to the third person if the agent (a) acts for an undisclosed principal (b) exceeds the authority granted by the principal (c) commits a tortious act (d) all of the above.

_____ 5. When a third party discovers the identity of an undisclosed principal, the third party may (a) hold either the principal or agent to performance of the contract (b) hold both liable for the contract (c) sue and get a judgment against both principal and agent (d) none of the above.

_____ 6. Ratification must be (a) communicated to the agent (b) communicated to the third person (c) manifested by words (d) none of the above.

_____ 7. When agents falsely represent to third persons that they are authorized by the principals to make contracts for them, the agents are (a) ultimately not liable (b) liable in tort (c) liable in contract (d) none of the above to the third party.

_____ 8. Under the Restatement, employee conduct within scope of employment includes actions (a) motivated to serve the employer (b) within set time and space limits (c) of the kind for which employees have been hired (d) all of the above.

_____ 9. When agents guarantee third persons that principals will carry out the terms of contracts, (a) the agents are liable for nonperformance by the principals (b) only principals are liable for their nonperformance (c) no suretyship exists between the agents and third persons (d) the principals have rights of reimbursement against the agent.

_____ 10. Actions by an agent that make the agent liable on the contract entered into between the principal and the third party include (a) making the contract in the principal's name only (b) committing any crime (c) making the contract in the agent's name only (d) all of the above.

_____ 11. When a third party obtains a judgment against an agent who represents an undisclosed principal whose identity and existence have become known to the third party, (a) the principal's liability remains intact (b) a right of reimbursement against the principal arises in the agent's favor (c) constructive ratification cuts off any rights the principal might have against the agent (d) none of the above.

_____ 12. Conditions that indicate a principal's intent to allow an agent to delegate authority to another include (a) prior dealings among the parties (b) presumption per se (c) constructive notice (d) all of the above.

_____ 13. Effective constructive notice is achieved through (a) radio announcements (b) statements in geographically proper newspapers of general circulation (c) billboard ads (d) handbills.

CASE PROBLEMS–SHORT ESSAY ANSWERS: Read each case problem carefully. When appropriate, answer by stating a Decision for the case and by explaining the rationale–Rule of Law–relied upon to support your decision.

1. For the past five years, agent A, acting on behalf of principal P, has purchased new model year cars from car dealership C for P's company fleet. Each year, A trades in the previous year's cars. The past year has been financially difficult for P's company so to reduce expenditures, P directs A not to purchase new model year cars but to retain last year's models for at least another year. C is not aware of P's changed plans nor does A inform C of this fact when, disregarding P's instructions, A trades in the last year's models and purchases new ones. When A refuses to pay for them and C seeks payment from P, may P validly avoid payment based on the express refusal to A for the authority to make the purchases? Explain.

    Decision: _____

    _____

    Rule of Law: _____

    _____

2. A, agent for P, is told by P to deliver an important paper to X immediately. Time is essential. Hoping to please P, A drove the company car at a high rate of speed and unfortunately struck T. Can T sue A? Explain.

    Decision: _____

    _____

    Rule of Law: _____

    _____

3. A, an agent for disclosed principal P, makes a contract with third party T on behalf of P for the purchase of property insurance from which A will be paid $500 by P. If T breaches the contract, can A sue T? Explain.

    Decision: _____

    _____

Rule of Law: _____

_____

4. In a case involving an undisclosed principal, an agent buys goods on credit but does not pay for them. Later the seller of the goods discovers the fact of the agency and the identity of the principal. The seller obtains a judgment against the principal, but the principal is insolvent. Can the seller recover from the agent? Explain.

Decision: _____

_____

Rule of Law: _____

_____

5. P, the owner of Blackacre, hires X, an independent contractor to build a hotel on P's land. When X begins to break the ground, X uses dynamite to loosen the earth. T, who lives three blocks away, has five windows broken due to the concussion from the explosions. Can T sue P even though X was an independent contractor? Explain.

Decision: _____

_____

Rule of Law: _____

_____

AGENCY UNIT RESEARCH QUESTIONS: Drawing upon information contained in the text, as well as outside sources, discuss the following questions:

1. In what areas of our business and personal lives are we likely to encounter principles of agency law?

2. How has legislative and administrative law pre-empted certain common law agency principles? What rationale underlies these changes?

Chapter 21

INTRODUCTION TO SALES AND LEASES

SCOPE NOTE

Sales and leases of goods are basic, significant parts of most commercial transactions. Contract law and Article 2 of the U.C.C. control transactions for selling or leasing goods. Sales law provides order and stability to the rights and duties of parties to a sales transaction, reducing costs and risks. Knowing basic terminology, the requirements for a valid sales/lease contract, and fundamental legal doctrines that control this area of law is vital for understanding the various specific areas of law that comprise the law of sales. Chapter 21 gives an overview of the fundamental provisions of Code Article 2 covering the law of sales and leases.

EDUCATIONAL OBJECTIVES

1. Distinguish common law and U.C.C. Article 2 approaches to sales contracts.

2. List various Article 2 doctrines controlling sales/lease contracts.

3. Explain the various requirements for a valid sales contract–mutual agreement, consideration, and various formality restrictions.

4. Discuss how sales/lease contracts differ from other non-goods contracts and transactions.

5. Know U.C.C. provisions that apply exclusively to sales between merchants.

6. Appreciate the significance of the doctrine of unconscionability in sales law.

7. Understand the major provisions of U.C.C. Article 2 covering leases.

CHAPTER OUTLINE

I. Nature of Sales Contracts–blend of contract and personal property law
  A. Sale: transfer of title to goods (movable, tangible, personal property and items attached to real property removed by seller) for a price
    1. Governing law–U.C.C. Article 2 and contract/tort law; employment contracts, service contracts, insurance contracts, real property contracts, contracts for sale of intangibles not included
    2. Nonsales transactions in goods–bailments, leases, and gifts are not sales, but affect goods: courts might apply Code provisions to these transaction
  B. Fundamental Principles of Article 2–Article 2 intended to modernize, clarify, simplify, and make uniform law of sales
    1. Good faith–for merchants includes honesty in fact or observing reasonable commercial standards of fair dealing
    2. Unconscionability–based on transaction's commercial setting, purpose, or effect; includes procedural unconscionability (unfairness of bargaining process) or substantive unconscionability (grossly unfairly, oppressive contract terms or provisions)
    3. Expansion of commercial practices–concepts used in interpreting agreements:
      a. Course of dealing–prior conduct between parties establishing a common basis of understanding the agreement
      b. Trade usage–method of dealing regularly observed and followed in particular market
    4. Sales by/between merchants–higher standards of conduct based on separate rules applying to transactions between merchants or involving a merchant (a dealer in goods or having special knowledge or skill peculiar to transaction)
    5. Liberal administration of remedies–intent to put aggrieved party in as good a position as if defaulting party had fully performed; where no specific remedy provided, courts should provide an appropriate remedy
    6. Freedom of contract–parties may vary, replace Code provisions except duties of good faith, diligence, reasonableness, and care
    7. Validation and preservation of sales contracts–formal requisites for contract reduced to a minimum; agreements should be upheld when parties intend to enter contract

II. Formation of a Sales Contract–Code emphasizes validating contracts where parties intend to contract
  A. Manifestation of Mutual Assent–based on offer and acceptance
    1. Definiteness of offer–Code changes common law; contract does not fail for indefiniteness over omitted terms; Code gives standards for filling in omitted terms
      a. Open price–reasonable price at time for delivery
      b. Open Delivery–must be made within reasonable time, in single delivery, at seller's place of business

    c. Open quantity (output and requirements contracts)–enforced by using objective standard based on good faith of both parties

    d. Code provisions cover terms of payment, duration of contracts, and other specifics of performance

2. Irrevocable offers–firm offer (signed writing) by merchant to hold offer open for stated period (up to three months) enforceable without consideration; similar to option contract (consideration given to keep offer open)

3. Variant acceptances–Code changes old common law "mirror image" rule in battle of forms problems, intent of parties now controls

    a. Both parties merchants–offeree's additional terms become part of contract if agreement not materially altered

    b. Neither party a merchant or additional terms materially alter offer–terms are proposals for additions to contract; different terms proposed by offeree not part of contract unless specifically accepted by offeror

    c. Acceptance expressly conditioned upon consenting to additional/different terms–no contract unless variant terms agreed to

4. Manner of acceptance–any reasonable manner under circumstances unless clearly stated otherwise

5. Auctions–*without reserve* precludes withdrawing articles from sale; unless stated otherwise, auction presumed *with reserve* (goods may be withdrawn at any time until sale completed)

B. Consideration–Code relaxes common law rule of consideration; modification, waiver, renunciation or firm offer are binding without separate consideration

C. Form of the Contract

1. Statute of frauds–Code requires contracts for sale of goods over $500 be in writing

    a. Modification of contracts–must be written if resulting contract within Statute; modification taking contract outside Statute may be oral

    b. Written compliance–indication that contract exists between parties; signed by party against whom enforcement sought; specifies quantity of goods; omitted or incorrectly stated terms do not necessarily invalidate contract

    c. Exceptions (oral contracts enforced)–admission that contract was made; specially manufactured goods; partial performance

2. Parol evidence–Code modifies common law rule by using course of dealing, usage of trade, course of performance, or evidence of consistent additional terms for changing terms of written contract

3. Seal–made inoperative under Code

D. Fundamentals of Leases Code Article 2A–attempts to codify all rules governing personal property leases

1. Lease defined–transfer of possession and use of goods for return consideration; no title transfer

2. Warranties–warranty provisions of Article 2 are carried over

3. Default remedies–parties free to create own rights, remedies for default in addition to, or substitution for those in Article 2A

4. Consumer leases defined–lessor regularly leases/sells goods as business; lessee an individual; lease primarily for personal, family, or household purpose; total lease payments not exceeding $25,000
5. Finance leases–lessor not party supplying goods; lessor's primary function to provide financing to lessee to acquire goods from supplier

TRUE–FALSE: Circle true or false.

T F 1. Employment contracts, service contracts and insurance contracts are not covered by Article 2 of the U.C.C.

T F 2. Contracts for the sale of goods costing $300 or more must be in writing to be enforceable.

T F 3. Under the Code, sales contracts containing omitted terms are unenforceable due to their lack of definiteness.

T F 4. Under the Code, merchants are held to a higher standard of commercial reasonableness than are non-merchants.

T F 5. A written memorandum, signed by a merchant seller, confirming an earlier oral contract falling within the Statute of Frauds, binds a merchant buyer unless the latter effectively objects.

T F 6. Retracted bids at auctions automatically revive the previously submitted bid.

T F 7. A contract for the sale of timber to be cut and removed by purchaser is a sale of goods under the U.C.C.

T F 8. Where both the CISG and the U.C.C. apply to a transaction, the CISG preempts the U.C.C.

T F 9. Unless the parties provide otherwise, place of delivery of goods is seller's place of business.

T F 10. Any modification of a contract originally within the Statute of Frauds must be in writing to be enforced.

T F 11. The Code reduces the importance of contracting parties complying exactly with the formal requirements of commercial law in validating and enforcing sales contracts.

T F 12. As a general rule, the remedial provisions of the Code are narrowly interpreted and applied to prevent unjust enrichment to the party injured by another's breach of contract.

KEY TERMS–MATCHING EXERCISE: Select the term that best completes each statement below.

1. Option
2. Mirror image rule
3. Seller
4. Sale
5. Possession
6. Consumer goods sales
7. Goods
8. Without reserve
9. CISG
10. Trade usage
11. Good faith
12. Implied warranty
13. Unconscionable
14. Merchants
15. Finance lease
16. Waiver
17. Firm offer
18. With reserve
19. Lease
20. Trust

_____ 1. A present transfer of title to goods in exchange for a price.

_____ 2. Movable, tangible personal property.

_____ 3. The performance standard controlling parties to sales contracts on their contractual duties.

_____ 4. Law governing international sales transactions involving parties from different countries.

_____ 5. Transaction in which lessor provides lessee with financing enabling acquisition of goods from a supplier.

_____ 6. A common method of doing business prevalent in a particular area of commerce.

_____ 7. An auction at which the auctioneer may not withdraw items put up for sale unless no bids are made.

_____ 8. The common law doctrine that required acceptances of offers to comply exactly with the terms of the offer.

_____ 9. Sales contracts that are harsh and unfair because of the unequal bargaining positions of the parties.

_____ 10. Transaction specifically excluded from CISG coverage.

_____ 11. A contract binding the offeror to keep the offer open for a specific time period.

_____ 12. Written statement signed by non-breaching party discharging breaching party for liability for non-performance.

_____ 13. Transfer of possession to another for a specific time for return payment.

_____ 14. Irrevocable offer made by a merchant.

_____ 15. Auctions at which auctioneer may withdraw goods at anytime until completion of the sale.

MULTIPLE CHOICE: Select the alternative that best completes each statement below.

_____ 1. Property included under the U.C.C.'s definition of goods includes (a) real property (b) negotiable instruments (c) growing crops (d) all of the above.

_____ 2. Which of the following is not a requirement for a valid consumer lease under U.C.C. Article 2A provisions? (a) merchant lessor (b) an individual lessee (c) value of the lease less than $25,000 (d) lease is primarily for business-commercial purposes.

_____ 3. Modifications of sales contracts must be (a) supported by consideration (b) made in good faith (c) witnessed in writing (d) all of the above spc. to be valid under the terms of the U.C.C.

_____ 4. Acceptance of the terms of a sales offer may be indicated by (a) conduct (b) words (c) presumed intention (d) all of the above.

_____ 5. Under the Code, merchants are persons who (a) deal in certain goods (b) hold themselves out to have special knowledge peculiar to certain goods (c) employ an agent who professes to have special knowledge peculiar to goods (d) all of the above.

_____ 6. A pattern of business relations existing between parties often doing business with one another is called a/n (a) trade pattern (b) course of dealing (c) usage of trade (d) none of the above.

_____ 7. Written contractual terms intended as the final, complete agreement of the parties may not be altered, contradicted or supplemented by prior or contemporaneous evidence under the (a) Parol Evidence Rule (b) Fair Interpretation Doctrine (c) Last In/First Out Rule (d) none of the above.

_____ 8. Consideration that the buyer promises the seller in exchange for the goods is referred to as the (a) cost minus depreciation (b) price (c) appreciation (d) pledge.

_____ 9. The Code expressly defines unconscionability as (a) criminal dishonesty (b) fraud in execution (c) deceit (d) none of the above.

_____ 10. An "open-price" term in a sales contract may be filled in by a/an (a) later agreement between the parties (b) bailment (c) auction (d) conditional sale.

_____ 11. The Code's sales provisions are (a) mandatory and must be strictly followed by contracting parties (b) monitored and enforced by the FTC (c) subject to change by contracting parties (d) none of the above.

_____ 12. The Code has changed general contract law regarding the formation of sales contracts (a) to bring more formality to this process (b) by allowing states greater freedom to apply their own rules of law (c) by favoring commercial over consumer interests (d) to modernize and promote fairness in contract law.

_____ 13. Under the Code, an oral contract for the sale of $850 worth of pencils is enforceable (a) if a party admits that negotiations for such a sale occurred (b) only to the extent of delivered and accepted units (c) totally as long as partial performance has occurred (d) only upon complete performance by both parties.

CASE PROBLEMS–SHORT ESSAY ANSWERS: Read each case problem carefully. Answer by stating a Decision for the case and by explaining the rationale–Rule of Law–relied upon to support your decision.

1. S, a nail wholesaler, offers to sell to B, a hardware dealer, 2 tons of nails for $600. S sends B a signed memo stating the offer will remain open for five business days. Two days later, S sends a telegram to B revoking the offer. B ignores the attempted revocation and transmits an acceptance that S refuses to honor. Do the parties have a contract? Explain.

Decision: _____

_____

Rule of Law: _____

_____

2. B enters a contract with S for the purchase of the entire production of S's mobile home manufacturing facility from March through June. Since the exact quantity of homes to be purchased is not stated, is this contract invalid due to indefiniteness?

Decision: _____

_____

Rule of Law: _____

_____

3. A financially strapped elderly retired couple, H and W, enter an installment purchase contract with S, a door-to-door salesperson, for a dishwasher, retail value of $180, calling for four payments of $220 each. After making two installment payments, H and W become dissatisfied, not with the dishwasher, but its price. Can they withdraw from this contract with S? Why or why not?

Decision: _____

_____

Rule of Law: _____

_____

4. Penny, pet store operator, receives an offer mailed from Yummy Pet Supplies, Inc., for the sale of 6 months' supply of Yummy pet food products to be sold in Penny's store. Penny, knowing Yummy's reputation for quality, reasonably priced products, believes this pet food line will increase her business and quickly accepts Yummy's offer, adding in her acceptance letter that she'd like samples of Yummy's grooming products to examine for possible sale in her store. A few days after Penny sends her acceptance letter, she receives a call from Yale Yummy, C.E.O. of Yummy, Inc., saying he considers Penny's letter a rejection and a counter offer that he finds unpalatable and refuses to do business with her. Penny thinks she has a contract. Who wins this dispute?

Decision: _____

_____

Rule of Law: _____

_____

5. Wally Widget is the only person who would want or could use wadgets. Wally places an oral order with the Wadget Company to make 10,000 wadgets at $2.00 each. Later, Wally refuses to accept the completed wadgets and alleges the Uniform Commercial Code Statute of Frauds as a defense to Wadget's suit for breach of contract against Wally. Who wins and why?

Decision: _____

_____

Rule of Law: _____

_____

Chapter 22

PERFORMANCE

SCOPE NOTE

The terms of the sales contract, as well as various provisions of the U.C.C., control the nature and interpretation of the mutually dependent rights/duties of the parties in performing on their sales agreement. The seller's obvious duty is to deliver conforming goods at the proper time and location. The buyer's obvious duty is to accept properly tendered, conforming goods and offer proper payment. The U.C.C. provisions controlling interpretation of contractual terms regarding performance give direction to how issues and disputes in this area are to be resolved. Besides outlining the broad performance rights/obligations of the parties, Chapter 22 covers the complex issues and guidelines for resolving disputes associated with improper performance.

EDUCATIONAL OBJECTIVES

1. Describe the "perfect tender" rule as it applies to both buyer and seller.

2. Discuss the seller's proper delivery obligation in terms of method, location and time.

3. Identify situations under which the seller's duties under the "perfect tender" rule are altered.

4. Explain the buyer's performance duties under the "perfect tender" rule in terms of payment and inspection.

5. Understand the buyer's rights upon improper delivery.

6. Define and discuss the significance of acceptance.

7. Differentiate between the buyer's right to reject non-conforming goods and to revoke acceptance.

8. Explain the doctrine of "cure" in the context of improper performance.

9. Know the significance of substituted performance.

10. Outline circumstances that excuse non-performance in the context of failure of conditions and damage to goods.

CHAPTER OUTLINE

I. Seller's Performance Duties–tender of delivery triggers buyer's payment duty; tender of delivery requires seller to put and hold conforming goods for buyer's inspection and acceptance; reasonable notice (time and place) to buyer to take delivery
  A. Time/Manner of Tender–reasonable time requirement: goods kept available for reasonable period enabling buyer to take possession; performance presumed not in installments unless parties agree otherwise
  B. Place of Tender–silent contract puts place for delivery at seller's place of business, residence, or location of goods; delivery terms determines place of delivery
    1. Shipment contracts–indicated by "F.O.B. seller's place of shipment," "FAS seller's port," "C.I.F.," and "C & F"; delivery occurs at point of shipment; seller delivers goods to carrier, makes reasonable transportation contract, obtains and promptly delivers or tenders to buyer title documents allowing buyer to obtain possession from carrier and promptly notifies buyer of shipment
    2. Destination contracts–indicated by "F.O.B. city of buyer," "ex-ship," and "no arrival, no sale"; conforming goods delivered at specified destination
    3. Goods held by bailee–seller tenders title document or obtains bailee's acknowledgment of buyer's right of possession
  C. Perfect Tender Rule–seller's delivery tender must conform exactly to contract terms; improper tender triggers buyer's right to reject whole lot, accept whole lot, or accept commercial unit or units and reject rest; qualifications of buyer's right of rejection include:
    1. Agreement by parties–parties limit perfect tender rule
    2. Seller's cure–seller may correct improper performance (nonconforming goods shipped) if time remains for proper performance
    3. Installment contracts–buyer's payment performance not triggered until entire contract quantity delivered or tendered unless contract expressly provides for delivery and payment in separate lots or installments; unless provided otherwise, payment due at each installment unless price can be apportioned; buyer's right to reject nonconforming installment if substantially impairs value and cure not feasible; non-conformity or default of one or more installments substantially impairing value of whole contract is breach of whole contract

II. Buyer's Performance–accept and pay for conforming goods; payment a condition to seller's duty of delivery
  A. Inspection–prior to payment or acceptance; determine whether goods conform to contract; C.O.D. contracts require payment prior to inspection, but payment is not

acceptance; inspection must be made within reasonable time; right to reject or revoke acceptance waived when no inspection made

  B. Rejection–includes buyer refusing acceptance, refusing to become owner; must occur within reasonable time after goods tendered or delivered; buyer must reasonably notify seller; for perishables or goods likely to decline in value, buyer obligated to make reasonable efforts to sell them for seller's account

  C. Acceptance–buyer's willingness to become owner, express or implied; acceptance precludes rejection; ownership statements include buyer telling seller that goods conform to contract, will take goods in spite of nonconformity, or failing to make an effective rejection; accepting part of commercial unit is acceptance of entire unit

  D. Revocation of Acceptance–buyer cancels acceptance based upon later discovery of nonconformity substantially impairing contract value; notice must be given seller within reasonable time after defect discovered, should have been discovered; buyer has same rights and duties as after rejection

  E. Payment Obligation–payment due at time/place of delivery

III. Obligations of Both Parties–Code provisions control unless parties allocate risks differently

  A. Casualty to Identified Goods–contract for goods identified at time of contract <u>totally lost</u> or damaged without parties' fault, before risk of loss passes to buyer, makes contract voidable; each party excused from performance obligation; goods <u>partially destroyed</u> gives buyer option to avoid contract or accept goods with price reduction for deterioration

  B. Nonhappening of Presupposed Condition–seller excused from contract duty on non-occurrence of presupposed conditions that were basic contract assumptions unless seller expressly assumed risk; Code excuses performance where commercially impracticable due to unforeseen supervening event

  C. Substituted Performance–neither party at fault, agreed manner of delivery commercially impracticable, substituted manner of performance must be tendered and accepted where commercially reasonable

  D. Right to Adequate Assurance of Performance–triggered by reasonable grounds for fearing other party might not perform; innocent party may demand written assurance and suspend own performance until assurance is secured from party causing fear; assurance not received within reasonable time, not exceeding thirty days, cancels contract

  E. Right to Cooperation–performance dependent upon cooperation not forthcoming excuses delaying own performance and may be treated as a breach

  F. Anticipatory Repudiation–clear indication of unwillingness to perform made before performance due; if substantially impairs value of contract, triggers rights to wait for commercially reasonable time or resort to remedy for breach

TRUE-FALSE: Circle true or false.

T   F   1. A sales contract may call for the seller to deliver goods prior to receiving payment.

T   F   2. Delivery may be tendered at any hour and conducted in any manner as the seller chooses.

T   F   3. Both parties to a sales contract are automatically excused from performance when the expressly provided for manner of delivery becomes impossible.

T   F   4. The buyer's acceptance of goods cuts off any right to reject them.

T   F   5. Parties to a sales contract may not alter the application of the perfect tender rule to their transaction through contractual provisions.

T   F   6. Unless the contract provides otherwise, payment is due at the time and place where the buyer is to receive the goods.

T   F   7. A C.O.D. shipment contract requires buyer payment for the goods prior to inspection.

T   F   8. Under the Code, acceptance of goods must always be in writing, signed by the buyer.

T   F   9. When the sales contract does not specify the location for delivery, the place for delivery is deemed the buyer's place of business.

T   F   10. When a buyer has rejected goods due to their nonconformity, the seller bears the burden of establishing that the goods conform to the contract.

T   F   11. Usually fires, strikes or lock-outs are sufficient to excuse contractual performance on the grounds of performance impossibility.

T   F   12. For a buyer to revoke acceptance, the seller's defective performance must substantially impair the value of the goods.

KEY TERMS–MATCHING EXERCISE: Select the term that best completes each statement below.

1. Shipment contract

2. Seller

3. Installment contract

4. Possession

5. Cure

6. Commercial unit

7. Performance

8. Revoke

9. Substituted performance

10. Perfect tender rule

11. Acceptance

12. Credit sale

13. Cancellation

14. Money damages

15. Rejection

16. Inspection

17. Commercial impracticability

18. Anticipatory repudiation

19. Tender

20. Contract rate

_____ 1. The act that fulfills the expectations of the parties to their contract and discharges their contractual duties.

_____ 2. A sales agreement calling for delivery and payment of goods in separate lots.

_____ 3. A unit of goods that is a single whole for the purposes of sale, a division of which substantially impairs its identity, value or use.

_____ 4. The buyer's refusal to accept and make payment on non-conforming goods.

_____ 5. A transaction under which the buyer is not required to make payment for the goods at the time they are received.

_____ 6. Seller's prompt, timely delivery of conforming goods, following buyer's rightful rejection of nonconforming goods.

_____ 7. The obligation facing the parties to a sales contract when the agreed manner of performance has become commercially untenable without fault of either party.

_____ 8. A sales contract containing C.O.D., C.I.F., and C.F. delivery terms.

_____ 9. Duty imposed on the seller under the Code requiring tender of delivery exactly conforming to contractual terms.

_____ 10. Buyer's expression of willingness to become owner of goods.

_____ 11. Consideration buyer must give seller upon accepting commercial unit of nonconforming goods.

_____ 12. Buyer's pre-acceptance right to examine goods to insure that they conform to the contract.

_____ 13. Seller's duty to make available to the buyer conforming goods.

_____ 14. U.C.C. doctrine that discharges performance when unforeseen events not anticipatable by parties make performance an extreme hardship.

_____ 15. Party's expression of unwillingness to perform on the contract prior to date of performance.

MULTIPLE CHOICE: Select the alternative that best completes each statement below.

_____ 1. When the sales contract does not mention time for delivery, the seller (a) has a reasonable time after entering the contract to deliver the goods (b) must deliver the goods on buyer's demand (c) has no more than 60 days to deliver the goods (d) none of the above.

_____ 2. Following a buyer's rejection of nonconforming goods, a seller may rightfully (a) hold the buyer in breach (b) sell the goods elsewhere and thus avoid all liability to the buyer (c) rightfully refuse to reimburse the buyer for inspection expenses (d) undo the defective tender by promptly delivering conforming goods within the allowed performance time.

_____ 3. Under a shipment contract, the seller must (a) deliver the goods to a carrier (b) issue a document of title for the goods to the buyer (c) make a reasonable contract of cartage (d) all of the above.

_____ 4. To be effective, revocation of acceptance must be made (a) within a year after the goods are delivered (b) within a reasonable time after the nonconformity of the goods is discovered (c) in writing only (d) by a receiver in equity.

_____ 5. Merchant buyers possessing rightfully rejected goods must (a) reship them (b) resell them (c) follow the reasonable instructions of the seller concerning their disposal (d) place them in trust.

_____ 6. When a party to a sales contract reasonably doubts whether the other party will be willing or have the ability to properly perform on the designated date, the threatened party may (a) cancel the contract (b) demand written assurance of proper performance (c) seek enforcement of the right of cooperation in equity (d) demand a cure.

_____ 7. Upon delivery of conforming goods, the buyer must (a) tender payment (b) issue a document of title in favor of the seller (c) warehouse the goods until the seller is paid (d) all of the above.

_____ 8. A buyer's right of inspection (a) can be exercised anytime (b) may not be eliminated by a clause in the contract (c) requires the buyer to bear inspection expenses (d) is usually nonexistent.

_____ 9. Acceptance takes place when the buyer (a) fails to reject the goods (b) informs the seller that the goods are conforming (c) tells the seller that, despite nonconformities, the goods are adequate (d) all of the above.

_____ 10. A sales contract containing the delivery terms "exship," "F.O.B. city of buyer," "no arrival, no sale," is a (a) substituted contract (b) destination contract (c) tendered contract (d) none of the above.

_____ 11. Upon delivery of nonconforming goods a buyer may (a) reject all of the goods (b) accept all of the goods (c) accept any commercial unit or units and reject the rest (d) all of the above.

_____ 12. Under an installment contract, when the seller has tendered nonconforming goods, the buyer (a) may reject the installment if its value is substantially impaired and the seller cannot cure the non-conformity (b) can immediately cancel the contract and hold the seller in total breach (c) has an absolute right of rejection (d) none of the above.

_____ 13. A sales contract is performable in installments (a) in all cases (b) only in commercial transactions between merchants (c) only if the parties so agree (d) none of the above.

CASE PROBLEMS–SHORT ESSAY ANSWERS: Read each case problem carefully. When appropriate, answer by stating a Decision for the case and by explaining the rationale–Rule of Law–relied upon to support your decision.

1. B orders two dozen personalized Halloween masks from Costume Supplies, Inc., delivery and payment at B's residence. While seller's truck is making the delivery, a flash flood strikes and sweeps the truck away. A few hours later, the truck and its driver are found, but the delivery items are a total loss. S informs B of the near tragedy and tells B, regrettably, that their contract is cancelled. B, needing the masks for an upcoming party, demands that S provide substitute masks or a lawsuit will follow. Is S required to provide replacement masks as B asserts? Discuss.

   Decision: _____

   _____

   Rule of Law: _____

   _____

2. B ordered 20,000 1/2-inch bolts from S, delivery in installments of 1,000 per month in 20 different shipments. Payment was to occur on the first day of each month. On the third shipment, B is a day late in making payment. S gives immediate notice of cancellation of the entire contract. Decision for whom and why?

   Decision: _____

   _____

   Rule of Law: _____

   _____

3. Henrietta Hunter purchases a new hunting rifle from Barney's sporting goods store. An avid sportswoman, Henrietta is ready to pay top dollar for top quality. Upon unpacking the rifle and readying it for use, she notices tiny scratches on the lever and nicks in the handle. A perfectionist, Henrietta is furious and storms back to Barney's demanding a full refund. Barney refuses her request, arguing that the gun is still suitable for hunting purposes and Henrietta's dissatisfaction is over mere cosmetic blemishes. Who wins this dispute and why?

   Decision: _____

   _____

Rule of Law: _____

_____

4. B, a merchant, receives a shipment of nonconforming bananas from S. B rejects them and notifies S to come and get them. S remains silent. B does nothing and the bananas spoil. In a suit by S against B for the loss of the bananas, who wins and why?

Decision: _____

_____

Rule of Law: _____

_____

5. B and S, American business executives, enter a sales contract for 5,000 Australian widgees at 50 cents apiece, to be delivered to B's place of business no later than August 14. Diplomatic relations between America and Australia become strained. By July 21, the countries cut off diplomatic relations, call home their respective ambassadors and place an embargo on all mutual trade. When S is unable to deliver the specified widgees at the appointed time and place, B sues for breach. Who wins and why?

Decision: _____

_____

Rule of Law: _____

_____

Chapter 23

TRANSFER OF TITLE AND RISK OF LOSS

SCOPE NOTE

At common law, buyer/seller rights and duties under a sales contract were determined by the concept of title. The U.C.C. takes a different approach. Title passage in various types of sales transactions and the factors used to determine title passing under the Code are discussed in Chapter 23. In addition to ownership considerations, parties to sales transactions must know their rights and duties at the various stages of their business dealings. In the event of damage or destruction to the goods sold, who bears the risk of loss? When may the parties to a sales transaction protect their interest in goods through insurance? The factors used to decide risk-of-loss issues, as well as the various U.C.C. provisions controlling this area, are also examined in this Chapter:

Another important aspect of the legal identities of parties to a sales transaction is knowing under what circumstances someone with less than full ownership may transfer title to purchasers of goods. What difficulties are created when an innocent buyer purchases another person's goods believing that the sale was authorized by and is made with the permission of the true owner? These issues are addressed in Chapter 23, which examines the rules used to determine the rights of adversary parties (usually the purchaser and the original owner) in cases of attempted title transfer by a non-owner of goods. The situations in which the innocent buyer prevails are discussed, as well as those cases where the original owner's title to the goods sold is protected. Chapter 23 closes with a discussion of the rights that creditors of the seller have in the goods sold. Principles for ranking the conflicting interests of buyers from, and creditors of, the seller are presented to assist in determining the priority of competing interests in these confusing situations.

EDUCATIONAL OBJECTIVES

1. Know the types of concerns directly related to location of title issues.

2. Identify the rules used in determining title passage and how they are influenced by type of goods, shipment terms, use of documents of title, and other related circumstances.

3. Explain the importance of identifying goods to the contract.

4. Define and point out the significance of a buyer's "special property interest."

5. Understand the various rules associated with determining risk of loss when no breach of contract has occurred.

6. Distinguish sale on approval from sale or return.

7. Describe how shipment terms, possession of the goods by a bailee, and breach of contract affect risk-of-loss issues.

8. Explain the legal policies in competition with one another in non-owner sales of goods.

9. Distinguish between void and voidable title transfers both at common law and under the U.C.C.

10. Define and describe the significance of a bona fide purchaser for value.

11. Discuss the treatment of an innocent buyer under the U.C.C.

12. Describe the importance of the U.C.C. doctrine of entrusting.

13. Define "bulk transfer" and list Code requirements applicable to such transactions.

14. List the type of transactions exempted from Article 6 control.

15. Discuss the effect of not complying with Article 6.

CHAPTER OUTLINE

I. Transfer of Title–title passes when existing goods are identified to contract
   A. Identification–designation of specific goods to contract; occurs at any time, in any manner parties agree to
      1. Where no prior agreement by parties
         a. Existing goods–when contract made
         b. Future goods–when seller ships, marks or designates goods
         c. Future crops or animals–when crops planted, offspring conceived
         d. Fungibles–for share of undivided goods, occurs when contract made
      2. Insurable interest–Code extends insurable interest to buyer; both buyer & seller can insure goods

3. Security interest–interest in personal property/fixtures intended to ensure payment; covered by Article 9

B. Passage of Title–when parties intend it to pass, or according to Code rules
 1. Physical movement of goods–title passes at time/place where seller completes delivery
  a. Shipment contract (seller tenders delivery to carrier)–title passes to buyer at time and place of delivery to carrier
  b. Destination contract (seller tenders delivery at a specified destination)–title passes on tender at destination
 2. No Movement of goods–title passes on delivery of title document at time/place of contracting for existing, identified goods; at time of identification for unidentified goods

C. Power to Transfer Title–contrary to general rule that non-owners, unauthorized sellers (thief, finder, or bailee) cannot transfer good title, certain buyers (bona fide, innocent, good faith purchasers for value) from non-owners may get good title; such buyers must act honestly, and take goods without knowledge of title defect
 1. Void and voidable title to goods–void title is no title (thief or finder has no title, can transfer none); buyer with voidable title acquired under circumstances permitting former owner to rescind transfer and regain title (cases of mistake, duress, undue influence, or incapacity) can pass good title to good faith purchaser for value that ends original seller's right of rescission and replevin (action to recover goods)
 2. Entrusting goods to merchant–Code protects buyers in ordinary course of business from merchants who deal in goods of the kind sold
  a. Merchant (in business of selling goods) wrongfully selling another's entrusted goods (voluntary transfer by owner)–buyer in ordinary course of business acquires title and original owner of entrusted goods no longer has title; original owner has conversion action for $ damages against merchant for wrongful sale; protection of bona fide purchaser does not apply to goods transferred to merchant by thief, finder or any other person not unauthorized to entrust them

II. Risk of Loss–allocation of loss between seller and buyer where goods damaged, destroyed or lost without fault of either party
 A. Risk of Loss Where There is a Contract Breach–Code places risk of loss on breaching party
  1. Breach by seller–non-conforming goods; risk of loss remains on seller until buyer accepts goods or seller cures defect
  2. Breach by buyer–conforming goods identified to contract wrongfully rejected by buyer who refuses payment (buyer repudiates contract)–seller may treat risk of loss as resting on buyer "for commercially reasonable time" to cover deficiency in seller's insurance protection
 B. Risk of Loss in Absence of Breach–risk of loss allocated by agreement of parties
  1. Trial sales–Code provisions for "sale on approval," "sale or return"
   a. Sale on approval–goods sold for buyer's use; possession, not title, passes to buyer for stated or reasonable period of time, title/risk of loss remain with seller until buyer's "approval" or acceptance

   b. Sale or return–goods sold for resale by buyer; buyer has option to return goods; risk of loss on buyer, who has title until revested in seller by return; Code treats consignments (delivery of possession to agent for sale) as sale or return
   2. Contracts involving carriers
       a. Shipment contract–risk passes to buyer when goods delivered to carrier
       b. Destination contract–risk passes to buyer at place goods tendered
   3. Goods in possession of bailee–risk of loss passes to buyer when buyer receives negotiable title document, when seller tenders nonnegotiable title document, when seller tenders written directions to bailee to deliver goods to buyer or when bailee acknowledges buyer's right to possession
   4. All other sales–risk of loss passes when buyer receives goods from a merchant or on tender of goods from a non merchant seller

III. Bulk Sales–covered by Code Article 6
   A. Definition–transfer of major part of inventory not in ordinary course of transferor's business
   B. Risk to Seller's Creditors–seller liquidates all or major part of assets by bulk sale, conceals/diverts sale proceeds from creditors
   C. Code Provisions–rules to protect creditor interest in sales proceeds; changes in business practices and legal contexts have reduced importance of Code bulk sales rules; revised Article 6 provides improved protection to creditors and reduces obstacles to good faith transactions

TRUE-FALSE: Circle true or false.

T   F   1. Parties to a sales contract may, by agreement, define who will assume risk of loss for damage or destruction of the goods.

T   F   2. Under the Code, buyers must own goods before they are insurable.

T   F   3. The U.C.C. does not use title location as the primary means to determine the rights of parties to a sales contract when goods are damaged.

T   F   4. The power and right to transfer title are one and the same.

T   F   5. In contracts for the sale of fungible goods, identification of a part or unit of the undivided whole occurs at the time the contract is made.

T   F   6. When a seller ships nonconforming goods to a buyer, risk of loss remains on the seller until the buyer accepts the goods.

T   F   7. Under the revised provisions of U.C.C. Article 6, buyers under bulk transfers who make good faith attempts to meet the requirements of the Article are still liable for non compliances that occurred.

T   F   8. A bulk sale is a transfer not in the ordinary course of business.

T   F   9. Under modern law, a minor seller may avoid a sale of goods and recover them from a third-party bona fide purchaser for value.

T   F   10. A risk faced by creditors of a debtor-seller of goods in bulk is that the latter may use the bulk sale to liquidate assets and keep the sale proceeds from the creditors.

T   F   11. The bulk sales provisions of the Code are designed to protect creditors of a merchant debtor from the latter's fraud.

T   F   12. A shipment contract requires a seller to deliver goods at a specified location.

KEY TERMS–MATCHING EXERCISE: Select the term that best completes each statement below.

1. Bulk sale	8. Identification	15. C. I. F.
2. Freight forwarder	9. Entrusting	16. Sale
3. Sale or return	10. F.A.S.	17. Good faith purchaser for value
4. Initial carrier	11. Buyer in the ordinary course	
5. Voidable title	12. Risk of loss	18. Tender
6. Bailee	13. Party intent	19. Destination
7. Security interest	14. Sale on approval	20. Thief

_____ 1. Steps taken by the seller to choose goods that meet contractual specifications.

_____ 2. A transfer of goods to a merchant dealing in the type of goods transferred.

_____ 3. An interest in personal property that protects performance of a promised, future obligation.

_____ 4. A good faith purchaser for value who purchased from a merchant during normal business hours.

_____ 5. The interest acquired under circumstances that allow former owner-vendors to revoke a sale and recapture their prior ownership.

_____ 6. Burden assumed by either party to a sales contract for destruction or damage to the goods.

_____ 7. Transfer of title to goods under which buyer retains an option to revest title in the seller.

_____ 8. Controls title passage for identified, existing goods.

_____ 9. Transfer of goods for a period of time during which buyer determines whether or not to purchase them.

_____ 10. A transfer for value not in the ordinary course of business, of a substantial portion of the equipment, materials, inventory, supplies or merchandise of a business.

_____ 11. Someone lacking both the power and right to sell goods.

_____ 12. One buying goods honestly without knowledge of any title problems.

_____ 13. Transferring title to goods for a price.

_____ 14. Contract requiring seller to ship goods to a specific location.

_____ 15. Duty of seller to make conforming goods available to the buyer for a reasonable time and notify the buyer of this fact.

MULTIPLE CHOICE: Select the alternative that best completes each statement below.

_____ 1. A reason for the legal policy to protect existing ownership of goods is to (a) make transfers easier (b) protect involuntary bailees (c) ensure that people are not required to retain possession or control of goods at all times to maintain their ownership in them (d) none of the above.

_____ 2. The controversy that commonly follows a non-owner's sale of goods pits a (a) non-owner against an owner (b) non-owner against a good faith purchaser for value (c) good faith purchaser for value against an owner (d) none of the above.

_____ 3. Bulk transfers exempted from U.C.C. Article 6 coverage include (a) transfers settling a security interest (b) sales by bankruptcy trustees (c) sales by personal representatives (executor/executrix) (d) all of the above.

_____ 4. Code requirements making bulk transfers valid against creditors of the bulk transferor include (a) central filing by the transferee (b) notice of the transfer by the transferee to all listed creditors of the transferor (c) a conditional pledge signed by the transferor (d) a recorded factor's lien.

_____ 5. When a buyer holding title to goods purchased from a merchant seller leaves them with the seller who then sells the goods to another party, the buyer (a) may reclaim the goods anytime after delivery to the subsequent purchaser (b) has given the seller both the right and power to make such a transfer (c) has 10 days after delivery to reclaim the goods from the subsequent purchaser (d) none of the above.

_____ 6. Persons holding void and therefore no title include (a) finders (b) bailors (c) people acquiring goods through undue influence (d) all of the above.

_____ 7. Examples of voidable title include acquisition through (a) mistake (b) fraud in the execution (c) sale or gift from someone under guardianship (d) all of the above.

_____ 8. A/n _____ is delivering personal property to an agent for sale by that person. (a) allocation (b) approval transfer (c) consignment (d) none of the above

_____ 9. Under a sale on approval, the buyer's failure to reasonably notify the seller of an election to return the goods is (a) identification (b) acceptance (c) ratification (d) consignment of the goods.

_____ 10. Under the U.C.C., risk of loss is determined by who (a) holds title to the goods (b) has greater control over the goods (c) occupies the position of equitable receiver (d) all of the above.

_____ 11. The Code's approach to risk of loss is (a) a transactional approach (b) based on state-secured credit laws (c) generally outmoded and antiquated (d) none of the above.

_____ 12. The Code treats consignment sales as (a) ones on approval (b) bailments (c) sales or returns (d) leases.

_____ 13. Generally, in cases of breach of contract, the Code places the risk of loss on (a) both parties equally (b) the offeror (c) the party financing the transaction (d) the non-performing party.

CASE PROBLEMS–SHORT ESSAY ANSWERS: Read each case problem carefully. Answer by stating a Decision for the case and by explaining the rationale–Rule of Law–relied upon to support your decision.

1. A makes a bulk transfer purchase of B's goods. B failed to comply with U.C.C. provisions regulating bulk sales. B turns over the net proceeds of the sale to creditors but the amount covers only 50% of the outstanding debt. The creditors seek to avoid the transfer to A and have the goods returned. A vigorously opposes the creditor's action. Who wins this dispute?

Decision: _____

_____

Rule of Law: _____

_____

2. A week after accepting delivery of a new $10,000 set of dining/living room furniture purchased from Ajax Home Furnishings, Mary discovers fabric tears and foundation cracks in most of the items. She quickly sends Ajax a revocation of acceptance notice and awaits their reply. Shortly thereafter a hurricane strikes, destroying Mary's house and all her belongings. Mary's homeowner's insurance policy covers 70% of losses to household furnishings caused by fire, storm, flooding or other unintentional causes. Who bears what risk of loss for the furniture purchased from Ajax?

Decision: _____

_____

Rule of Law: _____

_____

3. A transfers a fur coat to retail furrier B for repair and storage. During B's regular business hours, C purchases the coat from B. What are A's rights against purchaser C? Explain.

Decision: _____

_____

Rule of Law: _____

_____

4. Owner of grain stored in E's elevator sells the grain to B. Every bushel of grain in the elevator is covered by an outstanding negotiable document of title evidencing ownership. Upon selling the grain in the elevator, owner delivers the title document to the buyer. Shortly thereafter, the elevator burns with all contents lost. Who bears the loss for the sold grain, elevator owner, grain owner or buyer? Explain.

Decision: _____

_____

Rule of Law: _____

_____

5. Francine goes to Mary's bridal shop to select her wedding gown. Francine chooses a gown to her liking and pays the purchase price of $1280. She leaves the gown with Mary so a train and waist ruffles can be sewn on. Mary completes her work and calls Francine telling her the dress is ready for pickup. Later that evening, vandals break into Mary's shop, causing considerable damage, including setting Francine's dress on fire, making it worthless. Advise Francine and Mary of their rights and responsibilities at this point.

Decision: _____

_____

Rule of Law: _____

_____

Chapter 24

PRODUCTS LIABILITY: WARRANTIES AND STRICT LIABILITY IN TORT

SCOPE NOTE

The purchaser of goods expects that they will conform to certain quality and title standards. When a seller's performance falls below such standards, when goods are defective, a breach of warranty usually exists, making the seller liable for resulting damages. What protection is given the buyer against title/quality defects? What guarantees run to innocent purchasers protecting them against unfair/dishonest business practices? In the following chapter, these issues are focused upon in terms of basic terminology and the principles of warranty law contained in the U.C.C. Because defective products may cause personal injury or property damage to the buyer or others, who is liable to whom, for what type of injury, based on what theory, is important to know. Manufacturer and seller liability in this area, based on contract, sales, tort, and statutory law, has grown. Chapter 24 examines this area of law in the context of warranty and strict liability principles.

EDUCATIONAL OBJECTIVES

1. Identify the types of transactions to which warranty law applies.

2. Distinguish between express and implied warranties and how they are created.

3. Discuss how the "Puffing Doctrine" and the Parole Evidence Rule affect warranty protection.

4. Analyze how "caveat emptor" interacts with warranty liability.

5. Explain the various U.C.C. requirements for validly excluding/limiting express and implied warranty protection.

6. Identify the roles that the doctrines of privity and trade usage, as well as the buyer's duty of examination, play in warranty considerations.

7. Understand the Code's application of warranty protection to third parties.

8. Know significant changes brought to warranty law by the enactment of federal warranty legislation.

9. Contrast the influence of contributory negligence and assumption of risk on warranty liability.

10. Define strict liability and its relevance to product liability cases.

11. Outline burden of proof requirements under strict liability and demonstrate how they apply to cases of personal injury caused by defective goods.

12. Review the impact of contributory negligence and assumption of the risk in product liability cases.

CHAPTER OUTLINE

I. Warranties–seller's obligation covering title, quality, characteristics, or condition of goods; seller not required to provide; Code prescribed implied warranties must be affirmatively disclaimed to avoid liability
   A. Types of Warranties–arise out of sale itself (warranty of title), seller's statement of fact or promise (express warranty), or circumstances of sale (implied warranty)
      1. Warranty of title–seller's duty to convey ownership without any lien; seller implicitly warrants good title, transfer is rightful, no security interest or other lien exists against goods which buyer has no knowledge of at time of contracting
      2. Express warranties–statement of fact or promise about goods; description of goods, sale by sample or model; becomes part of basis of bargain; no formal words ("warrant," "guarantee") required; seller not required to know statement is untrue
         a. Creation–created by seller orally, in writing; making statement (not value or opinion) of fact or promise; covers quality, condition, capacity, performability, or safety
         b. Basis of bargain–crucial to buyer's expectation of value or assumption underlying contract
      3. Implied warranties–contractual obligation arising out of circumstances of sale; exist by operation of law; not found from contract language; both types may apply
         a. Merchantability–Code requires merchant sellers to impliedly warrant that goods are reasonably fit for ordinary purposes for which they're manufactured and sold; that they're of fair, average quality
         b. Fitness for particular purpose–any seller impliedly warrants that goods are fit for stated purpose; seller selects product knowing buyer's intended use; buyer relies on seller's judgment in selecting goods; applies to specific, not ordinary, purpose

B. Obstacles to Warranty Based Recovery–limits on effectiveness of warranty protection
  1. Disclaimer of warranties–elimination of protection; Code provides reasonable construction of words/conduct for disclaimers, limitations to apply
    a. Express exclusions–title warranty excluded by specific language or certain circumstances (judicial sale, sale by sheriff, executor, foreclosure; seller sells only such title as he has)
    b. Implied warranty–disclaimer, modification language for implied merchantability must mention "merchantability" and be conspicuous; disclaimer of fitness for particular purpose must be written and conspicuous; implied warranties disclaimed by "as is," "with all faults," or similar language reasonably conveying meaning of exclusion, by course of dealing, course of performance or usage of trade doctrines
    c. Buyer's examination or refusal to examine–inspecting goods before entering contract waives implied warranties for apparent, knowable defects; failure to inspect may void consumer warranty protection
    d. Federal legislation covering consumer warranties–Federal Trade Commission administers/enforces Magnuson-Moss Warranty Act; designed to protect consumer purchasers; requires clear, useful warranty information covering consumer goods (used for personal, family, or household purposes); seller making written warranty cannot disclaim any implied warranty
  2. Limitation/modification of warranties–Code permits seller to limit or modify buyer's remedies for breach of warranty; limitations cannot be unconscionable or exclude consequential damages language
  3. Privity of contract–19th Century legal doctrine requiring contractual relationship between plaintiff-buyer and defendant-seller for warranty recovery
    a. Horizontal privity–noncontracting nonpurchaser (user, consumer, bystander) injured by defective goods; the Code lists recognized plaintiffs; seller's warranty, express or implied, extends to any natural person in family, household or guest of buyer at home; must be reasonable to expect that injured person would use, consume, be affected by product; Code prohibits seller from excluding or limiting warranty protection
    b. Vertical privity–who is liable for breach of warranty; covers remote sellers (manufacturers, wholesalers, retailers) within chain of distribution with whom consumer purchaser has not contracted; most states have eliminated requirement of vertical privity to maintain warranty actions
  4. Notice of breach of warranty–buyer must notify seller of warranty breach within reasonable time to have remedy against seller
  5. Plaintiff's conduct–buyer's contributory negligence not a defense in action against seller for breach of warranty; buyer discovering defect that might cause injury and proceeds to use goods waives rights to recover against seller based on voluntary assumption of risk

II. Strict Liability in Tort–Section 402A of Restatement Torts; applies liability to merchant sellers for personal injuries and property damage; covers unreasonably dangerous defect; strict liability does not require proof of seller's negligence; seller's reasonable care not a defense

   A. Requirements of Strict Liability–merchant seller; defective product; unreasonable danger to user or consumer; defect existed at time of sale; defect attributable to seller; plaintiff injured by using/consuming product; defect proximately caused injury

      1. Merchant sellers–liability only on person in business of selling product

      2. Defective condition–plaintiff need not prove how, why product became defective; defect includes faulty manufacture, design, warning, labeling, packaging, or instructions

         a. Manufacturing defect–product not properly made, fails to meet manufacturing specifications

         b. Design defect–product made as specified but dangerous or hazardous because design inadequate; poor engineering, choice of materials, packaging

         c. Failure to warn–seller's duty to provide adequate warning of possible danger, provide appropriate directions for safe use, package product in suitable safe manner

      3. Unreasonable danger–danger beyond what would be reasonably anticipated by ordinary consumers who buy with common knowledge of product characteristics; courts let jury decide what are reasonable expectations by consumers

   B. Obstacles to Recovery–warranty obstacles not generally applied in strict liability actions

      1. Disclaimers and notice–strict liability based on tort law and not subject to contractual defenses, not governed by Code, not affected by contractual limitations or disclaimers, not subject to notice requirement; in commercial transactions, between merchants of equal bargaining power, clear and specific disclaimers are enforceable

      2. Privity–horizontal privity extends to buyers, users, consumers and bystanders; vertical privity extends to any merchant seller (wholesalers, distributors, manufacturers, retailers, manufacturers of component parts)

      3. Plaintiff's conduct–did plaintiff's conduct play role in causing injury (is it fair to blame seller for plaintiff's product misuse); defendant bears burden of proof

         a. Contributory negligence–plaintiff's conduct falls below standard of care for self protection; not a defense for strict liability.

         b. Comparative negligence–damages apportioned between parties based on degree of fault found against each; recognized as strict liability defense

         c. Voluntary assumption of risk–plaintiff's express/implied consent to encounter known danger; recognized as a defense; burden of proof on defendant

         d. Misuse/abuse of product–plaintiff knows, should know, that product is defective or used improperly; a recognized defense; foreseeable misuse of product with no warning by seller waives defense

      4. Subsequent alteration–recognized defense; covers substantial change in product's condition after sold

    5. Statute of repose–how long should manufacturer face potential liability after product sold; some state laws limit time for which manufacturer liable; after statutory time period expires, manufacturer no longer liable

TRUE-FALSE: Circle true or false.

T   F   1. To reduce the likelihood that plaintiffs in product liability suits might seek recovery of punitive damages for improper or unjustified reasons, some states require that all or part of any punitive damages award be paid directly to the state and not the plaintiff.

T   F   2. Sellers are always required to warrant goods they sell.

T   F   3. Extending products liability to manufacturers of goods has not reduced the liability of sellers to purchasers of defective goods.

T   F   4. All sellers impliedly warrant the merchantability of the goods they sell.

T   F   5. For the implied warranty of fitness for a particular purpose to apply, the buyer must specifically inform the seller of the express purpose for which the goods are purchased.

T   F   6. The U.C.C. reduces the controlling influence that contractual privity has in breach of warranty disputes.

T   F   7. Under the theory of strict liability, a plaintiff must show how and why a product became defective to establish a recovery right.

T   F   8. Strict liability may not be disclaimed, excluded or modified by contract.

T   F   9. Manufacturers or sellers must warn purchasers of all possible hazards associated with any use of products sold.

T   F   10. Contributory negligence is not an effective defense in a suit against a seller of goods for breach of warranty.

T   F   11. Implied warranties arise by acts of parties and not through operation of law.

T   F   12. Liability for personal injuries caused by unreasonably dangerous, defective goods extends to lease transactions.

KEY TERMS–MATCHING EXERCISE: Select the term that best completes each statement below.

---

1. Sales acts
2. Contributory negligence
3. Comparative negligence
4. Expert
5. Disclaimer
6. Strict liability
7. Puffing

8. Reliance
9. Express warranty
10. Assumption of risk
11. Consumer products
12. Inspection of goods
13. By sample

14. Privity
15. Magnuson-Moss Act
16. Trade usage
17. Sale on approval
18. Merchantable
19. Waiver
20. Statutes of repose

_____ 1. Buyer's act of accepting seller's superior skill, knowledge or judgment in choosing a product to meet the buyer's stated needs.

_____ 2. Action on the part of a buyer that nullifies the seller's implied warranty liability for obvious defects.

_____ 3. Statements of opinion or value made by a seller that are not a basis for warranty liability.

_____ 4. A seller's statement amounting to a definite assurance regarding the description, quality or condition of goods sold.

_____ 5. Liability without fault imposed by law as a matter of public policy in sales of defective products posing unreasonably dangerous hazards.

_____ 6. Voluntarily using a known defective product in the face of danger.

_____ 7. The contractual relationship that early common law required between a plaintiff and defendant before recovery based upon breach of warranty could be obtained.

_____ 8. A tort defense that completely bars plaintiffs from any recovery due to self-carelessness.

_____ 9. An act of Congress seeking to prevent deception and protect consumer purchasers by providing for competent product warranty information.

_____ 10. The tort doctrine applicable to reduce a plaintiff's damage recovery by the degree of the plaintiff's contributory fault.

_____ 11. One whose statements of opinion may create warranty liability.

_____ 12. Of fair, average and medium quality.

_____ 13. Regular industry customs that may create warranty liability.

_____ 14. Positive, explicit, unequivocal statements eliminating warranty liability.

_____ 15. Legislation limiting the time during which manufacturers are liable for injuries caused by products.

MULTIPLE CHOICE: Select the alternative that best completes each statement below.

_____ 1. The duty to warn of dangers or hazards associated with the use of products arises from (a) the duty of due care (b) specific statutory provisions (c) the spreading of the risk theory (d) none of the above.

_____ 2. Of the following, who is normally not subject to strict liability in tort? (a) supplier of component parts (b) manufacturer of finished goods (c) purchaser (d) retailer

_____ 3. Under the Code, liability of the seller for express warranty is made dependent on whether the statement in question was (a) the basis for the bargain (b) a repudiation of the contract (c) the basis for damages (d) made with the necessary intent.

_____ 4. The Code's extension of seller warranty applies to (a) employees of the buyer (b) household guests of the buyer (c) guest passengers in the buyer's car (d) all of the above.

_____ 5. A defense in tort that may be successfully used by the seller against an injured buyer of defective goods in a breach of warranty suit is (a) assumption of the risk (b) res ipsa loquitur (c) contributory negligence (d) equitable cloture.

_____ 6. Sellers of products are liable for injuries that result from (a) any misuse of a product (b) unanticipatable product abuse (c) foreseeable misuse of a product (d) all of the above.

_____ 7. Which of the following is not a required element of proof for strict liability under Section 402A, Restatement of Torts, Second Edition? (a) merchant seller (b) life expectancy of product (c) defective condition (d) unchanged condition of the product.

_____ 8. Implied warranties are excludable by (a) the words "as is" (b) usage of trade (c) course of dealing (d) all of the above.

_____ 9. When a product is changed significantly after leaving the manufacturer, the defense of _____ is available in a strict liability action brought against the manufacturer. (a) privity (b) estoppel (c) subsequent alteration (d) none of the above.

_____ 10. Warranties of quality under the Code generally do not apply to sales of (a) land (b) services (c) stocks (d) all of the above.

_____ 11. Situations where title warranties do not run with the transaction include (a) sheriff's sales (b) foreclosure sales (c) judicial sales (d) all of the above.

_____ 12. To maintain a warranty action, a buyer must prove (a) the seller has been notified of the breach (b) no contributory negligence occurred (c) the seller was a merchant (d) all of the above.

_____ 13. _____ privity concerns sellers in the product distribution chain with whom the buyer did not deal. (a) equitable (b) vertical (c) horizontal (d) constructive

CASE PROBLEMS–SHORT ESSAY ANSWERS: Read each case problem carefully. Answer by stating a Decision for the case and by explaining the rationale–Rule of Law–relied upon to support your decision.

1. B, a sportsperson, purchases a handwarmer from a non-merchant neighbor, M. B carries the handwarmer in a coat pocket while hunting and suffers burns when the handwarmer explodes. May B bring suit against M using a strict liability theory for the injuries caused by the defective handwarmer? Explain.

   Decision: _____

   _____

   Rule of Law: _____

   _____

2. B buys a used car from S, a used car dealer. B drives the car for two days when suddenly, all four wheels fall off and the steering mechanism collapses. What rights has B against S? Discuss.

   Decision: _____

   _____

   Rule of Law: _____

   _____

3. B purchases a bottle of hair coloring. The label contains a conspicuously typed and displayed caution: "WARNING. Always make a patch test before using this product." B applies the coloring, according to its directions, to a table top in an attempt to remove a water stain. The next day, the table is ruined. B sues the manufacturer for the damages to the table. Who prevails and why?

   Decision: _____

   _____

Rule of Law: _____

_____

4. B purchased 40 lbs. of 1/8" steel rods cut to six-foot lengths. The contract price was $800. When the rods arrived, B accepted them. Sometime later, B discovers that some of the rods are not 1/8" and others are more than six feet. B sues for breach of warranty. The value of the rods accepted was $700. Their value, had they conformed to the contract, would have been $1,000. What is the level of B's damages? Explain.

Decision: _____

_____

Rule of Law: _____

_____

5. While eating pieces of fried chicken at Chuck's Chicken Coop, customer C chokes on a chicken bone which becomes stuck in her throat. C sues restaurant owner B for her injuries, arguing that the presence of the inedible bone was a breach of the implied warranties of fitness and merchantability. Evaluate C's argument.

Decision: _____

_____

Rule of Law: _____

_____

Chapter 25

SALES REMEDIES

SCOPE NOTE

What happens when parties to a sales contract fail to properly perform their contractual duties–the seller fails to deliver conforming goods; the buyer refuses to pay for or accept conforming goods? Chapter 25 closes our study of sales law by examining the remedies available to parties confronting inadequate performance under the terms of their agreement. The breadth of remedies available under the U.C.C. to non-breaching parties is intended to enable them to gain the position they would have occupied had the breaching party performed properly. It is important to note the key factors associated with a breach that dictate which choice of remedies will be available to the aggrieved party as well as the Code's liberal application of the remedies.

EDUCATIONAL OBJECTIVES

1. Describe the pre-acceptance remedies made available to both non-breaching buyers and sellers.

2. Outline the pre-acceptance breaching party's rights and duties.

3. Explain the non-breaching party's choice of remedies following acceptance.

4. Define and discuss the implications of anticipatory repudiation.

5. Identify how insolvency of the breaching party affects the choice-of-remedies question.

6. Understand choice-of-remedy issues in installment contracts.

7. Define the role of liquidated damages regarding limiting or expanding choice of remedies in an agreement.

8. Identify the choice of remedies available in equity for enforcing sales contracts.

9. Know how parties to a sales contract, under Code limitations, may alter their choice of remedies by agreement.

CHAPTER OUTLINE

I. Seller's Remedies–triggered by buyer's default (wrongful rejection, wrongful revocation of acceptance, no payment when due, or contract repudiation)
   A. Goods Oriented Remedies–include withholding delivery, stopping delivery by carrier, identifying conforming goods to contract, reclaiming goods from insolvent buyer
   B. Money Oriented Remedies–include reselling goods and recovering damages, recovering damages for nonacceptance or repudiation, recovering price, recovering incidental damage
   C. Code's Remedies–cumulative; more than one may be used
      1. Withhold delivery–applies to any breach; breach of installment that impairs value of whole contract permits seller to withhold entire undelivered balance; when buyer insolvent, seller may refuse delivery, demand cash payment
      2. Stop delivery–applies to any breach; timely notification to carrier or bailee for effective stop order; carrier or bailee must follow seller's reasonable directions; seller pays carrier/bailee damages or charges
      3. Identify goods to contract–applies to any breach; seller completes manufacture of unfinished goods, identifies them to contract or ceases manufacture and sells unfinished goods for scrap or salvage value; seller's duty to exercise reasonable judgment to minimize losses (mitigate damages)
      4. Resell goods/recover damages–resale must be in good faith, commercially reasonable manner; seller recovers difference between contract price and resale price plus incidental damages, less expenses saved; seller not accountable for any resale profits; good faith purchaser takes free of original buyer's rights
      5. Recover damage for non-acceptance/repudiation–applies to any breach; damages measured by difference between unpaid contract price and market price at time, place of delivery plus incidental damages, less expenses saved
      6. Recover price–Code permits this recovery when buyer has accepted goods, goods are lost, damaged after risk of loss passed to buyer; where identified goods have no reasonable resale value
      7. Recover incidental damages–include any commercially reasonable charges, expenses, or commissions resulting from breach
      8. Cancel contract–ending contract by reason of breach
      9. Reclaim goods upon buyer's insolvency–unpaid seller pursues reclamation by making demand on buyer within 10 days after receiving goods to return them; 10 day limitation waived upon buyer's written, fraudulent assurance of solvency made to seller within three months prior to delivery; reclamation cut off by buyer in ordinary course of business or other good faith purchaser; using this remedy precludes using other remedies

II. Buyer's Remedies–triggered by seller's default; includes repudiating contract, failure to deliver conforming goods

   A. Money Oriented Remedies–recover payments made, "cover" and seek damages, seek damages for nondelivery, breach of warranty damages, incidental damages, and consequential damages

   B. Goods Oriented Remedies–recover identified goods from insolvent seller, replevy goods, seek specific performance or obtain security interest in goods

   C. Cancel Contract–applies to any breach; breach affecting whole contract triggers buyer's right to cancel entire contract; buyer must give notice of cancellation, is freed from further performance.

   D. Code's Remedies–cumulative; more than one may be used

      1. Recover payments made–recover any part of price paid

      2. Cover–buyer, in good faith, without unreasonable delay, purchases replacement goods elsewhere or makes contract to purchase such substituted goods; buyer recovers difference between cost of cover and contract price, plus incidental and consequential damages, less expenses saved; not "covering" does not bar any other Code remedies; not "covering" bars consequential damages that could have been prevented by cover

      3. Recover damages for non-delivery/repudiation–damages measured by difference between market price at time when buyer learned of seller's breach and contract price, plus incidental/consequential damages, less expenses saved; an alternative to cover available only if buyer has not yet covered

      4. Recover identified goods on seller's insolvency–applies to existing identified goods; gives buyer special property interest in goods, even if they are non-conforming; buyer retains right to return, reject nonconforming goods; identification made by either buyer or seller; right to recover goods from insolvent seller protected by a special property interest; right applies where seller has possession or control of goods, becomes insolvent within ten days after receipt of buyer's first payment; buyer must pay full price to recover goods; where buyer identified goods, recovery can occur only if they conform to contract

      5. Sue for replevin–equitable action to recover specific goods in seller's, carrier's or bailee's possession

      6. Sue for specific performance–equitable remedy compelling breaching party to perform according to contract terms; available when other remedies are inadequate (unique, not obtainable elsewhere)

      7. Enforce a security interest–buyer possesses nonconforming goods and has made partial payment on price; security interest covers extent of payment made and inspection, receipt, transportation, care and custody expenses; buyer may hold or resell goods; buyer must account to seller for any resale proceeds beyond amount of security interest

      8. Recover damages for breach after goods accepted–nonconforming goods are accepted and timely notification given seller; buyer recovers damages resulting in ordinary course of events; breach of warranty damages measure is difference between value of nonconforming accepted goods and their value as warranted; incidental and consequential damages also recoverable

9. Recover incidental damages–includes reasonable expenses in inspection, receipt, transportation, care and custody of goods rightfully rejected and any commercially reasonable cover expenses

10. Recover consequential damages–includes losses resulting from buyer's needs/ requirements seller aware of at time of contracting which could not reasonably be prevented by cover

III. Contractual Provisions Affecting Remedies–parties may modify, exclude, or limit Code remedies or damages.
   A. Liquidation/Limitation of Damages–parties specify amount, measure of damages recoverable; stated damages amount must be reasonable in light of difference between anticipated and actual loss, difficulties of proving loss, and inconvenience or lack of feasibility of another adequate remedy; unreasonably large or small stated amount is void as a penalty
   B. Modification/Limitation of Remedy–parties may provide for remedies beyond Code's; parties may limit or change measure of damages; contract remedy optional unless expressly made exclusive; exclusive remedy that fails its purpose triggers Code remedies; consequential damage can be limited/excluded unless unconscionable (limitation of consequential damages for personal injury from breach of warranty in consumer sales)
   C. Statute of Limitations (time in which to bring action against another)–parties may not change to less than one, nor more than four, years; cause of action begins at time of breach regardless of parties' awareness

TRUE-FALSE: Circle true or false.

T F 1. An unpaid seller, faced with a buyer's material breach of the contract or insolvency may properly withhold or stop delivery of the goods.

T F 2. When a buyer has breached the sales contract, the seller may resell the goods at either a public or private sale.

T F 3. A bona fide purchaser at a resale takes title to the goods subject to the superior interests of the original buyer when the seller fails to properly notify the breaching original buyer of the time, date and location of the resale.

T F 4. Failure of a buyer to "cover" upon the seller's breach will bar the buyer from seeking other remedies.

T F 5. A buyer acquires a special property interest in existing goods when they are identified to the contract.

T   F   6. A provision in a sales contract providing for liquidated damages is void per se.

T   F   7. A sales contract may validly limit consequential damages for commercial loss.

T   F   8. The Code places a four-year statute of limitations for sales contract breaches commencing at the time the non-breaching party learned of the breach.

T   F   9. An unpaid seller may reclaim goods delivered to a buyer any time after the seller has learned of the buyer's insolvency.

T   F   10. The Code has adopted the common law approach to specific performance.

T   F   11. The goal of Code remedy provisions is to place the non-breaching party in as good a position as if the breaching party had properly performed.

T   F   12. The Code uses both equity and bankruptcy definitions of insolvency.

KEY TERMS–MATCHING EXERCISE: Select the term that best completes each statement below.

1. Equitable insolvency	8. Liquidated damages	15. Dilatory
2. "Cover"	9. Cancellation	16. Punitive damages
3. Bankruptcy insolvency	10. Reclamation	17. Profit
4. Specific performance	11. Highest standard of care	18. Election of remedies
5. Consequential damages	12. Incidental damages	19. Commercial reasonableness
6. Replevin	13. Public sale	20. Breach
7. Penalty	14. Speculative damages	

_____ 1. Inability to meet debts as they come due.

_____ 2. Resale of goods at which a non-breaching, unpaid seller may be a purchaser.

_____ 3. The buyer's remedy to purchase substitute goods elsewhere following the seller's failure to perform properly.

_____ 4. Remedy available for injury resulting to a person or property caused by breach of warranty.

_____ 5. An action to recover goods in the possession of and wrongfully withheld by another.

_____ 6. A provision in a sales contract calling for liquidated damages at an unacceptably high level.

_____ 7. The non-breaching party's termination of the contract in response to the breaching party's failure of performance.

_____ 8. Unpaid seller's right to retake goods from an insolvent buyer.

_____ 9. Commercially reasonable expenses incurred by a seller in connection with the remedies available following a buyer's breach.

_____ 10. Buyer's equitable remedy compelling seller to deliver conforming goods as described in the sales contract.

_____ 11. Failure of a contracting party to properly perform contractual duties.

_____ 12. Seller's remedy when the market price/contract price difference fails to place seller in as good a position as if buyer had performed properly.

_____ 13. Damages generally not recoverable under the Code.

_____ 14. Standard merchants must follow when deciding whether to finish manufacturing goods or cease manufacturing or sell the partially finished goods for scrap value.

_____ 15. Common law doctrine requiring non-breaching party to choose a single remedy to the exclusion of all others.

MULTIPLE CHOICE: Select the alternative that best completes each statement below.

_____ 1. A seller's right to stop delivery ceases when (a) a carrier acknowledges that goods are held for the seller (b) a bailee acknowledges that goods are held for the buyer (c) goods are rejected by the buyer (d) all of the above.

_____ 2. A seller may recover as damages against a breaching buyer (a) the difference between the market price and the contract price plus incidental damages (b) the profit that would have been received had the deal gone through plus incidental damages (c) liquidated damages as provided for in the contract (d) any of the above.

_____ 3. A buyer may exercise a right of cover when (a) conforming goods have been wrongfully rejected (b) the seller has made proper delivery of conforming goods (c) the seller has repudiated the sales contract (d) the buyer has improperly revoked acceptance.

_____ 4. Identification of goods to the contract may be made by (a) the seller only (b) the buyer only (c) either the seller or buyer (d) the court after an action at law has been brought.

_____ 5. A sales contract between buyer and seller may (a) not limit a remedy provided for by the Code (b) provide for fewer remedies than those specified in the Code (c) allow for penalties in lieu of stipulated damages (d) none of the above.

_____ 6. In deciding whether to liquidate goods through public or private sale, a seller (a) must follow normal trade practices and usage (b) need not be concerned about the nature of the goods (c) is generally free to make the choice without any restrictions (d) must follow Code provisions exactly and is allowed no deviation.

_____ 7. Upon cancellation of a sales contract, (a) the canceling party's duty of future performance is discharged (b) all security interests in the goods are voided (c) a trustee in bankruptcy is treated as an assignee of the contract (d) none of the above.

_____ 8. A seller's reclamation right is always subject to (a) the buyer's business partners (b) an equitable receiver (c) a buyer in the ordinary course of business from the non-performing purchaser (d) a bank.

_____ 9. Following buyer's breach, an unpaid seller may recover the contract price when the (a) buyer has rejected the goods (b) goods are damaged and the risk of loss remains with the seller (c) goods are identified to the contract and they have no resale market value (d) none of the above.

_____ 10. Insolvency for the purposes of federal bankruptcy law occurs when (a) a receiver is appointed to take control of the debtor's assets (b) the debtor's total liabilities exceed total assets (c) the debtor has stopped making payments on debts during the normal course of business (d) a fraudulent conveyance has been made.

_____ 11. When the buyer has breached the sales contract, the seller _____ unfinished goods (a) may cease manufacture and resell them for scrap (b) may finish their manufacture and identify them to the contract (c) must use reasonable judgment to minimize losses (d) all of the above.

_____ 12. When liquidated damages are provided for they must be (a) provable through appraisal (b) commensurate with the anticipated or actual losses (c) no more than $500 (d) supported by affidavits of value.

_____ 13. A buyer who has "covered" the seller's breach may recover (a) all losses (b) the difference between the cost of "cover" and the contract price plus incidental or consequential damages (c) b above minus expenses saved as a result of the seller's breach (d) none of the above.

CASE PROBLEMS–SHORT ESSAY ANSWERS: Read each case problem carefully. When appropriate, answer by stating a Decision for the case and by explaining the rationale–Rule of Law–relied upon to support your decision.

1. B breaches a sales contract and S elects to resell the goods. The contract price called for a $10,000 payment from B. The resale realized $18,000 for S. In a suit by B against S for the excess above the contract price, what might B recover and why?

   Decision: _____

   _____

   Rule of Law: _____

   _____

2. B ordered $10,000 worth of grade A grotaberries from S. On May 1, S shipped grade A wingaberries that were rightfully rejected by B. The following day, B bought grade A gro-taberries on the open market from another supplier for $9,000. In a suit against S for the breach, what are the damages recoverable by B? Explain.

   Decision: _____

   _____

   Rule of Law: _____

   _____

3. B enters a contract with S for the sale of $10,000 worth of feather dusters. The dusters were labeled with B's name at S's warehouse. On July 10, B makes a $2,500 advance to S. A day later, B learns that S is insolvent. Fearing a loss of both the money and the goods, B seeks your advice. What should be done to protect B's interests?

   Decision: _____

   _____

   Rule of Law: _____

   _____

4. B receives a shipment of nails from building materials supplier S that are nonconforming to the contract. B had made a down payment of $200 on the contract. B writes to S and notifies S of an intent to reject the nails. Three months pass without B receiving any reply from S. What may B do? Discuss.

Decision: _____

_____

Rule of Law: _____

_____

5. Art dealer A contracts with art collector C to purchase one of C's Rembrandt paintings. Later, because of the painting's sentimental value, C repudiates the contract. In a suit by A against C, what remedy will A most likely seek? Explain.

Decision: _____

_____

Rule of Law: _____

_____

SALES UNIT RESEARCH QUESTIONS: Drawing upon information contained in the text, as well as outside sources, discuss the following questions.

1. In response to performance breakdowns in new cars, some states have adopted what is popularly known as new car Lemon Laws. Explain the rationale for these laws and identify their significant provisions. What are the advantages and disadvantages of these laws? Does your state have such a law? Explain why you support or oppose your state's position on this issue?

2. In response to the increases in product liability litigation over the past few decades and the financial, insurance, business, and judicial costs associated with these lawsuits, some states have adopted laws that limit the availability of punitive damages in these suits. What rationale underlies these limitations? Do you support or oppose these restrictions and why? Has your state enacted such a law? If so, what are its provisions and do you support this approach? Why or why not? If your state has not passed such legislation, what are the reasons and do you support this position? Why or why not?

Chapter 26

FORM AND CONTENT

SCOPE NOTE

Commercial paper–negotiable instruments including checks, drafts, promissory notes and deposit certificates–occupies a crucial position in today's marketplace. Commerce moves on written contracts to pay sums of money that pass freely and are enforceable as money. Chapter 26 introduces the law regulating the issuance and use of commercial paper. The development of the law of negotiable instruments is traced and the most commonly used forms of commercial paper are explained. Also discussed is the key concept of negotiability. The terminology and rules addressed in Chapter 26 form a useful basis for understanding the subsequent chapters on negotiable instruments that focus on specific aspects of law.

EDUCATIONAL OBJECTIVES

1. Explain the importance and function of negotiable instruments in today's business.

2. Contrast creating commercial paper performance duties to contractual performance duties.

3. Define and discuss the significance of negotiability.

4. Identify the essential elements of negotiable instruments.

5. Differentiate contractual assignment from negotiating commercial paper.

6. Discuss the effect on negotiability of various provisions/omissions in a written promise to pay.

7. Distinguish the essential characteristics of the various forms of negotiable instruments.

8. Identify the rights/duties of parties under the various types of commercial paper.

CHAPTER OUTLINE

I. Concept of Negotiability
   A. Importance–instruments accepted as money substitute; promotes marketability of commercial paper
   B. History of Law
      1. Early period–payment rights non-transferable
      2. Assignment period–transferable payment rights puts assignee in assignor's shoes subject to payment defenses; assignee's risk of nonpayment from claims and defenses
      3. Current U.C.C and HDC status–good faith purchase for value of instrument assumes protected position, free of defenses/claims assertable against transferor
   C. Applies to commercial paper, title documents, investment securities

II. Negotiable Instruments
   A. Types
      1. Order, direction to pay–drafts/checks
      2. Promise to pay–notes/deposit certificates
   B. Draft–drawer/payee/drawee; sum certain in money
      1. Time–payment at specified date
      2. Sight–payment on presentation
      3. Trade acceptance–time draft for credit purpose
   C. Check–specialized draft; payable on demand
   D. Note–maker's promise to pay sum certain on demand or by stated date to order of payee
   E. Deposit Certificate–bank's note; bank is maker

III. Negotiable Instrument Requirements
   A. Four Corners Rule–all vital information must be on paper's face
   B. Specific Vital Information and Form: failure to comply destroys negotiability
      1. Signed writing–any tangible expression of intention to pay; by maker or drawer; location of signature not material; any mark intended as signature is sufficient
      2. Promise/order to pay–I.O.U., authorization of, request for payment not sufficient
      3. Unconditional payment–absolute, unqualified payment obligation; no contingencies
         a. Reference to another agreement–right of payment determined from instrument alone; payment tied to another document destroys negotiability
         b. Particular fund rule–Payment from specified account does not destroy negotiability–once considered a conditional order destroying negotiability
         c. No obligation other than payment
      4. Sum certain in money–determinable from face of instrument
         a. Fixed amount–from holder's perspective; determined minimum amount; interest/discount rates, collection costs/fees are proper
      5. Payment on demand or specific date
         a. Demand paper–payable on sight, presentation
         b. Time paper–payable on definite date; examples include

            (1) Fixed period after sight
            (2) Subject to acceleration
            (3) Option for maturity extension
      6. Payable to order or bearer
         a. Payee identified–order paper
         b. No payee identified–bearer paper

IV. Terms, Omissions, Conditions Affecting Negotiability
    A. Dating–negotiability not affected by post, un- or antedating
    B. Incompleteness–omitting material requirement ends negotiability until proper completion
    C. Confusion/ambiguity/uncertainty–Code rules to promote negotiability
       1. Handwritten > typewritten words
       2. Typewritten > printed words
       3. Words > figures

TRUE-FALSE: Circle true or false.

T   F   1. A promise to pay out of a specific fund is not conditional and does not make an instrument non-negotiable.

T   F   2. An acceleration clause in commercial paper destroys negotiability because of the uncertainty of the due date.

T   F   3. A certificate of deposit is a written receipt for deposited money with a financial institution that the latter promises to pay out at some future date.

T   F   4. The location of a maker's signature on a promissory note affects its enforceability and negotiability.

T   F   5. The U.C.C. requires that for instruments to be negotiable, they must be payable on demand or at a definite time.

T   F   6. Antedating or postdating commercial paper destroys its negotiability.

T   F   7. Failure to state on an instrument an essential element makes it non-negotiable until properly completed.

T   F   8. Omitting the words "order," "bearer" or their equivalent makes a note non-negotiable.

T   F   9. A note payable "Sixty days after Maker's death" is negotiable under the U.C.C.

T   F   10. An instrument made payable "to order of cash" is a bearer instrument.

T   F   11. The negotiability of an instrument must be determined on its face without further inspection, inquiry or reference to another source.

T   F   12. A bank draft is a form of promissory note.

KEY TERMS–MATCHING EXERCISE: Select the term that best completes each statement below.

1. Trade acceptance	8. Negotiability	15. Drawee
2. Money	9. Credit device	16. Variable interest rate
3. Acceleration	10. Assignment	17. Promissory note
4. Time draft	11. Fixed amount	18. Check
5. Sight drafts	12. Cashier's check	19. Time paper
6. Installment	13. Collateral note	20. Barter
7. Bearer	14. Non-negotiable	

_____ 1. Instruments payable immediately upon presentation to the drawee.

_____ 2. A medium of exchange adopted by a government as its currency.

_____ 3. An instrument payable only upon the occurrence of a future, uncertain event or act.

_____ 4. A check drawn by a bank on itself payable to the order of a named payee.

_____ 5. A three-party instrument payable on a specific future date.

_____ 6. A legal concept that allows written documents to be easily used as money substitute forms of payment.

_____ 7. The specified minimum payment to be made on commercial paper.

_____ 8. The person ordered to pay a draft.

_____ 9. A clause that gives a payee the right to demand payment before a note is mature.

_____ 10. An instrument drawn by the seller of goods on their purchaser made payable to the seller.

_____ 11. A use for negotiable instruments other than as a substitute for money.

_____ 12. A two-party negotiable instrument.

_____ 13. Instruments payable at a definite time.

_____ 14. Provision in commercial paper judicially interpreted to make the instrument non-negotiable.

_____ 15. The most common form of commercial paper.

MULTIPLE CHOICE: Select the alternative that best completes each statement below.

_____ 1. An order to pay a sum certain is conditional if an instrument (a) states its consideration (b) specifies it is subject to another agreement (c) indicates it is secured by a mortgage (d) refers to the transaction that created it.

_____ 2. The signature of the maker of a note may be (a) under an assumed name (b) a thumb print (c) made by an authorized agent (d) all of the above.

_____ 3. The primary obligor on a promissory note is the (a) acceptor (b) cosigner (c) payee (d) none of the above.

_____ 4. An instrument that is an order by one party upon another party to pay a third party is a (a) promissory note (b) draft (c) bond (d) collateral note.

_____ 5. Negotiability of an instrument is adversely affected by (a) not dating the instrument (b) a clause authorizing payment in goods (c) a clause providing for extension of the maturity date (d) its being made under seal.

_____ 6. To be negotiable, an instrument must be (a) signed by its maker (b) an unconditional promise to pay a sum certain (c) payable on demand or at a definite time (d) all of the above.

_____ 7. Clauses in an instrument that do not make it non-negotiable include (a) confessions of judgment (b) creating an interest in collateral (c) providing for disposal of collateral (d) all of the above.

_____ 8. Negotiability makes commercial paper (a) highly marketable (b) less commercially useful (c) not as valuable as contract assignments (d) none of the above.

_____ 9. An undated instrument made payable "two days after the date" (a) is negotiable (b) lacks consideration (c) is not negotiable (d) is complete on its face.

_____ 10. An instrument that does not specify a payment date is (a) demand paper (b) non-negotiable (c) fatally incomplete (d) all of the above.

_____ 11. Which of the following is not a type of negotiable instrument? (a) certificate of deposit (b) bill of lading (c) draft (d) promissory note

_____ 12. The bank upon which a check is drawn is the (a) drawer (b) drawee (c) payee (d) accommodation party.

_____ 13. An instrument payable to "John Doe, County Collector of Cook County" is payable (a) to order (b) to bearer (c) on condition (d) to accommodation.

CASE PROBLEMS–SHORT ESSAY ANSWERS: Read each case problem carefully. When appropriate, answer by stating a Decision for the case and by explaining the rationale–Rule of Law–relied upon to support your decision.

1. B purchases a television set from S and executes a 30 day note that reads, "nine hundred ($90) dollar purchase price." S accepts the note and is later faced with B asserting the $90 is the cost of the transaction. B steadfastly refuses to pay $900. S sues B for the $810 difference. Who wins the dispute?

    Decision: _____

    _____

    Rule of Law: _____

    _____

2. M executes a promissory note payable to P in 25 days. The note contains a provision allowing M to extend the maturity date for an additional fifteen days. What effect does the extension option have on the note's negotiability? Explain.

    Decision: _____

    _____

    Rule of Law: _____

    _____

3. M's 90 day $100 note at 6% interest, payable to P, provides for the addition of collection costs to the amount due if the holder has to resort to legal procedures for collection. Is this a negotiable instrument? Explain.

    Decision: _____

    _____

    Rule of Law: _____

    _____

4. M executes a promissory note by typing the necessary information on a sheet of paper and signing it with a rubber stamp. Has the note been properly signed? Discuss.

Decision: _____

_____

Rule of Law: _____

_____

5. M writes out in longhand, with an affixed signature, "I owe C $150," and dates the instrument. C transfers the memorandum to D to discharge a debt C owed D. Does D have an enforceable right of payment against M? Explain.

Decision: _____

_____

Rule of Law: _____

_____

Chapter 27

TRANSFER

SCOPE NOTE

Negotiable instruments will usually have useful lives extending beyond the transaction that created them. The first taker of commercial paper most likely will transfer it to another person. The process effectively transferring the rights/duties contained in negotiable instruments to other parties is the focus of Chapter 27. Requirements for a valid transfer–negotiation–are explained in relation to the different types of instruments, order and bearer paper.

EDUCATIONAL OBJECTIVES

1. Distinguish the definitional elements and effects of transfer by assignment from those of negotiation.

2. Define the concept "holder" and explain how this status is acquired.

3. Identify the various types of indorsement and their respective uses.

4. Know the significance of the imposter and fictitious payee rules.

5. Summarize the rights/duties of the parties to an indorsement.

6. Explain the formal requirements of negotiation.

CHAPTER OUTLINE

I. Transfer: by assignment or negotiation
   A. Assignment–voluntary transfer of non-negotiable paper contract rights to another
      1. Assignee acquires assignor's rights, subject to claims/defenses posing non-payment risk

    B. Negotiation–voluntary transfer of negotiable paper: transferee becomes "holder"–possessor–of order or bearer instrument
       1. Transferee may acquire more rights than transferor under HDC status–free of assignee non-payment risks
       2. Negotiation requirements –depends on type of instrument
         a. Bearer paper–delivery, possession alone (equivalent of cash) triggers payment rights
           (1) Finder, thief entitled to payment
         b. Order paper–possession and proper indorsement (payee's valid signatures) required
           (1) Transfer for values triggers right to receive transferor's unqualified indorsement
           (2) Negotiation occurs on proper indorsement
           (3) Transfer without proper indorsement is an assignment
       3. Order paper transfer problems
         a. Impostor rule–invalid signature by impersonator of named payee is effective
         b. Fictitious payee–agent/employee of maker/drawer fraudulently issues paper to nonexisting payee and indorses to self triggering payment rights
       4. Contract recission issue–proper negotiation triggers payment rights regardless whether transaction originating instrument is void/voidable

II. Indorsements
    A. Defined–signatures by non-maker, non-drawer, non-acceptor made to negotiate paper that restrict payment or assume liability
    B. Types of Indorsement–affect proper negotiation
       1. Blank–no specified indorsee; bare signature; converts order paper to bearer paper
       2. Special–indorsee specifically designated; further negotiation requires named person's signature; converts bearer paper into order paper
       3. Restrictive–limits indorsee's rights
         a. Conditional–indorsee's rights tied to specific event; Code nullifies restriction; payment rights free of stated condition
         b. Prohibiting further transfer–nullified by Code; payment rights unrestricted
         c. For deposit/collection–place paper in banking system; limits further negotiation
         d. In trust–for benefit of indorser, another; payee owes fiduciary duties to beneficiary
       4. Unqualified–payment guaranteed
       5. Qualified–"without recourse" indorsement; payment liability disclaimer effective for contract but not warranty liability
    C. Formal Requirements
       1. Place–on instrument or an "allonge" (attached paper)
       2. Mistakes–misspellings, misnamings, give holder option to demand indorsement in either or both names

TRUE-FALSE: Circle true or false.

T   F   1. A finder of lost bearer commercial paper can become a holder.

T   F   2. An indorsement "pay to the order of Mary" is a blank indorsement.

T   F   3. The usual way to disclaim indorser's liability is to add the words "without recourse" along with the indorsees signature.

T   F   4. The transferee of an instrument can be a holder either by negotiation or by assignment.

T   F   5. Trust indorsements make the indorser a fiduciary.

T   F   6. Under the U.C.C., a properly worded restrictive indorsement may prevent further transfer or negotiation of the instrument.

T   F   7. A conditional indorsement is a type of restrictive indorsement.

T   F   8. A blank indorsement transforms a bearer instrument into an order instrument.

T   F   9. An indorsement "for collection" places the instrument within the banking system for deposit or collection.

T   F   10. A qualified indorsement terminates negotiability and stops further negotiation of the paper.

T   F   11. Absent any agreement of assignment, it is presumed that in transfers for value, the parties intend for a negotiation to occur.

T   F   12. It is preferable from the transferee's standpoint to take an instrument by assignment and not by negotiation.

KEY TERMS–MATCHING EXERCISE: Select the term that best completes each statement below.

1. Holder	8. Payor	15. Negotiation
2. Shelter Rule	9. Qualified	16. Order paper
3. Transfer	10. Conditional indorsement	17. Equitable
4. Blank	11. Collection indorsement	18. Assignment
5. Signature	12. Trust indorsement	19. Warranty
6. Imposter Rule	13. Special indorsement	20. Restrictive
7. Bearer paper	14. Allonge	

_____ 1. An indorsement bearing only the indorser's signature, designating no indorsee.

_____ 2. A separate document containing an indorsement firmly affixed to commercial paper.

_____ 3. Simplest form of indorsement.

_____ 4. One possessing an instrument drawn, issued or indorsed to the possessor, the possessor's order, or in blank.

_____ 5. Transferring an instrument that makes the transferee a holder.

_____ 6. An act specifying the person to whom or to whose order an instrument is payable.

_____ 7. An act that makes the rights of an indorsee subject to the occurrence of a certain event.

_____ 8. The legal doctrine granting a non-holder transferee the rights of a holder if the transferee takes the instrument from a holder in due course.

_____ 9. Indorsing an instrument with the words "payment to A for B".

_____ 10. Commercial paper transferred by possession alone, making it equivalent to cash.

_____ 11. Transferring commercial paper in a manner that does not make the transferee a holder.

_____ 12. A "for deposit only" indorsement.

_____ 13. Commercial paper that must be indorsed for proper transfer.

_____ 14. An exception to the rule that proper negotiation on an order instrument can occur only if it has been validly indorsed by the person to whom it is payable.

_____ 15. Liability of the indorser that is not affected by a qualified indorsement.

MULTIPLE CHOICE: Select the alternative that best completes each statement below.

_____ 1. Transferring non-negotiable instruments operates as a/n (a) negotiation (b) indorsement (c) accommodation (d) assignment.

_____ 2. An indorsement reading "Pay Sue only" is treated as a/n (a) conditional indorsement (b) assignment (c) unrestricted indorsement (d) subsequent cancellation by the Code.

_____ 3. All indorsements disclose the (a) type of interest transferred (b) liability of the indorser (c) method of subsequent negotiation (d) all of the above.

_____ 4. Fraud (a) has no effect on a properly negotiated instrument (b) invalidates negotiation (c) prevents the transferee from becoming a holder (d) makes an instrument void.

_____ 5. An indorsement must always be (a) in ink (b) witnessed by at least two other people (c) either written on the instrument or on an allonge (d) written twice wherever used.

_____ 6. When the payee of a check simply signs a name on the back of the check without anything more, the indorsement is (a) special, qualified and nonrestrictive (b) blank, unqualified and nonrestrictive (c) conditional, special and in trust (d) none of the above.

_____ 7. When an instrument has been made payable to the order of its holder and the holder's name is misspelled, the holder may (a) do nothing since all rights have ceased (b) bring suit and recover against the indorsee (c) legally and equitably change her name for the purpose of securing the instrument (d) indorse the instrument in the misspelled name, in her own name or both.

_____ 8. Indorsements may be (a) equitable or civil (b) restrictive or nonrestrictive (c) logical or sequential (d) chronological or baited.

_____ 9. An indorsement containing the words "without recourse" is a/n (a) blank (b) qualified (c) Drach (d) unqualified one.

_____ 10. An unqualified indorser guarantees (a) payment only if specific conditions have been met (b) that value has been given for the instrument (c) payment on the instrument (d) that all persons named on the instrument had good title.

_____ 11. Generally, subject to specified exception, the transfer of an instrument vests in the transferee (a) only those rights the transferor has (b) no new rights (c) fifty percent of the transferor's rights (d) none of the above.

_____ 12. An order instrument (a) may never be changed to bearer paper (b) may be changed to bearer paper by a blank indorsement (c) may be changed to bearer paper only if done within 24 hours after receipt (d) none of the above.

_____ 13. The words "Pay Alex" (a) are sufficient to make an instrument negotiable (b) fail the specificity test for valid indorsement (c) make an instrument bearer paper (d) are sufficient to make an order indorsement.

CASE PROBLEMS–SHORT ESSAY ANSWERS: Read each case problem carefully. When appropriate, answer by stating a Decision for the case and by explaining the rationale–Rule of Law–relied upon to support your decision.

1. X issued a note "payable to the order of Y." Y indorses the note "Pay to Z only if Safe-Way Airlines Flight 602 arrives at Hollman Field by 2:30 p.m., August 23, 2000." On August 20th, 1999, Z presents the note to X for payment. X refuses to honor the note, arguing the controlling influence of Y's indorsement. Z sues X for wrongful dishonor of the note. What result?

   Decision: _____

   _____

   Rule of Law: _____

   _____

2. Frank, a bookkeeper in Fran's accounting firm, has authority to issue checks on Fran's behalf to pay the firm's operating expenses. Frank writes a $600 check in Fran's name payable to Ralph Newbar, not a real person. Frank, using Ralph's name, indorses the check to himself and presents it for payment at Fran's bank. If the bank were to pay the $600 and debit Fran's account, could she seek reimbursement alleging wrongful payment by the bank?

   Decision: _____

   _____

   Rule of Law: _____

   _____

3. M executes a $500 note "payable to bearer" and delivers it to P. P indorses the note "Pay to the order of X." Sometime later, P loses the note and F finds it. F presents the note to M for payment. Must M honor F's presentment? Explain.

   Decision: _____

   _____

   Rule of Law: _____

   _____

4. T steals a $250 bearer note from P. T sells the note to B who presents it for payment. Is B rightfully entitled to payment?

Decision: _____

_____

Rule of Law: _____

_____

5. A indorses an instrument to B in blank. Assuming B is the holder, what can B do to prevent the instrument from being treated as cash? Discuss.

Decision: _____

_____

Rule of Law: _____

_____

Chapter 28

HOLDER IN DUE COURSE

SCOPE NOTE

Under contract law, assigning rights under a contract not only creates in the assignee the same rights held by the assignor but also exposes the assignee to liability on the defenses to performance that could have been validly asserted against the assignor. This fact, in the marketplace of commercial paper, would constitute a substantial cloud on the marketability and usefulness of these instruments. Chapter 28 addresses the circumstances under which such vulnerability of the taker of a negotiable instrument is removed, thus enhancing the transferability of the instrument, the Holder in Due Course doctrine. Under this doctrine, the holder of a non-consumer credit instrument takes it free of most defenses to or claims against payment. How must the taker of a negotiable instrument acquire it to achieve such a preferred status? What are the benefits of such status? Under what circumstances may a holder in due course still face non-payment vulnerability? These are the type of issues that are the focus of Chapter 28.

EDUCATIONAL OBJECTIVES

1. Identify and discuss the significance of the requirements that must be met to acquire holder in due course status.

2. Explain situations where, even though holder in due course requisites have been met, the status will be denied the holder.

3. Define and discuss the significance of the Shelter Rule.

4. Contrast the definitional elements and the consequences of real and personal payment defenses.

5. Know the effect of the FTC rule on holder in due course status in consumer transactions.

CHAPTER OUTLINE

I. Holder in Due Course
   A. Significance–preferential payment rights
   B. Status acquired through shelter rule or Code requirements

II. Code Requirements
   A. Holder–possessor of paper with necessary indorsements; bearer or order paper
   B. Value–paper acquired through purchase, not gift
      1. Different from contractual consideration
      2. Types: performing agreed upon promise; gaining security interest; accepting paper as debt payment; giving a negotiable instrument
      3. Executory promise, unperformed obligation, not sufficient
      4. To extent of security interest
   C. Good faith–honesty in fact, fair dealing, commercially reasonable practices
   D. No notice–overdue, dishonor, subject to claim or defense
      1. Notice–actual knowledge, reason to know, notification
      2. Effectiveness of notice–time, understandable, opportunity to act on
      3. Various situations
         a. Time paper–stated due date if business day
         b. Demand paper–not paid after unreasonable length of time (90 days for checks)
         c. Claim (ownership assertion) vs. defense (justification for nonpayment)
         d. Authenticity issue–indicators of material alteration, forgery, irregularity, incompleteness–degree apparent and reason to know

III. HDC Status
   A. Payee as HDC–satisfies Code requirements
   B. Shelter Rule–transferee becomes HDC through earlier HDC
      1. Exceptions to rule–fraud, notice of claim or defense and reacquires instrument, taking instrument through non-commercial channels

IV. HDC Preferred Payment Position–applies in non-consumer transactions
   A. Payment not subject to claims, personal defenses (voidable contract duties)
   B. Payment Subject to Real Defenses–HDC not protected against
      1. Infancy–to extent a contract defense under state law
      2. Void contract
      3. Fraud in execution (not in inducement)–misrepresentation of terms, character, purpose of paper
      4. Insolvency discharge–bankruptcy making debt unenforceable
      5. Notice that all prior parties have been discharged
      6. Unauthorized, forged signatures
         a. Estoppel, ratification bars named party's payment defense
         b. Signer liable
      7. Material alteration–negligence, consent of obligor bars defense

    C. Personal Defenses–not affective against HDC; effective against holders and assignees
      1. Contract breach
      2. Failure of consideration
      3. Fraud in inducement (not in execution)
      4. Voidable instruments–incapacity, illegality, mistake, fraud, duress, undue influence
      5. Counter claim/set off
      6. Non-delivery of paper
      7. Improper completion
      8. Theft of bearer paper
      9. Agent lacks authority

V. Consumer Credit Transaction Limitations on HDC status
    A. Source–FTC rule applies to consumer goods/services (family, household, personal use)
    B. Effect–defrauded consumer's payment obligation to seller, lessor, financer, discharged for defective goods/services and fraud in inducement
      1. Personal defenses of buyer available vs. HDC (holds position of assignee)

TRUE OR FALSE: Circle true or false.

T   F   1. The U.C.C.'s definition of good faith stresses both objective and subjective tests for honesty.

T   F   2. An example of failure to give value for the purposes of determining holder in due course status occurs when a holder of an instrument gives it to another person.

T   F   3. Value for the purposes of negotiable instrument law is the same as consideration in the law of contracts.

T   F   4. According to the U.C.C., one who purchases an instrument for less than its face value has notice of a claim or defense and therefore can never become a holder in due course.

T   F   5. The Code does not specify what is reasonable time for the purposes of determining whether a note is overdue.

T   F   6. The U.C.C. specifically states when minority is available as a defense on an instrument and under what circumstances it may be claimed.

T   F   7. Under the Code, holders give value when an instrument is received as payment of or security for antecedent debts.

T   F   8. A person whose signature has been forged on an instrument is usually liable for payment to holders in due course.

T   F   9. Under the Code, a reasonable time for presentment. on a check is 30 days.

T   F   10. The FTC has changed the effect of the holder in due course doctrine in consumer credit transactions.

T   F   11. One who takes an instrument knowing that all previous parties have been discharged may still acquire the status of holder in due course.

T   F   12. A transferee of a stolen instrument taken from the thief cannot become a holder in due course.

KEY TERMS–MATCHING EXERCISE: Select the term that best completes each statement below.

1. Shelter Rule	8. Acceleration	15. Cancellation
2. Objective	9. Void	16. Alteration
3. Forgery	10. Ratification	17. Dishonor
4. Holder	11. Real	18. Claim
5. Subjective	12. Bankruptcy	19. Holder in due course
6. Fraud in the execution	13. Personal	20. Certification
7. Negligence	14. Valid	

_____ 1. The possessor of a negotiable note who, by its terms, is entitled to payment.

_____ 2. The test for good faith adopted by the Code emphasizing commercial reasonableness.

_____ 3. Doctrine making signer liable on the instrument even though their signature is forged.

_____ 4. The act of affixing another person's signature to an instrument without actual, apparent or implied authority.

_____ 5. Factual misrepresentation inducing a party to sign a note without knowing or having an opportunity to know its nature or material terms.

_____ 6. Defenses effective against all holders except those in due course.

_____ 7. Process by which an unauthorized signature is transformed into a valid one.

_____ 8. Defenses available against any holder, including one in due course.

_____ 9. Doctrine that transforms a non-due-course holder into a holder in due course if they have taken the instrument from a holder in due course.

_____ 10. Insolvency proceedings that can operate to discharge a party from any liability on a note to all holders, including those in due course.

_____ 11. Transferee of a negotiable instrument who takes it for value, in good faith and without notice of dishonor, outdatedness or defenses to payment.

_____ 12. Unauthorized changing of the rights and responsibilities of parties to an instrument.

_____ 13. An assertion of ownership.

_____ 14. Refusing to pay or accept commercial paper that has become due.

_____ 15. Type of contractual obligation giving rise to commercial paper that triggers valid payment defenses against a holder in due course.

MULTIPLE CHOICE: Select the alternative that best completes each statement below.

_____ 1. Mae holds a $1,500 note payable to her in six months. When she uses the note to secure a $1,000 loan from Mary, Mary is a holder (a) to the full extent of the note's value–$1,500 (b) based on the Executory Promise Rule (c) due to the application of the estoppel doctrine (d) to the extent of the amount–$1,000.

_____ 2. Personal defenses include (a) fraud in the inducement (b) forgery (c) bankruptcy discharge (d) all of the above.

_____ 3. According to the U.C.C., notice of an event is (a) actual awareness of it (b) notification of it (c) reason to know of it (d) all of the above.

_____ 4. The purpose of the Shelter Rule is to (a) provide marketability of instruments to holders in due course (b) guarantee rights of cloture to holders of instruments (c) protect interests of all transferees of instruments (d) guard against the hardships associated with equitable discharge.

_____ 5. Real defenses include (a) duress making the transaction void (b) minority (c) fraud in the execution (d) all of the above.

_____ 6. Material alteration discharges a party on the note when (a) it is made for any purpose (b) done with intent to defraud (c) it specifies payment more than 25 days after the initial payment date (d) done for no value.

_____ 7. To qualify as a holder in due course, a transferee must acquire an instrument (a) for no value (b) hold possession of it for at least ninety days (c) without notice of certain specified matters (d) for the purpose of subsequent transfer to an heir.

_____ 8. Signing a negotiable instrument by carbon copy in the induced belief that only an autograph is being given is an example of (a) failure of consideration (b) fraud in the execution (c) nondelivery (d) fraud in the inducement.

_____ 9. The effect of the FTC rule applying to consumer credit transactions is to make transferees of negotiable paper associated with the transaction (a) holders in due course (b) trustees (c) receivers (d) assignees.

_____ 10. Shortening the time for payment on a note by operation of a provision in the note is (a) ademption (b) abatement (c) acceleration (d) none of the above.

_____ 11. Which of the following does not constitute value given? (a) an executory promise (b) a check as security for a debt (c) a check as payment for a debt (d) exchanging negotiable instruments

_____ 12. A _____ is protection against liability. (a) claim (b) defense (c) allonge (d) privilege

_____ 13. The doctrine that prevents someone from asserting a defense to liability because their conduct caused another person to change their position to their own loss or hardship is (a) negligence (b) laches (c) estoppel (d) trust.

CASE PROBLEMS–SHORT ESSAY ANSWERS: Read each case problem carefully. When appropriate, answer by stating a Decision for the case and by explaining the rationale–Rule of Law–relied upon to support your decision.

1. M issues a $1,000 note payable to P and delivers it. P negotiates the note to H who promises to pay $850 for it by the end of the month, which H does. On payment of the $850, what rights to payment has H acquired, the original value of $1,000 or the $850 that was paid? Explain.

Decision: _____

_____

Rule of Law: _____

_____

2. P fraudulently induces M to execute a $1,000 note payable to P. Following delivery of the instrument, P negotiates the note to holder in due course H, who in turn renegotiates the note back to P. Has P acquired the status of a holder in due course? Discuss.

Decision: _____

_____

Rule of Law: _____

3. M buys a new car with a note payable to seller S reading "thirty-five hundred dollars ($350)." S changes the figure to $3,500 and negotiates the note to H, who attempts to collect from M. M refuses to make payment asserting material alteration by S. Who wins this dispute and why?

    Decision: _____

    _____

    Rule of Law: _____

    _____

4. M draws a check on bank B payable to P. P presents the check to bank B for payment. Shortly before a teller at bank B cashes the check, bank B learns that M has issued a stop payment notice due to fraud. Has bank B acquired notice sufficient to preclude it from becoming a holder in due course?

    Decision: _____

    _____

    Rule of Law: _____

    _____

5. B purchases for home use, on an $850 installment contract, a riding mower from S. As part of the transaction, B issues a $750 note payable to S for the balance remaining after B's $100 down payment. S negotiates the note to holder in due course H. After three weeks of frustrating, breakdown-ridden use of the new mower, marred by S's refusal to service the defects, B revokes acceptance of the mower and notifies H that the note is being canceled. H refuses to accept B's cancellation, asserting that as a holder in due course, the defense of defective goods is not valid against him. Is H correct?

    Decision: _____

    _____

    Rule of Law: _____

    _____

Chapter 29

LIABILITIES OF PARTIES

SCOPE NOTE

Payment on negotiable instruments is the eventual goal of the parties using them. A basic rule regarding payment liability is that no one faces a duty of payment unless their signature appears on the instrument. But, with all names that might appear on an instrument following a series of negotiations, how is the order of payment obligation determined? In Chapter 29, U.C.C. rules controlling liability for payment are developed. Special attention must be given to the type of instrument used and the relation of the parties to that instrument. The two types of liability, contractual and warranty based, are examined in the context of primary and secondary payment obligations.

EDUCATIONAL OBJECTIVES

1. Differentiate primary from secondary parties and their respective payment obligations.

2. Distinguish liability for authorized from unauthorized signatures.

3. Identify the types of instruments in which the payment obligation is triggered by acceptance.

4. Outline the procedure for acceptance.

5. List the various conditions that must be met, and their respective procedures, before secondary parties are liable on the instrument.

6. Discuss when the conditions precedent for secondary party liability are waived or excused.

7. Distinguish transfer and presentment warranties and explain party liability for breach of those warranties.

8. Explain the effect on payment liability of the problem of conversion.

9. Enumerate the various circumstances that terminate a party's payment obligations on the instrument.

CHAPTER OUTLINE

I.   Contractual Liability–payment obligation
    A.   Basis–signature on instrument; can be disclaimed
    B.   Types
        1.   Primary–absolute, unconditional payment duty for makers of notes/acceptors of drafts
        2.   Secondary–payment duty conditioned on non-payment by above parties; applies to check drawers/indorsers
            a.   Duty dependent on presentment, dishonor, notice of dishonor and protest
    C.   Accommodation Party–signature for credit purpose; have primary or secondary liability
    D.   Signature Requirement–mark, word, name, in any form, intended to validate instrument, by person or agent
        1.   Authorized–relationship of principal, agent and payment duty
            a.   Agent has no payment duty–disclosure of principal's name and agency status; agent draws check on identified principal's account
            b.   Agent has sole payment duty–nondisclosure of agency status and principal's name
            c.   Principal/agent share payment duty–both agent's and principal's names appear without agency status disclosed; agent may prove agency status with parol evidence to avoid payment
        2.   Unauthorized signatures–forgeries by authorized agent, signatures of non-agent
            a.   Payment duty on signer unless negligence of named party contributes to wrongful signature or signature is ratified
            b.   Ratification–triggers payment duty by party named; ratifier has reimbursement rights against signor
            c.   Negligence–by named party; substantial contribution to making signature triggers payment liability
            d.   Not a valid payment defense against HDC
    E.   Primary party liability
        1.   Makers–payment duty on terms at time note issued or as completed; applies to cashier check issuers and drafts drawn on drawer
        2.   Acceptors–acceptance by drawee triggers payment duty; applies to certification of checks
    F.   Secondary party liability–triggered by non-payment by primary party
        1.   Liability disclaimer–"without recourse" drawing/indorsing; check drawer's contractual liability not disclaimable since faces breach of warranty liability
        2.   Requirements–conditions precedent to payment duty
            a.   Dishonor–payment refusal; applies to unaccepted draft drawer
                (1)   Demand note–refusal on presentment
                (2)   Time note–refusal at maturity

          (3) Drafts–refusal when presented

          (4) Checks–refusal when presented to drawee

      b. Notice of dishonor/presentment

          (1) Conditions excusing requirement: cannot reasonably be made; repudiation; death or insolvency of maker/acceptor; waiver; drawee instructed to refuse

    3. Conversion liability–damages for exercising wrongful control over another's personal property

II. Liability Termination

    A. Payment Duty Discharged–primary/secondary parties

    B. Methods for Discharging

      1. Payment–to properly entitled party

      2. Payment tender–discharges subsequent interest, not accrued interest or face value

      3. Intentional, authorized cancellation/renunciation–not accidental destruction or improper cancellation

III. Warranty Based Liability

    A. Types–transferor/presenter whether or not they have signed

    B. May be validly disclaimed

    C. Transfer Warranties–by transferor receiving consideration; transfer by delivery warranties apply only to immediate transferee; transfer by indorsement warranties apply to any good faith holder

      1. Enforcement–rightful transfer

      2. Authentic, authorized signatures

      3. No material alteration

      4. No defense/claims

      5. No knowledge of insolvency

    D. Presentment warranties–payor/acceptor must follow terms of instrument; wrongful payment by note maker does not discharge duty to pay correct person; wrongful payment by drawee precludes charging drawer's account

      1. Genuine signatures–no knowledge of unauthorized signatures

      2. No material alteration–protected status for good faith HDC

      3. Payment entitlement

    E. Impairment of Collateral/Recourse

    F. Re-acquisition–discharge against intervening subsequent parties but not good faith HDC

    G. Payment Duty Discharged

      1. Fraud

      2. Material alteration

      3. Certification

      4. Delays in presentment, notice of dishonor

      5. Purchasing discharge

TRUE-FALSE: Circle true or false.

T   F   1. Generally, a person is not contractually liable on an instrument unless his signature appears on it.

T   F   2. The two recognized types of payment liability for instruments are contractual and warranty.

T   F   3. When a draft is accepted by a bank, the drawer is discharged but not indorsers.

T   F   4. Presentment for payment is a prerequisite for a primary party to be liable on a negotiable instrument.

T   F   5. Presentment of a check must be made within thirty days after an indorsement in order to hold the indorser liable.

T   F   6. A time note has not been dishonored when a bank refuses payment following presentment before the note's due date.

T   F   7. Notice of dishonor of an instrument must be given in writing.

T   F   8. Someone whose own negligence substantially contributed to her unauthorized signature appearing on an instrument can be liable for payment.

T   F   9. Transfer warranties run to any subsequent good faith holder of the instrument when transfer is by delivery alone without endorsement.

T   F   10. Transferors of negotiable instruments warrant that they have no knowledge of insolvency proceedings pending against the maker, acceptor or drawer of an instrument.

T   F   11. Under the Code, the requirements of presentment and notice of dishonor may be waived.

T   F   12. When a forged instrument has been paid by the drawee, the loss can be shifted to the drawer by charging the latter's account.

KEY TERMS–MATCHING EXERCISE: Select the term that best completes each statement below.

1. Drawer	5. Acceptor	9. Dishonor
2. Conversion	6. Presentment	10. Signature
3. Drawee	7. Accommodation parties	11. Breach of contract
4. Certification	8. Acceptance	12. Insolvency proceedings

13. Payment   16. Primary   19. Disclosure

14. Cancellation   17. Renunciation   20. Notice of dishonor

15. Secondary   18. Warranty

_____ 1. The promise of a bank to honor a check when it is subsequently presented for payment.

_____ 2. Basis of the drawee bank's liability to drawer for refusing to pay or accept a check.

_____ 3. An act by the holder discharging all parties to an instrument.

_____ 4. The act that makes the drawee of a draft primarily liable.

_____ 5. Refusing to pay an instrument presented for payment.

_____ 6. Persons who sign a negotiable instrument for the purpose of lending their credit to another party on the note.

_____ 7. The tort of wrongfully exercising control over another's personal property.

_____ 8. The demand made by a holder on the maker or drawee for acceptance or payment of the instrument.

_____ 9. The most obvious way for a party to discharge liability on an instrument.

_____ 10. A situation totally excusing presentment but not notice of dishonor.

_____ 11. Liability imposed on signers and non-signers of commercial paper as a result of the transfer, payment or acceptance of the instrument.

_____ 12. The type of payment obligation assumed by makers of promissory notes and acceptors of drafts.

_____ 13. Someone secondarily liable for payment on a check.

_____ 14. An act making an indorser's payment obligation enforceable.

_____ 15. Written statement by a holder giving up right of payment.

MULTIPLE CHOICE: Select the alternative that best completes each statement below.

_____ 1. Indorsers and drawers of checks have _____ liability for payment (a) primary (b) no (c) secondary (d) tertiary.

_____ 2. Acceptance of an instrument is effective only when it is (a) in the drawee's own handwriting (b) oral (c) made within 14 days after issuance (d) none of the above.

_____ 3. The conditions precedent to the liability of secondary parties do not include (a) protest (b) default (c) notice of dishonor (d) presentment.

_____ 4. _____ indicates the intent to accept and be bound by an unauthorized signature. (a) Protest (b) Ratification (c) Presentment (d) Repudiation.

_____ 5. Notice of dishonor must be given by a bank on or before midnight (a) on the day of dishonor (b) three days after dishonor (c) on the next banking day following receipt of a dishonor notice (d) within 24 hours after certification.

_____ 6. Check drawers are discharged from payment obligations when presentment delay (a) results in the drawer having insufficient funds in their account due to a bank failure (b) occurs more than 30 days after an indorsement (c) extends beyond midnight of the third banking day after issuance (d) results in an account funds shortage caused by payment of subsequently issued checks.

_____ 7. Examples of conversion include (a) waiver of presentment (b) adoption by protest (c) payment on an instrument bearing a forged indorsement (d) none of the above.

_____ 8. Check drawers and indorsers may avoid their usual secondary contractual payment obligation by making or indorsing the paper (a) without recourse (b) as accommodation parties (c) without certification (d) none of the above.

_____ 9. Any mark, made in any manner, that indicates a present intent to validate commercial paper is a (a) protest (b) signature (c) contribution (d) payment.

_____ 10. A party discharged on an instrument (a) no longer faces any payment obligation (b) still faces payment obligation to any holder in due course (c) might still face a payment obligation under constructive estoppel (d) none of the above.

_____ 11. Examples of unauthorized signatures include (a) using rubberized stamps (b) mechanized signatures (c) an agent exceeding authority (d) all of the above.

_____ 12. Code warranties running with the sale of instruments include (a) drawee and payee warranties (b) presenter and transferor warranties (c) statutory and judicial warranties (d) none of the above.

_____ 13. When bearer paper is transferred by delivery alone, the transferor warrants to all subsequent holders (a) nothing, since warranties in the case run only to an immediate transferee (b) good title (c) no defense (d) no dishonor.

CASE PROBLEMS–SHORT ESSAY ANSWERS: Read each case problem carefully. When appropriate, answer by stating a Decision for the case and by explaining the rationale–Rule of Law–relied upon to support your decision.

1. A maintains a checking account at XYZ Bank, having $1,000 on deposit. A draws a check for $500 in favor of M and gives it to M. Before M presents the check for payment, XYZ Bank ceases operations due to insolvency. When M makes presentment for payment, the bank refuses to pay. What can M do? Explain.

    Decision: _____

    _____

    Rule of Law: _____

    _____

2. A makes a promissory note in favor of B payable at State Bank in 60 days at 10% interest per month. After 60 days, A is willing and able to pay the note at the bank. B takes a round-the-world tour for a year while the interest builds on the note. A asks your advice about liability on the note and interest. Explain.

    Decision: _____

    _____

    Rule of Law: _____

    _____

3. M issues a $500 note "payable to P." P's briefcase containing the note is stolen by thief T, who, finding the note, forges P's indorsement. T sells the note to B for $400. B in turn sells it to H for $450. When H presents the note, the bank discovers P's forged indorsement and refuses payment. What rights does H have? Explain.

    Decision: _____

    _____

    Rule of Law: _____

    _____

4. M, executing an instrument on behalf of P, signs it "M, as agent" without naming P. The instrument is negotiated to H, who seeks payment from M. Who is liable on this document? Explain.

    Decision: _____

    _____

Rule of Law: _____

_____

5. M issues a check drawn on bank B payable to P for $800. P raises the amount to $1,800 and negotiates the check to holder H. H presents the check for payment to B, who pays the $1,800. Discovering the error a short time later, B seeks reimbursement of the $1,000 over-payment from H. H refuses to pay. Who wins? Explain.

Decision: _____

_____

Rule of Law: _____

_____

Chapter 30

BANK DEPOSITS, COLLECTIONS, AND FUNDS TRANSFERS

SCOPE NOTE

The past four chapters focused on the life cycle of negotiable instruments, from drafting the paper through negotiating it and discharging the parties. Chapter 30 concludes the cycle by examining placement of certain instruments–checks–in the banking deposit-collection-payment-process. The rights/duties of the various banks in the chain of collection, and those of the parties to the instrument as well, controlled by U.C.C. Article 4, are the focus of this chapter. Chapter 30 closes with a discussion of the laws regulating electronic funds transfers, including consumer and wholesale funds transfers.

EDUCATIONAL OBJECTIVES

1. Discuss the collection process and the relationship of depositary, payor, intermediary and collecting banks.

2. Distinguish provisional from final credit.

3. Describe the contractual relationship between a bank and its customers.

4. Explain bank liability for wrongfully dishonoring a check.

5. Identify the approaches to and effect of stopping payment.

6. Understand the meaning and importance of the customer's duty to examine monthly statements.

7. Know collection alternatives following the death or incompetence of a customer.

8. List the requirements for and effect of final payment.

9. Explain the importance of electronic fund transfers.

10. Outline the major provisions of the Electronic Fund Transfer Act.

11. Know the scope, importance and regulatory impact of U.C.C. Article 4A covering wholesale funds transfers.

CHAPTER OUTLINE

I. Bank Deposits/Collections
   A. Governing Authority–U.C.C. Article 9

II. Collection Process
   A. Depositary Bank–where check deposited for credit
      1. Provisional credit–tentative deposit credit; drawee bank becomes HDC upon paying payee
   B. Competitive Equality Banking Act–quickens funds' availability; time limits for banks holding items
   C. Intermediary Banks–collecting bank other than depositary or payor
   D. Clearinghouse–bank association involved in daily account settling
   E. Payor Bank–final obligation to pay item, debit drawer's account (provisional credits on collection chain become final)
      1. Payment refusal–process reversed (charge backs); depositary bank debits depositor's account, who seeks recourse against drawer/endorser
   F. Collecting Bank–all non-payor item handling banks
      1. Check owner's agent pending final payment
      2. Final payment makes depositary bank debtor to depositor
      3. Duties relating to handling/forwarding items
         a. Ordinary care
         b. Timely action–midnight deadline rule; reasonable cut-off times
         c. Follow indorsement
         d. Presentment and transfer warranties
      4. Final payment–occurs upon cash payment, irrevocable settlement or unrevoked provisional settlement
   G. Payor Banks Duties–contract based
      1. Pay drawer's checks subject to sufficient funds/stop order restrictions

III. Customer/Payor Bank Relationship–contract based
   A. Prohibited Terms–good faith/negligence disclaimers and damages limitation for duty breaches
   B. Payment–drawer's properly drawn checks
      1. Triggered by acceptance of item
      2. Improper refusal (dishonor)–no stop order; account has sufficient funds; liable to customer/drawer for damages
      3. Over six-months-old checks can be refused

     4. Account with insufficient funds–refuse and return item; pay, charge customer's account and impose overdraft

  C. Stop Payment Order–timely receipt (chance to act on request) requirement

     1. Oral–14 days effectiveness

     2. Written–6 months effectiveness; renewable

     3. Drawer risks damages liability

     4. Subrogation of payor bank–triggered by payment over a stop order

  D. Disclosure Requirements–Truth in Savings Act; conspicuous, understandable, written notification of essential information/contract terms

  E. Death/Incompetence of Customer–no effect until timely (chance to act on information) knowledge

     1. 10-day period after notice of death in which payment can occur subject to interested parties (heir/creditor) valid stop order

  F. Customer Duties–U.C.C. defined

     1. Reasonable care/promptness–notice to bank for discoverable unauthorized signatures, material alteration

     2. Examine monthly statements–14 day limit for forgery/alteration notice

     3. 1-year notice limitation for forgeries/alteration from time statements are available

     4. 3-year notice limitation for wrongful indorsement

IV. Electronic Fund Transfers

  A. Regulated by EFTA–covers only consumer transfers

  B. Advantages–eliminates paperwork, saves time, no "float" (check processing between issuance and final payment)

  C. Types of Transfers

     1. ATM–full banking services

     2. Point of sale–direct from account to seller at store

     3. Phone access to accounts

     4. Commercial wholesale transfers–between business and financial institutions

  D. Consumer Funds Transfers–regulations under EFTA

     1. Disclosure of contract terms/account activity

     2. Periodic statements/documentation (receipt) for transactions

     3. Preauthorized Transfers–based on written authorization with 3 days advance stop notice

     4. Resolving errors

        a. Notification duty–within 60 days after statement received

        b. Bank's investigation duty within 10 days of error notification

        c. Bank liability for failure to investigate, correct error

     5. Customer liability for unauthorized card use–loss/theft

        a. $50 limit if notice within 2 days after knowledge of

        b. $500 limit if no proper notice within 2 days

        c. Unlimited if no notice after 60 days

     6. Bank's liability

        a. Unlimited for breach of contract terms

  b. Excluded by–circumstances beyond their control; insufficient funds in account; legal process freezing funds; credit limits

V. Wholesale Funds Transfers–regulated by Code Article 4A
  A. Scope of Article 4A–commercial transfer of funds between businesses
    1. Parties may vary Code provisions by contract
    2. Transfer factors
      a. Payment order–instruction to bank to pay a specific amount
      b. Parties–originator sender; payee-beneficiary originator's bank; intermediary bank; beneficiary's bank
    3. Does not apply to EFTA, debit transactions
  B. Acceptance–agreeing to paying order; beneficiary's bank becomes debtor of beneficiary
  C. Payment of Unauthorized (greater than authorized) Amount–beneficiary liable to bank for excess
    1. Customer liability if bank follows commercially reasonable security measures

TRUE-FALSE: Circle true or false.

T F 1. Parties to a funds transfer may change their Code Article 4A rights and duties by contract.

T F 2. Under the Code, deposits made by check are available for immediate drawing by the depositing customer.

T F 3. Holders of checks have no right to force drawee banks to pay them even when sufficient funds are in the drawer's account to cover the checks.

T F 4. Any day a bank is open constitutes a banking day

T F 5. A stop payment order is never renewable.

T F 6. A bank may continue to certify or pay checks drawn by a deceased customer for up to ten days after the customer's death, regardless of the bank knowing of the death.

T F 7. The customer bears a duty of reasonably prompt and careful examination of both the account statements and the paid items made available by the bank.

T F 8. There are no exceptions to the "midnight deadline" rule in determining whether a bank has acted seasonably.

T F 9. When an item received by a depositary bank has no indorsement, the only recourse open to the bank is to return the item to its customer.

T F 10. A receiving bank that mistakenly makes payment to an improper beneficiary has no reimbursement recourse against prior sender banks.

T   F   11. Collecting banks must use extraordinary care in handling items transferred to it for collection.

T   F   12. A collecting bank has the duty to act in a timely manner.

KEY TERMS–MATCHING EXERCISE: Select the term that best completes each statement below.

1. Depositary	8. Point of sale transfer	15. Stop payment order
2. Float	9. Two years	16. Agency
3. Payor	10. Check	17. Clearinghouse
4. Banking day	11. Pay any bank	18. Intermediary
5. Renunciation	12. Collection guaranteed	19. Examination and notice
6. Posting	13. Provisional	20. One year
7. Midnight deadline	14. Final payment	

_____ 1. The bank at which an item is presented for credit to the payee's account.

_____ 2. The bank on which an item is drawn.

_____ 3. The type of initial credit given to a bank's customer before an item is finally paid.

_____ 4. The concept underlying the determination of whether a bank has met its duty to act in a timely manner.

_____ 5. Terminal point in the collection process constituting the turnaround point from which the proceeds of the item begin their return flow.

_____ 6. A statement countermanding the drawer's order to the bank authorizing it to pay a certain sum of money and charge the amount to the drawer's account.

_____ 7. An automatic transfer of funds from a bank to a merchant completed through machines at the merchant's place of business.

_____ 8. The normal indorsement made when a bank forwards an item for collection.

_____ 9. The term describing a check drawer's use of funds between time of issuance of and final payment on the check.

_____ 10. The procedure followed by the payor bank in deciding to pay an item and making a record of the payment.

_____ 11. A group of banks cooperating together to settle accounts with one another on a daily basis.

_____ 12. Time period in which a customer must report alterations or unauthorized signatures after statements or items are made available to preserve rights against a bank.

_____ 13. Any bank, other than an originator's or beneficiary's bank, receiving a payment order.

_____ 14. Relationship between collecting banks and owner of an instrument pending final settlement.

_____ 15. General duties of bank customers regarding their own accounts.

MULTIPLE CHOICE: Select the alternative that best completes each statement below.

_____ 1. Customers or collecting banks transferring items in return for settlement or consideration warrant that (a) signatures on the instrument are genuine and authorized (b) no parties in the collection chain have filed for bankruptcy (c) no restrictive endorsements have been made (d) all of the above.

_____ 2. Reasons why a bank would dishonor a check and return the item include (a) the drawer not holding an account at the bank (b) a forged signature on the item (c) insufficient funds in the drawer's account (d) all of the above.

_____ 3. Electronic funds transfers are preferred over checks because they (a) eliminate the check drawer's float of funds (b) reduce the time and expense of processing checks (c) both a and b (d) neither a nor b.

_____ 4. Items received after the cutoff hour fixed by the bank for receipt of such items may be treated as having been received at the (a) beginning of the day of actual receipt (b) opening of the day after the next banking day (c) opening of the next banking day (d) none of the above.

_____ 5. A payor bank is under no obligation to pay an uncertified check that is over (a) six weeks old (b) six months old (c) sixty days old (d) none of the above.

_____ 6. The _____ requires that all depository financial institutions provide their customers a detailed description of their contractual terms and conditions. (a) Banking Disclosure Act (b) Uniform Banking Law (c) Truth in Savings Act (d) Banking Fair Dealing Act

_____ 7. Where the customer's account is not sufficient to pay all items presented, the bank must charge them against the account in (a) the order of their arrival (b) any order deemed reasonable by the bank (c) reverse order of their arrival (d) accordance with their date of issuance.

_____ 8. When a customer believes that a monthly statement from her bank contains errors, the customer must notify the bank within _____ days of the error. (a) 60 (b) 30 (c) 45 (d) 14.

_____ 9. The steps taken by a bank in presenting an item for collection include (a) choosing a reasonable method of forwarding the item (b) acting within a reasonable time after receipt of the item (c) careful routing of the item (d) all of the above.

_____ 10. When a bank mistakenly pays a check over a customer's valid stop order, it is liable to the customer for the (a) customer's losses resulting from the payment (b) amount of the payment (c) incidental loss to the bank (d) none of the above.

_____ 11. Electronic transfers not regulated by E.F.T.A. include transactions between (a) businesses (b) financial institutions (c) businesses and financial institutions (d) all of the above.

_____ 12. Situations in which a financial institution is not liable for E.F.T. errors include (a) employee negligence (b) equipment failure (c) customer account subject to legal process (d) all of the above.

_____ 13. The type of relationship between collecting banks and an owner of an item after final settlement is (a) agency (b) debtor-creditor (c) conservatorship (d) none of the above.

CASE PROBLEMS–SHORT ESSAY ANSWERS: Read each case problem carefully. When appropriate, answer by stating a Decision for the case and by explaining the rationale–Rule of Law–relied upon to support your decision.

1. A issues a $750 check to B drawn on A's $600 account with bank C. C honors the item when presented for payment and charges A's account. The bank then seeks the $150 difference from A plus service charges for the overdraft created. A refuses to pay, maintaining that it was the bank's obligation to dishonor the check since it knew sufficient funds were lacking to cover it. Who wins this dispute? Explain.

Decision: _____

_____

Rule of Law: _____

_____

2. Cathy Consumer, short of cash, decides to withdraw money from her bank account by using her bank card at an automated teller. She discovers, however, that both the bank card and her PIN card are missing from her purse. Searching at home, in her car, at friends' houses and at work leads to nothing. She cannot find the card anywhere. Meanwhile, Frank Fraud, having found Cathy's cards, has made $200 in withdrawals from her account. To what extent, if at all, is Cathy liable for these withdrawals?

Decision: _____

_____

Rule of Law: _____

_____

3. B purchases $20,000 worth of lumber from S, for use in homes B is constructing, with a check drawn on B's $40,000 checking account at PQR Bank. S negotiates the check to holder in due course, H. Much of the lumber B received from S is rotten so B notifies PQR Bank to stop payment. H presents B's $20,000 check for payment, and the bank honors the stop payment notice. What may H do to realize payment on the item? Explain.

Decision: _____

_____

Rule of Law: _____

_____

4. A presents an item to bank R for collection at 2:30 on Friday afternoon. The bank has a 2:00 p.m. cut-off time. On the following Wednesday, bank R forwards the item for collection. The person who was ultimately liable for the item files a bankruptcy petition one day before the item is presented to the person for payment. A claims the bank did not act seasonably. Decide.

Decision: _____

_____

Rule of Law: _____

_____

5. Millionaire spendthrift D issues a check drawn on an account with bank P payable to R for $10,000. Two days earlier, D's relatives had instituted an incompetency proceeding against D seeking to remove his financial responsibility. The court declares D incompetent a day before R presents the $10,000 check to bank P for payment. Unaware of D's adjudication of incompetence, bank P honors the check and charges D's account. The relatives learn of this fact and bring suit against the bank for wrongful payment. Who wins? Explain.

Decision: _____

_____

Rule of Law: _____

_____

NEGOTIABLE INSTRUMENTS UNIT RESEARCH QUESTIONS:
Drawing upon information contained in the text, as well as outside sources, discuss the following questions:

1. What effects have advancements in computer technology had on the principles and practice of negotiable instruments and banking law? What changes have occurred/need to occur in the law to accommodate further developments in computer technology and vice versa?

2. Congress passed legislation overhauling regulation of the banking industry. Identify the Act and its major provisions. What rationale underlies the revision and what are the anticipated benefits? What are the drawbacks to the changes and how might people, business, and the economy be hurt by them?

Chapter 31

FORMATION AND DISSOLUTIONS OF GENERAL PARTNERSHIPS

SCOPE NOTE

Businesses are usually organized in one of three different forms: a sole proprietorship, a partnership, or a corporation. Chapters 31 through 33 develop the law of partnerships, limited partnerships, and other unincorporated business associations, and Chapters 34 through 37 discuss corporate law.

The basis for the discussion of the law of partnership is the Uniform Partnership Act (UPA) and its revision (RUPA). In Chapter 31, which includes the legal principles associated with the nature and formation of a partnership, we focus our attention on the character of the property interest related to a partnership, and the comparative advantages and disadvantages associated with this form of an unincorporated business organization. The chapter also examines the legal doctrines and principles that control the operations and termination of a partnership. What happens when a partnership ends? These and other topics dealing with the management and dissolution of the partnership are the primary themes of Chapter 31.

EDUCATIONAL OBJECTIVES

1. Define and discuss the criteria for determining partnership existence.

2. Contrast the types of partnerships and partners.

3. Explain the substantive and procedural requirements for establishing a partnership.

4. Discuss the nature of the property interest held by a partnership.

5. Understand the theories and principles of partnership law included in the Articles of Partnership.

6. Develop the importance of contract law in the formation of a partnership.

7. Trace the various categories of partnership authority and discuss the extent of responsibilities associated with each upon dissolution and termination of the partnership.

8. Compare and contrast dissociation with dissolution and their respective causes and implications.

9. Explain and discuss the rights of partnership creditors.

10. Outline the specific rights partners have during and after dissolution.

11. Contrast partnership dissolutions harmonious with and contravening to the partnership contract.

12. Discuss circumstances and procedures associated with "winding up" a partnership.

13. Explain the implications of continuing a partnership after dissolution.

CHAPTER OUTLINE

I.   Choosing a Business Association
      A.   Factors Affecting the Choice
           1.   Ease of formation–business associations differ as to the formalities and expenses of formation
           2.   Taxation–IRS regulations allow unincorporated entities to elect whether or not to be taxed as a separate entity
           3.   External liability–most commonly occurring are tort and contract liability
           4.   Management and control–depends on the type of entity
           5.   Transferability–depends on the type of entity
           6.   Continuity–depends on the type of entity
      B.   Forms of Business Associations
           1.   Sole Proprietorship–unincorporated business consisting of one person who owns and controls the business
           2.   General partnership–unincorporated business consisting of two or more persons who co-own a business for profit
           3.   Joint venture–unincorporated business of short duration composed of persons who combine their property, money, efforts, skill, and knowledge for the purpose of carrying on a business for profit
           4.   Limited partnership–unincorporated business consisting of at least one general partner and one limited partner
           5.   Limited liability company–unincorporated business that provides limited liability to all members and permits all members to participate in the management
           6.   Limited liability partnership–registered general partnership that limits the liability of its partners for some or all of the partnership's obligations

7. Limited liability limited partnership–limited partnership in which the liability of the general partners has been limited to the same extent as in an LLP
8. Corporation–legal entity separate from its owners; taxed as a separate entity; shareholders taxed on corporate distributions to them
9. Business trusts–devised to avoid the burdens of corporate regulation

II. Formation of General Partnerships
  A. Nature of Partnerships
    1. Definition–partnership is an association of two or more persons as co-owners to carry on a business for profit
    2. Entity theory–legal entity is a unit with the capacity of possessing legal rights and being subject to legal duties independent from its members
      a. Partnership as a legal entity–UPA recognizes a partnership as a legal entity distinct from its members for most purposes
      b. Partnership as a legal aggregate–partnership is an aggregate for some purposes and thus cannot sue or be sued in the firm name unless a statute allows it
    3. Types of partnerships–"term" contrasted with "at will"
  B. Formation of a Partnership
    1. Partnership agreement–written agreement creating a partnership
      a. Statute of Frauds–not usually applied to a contract for the formation of a partnership; no writing required to create unless partnership to continue for more than one year
      b. Firm name–some restrictions on the choice of a name for the partnership
    2. Tests of partnership existence–formation requires presence of each of the following
      a. Association–two or more persons agree to be partners
      b. Business for profit
      c. Co-ownership–sharing profits and control
    3. Partnership capital–total money and property contributed by the partners
    4. Partnership property–sum of all of the partnership assets, including capital
    5. Partners' interest in partnership–covers partners' transferable interests and management rights
      a. Assignability–partner may sell, assign transferable interest in the partnership; does not cause dissolution; new owner or assignee does not become a partner
      b. Transferable interest–profit/loss share and distribution rights
      c. Creditors' right–partner's interest is subject to the claims of that partner's creditors who may obtain a charging order (a type of judicial lien) against the partner's interest

III. General Partnership Dissociation and Dissolution
    A. Dissociation–partnership relation changed by partners leaving the business; ends rights/duties related to business
        1. Wrongful–breaching express provision in agreement
            a. Term partnership–before designated end date or completing purpose; voluntary departure, judicial expulsion, partner becomes bankruptcy debtor
            b. Rightful–all other dissociations (death, leaving "at will" partnership)
    B. Dissolution–partnership ends under RUPA provisions
        1. Causes of dissolution
            a. Dissolution by act of the partners–"at will" partnership partner leaves; triggered by condition stated in agreement; end of term partnership
            b. Dissolution by operation of law–subsequent illegality dissolves partnership
            c. Dissolution by court order
        2. Effects of dissolution–partnership continues until winding up process completed
            a. Authority–dissolution terminates partner's actual authority to act for the partnership; apparent authority continues until notice to third party
            b. Existing liability–dissolution does not itself discharge the existing liability of any partner
    C. Winding Up Process–liquidation; completing unfinished business
        1. Winding up required–upon dissolution unless waived by all partners; participation by any not wrongfully dissociating partner
        2. Distribution of assets–assets reduced to cash, distributed to creditors and partners
            a. Non-partner and partner creditors paid first
            b. Amounts owing on partner accounts paid next
            c. Contribution of partner upon insolvency–generally, partners contribute equally to the partnership losses
        3. Marshaling of assets doctrine–segregating partnership assets/liabilities from those of individual partners; different rules for bankruptcy partnership
    D. Dissociation without Dissolution–RUPA triggered changes in effects of dissociation on partnership; dissolution no longer required
        1. Non-dissolving dissociations
            a. Partnership at will–death, incapacity, bankruptcy, expulsion; personal to affected partner
            b. Term partnership–more than 50% of partners oppose dissolution
        2. Continuation after dissociation–remaining partners refuse dissolution, support buying out departing partner
            a. Creditor claims against ongoing partnership
            b. Dissociated partner's binding power–actual authority ends; apparent authority lasts 2 years
            c. Dissociated partner's third party liability–continues for both pre and post (up to 2 years) dissociation partnership obligations

    E.   Continuation after Dissolution–remaining partners continue firm under certain circumstances
         1.   Continuation after wrongful dissolution–firm continues by injured partners paying departed partner value of respective % interest less damages caused by breach; departed partner indemnified for present/future liabilities
         2.   Continuation after expulsion–payment/novation discharges expelled partner; cash payment of net amount owing
         3.   Continuation by partners' agreement–remaining partners keep partnership property, conduct business, specify settlement with departed partners
         4.   Creditor rights–old partnership creditor rights against continuing partnership; creditors proceed against all partners, including departed ones, for claims existing prior to dissolution; notice (actual/constructive) protects departed partners against liability

TRUE–FALSE: Circle true or false.

T   F   1.   Partnerships pay Federal income tax on the profits they acquire.

T   F   2.   Under the UPA, a partnership cannot sue or be sued in its own name in the absence of a permissive statute.

T   F   3.   Upon dissolution, the partnership is automatically terminated.

T   F   4.   A partnership cannot acquire title to real property in its own name.

T   F   5.   A partnership must be organized as a business for profit.

T   F   6.   The fact that two or more persons own property jointly in itself establishes a partnership.

T   F   7.   Unless each partner takes an active part in the management of the firm, a partnership does not exist.

T   F   8.   The RUPA provides that property bought with partnership assets is not treated as partnership property if title was acquired under an individual partner's name.

T   F   9.   Under the RUPA, two or more co-owners of a business operated for profit create a partnership only if the parties intend to do so.

T   F   10.   Dissociation does not automatically require the termination and winding up of a partnership.

T   F   11.   A partner may not sell or assign her interest in the partnership.

T   F   12.   Dissociation does not end the dissociating partner's rights to share in managing and conducting partnership business.

KEY TERMS–MATCHING EXERCISE: Select the term that best completes each statement below.

1. Partnership	8. Capacity	15. Equitable partner
2. Capital	9. Marshaling of assets	16. Continuation
3. Novation	10. Contribution	17. Surplus
4. Winding up	11. Joint stock company	18. Charging order
5. Business trust	12. Partnership at will	19. Constructive notice
6. Nominal partner	13. Partnership property	20. Dissociation
7. Dissolution	14. Term partnership	

_____ 1. The sum of all of the partnership assets.

_____ 2. Partnership not ended by completing a specific purpose or the expiration of a specific time period.

_____ 3. A group of persons acting as co-owners to carry on a business for profit.

_____ 4. The process of liquidating a partnership.

_____ 5. Change in partner relationship triggering liquidation and termination of the partnership.

_____ 6. The right a partner who pays all the partnership debts has against the other non-paying partners.

_____ 7. Partnership created to accomplish a specific purpose or last for a specific period of time.

_____ 8. A key factor determining whether a natural person may become part of a partnership.

_____ 9. An agreement among a departing partner, continuing partners, and creditors that discharges the departing partner from existing partnership liabilities.

_____ 10. Aggregate total of money and property committed to the operation of a business enterprise.

_____ 11. Partner's withdrawal from participation in conducting partnership business.

_____ 12. Agreement used to guarantee the ongoing operations of a partnership following the death, disability or retirement of a partner.

_____ 13. A type of judicial lien a creditor may obtain against a partner's interest.

_____ 14. A business association formed to securely manage pooled income-producing assets.

_____ 15. Separating partnership assets and liabilities from those of the individual partners.

MULTIPLE CHOICE: Select the alternative that best completes each statement below.

_____ 1. Under the RUPA, a partnership at will is dissolved by a partner's (a) giving notice of intent to withdraw (b) death (c) bankruptcy (d) all of the above.

_____ 2. Which of the following is not a test for determining the existence of a partnership? (a) co-ownership (b) conducting a business (c) profit sharing (d) business experience.

_____ 3. One of the following could be a partnership: a (a) medical clinic (b) social club (c) literary society (d) charitable foundation.

_____ 4. A partnership terminates upon (a) completion of the winding-up process (b) issuance of a termination order from the court (c) creditors executing a liability waiver releasing partners from partnership debts (d) none of the above.

_____ 5. Which of the following does not occur during the winding up period of a partnership? (a) termination of the partners' liabilities (b) payment of creditors (c) distribution of assets (d) collection of debts

_____ 6. Dissolution by act of the partners occurs when a (a) partner withdraws (b) partner dies (c) judge dissolves the partnership (d) partner becomes insane.

_____ 7. The partnership name (a) must include the name of all the partners (b) may be a fictitious name (c) must include the name of at least one of the partners (d) may be the same name as an existing corporation.

_____ 8. The RUPA holds that no inference that a partnership exists can be made where profits are received in payment of a/n (a) debt (b) employee wages (c) interest on a loan (d) all of the above.

_____ 9. A court will order the dissolution of a partnership if (a) a partner is incompetent (b) a partner is guilty of conduct prejudicial to the business (c) the business cannot operate profitably (d) all of the above.

_____ 10. Placing an advertisement in a newspaper of general circulation calling attention to the dissolution of a named partnership is called _____ notice. (a) actual (b) equitable (c) vicarious (d) constructive

_____ 11. Circumstances triggering the dissolution of a partnership under the RUPA include (a) court order (b) act of the partners (c) operation of law (d) all of the above.

_____ 12. Under Federal bankruptcy law, the person who is appointed to administer the assets of the partnership is the (a) general partner (b) marshal (c) trustee (d) none of the above.

_____ 13. The transferee of an assignable partnership interest has rights to (a) participation in conducting partnership business (b) receive asset distributions which the transferor could have received (c) inspect partnership financial records (d) all of the above.

CASE PROBLEMS–SHORT ESSAY ANSWERS: Read each case problem carefully. When appropriate, answer by stating a Decision for the case and by explaining the rationale–Rule of Law–relied upon to support your decision.

1. A and B are nieces of X. X dies and under a will leaves apartment buildings to A and B as tenants in common. A and B continue to manage and lease the apartments together. They share equally the costs of managing the building as well as the profits. Do A and B have a partnership? Explain.

Decision: _____

_____

Rule of Law: _____

_____

2. X, Y and Z are partners. Z wants to retire from the partnership and end her liability to its existing creditors. X and Y want to continue their business partnership. Are these desires possible? Explain.

Decision: _____

_____

Rule of Law: _____

_____

3. A has been declared mentally incompetent by a court decision. The judge appointed a guardian for A. If A enters into a partnership agreement with B, does a partnership exist? Explain.

Decision: _____

_____

Rule of Law: _____

_____

4. Without authority from his co-partners, B and C, and in breach of their partnership agreement, A assigns five trucks owned by the firm to Z, an individual creditor of A. Z demands the trucks. The partners B and C refuse to relinquish them. Can the partnership be dissolved? Explain.

Decision: _____

_____

Rule of Law: _____

_____

5. A, B and C are partners. With A's and B's consent, C retires. Pursuant to their agreement, A and B agree to assume all the old debts and obligations of the firm and proceed with the accounting and dissolution. X, a creditor of the firm before dissolution, has a debt that A and B cannot satisfy, so X sues C. C refuses to pay X, arguing the controlling influence of C's agreement with A and B. Who prevails? Explain.

Decision: _____

_____

Rule of Law: _____

_____

Chapter 32

OPERATION OF GENERAL PARTNERSHIPS

SCOPE NOTE

Chapter 32 continues our discussion of partnership law. The chapter examines the legal doctrines and principles that control the operations of a partnership. What are the rights/duties existing among the members of the partnership? What are the rights/duties of people doing business with the enterprise? These and other topics are the primary themes of Chapter 32.

EDUCATIONAL OBJECTIVES

1. Trace the various categories of partnership authority and discuss the extent of responsibilities associated with each.

2. Explain the liability of partners in terms of contract, tort and agency theories.

3. Define and discuss the significance of a partnership by estoppel.

4. Understand the nature and substance of duties partners owe one another.

5. Outline the specific rights partners have with one another.

CHAPTER OUTLINE

I. Relationships Among Partners
   A. Duties Among Partners–the legal duties imposed upon partners are listed below
      1. Fiduciary duty–each partner owes a duty of absolute and utmost good faith and loyalty to his partners: not appropriate opportunities; not compete; protect confidential information; no conflict of interest

2. Duty of obedience–each partner must act in obedience to the partnership agreement
3. Duty of care–each partner owes a duty of faithful service to the best of her ability to the partnership: act without gross, reckless, intentional misconduct

B. Rights Among Partners–use, possess property; transferable rights
   1. Right to share in distributions–transfers of partnership property from the partnership to the partners
      a. Right to share in profits–each partner is entitled to a share of the profits
      b. Right to return of capital–only upon partnership withdrawal or partnership liquidation
      c. Right to return of advances–if a partner makes loans to the firm, she is entitled to repayment plus interest
      d. Right to compensation–generally, no partner is entitled to payment for services provided to the partnership
   2. Right to participate in management–each partner has an equal voice in management
   3. Right to choose associates–no person can become a partner without the consent of all the partners
   4. Enforcement rights–the law provides partners with the means to enforce rights and duties
      a. Right to information and inspection of the books–is a right of each partner
      b. Legal actions–direct suit for enforcing rights by partner against partnership or other partner, and vice versa

II. Relationship Between Partners and Third Parties
   A. Contracts of Partnership–the act of every partner binds the partnership to transactions within the scope of partnership business unless the partner does not have actual or apparent authority: individual partners have joint and several unlimited personal liability
      1. Authority to bind partnership–a partner may bind the firm by her act if she has any of the kinds of authority listed below
         a. Actual express authority–may be oral or written and it is usually included in the partnership agreement
         b. Actual implied authority–is authority that is reasonably deduced from the partnership nature or terms of the partnership agreement
         c. Apparent authority–partner apparently acting in ordinary business partnership and a third person who has no knowledge or notice of the lack of actual authority
      2. Partnership by estoppel–imposes partnership duties and liabilities upon a person who is not a partner but who has either represented herself or consented to be represented as a partner
   B. Torts and Crimes of Partnership–a partnership is liable for any loss or injury caused by a wrongful act or omission of any partner while acting within the ordinary course of the business or with authority of the co-partners; a partner is not criminally liable for the crimes of her partners unless she authorized or participated in them
      1. Breach of trust–partnership liability for partner's misappropriating money or property given by a third person
      2. Joint/several liability–for tort, breach of trust

    C. Notice to a Partner–notice to any partner of any matter relating to the firm's affairs binds the partnership; notice is actual knowledge, reason to know, or notification of facts

    D. Liability of Incoming Partner–a person admitted as a partner into an existing partnership is liable for all of the obligations of the partnership arising before her admission, but this liability may be satisfied only out of partnership property

TRUE-FALSE: Circle true or false.

T   F   1. Each partner owes a duty of good faith and loyalty to the other partners.

T   F   2. Upon termination of the partnership, partners are entitled to the return of their capital contributions after all debts have been paid.

T   F   3. Generally, when partners are repaid their capital contributions, they also receive interest on the contribution.

T   F   4. In most cases, the proportion in which partners bear business losses depends on their relative capital contributions.

T   F   5. An incoming partner has unlimited liability for all obligations arising after the partner's admission.

T   F   6. Partners who loan money to the partnership beyond their capital contribution become creditors of the firm.

T   F   7. Generally, a partner is entitled to compensation for services performed for the firm.

T   F   8. In an action on tort liability, the plaintiff must sue all the partners jointly.

T   F   9. A partnership is not bound by notice to a partner of a matter relating to partnership affairs since such notice must be given to all partners.

T   F   10. Much of the law of partnership is based on the law of agency.

T   F   11. If a partner has neither actual authority nor apparent authority, the partnership is bound only if it ratifies the act of the partner.

T   F   12. Any lawsuit based upon breach of contract brought against the partners must name all the partners as defendants.

KEY TERMS–MATCHING EXERCISE: Select the term that best completes each statement below.

1. Indemnification	8. Delectus personae	15. Partnership by estoppel
2. Joint and several liability	9. Court of equity	16. Contributory negligence
3. Agency law	10. Change in membership	17. Respondeat superior
4. Express authority	11. Fiduciary	18. Ratification
5. Limited personal liability	12. Apparent authority	19. Duty of obedience
6. Distribution	13. Court of law	20. Gross negligence
7. Account	14. Implied authority	

_____ 1. A principle that establishes the right of persons to select their own partners.

_____ 2. The right one partner who pays partnership debts has against the other non-paying partners.

_____ 3. All partners may be sued together or separately.

_____ 4. A major basis for partnership law and liability.

_____ 5. Actual partnership authority that is oral or written.

_____ 6. The court in which a partner sues for an accounting.

_____ 7. The partnership created when persons not partners hold themselves out as partners.

_____ 8. Partnership authority reasonably deduced from the partnership itself or from the relations of the partners.

_____ 9. The duties of fair dealing and honesty owed among partners.

_____ 10. A transfer of partnership property from the partnership to a partner.

_____ 11. A type of misconduct breaching partner's duty of care.

_____ 12. Doctrine holding employer liable for unauthorized acts of employees.

_____ 13. A detailed statement of financial transactions.

_____ 14. An act that requires the consent of all of the partners.

_____ 15. The duty violated by a partner who extends credit to an insolvent relative using partnership funds.

MULTIPLE CHOICE: Select the alternative that best completes each statement below.

_____ 1. Upon termination of a solvent partnership, partners are entitled to the (a) return of their capital contributions (b) interest on their capital contributions by right of implication (c) repayment of their loans to the partnership without interest (d) none of the above.

_____ 2. Decisions that require unanimous agreement of the partners include (a) disposal of the good will of the business (b) adding a new partner (c) submitting a dispute to arbitration (d) all of the above.

_____ 3. The duties of a partner include the duty of (a) care (b) loyalty (c) obedience (d) all of the above.

_____ 4. Authority of a partner to act that is specifically provided for in the partnership agreement is (a) apparent (b) equitable (c) express (d) apportioned.

_____ 5. A partner has implied authority to (a) hire employees (b) enforce partnership claims (c) purchase property for the business (d) all of the above.

_____ 6. A partner does not have apparent authority to (a) pay personal debts out of partnership assets (b) indorse checks (c) give warranties in selling goods (d) enter into contracts for advertising.

_____ 7. The rights of a partner do not include the right to (a) compensation for performing partnership business (b) payment of a debt to a partner before payment to creditors of the partnership (c) add a friend or relative to the partnership without consent of all the partners (d) all of the above.

_____ 8. Liability of general partners for valid partnership contracts is (a) limited personal liability (b) joint liability (c) joint and several liability (d) none of the above.

_____ 9. Liability of general partners for torts of a partner or an employee doing company business is (a) limited personal liability (b) joint liability (c) joint and several liability (d) none of the above.

_____ 10. The rights of a partner include the right to (a) share profits (b) participate in managing the business (c) a repayment of capital contributions (d) all of the above.

_____ 11. A partner may not (a) compete with the partnership business (b) acquire for himself a partnership asset without copartner consent (c) make exclusive profit from the partnership business for himself (d) all of the above.

_____ 12. A partnership agreement cannot eliminate the duties of (a) obedience (b) loyalty (c) accounting (d) all of the above.

_____ 13. Partners making capital contributions to the partnership more than their agreed proportionate share have _____ rights against the partnership. (a) equitable distribution (b) dissolution (c) reimbursement (d) none of the above.

CASE PROBLEMS–SHORT ESSAY ANSWERS: Read each case problem carefully. When appropriate, answer by stating a Decision for the case and by explaining the rationale–Rule of Law–relied upon to support your decision.

1. Floral Designs is a partnership among A, B and C. A sells his partnership interest to P, who alleges that as a result of the purchase, she is now a co-partner with B and C. Accordingly, she demands a voice in managing the firm, and B and C refuse. P threatens suit. Who wins? Explain.

   Decision: _____

   _____

   Rule of Law: _____

   _____

2. Futuristic Concepts is a partnership owned by P, B and Q, who have provided in the Articles of Partnership that profits should be shared equally. P and B decide to change the method of sharing profits. Q finds the change in method unacceptable and demands that the original equal-share method be retained. P and B resist, asserting "majority rules." What result? Explain.

   Decision: _____

   _____

   Rule of Law: _____

   _____

3. While acting for the partnership, A completes a business transaction that nets the firm over $50,000. A demands payment for the work or an increase in the partnership profits. The other partners refuse. What result? Explain.

   Decision: _____

   _____

   Rule of Law: _____

   _____

4. Elizabeth is a partner in a law firm. Her father has named Elizabeth the executor of his will. He dies. If Elizabeth does not account for her executor fees to the partnership (the law firm), is this a breach of her fiduciary duty to the firm? Explain.

   Decision: _____

   _____

Rule of Law: _____

_____

5. A, B and C are partners. B is wrongfully excluded from the management of the partnership business. B commences a lawsuit against the partnership seeking damages. Is B entitled to this remedy? Explain.

Decision: _____

_____

Rule of Law: _____

_____

Chapter 33

LIMITED PARTNERSHIPS AND LIMITED LIABILITY COMPANIES

SCOPE NOTE

Chapter 33 ends our discussion of partnership law with a review of some of the fastest growing forms of partnership: the limited partnership. This chapter identifies the rights/duties that exist among the members of the limited partnership, explains the procedures for the formation and dissolution of the limited partnership, and discusses the advantages/disadvantages of this partnership as well as other forms of unincorporated business associations, e.g., limited liability companies, limited liability partnerships, and limited liability limited partnerships.

EDUCATIONAL OBJECTIVES

1. Discuss the criteria for the formation and dissolution of a limited partnership.

2. Explain the liability of limited partners concerning torts or contracts of the partnership.

3. Discuss the rights and duties of limited partners.

4. Identify the advantages and disadvantages of other forms of unincorporated business associations.

CHAPTER OUTLINE

I. Limited Partnerships
    A. Definition–a partnership formed by two or more persons under the laws of a state and having at least one general partner and one limited partner
    B. Formation–requires substantial compliance with the limited partnership statute
        1. Filing of certificate–of the limited partnership with the Secretary of State is required

2. Name–of the limited partnership may not contain the surname of the limited partner in most cases
3. Contributions–may be in the form of cash, property, or services
4. Defective formation–the limited partnership is formed when the certificate is filed; if not done or done improperly, liability of the limited partners may be in jeopardy
5. Foreign limited partnerships–are considered foreign in any state in which they have not been formed

C. Rights–limited partnership general partner has same rights/powers as a general partnership partner
1. Control–is in the hands of the general partners
2. Voting rights–the partnership agreement may grant voting rights to some or all of the general or limited partners
3. Choice of associates–no partner can be added without the consent of all partners
4. Withdrawal–the certificate determines the right and method of withdrawal, although a general partner may withdraw at any time by giving written notice to the other partners
5. Assignment of partnership interest–the interest is the partner's share in the profits and her right to distribution of partnership assets
6. Profit and loss sharing–is allocated among the partners, except limited partners who are generally not liable for losses beyond their contribution of capital
7. Distributions–of assets are shared by partners as provided in their partnership agreement
8. Loans–all partners may be secured or unsecured creditors of the partnership
9. Information–all records must be kept at the partnership office and each partner has the right to inspect the records
10. Derivative actions–limited partners may sue on behalf of the partnership if general partners refuse to bring the action

D. Duties and Liabilities
1. Duties–general partners have a fiduciary duty to limited and other general partners
2. Liabilities–limited partners have limited personal liability

E. Dissolution
1. Causes–except through judicial decree, limited partners do not have the right to dissolve the partnership; causes are time period expiring, general partner withdraws, or judicial decree
2. Winding up–generally this is done by the general partners
3. Distribution of assets–the priorities in distributing the assets of a limited partnership are listed

II. Limited Liability Companies–noncorporate business organization limiting liability of owners
A. Formation–requires substantial compliance with the limited liability company statute
1. Filing–the articles of organization are required to be filed in a designated state office
2. Name–statutes generally require the name to include the words limited liability company or LLC
3. Contribution–may be in the form of cash, property, or services

4. Operating agreement–the basic contract governing the affairs of the LLC and stating the rights and duties of the members
5. Foreign limited liability companies–are considered foreign in any state in which they have not been formed

B. Rights of Members–consist of financial and management interests
1. Profit and loss sharing–is determined by the operating agreement, but typically is allocated on the basis of the value of the members' contributions
2. Distributions–of assets are shared by members as provided in the operation agreement or on basis of respective contributions
3. Withdrawal–statutes determine the right and method of withdrawal
4. Management–statutes permit management by one or more managers who may, but need not, be members
5. Voting–the operating agreement or statutes specify the voting rights of members
6. Derivative actions–a member may sue on behalf of the LLC if the managers refuse to bring the action
7. Assignment of LLC interest–a member may assign her financial interest in the LLC

C. Duties
1. Manager-managed LLCs–statutes impose a duty of care and a fiduciary duty upon the managers
2. Member-managed LLCs–members have the same duties of care and loyalty that managers have

D. Liabilities–statutes provide that no member or manager shall be personally obligated for LLC liabilities by reason of being a member or acting as a manager

E. Dissolution
1. Dissociation–means that a member has ceased to be associated with the company
2. Distribution of assets–default rules for distributing assets are listed

III. Other Types of Unincorporated Business Associations
A. Limited Liability Partnerships
1. Formalities–to become an LLP, a general partnership must file an application containing specified information with the Secretary of State
2. Designation–statutes require LLPs to include the LLP designation in the name
3. Liability limitation–statutes limit the liability of partners for the partnership's obligations

B. Limited Liability Limited Partnerships–are limited partnerships in which liability of the general partner has been limited to the same extent as in an LLP

TRUE-FALSE: Circle true or false.

T   F   1. The amount of capital invested in limited partnerships has declined substantially since 1916.

T   F   2. The major advantage of limited partnerships is that the sale of such partnerships is not subject to governmental regulations.

T   F   3. Members of a limited partnership association are not personally liable for the debts of the business association.

T   F   4. All states have enacted limited liability company statutes.

T   F   5. The causes of dissolution and the priorities in the distribution of assets are the same for the limited partnership as they are for the general partnership.

T   F   6. A general partner has a fiduciary duty to the limited partners, but it is unclear whether the limited partners have a fiduciary duty to the general partners.

T   F   7. A general partnership and a limited partnership have the same formal requirements for their formation.

T   F   8. The personal liability of a limited partner for partnership debts is limited to the amount of capital the limited partner has contributed.

T   F   9. A limited partner has no right to participate in the management of the limited partnership.

T   F   10. Limited partners always share the profits of the limited partnership equally.

T   F   11. Today, a promise by a limited partner to contribute to the limited partnership is not enforceable unless it is written and signed.

T   F   12. An existing general partnership may become a limited liability partnership without forming a new organization.

KEY TERMS–MATCHING EXERCISE: Select the term that best completes each statement below.

1. General partnership

2. Limited liability partnership

3. Limited personal liability

4. Fiduciary duty

5. Limited partnership

6. Dissolution

7. Capital contribution

8. Foreign limited partnership

9. Certificate of cancellation

10. Certificate of limited partnership

11. Constructive trust

12. Assignee

13. Dissociation

14. Derivative action

15. Operating agreement

16. Assignor

17. Equity participant

18. Attorney General

19. Secretary of State

20. Assignment

_____ 1. A partnership composed of one or more general partners and one or more limited partners.

_____ 2. A kind of limited partnership that cannot enforce actions in a state's courts for business transactions until it registers.

_____ 3. The first step in the extinguishment of a general or limited partnership.

_____ 4. The document that must be filed when the limited partnership is dissolved.

_____ 5. The document that is filed in the Secretary of State's office in the state in which the limited partnership has its principal office.

_____ 6. The method a member of a limited liability company uses to cease to be associated with the company through voluntary withdrawal.

_____ 7. The type of partnership in which death or insanity of a partner causes dissolution of the partnership.

_____ 8. All statutes require this type of unincorporated business association to designate itself as such.

_____ 9. The extent or the amount of liability of a limited partner for losses of the partnership.

_____ 10. The basic contract governing the affairs of a limited liability company.

_____ 11. A method a partner can use to transfer her partnership interest.

_____ 12. The kind of obligation a general partner owes a limited partner.

_____ 13. The person to whom a limited partner may transfer her partnership interest.

_____ 14. The person who contributes to the capital of a business in a good faith but erroneous effort to become a limited partner.

_____ 15. The office or person with whom a foreign limited partnership must register before transacting any business in a state.

MULTIPLE CHOICE: Select the alternative that best completes each statement below.

_____ 1. In a limited partnership, the definition of the word person includes a (a) natural person (b) corporation (c) partnership or limited partnership (d) all of the above.

_____ 2. Which of the following uniform laws governs the creation and operation of limited partnerships? (a) U.P.A. (b) U.L.P.A. (c) R.U.L.P.A. (d) all of the above.

_____ 3. Both general and limited partners (a) have limited personal liability (b) have the right to manage the partnership (c) must unanimously consent to add a general partner to the partnership (d) all of the above.

_____ 4. A basic difference between a general partnership and a limited partnership is (a) a statute must exist that provides for the formation of the limited partnership (b) the limited partnership must comply with statutory requirements (c) the limited partners' liability is limited to their capital contributions (d) all of the above.

_____ 5. The uniform laws provide that a limited partner shall have the same rights as a general partner to (a) inspect the partnership books (b) copy records of the firm's business (c) obtain tax returns of the limited partnership (d) all of the above.

_____ 6. Failure of a limited partnership to comply with the statutory requirements for its formation may result in (a) a name change of the firm (b) the loss of limited liability for the limited partners (c) the loss of the limited partner's right to manage the partnership (d) all of the above.

_____ 7. The management interest of a member of a limited liability company includes the right to (a) manage the company (b) vote (c) obtain information (d) all of the above.

_____ 8. A member of a limited liability company does not have a (a) property interest in property owned by the company (b) financial interest (c) management interest (d) all of the above.

_____ 9. Death or bankruptcy (a) of a limited partner dissolves the partnership (b) of a general partner dissolves the partnership (c) never has any effect on the limited partnership (d) none of the above.

_____ 10. Limited partners (a) must share the profits of the partnership equally (b) must receive the return of their capital contributions at the same time (c) may contribute cash, property or services under the revised act (d) all of the above.

_____ 11. A limited partnership requires that (a) all partners be limited partners (b) the number of limited and general partners be equal (c) the partnership be created according to statutory law (d) none of the above.

_____ 12. If the surname of a limited partner is used in the partnership name, the limited partner (a) is entitled to a higher percentage of the partnership profits (b) may participate in the management of the partnership (c) may be liable to creditors who are unaware of the limited partnership (d) all of the above.

_____ 13. A limited liability company (a) is a noncorporate business organization (b) provides limited liability to all of its owners (members) (c) permits all members to participate in management of the business (d) all of the above.

CASE PROBLEMS–SHORT ESSAY ANSWERS: Read each case problem carefully. When appropriate, answer by stating a Decision for the case and by explaining the rationale–Rule of Law–relied upon to support your decision.

1. For 1999, XYZ Limited Partnership has a $50,000 loss. Carol is a limited partner of the firm. Must Carol pay for a share of this loss from her personal assets? Explain.

   Decision: _____

   _____

   Rule of Law: _____

   _____

2. A and B form a limited partnership. A is the general partner, B is the limited partner. The name of their company is A and B Partnership. C agrees to make a loan to the partnership. If the partnership defaults on this loan, whom can C sue? Explain.

   Decision: _____

   _____

   Rule of Law: _____

   _____

3. A, B and C are members of a limited partnership. A is the limited partner. They buy a large tract of land surrounding a lake, subdivide it, and begin selling the lots at a generous profit. If A goes bankrupt, is the limited partnership dissolved? Explain.

   Decision: _____

   _____

   Rule of Law: _____

   _____

4. A, B and C form a limited partnership. A and B want to add D to the partnership as a new general partner. Can this be done? Explain.

   Decision: _____

   _____

   Rule of Law: _____

   _____

5. Bob, Carol, Ted and Alice agree to form a limited partnership. They are prepared to execute and sign a certificate but are unsure what is required by the Uniform Limited Partnership Act. Explain to them what the certificate of limited partnership contains.

    Decision: _____

    _____

    Rule of Law: _____

    _____

PARTNERSHIP UNIT RESEARCH QUESTIONS: Drawing upon information contained in the text, as well as outside sources, discuss the following questions:

1. You and your best friend want to form a business. The form of business enterprise the two of you select is a partnership. Although partnerships may be created by an oral agreement, you prefer a written partnership agreement.
    A. Explain the steps and processes you would complete to establish a formal partnership.
    B. Include in your explanation a sample partnership agreement (articles of partnership) that would be appropriate for your business.

2. Denny and Forrest are partners in a corner grocery store. Forrest makes some bad personal investments and has to file for bankruptcy. What effect will this have on the partnership? Explain. What would be the advantage if the above business was a corporation and an owner (stockholder) had to file for personal bankruptcy? Would this affect the other stockholders? Explain?

Chapter 34

NATURE, FORMATION, AND POWERS

SCOPE NOTE

The most common form of business organization among modern industrial businesses is the corporation. It is a major institution of the private sector. In today's economy, corporations occupy a significant position as employers, taxpayers, and primary participants in the flow of goods and services constituting G.D.P. How did this form of business organization evolve? Why is it so popular in certain sectors of the marketplace? These and other related concerns are the subject of Chapters 34-37. In these chapters, the law of corporations is discussed, including its basic doctrines, principles and terminology.

Chapter 34 focuses upon what corporations are, the functions they perform, how they are created, and the types of powers they can hold. This chapter serves as a general introduction to corporate law that can help in understanding the subsequent chapters that address particular aspects of a corporation's operational identity.

EDUCATIONAL OBJECTIVES

1. Trace the historical development of corporations.

2. Define and explain the basic attributes of a corporation.

3. Compare the advantages/disadvantages of the corporate form of business organization.

4. Outline the various rights/duties associated with a corporate legal identity.

5. Differentiate among the various kinds of corporations.

6. Enumerate the substantive and procedural formalities associated with effectively establishing a corporation.

7. Understand the consequences of ineffective formation of a corporation.

8. Identify the meaning and importance of the phrase "piercing the corporate veil."

9. Discuss the sources, nature and kinds of operational powers a corporation holds.

10. Define and develop the importance of "ultra vires."

11. Know the tort and criminal liability of a corporation.

CHAPTER OUTLINE

I. Nature of Corporations
    A. Corporate Attributes
        1. Legal entity–makes the corporation separate and apart from its shareholders with rights and liabilities entirely distinct from theirs and it allows the corporation to sue or be sued
        2. Creature of the state–a corporation must be formed by compliance with a state incorporation statute
        3. Limited liability–means the shareholders are not personally liable for corporate debts beyond the amount of their investment
        4. Free transferability of corporate shares–may be done by sale, gift, or pledge
        5. Perpetual existence–is common and included in the articles of incorporation
        6. Centralized management–the shareholders elect the board of directors, who manage the business
        7. As a person–a corporation is considered a person under most of the Federal Constitution Amendments
        8. As a citizen–a corporation is considered a citizen of the state of its incorporation and of the state of its principal place of business
    B. Classification of Corporations
        1. Public or private–a corporation is formed for both purposes
        2. Profit or nonprofit–a corporation is formed for profit or for charitable, educational, or scientific (nonprofit) purposes
        3. Domestic or foreign–it is domestic in the state in which it is incorporated and foreign in all others
            a. Doing business–generally, any regular, systematic, or extensive conduct constitutes the transaction of business unless excluded under the Revised Act
            b. Scope of regulation–it is a common and accepted principle that local courts will not interfere with the internal affairs of a foreign corporation
            c. Sanctions–a foreign corporation transacting business without having first qualified may be subject to penalties
        4. Publicly held or closely held–a corporation owned by a large number of persons is publicly held; if owned by a small number of persons is closely held
        5. Subchapter S corporation–is taxed like a partnership
        6. Professional corporations–corporations formed by duly licensed professionals

II. Formation of a Corporation
   A. Organizing the Corporation
      1. Promoters–persons who originate and organize the corporation
         a. Promoters' contracts–contracts created by promoters before the corporation is formed; promoters remain liable on preincorporation contracts
         b. Promoters' fiduciary duty–is due to the fiduciary relationship among themselves as well as to the corporation, its subscribers, and its initial shareholders
      2. Subscribers–the persons who offer to purchase capital stock in a corporation yet to be formed
         a. Irrevocability of preincorporation subscription
         b. Revocability of postincorporation subscription
      3. Selection of state for incorporation–generally is the state in which the corporation intends to be located and do business
   B. Formalities of Incorporation
      1. Selection of name–it must contain a word or words that indicate it is a corporation
      2. Incorporators–persons who sign and file the articles of incorporation
      3. Articles of incorporation–the charter or basic governing document of the corporation
      4. Organizational meeting–the first meeting to adopt corporate bylaws and elect officers
      5. Bylaws–the rules that govern the internal management of the corporation

III. Recognition or Disregard of Corporateness
   A. Defective Incorporation
      1. Common law approach–a defectively formed corporation was accorded corporate attributes
         a. Corporation de Jure–a corporation formed in substantial compliance with the statute
         b. Corporation de Facto–a corporation not formed in compliance with the statute but recognized as a corporation
         c. Corporation by estoppel–estoppel does not create a corporation
         d. Defective corporation–the courts deny the associates the benefits of incorporation
      2. Statutory approach–if the articles are filed or accepted, that is generally conclusive proof of proper incorporation under the statute
         a. RMBCA–liability only on person acting with knowledge of defective incorporation
         b. MBCA–unlimited personal liability for all persons
   B. Piercing the Corporate Veil–courts disregard corporate entity to promote public good
      1. Closely held corporations–its shareholders may relax the traditional corporate formalities without courts piercing the veil
      2. Parent-subsidiary corporations–courts will pierce the corporate veil and hold the parent liable for the debts of its subsidiary under certain circumstances
IV. Corporate Powers
   A. Sources of Corporate Powers
      1. Statutory powers–provided by the Revised Act, including perpetual existence, holding property, and all others necessary to carry out purposes

2. Purposes–only lawful ones unless more limited as are stated in the articles of incorporation

B. Ultra Vires Acts–act or contract beyond express or implied powers

    1. Effect of Ultra Vires Acts–most statutes abolish the defense of ultra vires in an action by or against a corporation; under RMBCA, such acts are not invalid

    2. Remedies for Ultra Vires Acts–three remedies are possible under the Revised Act

C. Liability for Torts and Crimes–a corporation is liable for the torts committed by its agents in the course of their employment (respondeat superior doctrine), and it may be convicted of a strict liability criminal offense for the conduct of its officers or directors

TRUE-FALSE: Circle true or false.

T   F   1. A corporation incorporated under the laws of one state is known as a foreign corporation in other states.

T   F   2. If the sole shareholder of a corporation willfully destroys corporate property by fire, the doctrine of "piercing the corporate veil" will protect the fire insurance company.

T   F   3. A corporation can have its principal place of business in one state and be incorporated under the laws of another state.

T   F   4. A corporation is "de jure" if it has failed to meet some of the technical requirements for incorporation.

T   F   5. A unanimous agreement among shareholders of a closely held corporation that does not strictly adhere to statutory guidelines is always void and unenforceable as a matter of public policy.

T   F   6. A corporation is liable for the torts of its agents and employees while they are engaged in company business.

T   F   7. A corporation may be formed only by substantial compliance with a state incorporation statute.

T   F   8. A corporation is a legal entity, and therefore it is liable for its debts.

T   F   9. A shareholder of a corporation is the owner, agent, and manager of the corporation.

T   F   10. Title to corporate property belongs to the shareholders.

T   F   11. A transfer of corporate stock by gift or sale from one shareholder to another causes dissolution of the corporation.

T   F   12. A corporation may be incorporated in one state and conduct all or most of its operations in another state.

KEY TERMS–MATCHING EXERCISE: Select the term that best completes each statement below.

1. Perpetual	8. Incorporator	14. Ultra vires
2. De jure	9. Respondeat superior	15."Inc." or "Ltd."
3. Limited liability	10. Subscriber	16. Officers
4. De facto	11. Diversity of citizenship	17. Dividends
5. Charter		18. Closely held corporation
6. Pierce the corporate veil	12. Bylaws	19. Municipal corporation
7. Promoter	13. Unlimited liability	20. Board of directors

_____ 1. The kind of liability shareholders usually have.

_____ 2. A corporation organized substantially in compliance with the statutes.

_____ 3. Another name for the articles of incorporation which authorizes a corporation to do business.

_____ 4. The procedure a court uses to disregard the corporate entity when it is wrongfully used to avoid personal accountability.

_____ 5. The person who signs and files the articles of incorporation.

_____ 6. The person who may be individually liable for contracts made prior to the corporation's existence.

_____ 7. Corporate acts that are beyond the scope of its powers.

_____ 8. The rules and regulations that govern a corporation's internal management.

_____ 9. The doctrine that imposes liability on a corporation for the torts committed by its agents and employees during their employment.

_____ 10. The term that signifies that the parties to a lawsuit are from different states.

_____ 11. Payments made to shareholders from profits of the corporation.

_____ 12. A corporation owned by a small number of persons such as family or friends.

_____ 13. The potential lifetime of a corporation.

_____ 14. Another name for a public corporation.

_____ 15. The individuals appointed to run the operations of a corporation on a day-to-day basis.

MULTIPLE CHOICE: Select the alternative that best completes each statement below.

_____ 1. The person who offers to buy stock in a nonexisting corporation is a(n) (a) promoter (b) incorporator (c) subscriber (d) none of the above.

_____ 2. The debts of a corporation are satisfied from (a) assets of the corporation (b) a shareholder's personal assets (c) an incorporator's personal assets (d) all of the above.

_____ 3. A shareholder is (a) personally responsible for corporation debts (b) an agent of the corporation (c) liable only for corporation torts (d) none of the above.

_____ 4. Most incorporation statutes require that a corporation name (a) not be the same as the name of an existing corporation doing business within the state (b) contain wording that indicates it is a corporation (c) both A and B (d) none of the above.

_____ 5. A promoter's profits may be allowed if they are (a) disclosed to the corporation (b) relatively small (c) secret (d) none of the above.

_____ 6. A corporation whose existence cannot be challenged by the state is a (a) corporation de facto (b) corporation by estoppel (c) corporation de jure (d) none of the above.

_____ 7. A corporation derives all of its power and its existence from (a) its charter (b) the state (c) the articles of incorporation (d) the bylaws.

_____ 8. To be eligible for Subchapter S treatment, a corporation must have (a) a minimal capitalization of $2.5 million (b) at least 125 shareholders (c) no more than 2000 employees (d) no shareholders who are business entities.

_____ 9. An ultra vires act by the corporation may be remedied by (a) an injunction brought by a shareholder (b) a representative suit by shareholders for the corporation against the officers (c) a proceeding to dissolve or enjoin the corporation brought by the Attorney General of the state (d) all of the above.

_____ 10. Generally, all of the following are proper names for a corporation except (a) Johnson and Son, Inc. (b) Merry Widow Corporation (c) A.B. Lincoln and Company (d) T. F. Elliot, Ltd.

_____ 11. The existence of a corporation is terminated by the (a) death of a shareholder (b) withdrawal or retirement of a director (c) addition of a new officer (d) none of the above.

_____ 12. Corporations may be classified as (a) public or private (b) profit or nonprofit (c) domestic or foreign (d) all of the above.

_____ 13. The following individuals need not be shareholders of the corporation (a) officers of the corporation (b) creditors of the corporation (c) members of the corporation's board of directors (d) all of the above.

CASE PROBLEMS–SHORT ESSAY ANSWERS: Read each case problem carefully. When appropriate, answer by stating a Decision for the case and by explaining the rationale–Rule of Law–relied upon to support your decision.

1. A, B and C plan to go into business together. A and B have limited assets. C is very wealthy. Would it be advantageous for C to insist upon a corporation? Explain.

   Decision: _____

   _____

   Rule of Law: _____

   _____

2. A bartender of an incorporated tavern illegally sells liquor to a minor. The act is a crime under the state law. If the bartender is a nonowner, can the tavern be criminally prosecuted for the illegal sale? Explain.

   Decision: _____

   _____

   Rule of Law: _____

   _____

3. A promoter contracts with B to engage B to manage ABC Corporation upon its incorporation. The directors of ABC Corporation refuse to accept the terms of the contract, and B refuses to be employed by ABC Corporation except on the terms of the contract with the promoter. What are B's rights? Explain.

   Decision: _____

   _____

   Rule of Law: _____

   _____

4. X, a promoter of a corporation created to do business as a shopping center, collects a 20% commission on the sale of land to the corporation. X does not inform the directors of the corporation. Can X keep the commission? Explain.

Decision: _____

_____

Rule of Law: _____

_____

5. A, B, and C hire attorney Y to incorporate their dry-cleaning partnership. All formal steps for incorporation are taken except publication of the articles in a legal newspaper and filing of the articles with the Register of Deeds in the county of the corporation's principal place of business. A, B, and C rely on Y to take all necessary steps and believe the procedures have been completed. Thereafter, a customer is seriously injured by dry-cleaning fumes. Can the customer sue A, B, and C personally on the theory that the corporation is not validly formed and A, B, and C are still operating as partners? Explain

Decision: _____

_____

Rule of Law: _____

_____

Chapter 35

FINANCIAL STRUCTURE

SCOPE NOTE

In Chapter 35, the financial structure of a corporation is discussed. The legal concepts and rules relating to corporate funding, stocks and bonds, payment of dividends, and transfer of ownership of shares are focused upon.

EDUCATIONAL OBJECTIVES

1. Identify the use and types of debt securities used as a source of corporate funds.

2. Distinguish among the various classes of stock commonly used in corporate financing.

3. Develop the difference between "par" and "no par" value.

4. Discuss the procedures related to issuing, redeeming, and acquiring stock.

5. Explain the nature of the shareholder's dividend rights and liabilities.

6. Differentiate among the several types of dividends.

7. Understand the dividend declaration and payment process.

8. Identify what is meant by wrongful and illegal dividends.

CHAPTER OUTLINE

I. Debt Securities–nonownership source of capital; corporate promise to repay money lent to it
   A. Authority to Issue Debt Securities–also called bonds, is a sole responsibility of the board of directors

B. Types of Debt Securities
  1. Unsecured bonds–or debentures, have only the obligation of the corporation backing them
  2. Secured bonds–are creditor claims enforceable against general corporate assets and also as a lien on specific corporate property
  3. Income bonds–are debt securities that condition the payment of interest on corporate earnings
  4. Convertible bonds–may be exchanged for other securities at a specified ratio
  5. Callable bonds–are bonds that are subject to redemption

II. Equity Securities–source of capital creating ownership interest
  A. Share–portion of ownership interest
  B. Treasury Stock–reacquired shares
  C. Issuance of Shares
    1. Authority to issue–is within the articles of incorporation
    2. Preemptive rights–a shareholder's right to purchase a proportionate part of a new share issue
    3. Amount of consideration for shares–depends on the type of shares being issued
      a. Par value stock–may be issued for any amount set by the directors or shareholders, but not less than par
      b. No par value stock–may be issued for any amount
      c. Treasury stock–shares that have been issued and then reacquired by the corporation, and may be sold for any amount; however, the Revised Act eliminated the concept of treasury shares
    4. Payment for shares–depends on two issues
      a. Type of consideration–may include cash, property, or services but not promissory notes or future services. The Revised Act allows future services and notes
      b. Valuation of consideration–exchanged for shares; is determined by the directors
    5. Liability for shares–a shareholder's only liability is to pay to the corporation the full consideration for the shares issued
  D. Classes of Shares
    1. Common stock–frequently the only class of stock issued with no special contract rights or preferences
    2. Preferred stock–has superior contract rights to common stock over dividends and assets upon liquidation
      a. Dividend preferences–means that preferred shareholders will receive full dividends before any are paid to common stockholders
      b. Liquidation preferences–after creditors are paid, preferred stockholders usually receive assets ahead of common stockholders
      c. Additional rights and limitations–preferred stock may have these
    3. Stock rights–rights of existing shareholders to purchase corporate shares of a specific class or classes

III. Dividends and Other Distributions
    A. Types of Dividends and Other Distributions
        1. Cash dividends–most common type of dividend
        2. Property dividends–a dividend of property
        3. Stock dividends–a ratable distribution of additional shares to the shareholders
        4. Stock splits–each of the issued and outstanding shares is split into a greater number of shares
        5. Liquidating dividends–a distribution of capital assets to shareholders upon termination
        6. Redemption of shares–the option of the corporation to repurchase its own shares
        7. Acquisition of shares–a corporation may acquire its own shares, called treasury shares
    B. Legal Restrictions on Dividends and Other Distributions
        1. Definitions–legal concepts and finance terms concerning corporation assets
        2. Legal restrictions on cash dividends–payment only if cash flow and balance sheet tests are met
            a. Cash flow test–insolvency precludes payment
            b. Balance sheet test–includes earned surplus, surplus, and net assets tests
        3. Legal restrictions on liquidating distributions–states usually permit distributions, or dividends, in partial liquidation from capital surplus
        4. Legal restrictions on redemption and acquisition of shares–redemption and the purchase of its own shares may not be made at a time when the corporation is insolvent or when the purchase would make it insolvent
    C. Declaration and Payment of Distributions–is accomplished at the direction of the board of directors
        1. Shareholders' right to compel a dividend–is done by a suit in equity seeking an injunction
        2. Effect of declaration–once a cash dividend is declared, it cannot be rescinded; debt owed to shareholders
    D. Liability for Improper Dividends and Distributions–the Revised Act imposes personal liability upon the directors to the corporation and to its creditors
        1. Shareholders–must return illegal dividends if knowledge of illegality, acquired through own fraud, or corporation is insolvent

TRUE-FALSE: Circle true or false.

T   F   1. Common and preferred stock are examples of debt investment securities.

T   F   2. Common stock shareholders generally bear the heaviest loss if a corporation fails.

T   F   3. A corporation's board of directors and shareholders share the responsibility for declaring dividends.

T   F   4. The current profits or net earnings of a corporation are the only lawful source of corporate dividends.

T   F   5. Generally, a stock dividend increases the shareholder's relative interest in the net worth of the corporation.

T   F   6. The purchaser of a bond issued by a corporation becomes an owner of the corporation like a shareholder.

T   F   7. Preferred shareholders have priority to the assets of the corporation over creditors of the corporation.

T   F   8. A shareholder has no right to transfer shares of stock by sale or gift.

T   F   9. Debenture holders are unsecured creditors and have equal rights with other general creditors.

T   F   10. Convertible bonds may be exchanged for other corporation securities at a specific ratio.

T   F   11. Modern statutes expressly authorize the articles of incorporation to deny or limit a shareholder's preemptive rights.

T   F   12. A stock split is a ratable distribution of additional shares of the capital stock of the corporation to its shareholders.

KEY TERMS–MATCHING EXERCISE: Select the term that best completes each statement below.

1. Indorsement	8. Blue-Sky laws	15. Liquidating dividend
2. Bonds	9. Preemptive rights	16. Debentures
3. Model Act	10. Equity securities	17. Prospectus
4. Shares	11. No par stock	18. Distribution
5. Cash dividend	12. Par value stock	19. Stock split
6. U.C.C. Article 8	13. Nimble dividend	20. Treasury stock
7. Stock certificate	14. Cumulative dividend	

_____ 1. The evidence of a shareholder's interest in a corporation.

_____ 2. The statute containing the rules applicable to stock transfer.

_____ 3. Another name for debt securities that are used by corporations as a source of funds.

_____ 4. A source of capital that creates a proportionate ownership interest in a corporation.

_____ 5. The state statute that regulates the issuance and sale of corporate securities.

_____ 6. The most customary type of dividend.

_____ 7. Stock in which the stated value is found in the articles of incorporation.

_____ 8. A shareholder's right to purchase a proportionate share of every new offering of stock by the corporation.

_____ 9. A source for financing corporations that includes common stock.

_____ 10. The dividend paid to preferred shareholders for all arrearages on their stock before any dividends are paid on the common stock.

_____ 11. Stock of a corporation that has been issued and subsequently reacquired by the corporation.

_____ 12. Another name for unsecured bonds.

_____ 13. A written offer made by corporations to interest people in buying stock.

_____ 14. A direct or indirect transfer of money or other property by a corporation to its shareholders in respect of any of its shares.

_____ 15. The breakup of outstanding shares of corporate stock into a greater number of shares, each representing a smaller interest in the corporation.

MULTIPLE CHOICE: Select the alternative that best completes each statement below.

_____ 1. A corporation (a) may acquire its own shares (b) may acquire treasury shares (c) may redeem preferred shares but not common stock (d) all of the above.

_____ 2. Valid consideration for the issuance of shares of a corporation generally includes (a) cash (b) property (c) services to the corporation (d) all of the above.

_____ 3. In many states, cash dividends may be paid from (a) stated capital (b) earned surplus (c) capital surplus (d) any surplus.

_____ 4. Preferred shareholders may be entitled to (a) liens on corporate assets (b) cumulative dividends (c) rights superior to creditors (d) none of the above.

_____ 5. The board of directors who vote for or assent to the distribution of an illegal dividend are (a) not liable to the corporation (b) liable only in equity (c) liable only to creditors (d) personally liable to the corporation.

_____ 6. When an unsuspecting shareholder receives an illegal dividend from a solvent corporation, the majority rule is the shareholder (a) may keep the dividend (b) must refund the dividend (c) may be sued by creditors of the corporation (d) none of the above.

_____ 7. Debt securities are (a) also called bonds (b) a source of corporate funds (c) issued by the corporation's board of directors (d) all of the above.

_____ 8. The type of bonds that may be exchanged for other securities of the corporation at a specified ratio are (a) debentures (b) callable bonds (c) income bonds (d) convertible bonds.

_____ 9. Which of the following is not liable for improper distributions of an insolvent corporation? (a) an innocent shareholder (b) a knowing shareholder (c) a nonbreaching director (d) a breaching director.

_____ 10. When voting for the declaration of a dividend, a director is entitled to rely in good faith upon financial statements made by the corporation's (a) officers (b) public accountants (c) finance committee (d) all of the above.

_____ 11. The term that constitutes the entire surplus of a corporation other than its earned surplus is (a) stated capital (b) net assets (c) capital surplus (d) none of the above.

_____ 12. Dividends are (a) prohibited from being paid if the corporation is insolvent (b) declared and distributed by the officers of the corporation (c) in the form of cash or stock but not other kinds of property (d) none of the above.

_____ 13. A corporation may finance its operations by (a) selling bonds (b) obtaining credit extended by its suppliers (c) short-term commercial paper (d) all of the above.

CASE PROBLEMS–SHORT ESSAY ANSWERS: Read each case problem carefully. When appropriate, answer by stating a Decision for the case and by explaining the rationale–Rule of Law–relied upon to support your decision.

1. The board of directors of XYZ Corporation issues 100 shares of no par stock valued at $10,000 to A and B in exchange for land valued in good faith by all parties to be worth $10,000. XYZ goes bankrupt and the land is sold for $6,000. Can A and B be held liable for the balance of $4,000 by the corporation's creditors? Explain.

Decision: _____

_____

Rule of Law: _____

_____

2. The XYZ Corporation intends to redeem its preferred stock. The company has $10,000 in cash, and it intends to use it to redeem part of its outstanding $100 par stock. Several creditors of XYZ seek to enjoin the redemption alleging that XYZ will have no money with which to pay its debts. Can the corporation redeem the stock? Explain.

Decision: _____

_____

Rule of Law: _____

_____

3. XYZ Corporation declared a cash dividend on common stock. Before the dividend was paid, the board of directors voted to revoke the dividend on grounds that, due to changed circumstances, the corporation needed the funds. Can holders of the common stock force the company to pay the dividend? Explain.

Decision: _____

_____

Rule of Law: _____

_____

4. A holds shares of XYZ Corporation but has not fully paid for them. B is an innocent purchaser (transferee) of A's shares. Is B personally liable to the corporation for the unpaid portion of the shares? Explain.

Decision: _____

_____

Rule of Law: _____

_____

5. A, a shareholder in XYZ Corporation, owns 500 shares with preemptive rights. The corporation has a total of 6,000 shares outstanding. The company decides to increase its capital stock by issuing 12,000 additional shares of stock. If A exercises her preemptive rights and purchases the maximum shares to which she is entitled, how many shares of stock will A own? Explain.

Decision: _____

_____

Rule of Law: _____

_____

Chapter 36

MANAGEMENT STRUCTURE

SCOPE NOTE

This chapter develops the nature of the relationship between a corporation, its directors, officers, and shareholders. What role do shareholders play in setting corporate policy? Particular attention is paid to the management functions of corporations. Who performs these functions? What is the source and nature of their authority? What limitations are placed on such authority? How is corporate policy established and executed? These and related issues are the focus of attention in Chapter 36 in its development of the rules and doctrines that control the management area of corporate law.

EDUCATIONAL OBJECTIVES

1. Identify and explain the rights and liabilities of shareholders.

2. Discuss proxy, cumulative, and trust voting.

3. Understand the nature and function of a board of directors.

4. Identify the qualifications for service on and the process of appointment to a board of directors.

5. Discuss the scope of powers/responsibilities held by corporate directors and explain the purpose of board meetings.

6. Know what management powers are delegated to corporate officers and outline the process of delegation.

7. List corporate officers and explain their responsibilities and basis for authority.

8. Outline the selection/removal procedure for corporate officers as well as how they are compensated.

9. Enumerate the kinds of duties and standard of care to which corporate officers are held.

CHAPTER OUTLINE

I. Corporate Governance

II. Role of Shareholders
    A. Voting Rights of Shareholders
        1. Shareholder meetings–shareholders may vote at both annual and special shareholder meetings
        2. Quorum and voting–generally, a majority of shares entitled to vote constitutes a quorum
        3. Election of directors–is the voting right of the shareholders
            a. Straight voting–normally, each shareholder has one vote for each share owned
            b. Cumulative voting–entitles shareholders to multiply the number of votes they are entitled to by the number of directors for whom they are entitled to vote and to cast the product for one candidate or distribute the product among two or more candidates
        4. Removal of directors–by a majority vote, shareholders may remove any director or the entire board
        5. Approval of fundamental changes–like amendments to the articles of incorporation, these require shareholder approval
        6. Concentrations of voting power
            a. Proxies–a shareholder may vote either in person or by written proxy
            b. Voting trusts–are devices designed to concentrate corporate control in one or more persons
            c. Shareholder voting agreements–shareholders may agree in advance to vote in a specific manner for the election or removal of directors or other matters
        7. Restrictions on transfer of shares–apply if adopted for a lawful purpose and do not unreasonably restrain or prohibit transferability. The Revised Act and several states require that restrictions be noted conspicuously on the stock certificate
    B. Enforcement Rights of Shareholders
        1. Right to inspect books and records–is a right of shareholders if demand made in good faith, for a proper purpose
        2. Shareholder suits–the ultimate recourse is a shareholder's suit against or on behalf of the corporation
            a. Direct suits–are brought to enforce a shareholder's claim against the corporation
            b. Derivative suits–are brought by one or more shareholders on behalf of the corporation
        3. Shareholder's right to dissent–concerns certain corporate actions such as mergers

III. Role of Directors and Officers
    A. Function of the Board of Directors
        1. Selection and removal of officers–the directors hire and can fire the officers
        2. Capital structure–and the financial policy of the corporation are determined by the directors
        3. Fundamental changes–such as amending and repealing bylaws are decided by the directors, unless reserved to the shareholders by the articles of incorporation
        4. Dividends–are declared by the directors, including the amount and type of dividends
        5. Management compensation–for both officers and directors is determined by the directors
    B. Election and Tenure of Directors
        1. Election, number, and tenure of directors–directors are elected at annual meetings of the shareholders and hold office for one year. State statutes usually set the number
        2. Vacancies and removal of directors–a vacancy may be filled by the shareholders or by a majority vote of the remaining directors while removal is done by the shareholders' vote
        3. Compensation of directors–Revised Act authorizes the board to fix the compensation for directors
    C. Exercise of Directors' Functions–directors bind corporation only when acting as a board
        1. Quorum and voting–a majority of the directors is a quorum, and it is necessary for a vote in most states
        2. Action taken without a meeting–requires written consent of all the directors
        3. Delegation of board powers–may be done by a majority vote of the full board of directors; committees appointed to carry out board functions
        4. Directors' inspection rights–include the right to inspect corporate books and records
    D. Officers–agents of corporation
        1. Selection and removal of officers–is done by the directors
        2. Role of officers–are set forth in the corporate bylaws
        3. Authority of officers
             a. Actual express authority–arises from the incorporation statute, the articles, the bylaws, and resolutions of the directors
             b. Actual implied authority–officers have this authority to do what is reasonably necessary
             c. Apparent authority–arises when a third party relies on the fact that an officer has exercised the same authority in the past
             d. Ratification–a corporation may ratify the unauthorized acts of its officers
    E. Duties of Directors and Officers
        1. Duty of obedience–directors and officers must act within their authority
        2. Duty of diligence–they must exercise ordinary care and prudence
             a. Reliance upon others–they are permitted to entrust important work to others
             b. Business judgment rule–precludes imposing liability upon the directors for honest mistakes of judgment based on reasonable good faith and due care
        3. Duty of loyalty–they owe a fiduciary duty to the corporation and its shareholders
             a. Conflict of interests–today, a contract between officers or directors and the corporation may be upheld under certain safeguards

  b. Loans to directors–by the corporation are not permitted without shareholder authorization

  c. Corporate opportunity–directors and officers may not usurp any corporation opportunity

  d. Transactions in shares–the issue of shares at favorable prices to management could constitute a breach of the fiduciary duty

  e. Duty not to compete–directors and officers may not compete with the corporation

 4. Indemnification of directors and officers–a corporation may indemnify a director or officer for liability incurred if he acted in good faith and he was not adjudged negligent or liable for misconduct

 5. Liability limitation statutes–forty states have authorized corporations, with shareholder approval, to limit or eliminate the liability of directors in some instances

TRUE-FALSE: Circle true or false.

T F 1. Bylaws may require a number greater than a simple majority of the directors for a quorum in order to transact corporate business.

T F 2. Shareholders elect the corporation's board of directors who manage the business of the corporation.

T F 3. Because they are so important to a publicly held corporation, directors are usually full-time employees who owe a fiduciary duty to the shareholders.

T F 4. The bylaws of a corporation set forth the duties of each officer of the corporation.

T F 5. Under the Revised Act, one person may be both the president and secretary of a corporation.

T F 6. Each corporation must comply with rigid common law requirements establishing the qualifications of directors.

T F 7. Although officers and directors are generally free from personal liability on contracts of the corporation, they are personally liable for breaching any duty they owe to the corporation and shareholders.

T F 8. According to the Revised Act, a vacancy on the board of directors may be filled by a majority vote of the remaining directors.

T F 9. Shareholders and directors generally do not have the right to inspect the books of the corporation.

T F 10. Cumulative voting works to the advantage of the majority shareholders.

T   F   11. The vast majority of corporations are closely held corporations.

T   F   12. Directors and officers of a corporation may not engage in their own private business interests during their tenure with the corporation.

KEY TERMS–MATCHING EXERCISE: Select the term that best completes each statement below.

1. Liability of directors	8. Fiduciary duty	15. Direct suit
2. Voting trust	9. Majority	16. Business judgment rule
3. Short-swing	10. Derivative suit	17. Secretary
4. Honorarium	11. Conflict of interest	18. Proxy
5. Bylaws	12. Interlocking directorate	19. Treasurer
6. Insider	13. Void	20. President
7. Quorum	14. Cumulative voting	

_____ 1. An action taken by a shareholder to enforce the right to inspect corporate books.

_____ 2. The small fee paid a director for attendance at meetings.

_____ 3. The essence of this obligation is the subordination of self-interest to the interest of the corporation.

_____ 4. The shareholder's remedy for breach of fiduciary duty by a director.

_____ 5. The problem of involvement when a contract is made between a director and the corporation.

_____ 6. The term that describes two corporations having common directors.

_____ 7. The number of directors usually necessary for a quorum.

_____ 8. An officer or director who has advance information not available to the public that may affect the future market value of stock.

_____ 9. A written agreement created when one or more shareholders transfer their shares to a trustee who is authorized to vote the shares.

_____ 10. The voting procedure that may allow a minority shareholder to obtain minority representation on the board of directors.

_____ 11. The principle that courts will not substitute their judgment for a good faith decision by the directors or officers of a corporation.

_____ 12. The principal executive officer of the corporation.

_____ 13. The minimum number of members necessary to be present at a meeting in order to transact business.

_____ 14. A shareholder's authorization to an agent to vote her shares at a particular meeting.

_____ 15. Rules adopted by a corporation to manage its internal affairs and establish the roles of the officers.

MULTIPLE CHOICE: Select the alternative that best completes each statement below.

_____ 1. Because of their positions of trust and loyalty, directors can best be described as (a) fiduciaries (b) trustees (c) salespersons (d) none of the above.

_____ 2. Generally, a corporation has the following officers, a (a) president (b) secretary (c) treasurer (d) all of the above.

_____ 3. Typically, bylaws include (a) the time and place of director's meetings (b) the compensation, if any, of directors (c) the number of directors needed for a quorum (d) all of the above.

_____ 4. Directors are most often elected for a term of (a) 3 years (b) 6 years (c) 5 years (d) 1 year.

_____ 5. A method of ridding the corporation of a poor director is (a) firing the director (b) removal by vote of the shareholders (c) removal by a quorum of the other directors (d) none of the above.

_____ 6. Officers of a corporation are (a) appointed by the shareholders (b) removed by the shareholders (c) agents of the corporation (d) all of the above.

_____ 7. The majority of the members of the board of directors constitutes a (a) quorum (b) bylaw directorate (c) proxy (d) all of the above.

_____ 8. Director power might include (a) fixing the selling price of newly issued shares (b) amending the bylaws (c) initiating merger proceedings (d) all of the above.

_____ 9. In an election of directors of a corporation, cumulative voting allows a (a) shareholder to distribute votes among many candidates (b) shareholder to give all votes to one candidate (c) minority shareholder to obtain minority representation on the board if a certain minimum number of shares are owned (d) all of the above.

_____ 10. Generally, shareholders of a corporation (a) may remove a director by a majority vote (b) may remove a director but only with cause (c) may not remove the entire board of directors (d) all of the above.

_____ 11. A closely held corporation has (a) a small number of shareholders (b) no ready market for its shares (c) shareholders who are often also the corporation's directors and officers (d) all of the above.

_____ 12. A "supermajority provision" (a) increases a corporation's voting requirements (b) in close corporations is frequently used to protect minority shareholders from oppression by the majority (c) is used by some publicly held corporations to defend against hostile takeover bids (d) all of the above.

_____ 13. The duties the directors and officers of a corporation are required to perform include the duties of (a) obedience (b) diligence (c) loyalty (d) all of the above.

CASE PROBLEMS–SHORT ESSAY ANSWERS: Read each case problem carefully. When appropriate, answer by stating a Decision for the case and by explaining the rationale–Rule of Law–relied upon to support your decision.

1. In a corporation with cumulative voting, X has only ten shares. Each share has one vote. There are three directors to be elected. Explain the possible voting methods X can follow.

   Decision: _____

   _____

   Rule of Law: _____

   _____

2. If A, as president of B Corporation, learns of a good buy in land that the corporation expected to buy and would use profitably, can A buy the land personally without informing the corporation? Explain.

   Decision: _____

   _____

   Rule of Law: _____

   _____

3. All the directors of X Corporation vote to convey, by deed, corporate land to Z. Each of the directors votes separately on the matter without a board meeting. Is such a vote binding on the corporation? Explain.

   Decision: _____

Rule of Law: _____

_____

4. X, director of Y Corporation, using X's best judgment, convinces the corporation to enter into a contract with Z Corporation. Y Corporation loses a lot of money on the contract. The shareholders bring suit against X for the loss. What result?

Decision: _____

_____

Rule of Law: _____

_____

5. X, an out-of-state director of Y Corporation, has not attended a directors' meeting for five years. The corporation suffers serious losses, and the shareholders seek to hold X liable. What result?

Decision: _____

_____

Rule of Law: _____

_____

Chapter 37

FUNDAMENTAL CHANGES

SCOPE NOTE

Chapter 37 brings our discussion of corporation law to a close. The chapter focuses on laws regulating the amending of the corporation's charter, the termination of the corporation's existence, and cases where independent business enterprises seek to join forces. Why would individual corporate enterprises wish to combine operations? What forms of combination are recognized by the law? How and why would a corporation terminate its existence? How are corporations regulated by the respective states in which they operate? These and other pertinent concerns complete our study of corporate law.

EDUCATIONAL OBJECTIVES

1. Discuss the methods and procedures for amending a corporation's charter.

2. Distinguish between the processes related to, the reasons for, and the effect of consolidation and merger.

3. Discuss shareholder rights/remedies related to opposing corporate combinations.

4. Contrast voluntary and involuntary dissolution procedures and their related effects.

CHAPTER OUTLINE

I. Charter Amendments–permitted by state statute
   A. Approval by Directors and Shareholders–the board of directors adopts a resolution setting forth the proposed amendment that then must be approved by a majority vote of the shareholders

B. Approval by Directors–the Revised Act permits directors to adopt certain amendments without shareholder action

II. Combinations
   A. Purchase or Lease of All or Substantially All of the Assets–of another corporation results in no change in the legal personality of either corporation
      1. Regular course of business–if sale or lease is in this manner, approval of the directors is required but not of the shareholders
      2. Other than in regular course of business–the sale or lease also requires approval of the shareholders
   B. Purchase of Shares–an alternative to the purchase of the assets of another corporation; does not change legal existence; no shareholder approval required
      1. Sale of control–the courts require that such sales be made with due care
      2. Tender offer–another method of purchasing shares of another corporation
   C. Compulsory Share Exchange–a method of share acquisition that is compulsory on all owners of the acquired shares; ownership of outstanding shares occurs; board and shareholder approval required
   D. Merger–of two or more corporations is the combination of all of their assets; shareholder and director approval required; short form merger does not require shareholder approval
   E. Consolidation–combines the assets of two or more corporations in which title is taken by a newly created corporation; requires shareholder and director approval; new corporation assumes assets and liabilities
   F. Going Private Transactions–a corporate combination that makes a publicly held corporation a private one
      1. Cash-out combinations–used to eliminate minority shareholders by forcing them to accept cash or property for their shares
      2. Management buyout–a transaction by which existing management increases its ownership of a corporation and eliminates its public shareholders
   G. Dissenting Shareholders–a shareholder's statutory right to dissent and receive payment for her shares when she objects to fundamental changes in the corporation
      1. Transactions giving rise to dissenters' rights–examples are listed
      2. Procedure–the corporation must notify the shareholders of the dissenter's rights before the vote is taken on the corporate action
      3. Appraisal remedy–payment by the corporation of the fair value of the dissenters' shares plus interest

III. Dissolution
   A. Voluntary Dissolution–effected by a resolution of the board with the approval of a majority of the shareholders
   B. Involuntary Dissolution–effected by administrative dissolution or by judicial dissolution
      1. Administrative dissolution–commenced by the Secretary of State
      2. Judicial dissolution–may be brought by the State, a shareholder, or a creditor
   C. Liquidation–the winding up of the corporation's affairs and liquidation of its assets
   D. Protection of Creditors–the statutory safeguards for creditors after dissolution of the corporation; payment priority according to contract or lien rights; any remaining assets paid to shareholders based on contract rights

TRUE-FALSE: Circle true or false.

T   F   1. It is illegal for one corporation to acquire all the assets, including the goodwill, of another corporation.

T   F   2. The purchase of all the assets of one corporation by another completely alters the legal existence of both.

T   F   3. Unlike a sale, mergers require one corporation to cease existence.

T   F   4. The surviving corporation in a merger assumes the merged corporation's debts and liabilities.

T   F   5. The dissenting shareholders in a merger have no recourse.

T   F   6. Dissolution terminates the corporation's existence and requires the corporation to liquidate its assets.

T   F   7. Shareholders of each corporation in a consolidation must receive new stock of the same class from the newly formed corporation.

T   F   8. Fundamental changes, such as amendments to the articles of incorporation, generally require the approval of the corporation's shareholders.

T   F   9. Dissenting shareholders in a merger or consolidation must notify the corporation in writing of their objections and of their demand for payment for their stock.

T   F   10. Involuntary liquidation of a corporation is usually conducted by the corporation's board of directors.

T   F   11. According to the Revised Act, all amendments to a corporation's articles of incorporation require shareholders' approval.

T   F   12. If acts of the directors are illegal or fraudulent, the shareholders may bring a court action for dissolution of the corporation.

KEY TERMS–MATCHING EXERCISE: Select the term that best completes each statement below.

1. Parent corporation	5. Par value	9. Fair value
2. Consolidation	6. Dissolution	10. Preferred shareholder
3. Merger	7. Creditors	11. Voluntary dissolution
4. Subsidiary corporation	8. Dissenting shareholder	12. Short-form merger

13. Liquidation	16. Leveraged buyouts	19. Articles of Incorporation
14. Interstate	17. Involuntary dissolution	20. Tender offer
15. Appraisal remedy	18. Secretary of State	

_____ 1. A combination of corporations leaving one survivor.

_____ 2. A combination of corporations leaving no survivors but instead a new corporation.

_____ 3. The right of dissenting shareholders to recover the fair value of their shares.

_____ 4. The name of a corporation owned or acquired by another corporation.

_____ 5. The value of the stock to which a dissenting shareholder is entitled.

_____ 6. The method of stopping the continuation of a corporation's business.

_____ 7. The persons who have the superior right to the corporate assets upon its dissolution.

_____ 8. A shareholder who does not agree with a plan of merger.

_____ 9. The kind of combination when a corporation owns at least 90% of the outstanding shares of another corporation (called a subsidiary) and combines the subsidiary into itself.

_____ 10. The procedure for turning into cash all assets for distribution first to the creditors of a corporation.

_____ 11. A general invitation to all the shareholders of a target company to offer their shares for sale at a specified price.

_____ 12. Another name for management buyouts that make extensive use of borrowed funds.

_____ 13. The name of a corporation that acquires another corporation.

_____ 14. Dissolution of a corporation without court action.

_____ 15. Dissolution by a court action brought by a creditor who shows that the corporation is unable to pay its debts as they become due.

MULTIPLE CHOICE: Select the alternative that best completes each statement below.

_____ 1. Which of the following requires shareholder approval? (a) the amendment of the corporate charter (b) merger (c) consolidation (d) all of the above.

_____ 2. The Revised Act permits the board of directors to adopt certain amendments without shareholder approval such as (a) making minor name changes (b) extending the duration of the corporation (c) splitting authorized shares if the corporation has only one class of shares (d) all of the above.

_____ 3. Dissolution (a) does not terminate the corporation's existence (b) requires the corporation to wind up its affairs (c) requires liquidation of the corporation's assets (d) all of the above.

_____ 4. Annual reports of a corporation must be delivered to the (a) county recorder (b) board of directors (c) Attorney General (d) Secretary of State.

_____ 5. Dissolution by court action may be brought by shareholders when acts of the directors are (a) illegal (b) oppressive (c) fraudulent (d) all of the above.

_____ 6. Dissolution of a corporation (a) may be voluntary or involuntary (b) does not terminate the corporation's existence (c) requires that the corporation wind up its affairs and liquidate its assets (d) all of the above.

_____ 7. Involuntary judicial dissolution of a corporation may be commenced by (a) creditors (b) the State (c) shareholders (d) all of the above.

_____ 8. Statutory provisions governing dissolution (a) do not preserve creditor claims against the corporation (b) require mailing of notice to known creditors (c) do not require notice of any kind (d) none of the above.

_____ 9. A corporation may be dissolved involuntarily if it failed to (a) pay its franchise taxes (b) extend its duration that now has expired (c) appoint and maintain a registered agent in the state in the prescribed time (d) all of the above.

_____ 10. A resolution adopted by the board of directors is required for a (a) merger (b) consolidation (c) compulsory share exchange between corporations (d) all of the above.

_____ 11. The procedural acts in amending a corporation's charter include the (a) vote of the shareholders (b) vote of the board of directors (c) filing of the articles of amendment (d) all of the above.

_____ 12. The directors of a corporation may adopt certain amendments to the articles of incorporation without shareholder approval except an amendment that (a) makes a minor name change (b) changes the voting rights of shareholders (c) extends the duration of the corporation (d) none of the above.

_____ 13. Shareholder approval is not required for (a) a merger (b) the sale of corporate assets in the usual and regular course of business (c) a consolidation (d) all of the above.

CASE PROBLEMS–SHORT ESSAY ANSWERS: Read each case problem carefully. When appropriate, answer by stating a Decision for the case and by explaining the rationale–Rule of Law–relied upon to support your decision.

1. X Corporation is dissolved by act of the legislature and A, as a creditor, wants to know what A's rights are to the assets. Explain.

   Decision: _____

   _____

   Rule of Law: _____

   _____

2. Abby is a dissenting shareholder to a merger between corporations X and Y. Abby wants nothing to do with the new corporation and wishes to get her money back. The state in which both corporations are located follows the Revised Act. Abby does nothing for 45 days, then seeks payment for the shares. Is Abby entitled to payment? Explain.

   Decision: _____

   _____

   Rule of Law: _____

   _____

3. A "short-form merger" takes place between parent Corporation X and subsidiary Corporation Y. Do the dissenting shareholders of each corporation have the right to an appraisal remedy? Explain.

   Decision: _____

   _____

   Rule of Law: _____

   _____

4. A, a director with X Corporation, and B, a director of Y Corporation, believe that their corporations are too much alike and that something ought to be done to eliminate their competition. What possible steps might be taken?

   Decision: _____

   _____

   Rule of Law: _____

   _____

5. X Corporation is a parent corporation to its subsidiary Y after a compulsory share exchange. Y owes A and B large sums of money but refuses to pay them after becoming the subsidiary. Can A and B sue Y Corporation? Explain.

Decision: _____

_____

Rule of Law: _____

_____

PARTNERSHIP AND CORPORATION UNIT RESEARCH QUESTIONS:

Drawing upon information contained in the text, as well as outside sources, discuss the following questions.

1. Assume you want to go into business. Your choice this time for the form of business organization is a corporation.
    a. Trace the steps and explain the process necessary to incorporate the business.
    b. Explain the differences between a corporation and a general partnership and those between a corporation and a limited partnership.
    c. List the advantages and disadvantages of selecting a corporation as the choice for the business enterprise rather than a partnership.

2. Since you have chosen to form a corporation, it is necessary for you to create articles of incorporation, hold the first organization or board of directors meeting, and adopt bylaws. Draft examples of the documents, including minutes of the organization meeting, necessary for the formation and operation of your corporation.

PART EIGHT: Debtor and Creditor Relations

Chapter 38

SECURED TRANSACTIONS AND SURETYSHIP

SCOPE NOTE

Buyers in today's marketplace neither expect nor are they expected to pay fully for the goods/services they purchase. When a seller/banker (creditor) performs completely for the buyer (debtor) who only partially performs, the unexecuted balance of the buyer's performance is credit from the seller/lender's perspective and debt from the buyer's. The importance of these credit arrangements is reflected in the hundreds of billions of dollars in outstanding commercial/consumer debt in America's economy. The exchange of the debtor's promised future performance for the creditor's present full performance creates a substantial risk of loss for creditors if the debtor fails to make proper payment–default. Chapter 38 examines the policy considerations and legal doctrines related to creditor alternatives to reducing the economic loss from nonpayment through security agreements, either property based (covered by U.C.C. Article 9), or contractual-cosigner based (covered under suretyship law). The advantages of secured credit over unsecured credit, competing interests among various parties over payment obligations and rights in collateral, as well as the requirements for creating valid, enforceable security interests, either property or reputationally based, are discussed.

EDUCATIONAL OBJECTIVES

1. Identify the sources of law that control the issuance and maintenance of secured debt.

2. Explain the requirements for creating a valid security agreement (attachment) in personal property.

3. Define and discuss the importance of a purchase money security interest.

4. Understand the significance and process of protecting (perfecting) personal property based security interests.

5. Distinguish among the various classifications of personal property in relation to attachment and perfection.

6. Explain the rules for determining priorities among conflicting interests–secured and unsecured creditors, purchasers, bailees, etc.–in shared collateral.

7. Discuss the rights/duties of the parties upon debtor defaulting proprietary security interests.

8. Identify and define the parties involved in a suretyship transaction.

9. Differentiate an absolute surety from a conditional guarantor and discuss what significance this difference has under the Statute of Frauds.

10. Explain the formal requirements for creating a surety contract.

11. Understand rights creditors have against sureties.

12. List various payment defenses available to sureties, the principal debtor and both.

13. Discuss alternative courses of action open to sureties after making debt payments.

CHAPTER OUTLINE

I.   Essentials of Secured Transactions–controlled by U.C.C. Article 9; debtor contractually consents to security interest in personal property to secure contractual (payment) duty
  A. Types–typical purchase money security interest–retail credit extender (seller retains security interest in goods sold); lender credit extender (lender acquires security interest in goods purchased with loan proceeds)
  B. Elements–debtor; creditor (secured party); security agreement; collateral (property used as payment security)

II. Collateral Classified–based on purpose, use, character of property
  A. Goods–tangible, movable property (consumer goods, farm products, inventory, equipment)
    1. Consumer goods–family, household, personal use
    2. Farm products–related to farming operations (livestock, crops, supplies)
    3. Inventory–products held for sale/lease; raw materials for manufacturing
    4. Equipment–primarily business use
    5. Fixtures–items attached to, considered part, of real property
      a. Conflicting interests in collateral–buyer, mortgage creditor, fixture creditor (usually prevails)
  B. Indispensable Paper–rights associated with commercial paper used as collateral; all transferable
    1. Chattel Paper–written evidence of debt, security interest in specific goods contained in security agreement
    2. Instruments–written evidence of right to payment (investment securities, bonds, stocks, commercial paper) used as collateral

3. Documents–written evidence of property ownership (bill of lading, warehouse receipt) used as collateral

III. Creating a Security Interest–Attachment
   A. Necessary Elements–value; property rights; payment duty/rights; debtor's signature
      1. Value–broad definition (contract consideration, letter of credit, antecedent debt, etc.)
      2. Debtor Property Rights–title, possession, in process of acquiring
      3. Security Agreement–contract gives creditor (secured party) security interest in specified property (collateral)
         a. Written
         b. Debtor signature
         c. Collateral description
   B. Pledge–creditor retains possession of collateral
   C. Consumer Goods–federal law prohibits nonpurchase money security interest, nonpledge security interest in household goods
   D. Code allows security interest in after–acquired property–10 day limitation
   E. Collateral Sale Proceeds–secured party right to
   F. Future Advances–debtor line of credit for yet to make advances

IV. Perfection of Security Interest–protecting security interest against competing interests in same collateral (buyers, creditors); occurs on attachment (creation of security interest) plus completing perfection process (filing, possession based on type of collateral)
   A. Methods of Perfection
      1. Filing financing statement–secured party's notice of security interest
         a. Content–names/addresses of parties; description of collateral; debtor's signature
         b. Effectiveness–initial five years; renewable within 6 months of expiration
         c. Motor vehicles–title certificate notation
         d. Location
            (1) Central filing–with secretary of state for all non "local" collateral
            (2) Local filing–farm products/equipment fixtures, real property based collateral
         e. Improper filing–ineffective except for good faith compliance with Article 9 or anyone having knowledge of financing statement
      2. Possession of collateral–documents, instructions, and pledges
      3. Automatic upon attachment–purchase money security interest in consumer goods
   B. Temporary Perfection–collateral sale proceeds; sale of instruments/documents; 21 day and 10 day protection periods

V. Priorities Among Competing Interests–creditors, buyers, and bankruptcy trustees with competing interests in same collateral; Article 9 rules determine who prevails
   A. Unsecured Creditors–general creditors without attached security interest subordinated to attached security interest
   B. Competing Secured Creditors–issues of perfection, type of collateral
      1. Perfected vs. unperfected–perfected prevails
      2. Competing perfected interests–first to file prevails

      a. Purchase money interest–priority depends on whether inventory (debtor notice to other creditor) or non-inventory collateral (10 day period for creditor to perfect by filing)

    3. Competing unperfected interests–first to attach prevails

  C. Competing Buyer's Interest–security interest follows sale of collateral, sale proceeds

    1. Ordinary course of business buyers–good faith commercial purchasers from merchant sellers cut off seller's inventory, perfected, secured creditors

      a. Farm products buyers protected under Federal Food Security Act

    2. Good faith non-commercial buyers of consumer products–cut off unfiled purchase money security interests in collateral

      a. Good faith purchasers cut off unperfected interests unless buyer has notice of security interest

    3. Purchasers of negotiable paper–cut off perfected/unperfected interests

  D. Lien Creditors–subordinate to perfected interest; prevail over unperfected interests

  E. Bankruptcy Trustee–prevails over unperfected interests, avoidable preferential transfers

    1. Purchase money security interest perfected by filing prevails over trustee

    2. Voidable preferential transfer–antecedent debt, insider trading based

VI. Rights/Duties on Debtor Default–creditor contractual/judicial payment enforcement options, debtor redemption option

  A. Repossession–take possession without judicial involvement; breach of peace issue

  B. Collateral Sale–creditor collateral disposal; commercially reasonable manner (time, method, place); debtor entitled to surplus (sale proceeds>debt balance), liable for deficiency (sale proceeds<debt balance)

  C. Collateral Retention–creditor written notice to debtor; debtor written objection to force disposal (collateral value exceeds debt balance); waivable prohibition against retention for consumer goods, 60% purchase price paid

VII. Surety Relationships–contractual duty to creditor to pay another's debt on debtor's default; three party contractual relationship (creditor, debtor, co-signing surety)

  A. Nature

    1. Absolute surety–primary obligor; immediate debt liability upon default; cannot compel creditor to seek payment from debtor

    2. Conditional (guarantor) surety–secondary obligor; creditor exhausts legal remedies against debtor before surety liable (creditor unable to collect on judgment against debtor); notice of default required

    3. Statute of frauds (written contract requirement)–applies to surety's promise to creditor

      a. Main purpose doctrine–exception making enforceable unwritten promise to creditor for surety's economic benefit

    4. Consideration requirement–surety's promise must be supported by consideration (either debtor's consideration or separate from creditor)

  B. Types of Sureties–creditor payment choice between debtor/surety

    1. Property purchase "assuming mortgage"–buyer becomes principal debtor/seller becomes secondary surety to mortgage holding creditor

      a. Contrast property purchase "subject to" mortgage–no surety relationship created

    2. Bonds–protection against negligence, non performance
      a. Fidelity–protection against employee dishonesty
      b. Performance–contract performance guaranteed
      c. Judicial–cover court costs, property loss tied to legal action
      d. Bail–assure defendant's appearance at criminal proceedings

C. Surety Rights–triggered by debtor default; asserted against debtor, co-sureties
    1. Exoneration–surety requires debtor/co-surety to pay; equity enforcement; creditor seeking payment from surety unaffected
    2. Reimbursement–repayment from debtor; limited to amount surety paid
    3. Subrogation–triggered by surety's full payment of debt; "stepping into creditor's shoes" assumes creditor's rights against debtor (bankruptcy priority, security interest, rights against co-sureties)
    4. Contribution–co-surety, joint/several liability; triggered by one co-surety's full payment; reimbursement from other co-surety up to amount of proportional share (contract specified, equal shares if no contract provision)

D. Payment Defenses–justified non-payment to creditor based on contract doctrines (modification of debtor's contract, variation of co-surety's risk, nonexistence/discharge of debt)
    1. Debtor personal defenses–not available to surety; assertable only by debtor
      a. Bankruptcy discharge
      b. Incapacity–age/mental incompetence
      c. Debtor's set off, counter claim vs creditor
    2. Surety personal defenses–assertably only by surety against creditor
      a. Contract based–surety's incapacity, Statute of Frauds non-compliance, no consideration or mutual assent
      b. Creditor's fraud/duress–creditor's concealment, non-disclosure of material fact but not debtor's fraud/duress
      c. No signature of surety
      d. Surety's set off, claim against creditor
      e. Unconsented to contract modification
      f. Creditor release/impairment of security interest
      g. Creditor release of surety
    3. Debtor/surety defenses–assertable against creditor by either party
      a. Forgery of signatures
      b. Creditor fraud/duress against debtor
      c. Creditor material alteration of contract
      d. No mutual assent consideration
      e. Contract illegality, impossibility of performance
      f. Creditor releases debtor
      g. Creditor refuses to accept payment

TRUE-FALSE: Circle true or false.

T   F   1. The creditor's refusal to accept an offer of payment from the debtor discharges both the debtor and the surety.

T   F   2. The Code defines "goods" as movable tangible personal property at the time of attachment.

T   F   3. A perfected security interest is not valid and enforceable against a trustee of a debtor in bankruptcy.

T   F   4. A security interest may be perfected by filing a financial statement or taking possession of the collateral.

T   F   5. Most states require the filing of a financing statement to perfect a security interest in a motor vehicle purchased for personal use.

T   F   6. Perfection of a purchase money security interest in consumer goods occurs without having to file a financing statement.

T   F   7. Examples of "general intangibles" that meet the Code's classification of collateral are goodwill, patent rights and trademark rights.

T   F   8. The code defines exactly what conduct undertaken by a debtor constitutes a default.

T   F   9. The principal debtor's incapacity based on mental incompetence or being under age does not discharge the surety.

T   F   10. A goal of Article 9 of the U.C.C. is to reduce the cost and foster the use of secured financing in commercial and consumer transactions.

T   F   11. For a security interest to attach, the security agreement must refer to and describe the transaction that gave rise to the debt.

T   F   12. Oral surety contracts are enforceable.

KEY TERMS–MATCHING EXERCISE: Select the term that best completes each statement below.

1. Financing statement	5. Equipment	9. Perfection
2. Acceleration clause	6. General intangibles	10. Consumer goods
3. Reimbursement	7. Collateral	11. Foreclosure
4. Contract rights	8. Attachment	12. Conditional guarantor

13. After acquired property	15. Contribution	18. Redemption
14. Mechanic's Lien	16. Mortgage assumption	19. Exoneration
	17. Floating lien	20. Pledge

_____ 1. Goods bought for business or professional use.

_____ 2. Property that is subject to a security interest.

_____ 3. The act of making a valid security interest in property enforceable against other creditors of a debtor.

_____ 4. Items primarily used for personal, family or household purpose.

_____ 5. A document filed to create a public record of the existence of a security interest in identified goods.

_____ 6. Items not presently owned by a debtor that might be obtained in the future.

_____ 7. The act of creating a valid enforceable security interest.

_____ 8. Clause in the security agreement giving the secured creditor rights to enforce payment of the full debt owing upon debtor's default of any installment payment.

_____ 9. One who promises to answer for another's debts only after the creditor has exhausted legal remedies against the debtor.

_____ 10. Surety's right against defaulting debtor after payment to the creditor.

_____ 11. Surety's right to require debtor to pay the creditor.

_____ 12. Purchasing mortgaged property in a manner that makes the buyer a principal debtor and the seller a surety.

_____ 13. Surety's right against co-sureties upon full payment of the debt.

_____ 14. Delivery of personal property to secure payment of a debt.

_____ 15. Debtor's right to pay off a default on a debt and regain an interest in collateral.

MULTIPLE CHOICE: Select the alternative that best completes each statement below.

_____ 1. Substantial changes in important contractual terms made by one or more parties to the contract is (a) spoilation (b) substitution (c) material alteration (d) none of the above.

_____ 2. One owing payment or performance on an obligation to another is the (a) secured party (b) debtor (c) attacher (d) perfector.

_____ 3. Refusal by the creditor to accept the debtor's offer of payment (a) constitutes a breach of fiduciary duty (b) often leads to criminal indictments (c) is usually grounds for defamation liability (d) terminates interest accruing on the debt.

_____ 4. A security agreement is enforceable between the creditor and debtor upon (a) perfection (b) attachment (c) filing (d) registering.

_____ 5. One who acquires title to property free of either known or unknown perfected security interests is a (a) trustee in bankruptcy (b) lien creditor (c) buyer in the ordinary course of business (d) all of the above.

_____ 6. Suretyships arise from (a) contract law (b) tort law (c) public policy considerations (d) Constitutional law.

_____ 7. _____ of the contract is conduct between the principal debtor and the creditor that results in discharge of the surety's contractual duties (a) execution (b) modification (c) apportionment (d) reimbursement.

_____ 8. A financing statement is automatically effective for a period of (a) 4 years (b) 8 years (c) 5 years (d) 10 years from the filing date.

_____ 9. When two security interests, both perfected by filing, are held by different creditors in the same collateral, priority is determined by (a) time of attachment (b) type of collateral (c) place of filing (d) time of filing.

_____ 10. Defenses discharging both the debtor's and surety's payment obligation include (a) impossibility of performance of debtor's contract (b) mental incompetence of debtor (c) extension of debt maturity (d) all of the above.

_____ 11. Examples of value as defined by the Code include (a) an antecedent debt (b) contractual consideration (c) a binding credit extension commitment (d) all of the above.

_____ 12. _____ extends the time period over which a financing statement is effective. (a) continuation statement (b) termination notice (c) release statement (d) filing statement.

_____ 13. Examples of lien creditors include (a) secured creditors (b) holders of pledges (c) trustees in bankruptcy (d) all of the above.

CASE PROBLEMS–SHORT ESSAY ANSWERS:

CASE PROBLEMS–SHORT ESSAY ANSWERS: Read each problem carefully. When appropriate, answer by stating a Decision for the case and by explaining the rationale– Rule of Law–relied upon to support your decision.

1. Dean Debtor has obtained an $1,850 loan from Casper Creditor. Their agreement, cosigned by Samantha Surety, calls for ten $185 monthly payments, final payment to be made no later than December of that year. Falling on financial hard times, Dean approaches Casper to extend the final payment date to March of the following year. Casper agrees. What effect does their action have on Samantha's payment obligations under the contract? Explain.

Decision: _____

_____

Rule of Law: _____

_____

2. Lawyer L receives a $1,500 loan from bank B collateralized by L's office library. L sells the books for $1,000 and deposits the money in an office account. Is B entitled to claim any of the $1,000?

Decision: _____

_____

Rule of Law: _____

_____

3. Charlie Creditor lends $2,100 to Debbie Debtor. Cosigning the agreement is Salvatore Surety. Under the agreement, Debbie has pledged a $2,500 diamond brooch to Charlie to secure her payment obligation. The brooch is a family heirloom and when other family members learn of Debbie's action, they approach Charlie requesting his release of the brooch. Sympathetic to their wishes, he agrees. What effect, if any, does this action have on Sal's suretyship status? Explain.

Decision: _____

_____

Rule of Law: _____

_____

4. Borrower B grants lender L a security interest in a sculpture that B owns for $3,500 that L
    advances to B. A financing statement is executed and filed by L. Sometime later, B pledges
    the sculpture to C for an additional $1,500. B defaults on both loans. Who has priority to the
    sculpture? Explain.

    Decision: _____

    _____

    Rule of Law: _____

    _____

5. B, an automobile assembly line worker, purchases from S a $2,500 TV/stereo entertainment
    unit under a conditional sales contract with S retaining a purchase money security interest in
    the unit. After properly making 17 of the 25 $100 monthly payments called for in the con-
    tract, B, laid off from the assembly plant, is unable to make any further payments and de-
    faults on the contract. S repossesses the unit with the intent to retain it as full satisfaction on
    the debt and so informs B. B believes S's actions are improper but S disagrees. Who is
    right? Explain.

    Decision: _____

    _____

    Rule of Law: _____

    _____

Chapter 39

BANKRUPTCY

SCOPE NOTE

Debtors encountering financial problems that prevent timely and proper debt payments have several options to resolve their troubles. Some debt resolution methods involve voluntary, informal agreements between a debtor and creditors (composition, assignments). Others take the shape of formal judicial proceedings under state insolvency laws (receivership). When all attempts to reach agreement between debtors and creditors fail, federal bankruptcy procedure is an option. Chapter 39 examines these choices with special emphasis on the historical development, substance and procedure of contemporary bankruptcy law. The terminology and the legal principles associated with the three types of bankruptcy proceedings (liquidation, reorganization and debt adjustments) are examined from an individual and a corporate perspective.

EDUCATIONAL OBJECTIVES

1. Differentiate among the various non-bankruptcy forms of debt resolution.

2. Distinguish pre-judgment creditor remedies from post-judgment ones.

3. Explain the commencement procedures for voluntary and involuntary bankruptcy proceedings.

4. Trace the steps in a typical debtor liquidation proceeding.

5. Outline the duties of the parties associated with debtor liquidation proceedings.

6. Contrast the rights of secured and unsecured creditors as well as priority and non-priority claims under federal bankruptcy.

7. Discuss how the debtor's estate may be enlarged or reduced in size and value by the conduct of creditors and the trustee.

8. List non-dischargeable debts and explain the significance of discharge and debtor denial of discharge.

9. Explain the grounds and procedure for Chapter 11 corporate reorganization plans.

10. Describe Chapters 12 and 13 debt adjustment processes and explain their debtor/creditor benefits.

CHAPTER OUTLINE

I.   Federal Bankruptcy Law (Bankruptcy Code)
     A. Purpose–equitable, orderly distribution of debtor's property; debtor has new financial start by discharge from debts

II. Case Administration (Chapter 3)–Code outlines case commencement, administration, officials and powers, creditor meetings
     A. Case Commencement–filing voluntary or involuntary petition
         1. Voluntary petitions–filing by any person eligible to be debtor; debtor insolvency not required; commencing voluntary case triggers automatic order for relief; petition lists all creditors (secured and unsecured), all debtor's property, property claimed as exempt, and statement of debtor affairs
         2. Involuntary petitions–filed under Chapter 7 for liquidation, Chapter 11 for reorganization
             a. Filed by 3 or more creditors with unsecured claims totaling $11,625 or more; if fewer than 12 creditors, by one or more creditors with claims totaling $11,625 or more
             b. Debtor does not contest petition–court enters order for relief
             c. Debtor opposes petition–court enters order for relief only if debtor not paying debts as they become due, or within 120 days before filing, custodian or receiver took possession of substantially all of debtor's property
     B. Automatic Stay–filing petition stays (prevents) creditor attempts to enforce liens, judgments, or claims; applies to secured/unsecured creditors
     C. Trustees–represents debtor's estate; can sue, be sued; elected by creditors or appointed by court
         1. Duties–collects, liquidates, distributes debtor's estate; authority to manage debtor's assets
     D. Creditor Meeting–debtor appears, submits to examination by creditors and trustee regarding financial situation

III. Creditors, Debtor and the Estate
     A. Creditors–any entity holding claim (payment right) against debtor
         1. Proof of claims–creditor not filing claim gives trustee or debtor right to file; filed claims allowed unless objection by interested party

a. Claims not allowed–unenforceable against debtor, unmatured, offset against a debt, for insider services or excessive attorney fees

2. Secured claims–lien against property of debtor; unsecured to extent security interest lesser value than allowed claim

3. Priority of claims–secured claims paid first; some classes of unsecured claims fully paid before payment of lesser claims; claimants within priority class share pro ratally when assets insufficient to satisfy entire class claims

4. Subordination of claims–court discretion to apply equitable priorities (based on fairness) to fully pay one claim before paying another of same class.

B. Debtors–face specified duties; exemptions for some property; discharge of most debts (become unenforceable)

1. Debtor's duties–file creditors list, assets/liabilities schedule, statement of financial affairs; cooperate with trustee, surrender all property, transfer property records

2. Debtor's exemptions–Code specifically exempts certain property from creditor claims; debtor's option to use either Code exemptions or state law exemptions

3. Discharge–no debtor liability for dischargeable debts; certain debts nondischargeable; discharge voids judgment against debt, enjoins commencement, continuation of recovery action

C. The Estate–all debtor's legal/equitable interests in nonexempt property at time of filing; estate enlarged by property acquired within 180 days after filing (inheritance, divorce property settlement, insurance proceeds), by trustee recovering as lien creditor, avoiding voidable preferences, fraudulent transfers, statutory liens

1. Trustee as lien creditor–trustee's creditor rights/powers for unsatisfied judicial lien against debtor, priority over creditor with unperfected security interest

2. Voidable preferences–Code invalidates "preferential transfers"; trustee recovers property of insolvent debtor, transferred to creditor for antecedent debt, made within ninety days before filing petition (within one year for "insider" creditor) giving creditor more payment than would have received under proceedings

a. Insolvency–total debt value exceeds total asset value

b. Nonvoidable transfers–exchanges for new value, gaining security interests, "ordinary course" payments, consumer debt, alimony/support payments

3. Fraudulent transfers–made on or within one year before petition filed

a. Types–debtor transfers property with intent to hinder, delay, or defraud creditors; property transfer for less than reasonably equivalent value, while debtor's insolvent or would make debtor so

4. Statutory liens–lien arising by statute not a security interest or judicial lien; avoidable if first becomes effective when debtor becomes insolvent, not perfected or enforceable on filing

IV. Liquidation–Code Chapter 7

A. Proceedings–apply to all debtors except railroads, insurance companies, banks, saving and loan associations, homestead associations and credit unions; filing petition triggers court order for relief and appointment of interim trustee (serves until permanent trustee selected)

B. Dismissal–court on own motion, after notice and hearing, may dismiss case filed by individual debtor with primarily consumer debts

C. Distribution of Estate–assets located, collected, distributed to creditors; remaining distributed to debtor

1. Order of distribution–secured creditors; priority creditors (paid in order provided); unsecured creditors with timely filed claims; creditors with no notice or actual knowledge of debtor's bankruptcy; late filing unsecured creditors; miscellaneous claims, interest on allowed claims from filing date; remainder to debtor

D. Discharge–relieves debtor of all debts arising before date of relief order except nondischargeable debts

1. Denial of discharge–debtor not an individual, destroyed or falsified records, committed fraud, transferred property defrauding creditors, granted a discharge within 6 years, refused to obey court order, failed to explain asset losses, executed a discharge waiver

V. Reorganization–Code Chapter 11–distressed business, value as a going concern, preserved through correcting mismanagement mistakes; applies to partnerships, corporations, sole proprietorships

A. Proceedings–any Chapter 7 debtor (except stockbrokers and commodity brokers) and railroads are eligible; voluntary or involuntary petitions

1. 1994 Reform Act–certain small businesses may elect streamlined procedures to expedite administration after order for relief

2. Committee of unsecured creditors–appointed by court; persons holding seven largest unsecured claims; court may appoint additional committees

3. Debtor possesses/manages estate property unless court appoints trustee to operate business

B. Plan of Reorganization

1. Submission–by debtor, trustee or creditor

2. Content–divide creditors' claims/shareholders' interest into classes, specify how each class will be treated, deal with each equally; show adequate implementation

3. Acceptance of plan–each class of claims accepts or rejects proposed plan

4. Confirmation of plan–by court; based on good faith, feasibility, cash payments to certain classes of creditors, and acceptance by at least one class of claims

C. Effect of Reorganization–confirmation makes plan binding on debtor and all creditors; final decree closes proceedings and discharges debtor.

VI. Family Farmer Debt Adjustment–Chapter 12

A. Scope–individuals, individuals and spouses, engaged in farming receiving 50 percent of gross income from farming, corporation or partnership may qualify

B. Provisions substantially same as Chapter 13

VII. Individual Debt Adjustments–Chapter 13

A. Scope–permits individual debtors to file repayment plan discharging debts when payments completed; applies to individual with regular income who owes liquidated, unsecured debts of less than $260,250 and secured debts of less than $876,750; sole proprietorships are eligible

B. Partnerships, corporations not eligible; case initiated by voluntary petition only, trustee appointed for every case

C. Procedure–debtor files plan, modifiable any time before confirmation; debtor submits all or portion of future earnings/income for executing plan; supervised, controlled by trustee; full payment on deferred basis of all claims entitled to priority unless claim holder objects; plan classifying claims must treat each claim in certain class equally; payments no longer than three years, unless court grants approval up to five years

D. Confirmation–by court if made in good faith
   1. Requirements–property distributed to unsecured creditors not less than what would receive under Chapter 7; secured creditors accept plan, or debtor surrenders collateral to secured creditors, or plan permits secured creditors to retain security interests; value of property distributed to secured creditors not less than allowed amount of their claim; debtor can make all payments, comply with plan; full payment to unsecured creditor objecting to confirmation

E. Effect of Confirmation–debtor free of any creditor's claim or interest provided for under plan; binds debtor and all creditors; plan modified after confirmation at debtor's, trustee's, or unsecured creditor's request

F. Discharge–after completing payments made under plan, debtor discharged of all debts except nondischargeable debts for alimony, maintenance, child support and certain long-term obligations; discharged debtor not subject to Chapter 7 six year limitation
   1. Hardship discharge–granted by court; based on debtor's failure to complete payments due to circumstances beyond debtor's control

VIII. Creditor's Rights/Debtor Relief Outside Bankruptcy–governed by state law; bankruptcy often seen as "last resort"; may be best for debtor/creditors to solve problems/claims outside bankruptcy law

A. Creditor's Rights–sue to collect defaulted debt; obtain judgment; collect on judgment
   1. Prejudgment remedies–stop debtor's disposing assets
      a. Attachment–property in debtor's hands seized, given to court
      b. Garnishment–creditor proceeding against third person holding debtor's property (owes money to debtor)
   2. Postjudgment remedies–creditor proceeds to trial, obtains judgment against debtor; debtor not voluntarily paying judgment triggers postjudgment collection remedies
      a. Writ of execution–sheriff's order demanding debtor pay judgment; nonexempt property seized by sheriff sold at public sale; proceeds of sale not sufficient to cover entire debt triggers deficiency action
      b. Supplementary proceedings–creditor instituted proceeding to locate debtor's property
      c. Garnishment–proceeding against debtor's employer or a bank in which the debtor has account; obtain property, apply to debt

B. Debtor's Relief–conflicts between creditors' rights/debtor relief; creditors pursue claims to judgment, satisfy judgments by sale of debtor's property; social policy to relieve debtor of debts unable to pay

1. Compositions–common law nonstatutory contract between debtor/creditors giving creditors proportional share of payment; debtor discharged from balance owing; requires contractual formalities

2. Assignments for benefits of creditors–common law, nonstatutory voluntary transfer by debtor of property to trustee who applies property to payment of all debtor's debts; prevents attachment, seizure of debtor's assets; halts creditor attachment race; does not require creditor's consent

3. Statutory assignments–attempt to combine assignment with discharge benefit of composition

4. Equity receiverships–court appointed disinterested person (or creditor) collecting, preserving debtor's assets, income; disposes assets at court's direction; court appointment of certain creditor's on showing just qualification

TRUE-FALSE: Circle true or false.

T   F   1. State courts have exclusive jurisdiction over bankruptcy proceedings.

T   F   2. A debtor need not be insolvent to file for voluntary bankruptcy.

T   F   3. All creditors of a debtor share equally in the assets of a debtor discharged in bankruptcy.

T   F   4. A debtor in bankruptcy has a choice of claiming exemptions either under federal bankruptcy law or state law.

T   F   5. Both intentional and negligent tort claims are nondischargeable in bankruptcy.

T   F   6. Creditor claims of equal statutory priority must always be dealt with equally by the bankruptcy court with no claim receiving priority over the others.

T   F   7. In cases of involuntary bankruptcy, a debtor must owe claims totaling at least $15,000 before a petition may be filed.

T   F   8. Not all cases of corporate rehabilitation under Chapter 11 will result in the court appointing a trustee to administer the proceedings.

T   F   9. The only-once-every-six-years limitation for Chapter 7 proceedings does not always apply to cases of wage-earner debtor-adjustment proceedings.

T   F   10. A successfully contested involuntary bankruptcy petition resulting in dismissal of the proceedings may lead to creditor liability for the costs, expenses and damages incurred by the debtor in attacking the petition.

T   F   11. Bankruptcy discharge of a debt does not extinguish any security interest held against the debt.

T   F   12. Once a Chapter 13 debt adjustment has been confirmed, it can only be changed upon a petition brought by secured creditors.

KEY TERMS–MATCHING EXERCISE: Select the term that best completes each statement below.

1. Estate	8. Attachment	15. Reorganization
2. Exemptions	9. Trustee	16. Discharge
3. Composition	10. Bank	17. Confirmation
4. Receiver	11. Straight bankruptcy	18. Writ of execution
5. Priority claim	12. Debt	19. Judicial lien
6. Preference	13. Referee	20. Claim
7. Garnishment	14. Assignment	

_____ 1. A specific sum of money owed to another person.

_____ 2. A contract between a debtor and creditors providing for the pro rata sharing of the creditors in the debtor's assets as satisfaction on the creditors claims.

_____ 3. One who gathers and protects assets of a debtor under an action in equity.

_____ 4. Termination and liquidation of a debtor's financial life.

_____ 5. Claims that must be fully satisfied before payment may be made to other creditors.

_____ 6. Aggregate equitable and legal property interests of the debtor when bankruptcy proceedings are commenced.

_____ 7. Assets that a bankrupt debtor retains title to that are beyond the reach of creditors.

_____ 8. A statutory debt satisfaction proceeding used to seize property of the debtor in the possession of another person.

_____ 9. Bankruptcy proceedings that provide an opportunity for a financially distressed business to preserve its existence by eliminating poor management policies, practices and personnel.

_____ 10. A debt enforcement process by which property of the debtor is taken into court custody and applied towards payment.

_____ 11. Right to payment enforceable against a bankruptcy debtor.

_____ 12. Release from payment obligation through bankruptcy procedure for certain debts.

_____ 13. Creditor's interest in debtor's property obtained through judicial process to secure payment on a debt.

_____ 14. Court approval of a plan for reorganization.

_____ 15. Document obtained by judgment creditor, served on the debtor by a sheriff ordering payment of the judgment debt

MULTIPLE CHOICE: Select the alternative that best completes each statement below.

_____ 1. The two types of petitions used for commencing bankruptcy proceedings are (a) equitable and legal (b) jurisdictional and stipulatory (c) voluntary and involuntary (d) none of the above.

_____ 2. Examples of unallowable claims are (a) ones for matured interest (b) those that are not enforceable against the debtor (c) reasonable attorney's fees (d) all of the above.

_____ 3. Which of the following is not a definitional element of a voidable preference? (a) a property transfer made within 90 days of filing a bankruptcy petition (b) intent to defraud creditors (c) insolvency of the debtor (d) payment on a debt owing before the transfer

_____ 4. The party whose duty is to gather, liquidate and distribute the assets of the debtor is the (a) trustee (b) referee (c) creditor (d) none of the above.

_____ 5. The purpose of bankruptcy is to (a) make equitable payments to creditors (b) discharge a debtor from unmeetable debts (c) enable a debtor to start a new financial life (d) all of the above.

_____ 6. A fraudulent conveyance requires (a) an intent to prefer one creditor over another (b) insolvency of the debtor (c) a transfer of property for little or no return value (d) payment on an antecedent debt.

_____ 7. Of the following claims, which are nondischargeable? (a) alimony payments (b) non-scheduled debts where the creditor had notice of the bankruptcy proceedings (c) payments made subject to a preferential transfer (d) moneys owed to foreign officials

_____ 8. A debtor in bankruptcy must (a) file a joint stipulation with the spouse (b) post a bond with the court amounting to no less than 20% of the aggregate value of all claims owed at time of filing (c) submit a statement of personal preference to the referee (d) file a schedule of assets and liabilities.

_____ 9. Requirements for a reorganization plan to be confirmed by the court include (a) filing petitions with the Secretaries of State for the residences of the creditors (b) feasibility of the plan (c) the plan providing for a minimal 45% return on a claim for each creditor (d) all of the above.

_____ 10. Under a plan of reorganization, creditors with rights of priority to have claims fully satisfied in cash are (a) business partners of the debtor (b) secured creditors (c) employees with wages owing (d) tax officials.

_____ 11. _____ occurs when a debtor voluntarily transfers property to a trustee with the understanding that these assets are to be used for payment on all debts then owing (a) fiduciary trust (b) general assignment (c) extension (d) consolidation loan.

_____ 12. Requirements for the validity of a Chapter 11 reorganization plan include (a) stating how each class of creditor interests/claims will be treated (b) insuring that all claims and interests share assets equally (c) notarized appraisal of the debtor's net worth (d) none of the above.

_____ 13. Automatic stays terminate when a/an (a) debtor is discharged (b) case is closed (c) case is dismissed (d) all of the above.

CASE PROBLEMS–SHORT ESSAY ANSWERS: Read each case problem carefully. When appropriate, answer by stating a Decision for the case and by explaining the rationale–Rule of Law–relied upon to support your decision.

1. Sara Student, finishing her last year of medical school, is worried about the $8,500 in student loans she has outstanding. She seeks advice from her first-year law-school friend, Darence Clarrow, who assures Sarah that if she files for bankruptcy, "all her financial troubles will be over." Is Mr. Clarrow correct? Discuss.

Decision: _____

_____

Rule of Law: _____

_____

2. D, recently discharged in bankruptcy, starts receiving calls from Ajax Appliance who urges D to reaffirm the $1,600 debt D had owed Ajax prior to the proceedings. D, worried about the "dire consequences" that Ajax had been referring to in the calls, decides to enter an agreement with Ajax for full payment on the debt. Is this contract with Ajax, who had notice of D's bankruptcy proceedings, enforceable? Explain.

Decision: _____

_____

Rule of Law: _____

_____

3. D has fallen upon complete financial disaster. With an estate valued at $45,000, D files a Chapter 7 petition listing the following creditors: a $17,000 debt to Creditor One, $10,000 of which is secured; $8,000 in back wages to Creditor Two; $6,000 in unpaid income taxes to the federal government, Creditor Three; a $12,000 unsecured negligence judgment to Creditor Four, who has filed this claim with the court; an unsecured $11,000 breach of contract judgment to Creditor Five, who has also filed a claim; and a $10,000 unsecured loan from D's in-laws who have not filed their claim although they had notice of the proceedings. List how D's $45,000 will be distributed among these creditors.

Decision: _____

_____

Rule of Law: _____

_____

4. Doodles Dingle, his finances in a shambles ($23,000 in liabilities, $4,200 in assets), is spending sleepless nights worrying over the creditor calls that constantly hound him. Having had enough, Doodles files for bankruptcy. At the creditor's meetings it is discovered that eight months prior to Doodles' filing, he had given his sister, Daphne, a $5,200 boat and his brother, Darby, a $7,500 car, both with the understanding that the property would be returned to Doodles when his financial woes were ended. Discuss the significance of Mr. Dingle's transfers.

Decision: _____

_____

Rule of Law: _____

_____

5. Paddywack has over $120,000 tied up in his Knick-Knack Estates realty business. He also has debts of $100,000. With an intent to prefer various creditors over others, Paddywack transfers property worth $15,000 to those creditors. The other creditors ask your advice. Discuss the significance of Paddywack's transfers.

Decision: _____

_____

Rule of Law: _____

_____

DEBTOR AND CREDITOR RELATIONS RESEARCH QUESTIONS:

Drawing upon information contained in the text, as well as outside sources, discuss the following questions.

1. Research your State's law on exempt property. Compare Federal exemptions with your State's exemptions. If you were to file for bankruptcy, which exemption path would you choose and why?

2. Over the past decade, major corporate reorganizations, based on similar financial scenarios, have occurred–Texaco, A.H. Robins, Johns-Mansville, Raybestos, W.R. Grace, and Dow Corning cases. What do these cases have in common? Why did these firms choose bankruptcy as a solution to their problems? Is this a proper use of bankruptcy law?

Chapter 40

PROTECTION OF
INTELLECTUAL PROPERTY

SCOPE NOTE

Since the late 19th century, "laissez-faire's" controlling influence over the proper role of government vis-à-vis business has all but disappeared. In response to the emergence of fraudulent, deceptive and anticompetitive business practices in the private sector (monopolies, contaminated food products, defective consumer products, and the like), the Federal government assumed an increasingly active role in regulating business practices that put competitors at an unfair disadvantage. Chapter 40 examines one aspect of such regulatory intervention intended to promote open, honest, and fair competition–protecting intellectual property rights. The important concepts and principles underlying the statutes, administrative regulations, and court rulings controlling this area of law are discussed in the context of trade symbol, trade secret, copyright and patent protection. Without these laws, America's economic growth and its competitive position in the world market would be threatened.

EDUCATIONAL OBJECTIVES

1. Evaluate policy considerations underlying proscription of false, deceptive and unfair commercial practices relating to intellectual property rights.

2. Distinguish common law doctrines from legislation and administrative regulation intended to protect and redress trade secret, trade symbol and trade name infringement.

3. Describe the purpose and protection mechanisms associated with copyright and patent laws.

4. Explain remedies available for copyright and patent infringement.

CHAPTER OUTLINE

I. Goal/Policy of Law: promote, protect research/innovation in products & services

II. Trade Secrets–commercially valuable, secret information (customer lists, secret formulas, production process)
   A. Employee Duty of Non-Disclosure/Loyalty–not reveal secret information to employer's competitors during time of employment
   B. Misappropriation–wrongful acquisition, use of secret information
      1. Owner's remedies–money damages, injunction
      2. Examples–employee breaches duty of loyalty; competitor's industrial espionage (electronic surveillance)
   C. Employee Rights to Compete With Former Employer
      1. Leave employment and work for competitor
      2. Use prior skills, knowledge unless valid contract restriction (reasonably limited) prevents working for competitor of former employer
   D. Loss of Trade Secrets Protection
      1. Independent inspection of finished product
      2. Independent research
      3. Voluntary disclosure
      4. Negligence of owner–no reasonable protection precautions

III. Trade Symbols–Lanham Act's protection against "palming off" (deception cashing in on competitor's good name, good will or reputation)
   A. Federal Trademark Act Protection
      1. Registration–distinctive marks, labels, designators for goods/services; exclusive use
      2. Infringement protection–money damages, injunctive relief for violating exclusive use
   B. Types of Trade Symbols–identifiers, descriptors
      1. Trademarks–goods
      2. Service marks–distinctive identification of services
      3. Certification marks–distinctive features of goods/services
      4. Collective marks–membership in organization or goods/services produced by specific group
   C. Registration Requirements
      1. Distinctiveness–identifying origin of goods/services (fanciful, arbitrary, unique symbols not description of use, quality, ingredients, or function)
      2. Effect–national, constructive notice of ownership; federal court protection
   D. Loss of Protection–owner fails to use symbol in ordinary course of trade
   E. Infringement–intentional/accidental unauthorized use of protected mark; use of indistinguishable mark causing confusion
      1. Factors examined–intent, degree of similarity, strength of meaning, marketing/sales channels, relation between marks and goods/services

2. Remedies–civil (damages/injunctions), criminal (fines/imprisonment)
   a. Damages–lost profits, attorney's fees, court costs, etc.
   b. Seizure, destruction of "pirate" products

IV. Trade Names–identification of business, occupation
  A. Secondary Meaning Protection–descriptive, personal, generic words, with a special, unique trade meaning
  B. Protection–not specifically in Lanham; damages/injunctive relief for action similar to "palming off"

V. Copyrights–federal legislation exclusively protecting ownership of originally created, authored work in any tangible medium (original expression of an idea)–music, literature, drama, dance, pictures, art, recordings, computer programs, architecture
  A. Procedure–registration not required; protection when work becomes tangible
    1. Registration–required for infringement protection
  B. Scope of Protection–exclusive ownership for creator's life plus 70 years
    1. Compulsory license–limited authorized use with royalty payments
    2. Fair Use Doctrine–limited free use (nature, type, purpose) for teaching, criticism, research, news reporting
  C. Ownership Transfer–sale/gift/inheritance
    1. Written, signed document required
  D. Infringement Remedies–civil damages, injunction (seizure and destruction), fines/imprisonment

VI. Patent–federal protection under Patent Act–creator/inventor's exclusive ownership right; produce, sell, use an invention
  A. Duration of Protection–not renewable; enters "public domain" on expiration
    1. Design–14 years
    2. Others–17 years
  B. License–authorized limited use for royalties
  C. Concept of "Patentability"–innovative process (manufacturing, composition, machine)
    1. Exclusions–basic truths, principles, natural substances, ideas
    2. Factors evaluated–creation's novelty, utility, non-obviousness
  D. Registration Procedure–Patent Office
    1. Application–specific description of operation, unique features, made by inventor
    2. Secret tests conducted by office
    3. Resubmission and appeal for rejection
  E. Infringement
    1. Types–depends on intent, adverse effect
      a. Direct–unauthorized use, sale; good faith mistake no defense
      b. Indirect–active encouragement of others to use/sell without permission
      c. Contributory–selling/supporting components without permission; good faith mistake a defense
    2. Remedies–civil damages and injunction
      a. Possible triple damages, court costs and fees if appropriate

TRUE-FALSE: Circle true or false.

T F 1. Trademark owners are not required to obtain federal registration before using the mark.

T F 2. Employees have a duty not to reveal their employer's secrets to competitors.

T F 3. A copyright lasts for a period of 17 years from the date of first publication.

T F 4. Exclusive monopoly rights exist at the time a patent seeker files an application with the Patent Office.

T F 5. Descriptive, personal and generic words and names may be protected as trade names.

T F 6. For a violation of copyright law to occur, the infringement of the exclusively protected right must be intentional.

T F 7. Patent protection is not renewable.

T F 8. Computer programs are not copyrightable under federal laws.

T F 9. Forces, substances and conditions of nature are not patentable.

T F 10. Copyright protection applies to new ideas or concepts.

T F 11. Trade symbol infringement does not require proof of intentionally caused or actual confusion.

T F 12. The owner of a collective mark is either the producer of the goods or service provider.

KEY TERMS–MATCHING EXERCISE: Select the term that best completes each statement below.

1. Misappropriation	8. Sherman Act	15. Trade name
2. Palming off	9. Economic Espionage Act	16. Compulsory license
3. Trade secret	10. Patent	17. Collective mark
4. Trademark	11. Vertical	18. Works for hire
5. Publication	12. Allonge	19. Service mark
6. Lanham Act	13. Cease & desist order	20. Direct infringer
7. Copyright	14. Infringement	

_____ 1. Unconsented to interference with protected intellectual property interests.

_____ 2. Wrongfully using a trade secret.

_____ 3. Business, vocation or occupation identification.

_____ 4. Federal legislation criminalizing the theft of trade secrets.

_____ 5. Falsely representing one's products as those of another.

_____ 6. Protection given authors of original creative works including music, novels, plays, paintings and sculptures.

_____ 7. A distinguishing symbol identifying tangible goods or products but not services.

_____ 8. Federal grant to an inventor of the exclusive right to produce and sell an invention for a specific period of time.

_____ 9. Federal legislation providing for protective registration of trade symbols.

_____ 10. Confidential information essential to the successful operation of a business.

_____ 11. Indication of trade union or association membership.

_____ 12. An unauthorized user, seller or maker of a patented invention.

_____ 13. Doctrine providing for copyright ownership to be held by non-creators of original works.

_____ 14. Symbol identifying and distinguishing one's services from others.

_____ 15. Permission to make limited use of copyrighted material, usually accompanied by payment of royalties.

MULTIPLE CHOICE: Select the alternative that best completes each statement below.

_____ 1. A process for protecting new distinctive fruits and vegetables is (a) presently nonexistent (b) called a plant patent (c) expressly banned by the Berne Convention (d) none of the above.

_____ 2. Trade secrets include (a) customer lists (b) product formulas (c) production methods (d) all of the above.

_____ 3. _____ meaning refers to the special significance acquired by descriptive, generic words through continued, extensive use connected to specific goods and services. (a) primary (b) popular (c) secondary (d) equitable.

_____ 4. Symbols that are denied protection under Federal registration include (a) titles of TV shows (b) insignia of the United States (c) identification of how products are manufactured (d) all of the above.

_____ 5. One who actively encourages another to commit a patent infringement is referred to as a/n _____ infringer. (a) indirect (b) contributory (c) direct (d) equitable

_____ 6. _____ amended the Lanham Act to prevent famous marks from losing their capacity to identify and distinguish goods or services with which they have been traditionally associated (a) Lanham II (b) Trademark Update Act (c) Trademark Dilution Act (d) Meyers-Moss Trademark Reform Act.

_____ 7. For a patent to be issued, a patent application must contain a/n (a) judicial certification of ownership (b) profit projection and market allocation (c) claims statement and specification (d) all of the above.

_____ 8. Remedies for unintentional violations of the Lanham Act include (a) accounting for profits (b) treble money damages (c) fine and/or imprisonment (d) all of the above.

_____ 9. To accomplish a valid transfer of copyright ownership, _____ is required. (a) consideration (b) a writing signed by the copyright owner (c) recording (d) all of the above.

_____ 10. _____ is the doctrine that allows reproduction of copyrighted works for the purpose of criticism, news reporting, teaching, comment or research without an infringement occurring. (a) Fair Use (b) Main Purpose (c) Reasonable Decency (d) Good Faith.

_____ 11. "U.L." is an example of a (a) service mark (b) tradename (c) collective mark (d) certification mark.

_____ 12. Patentability depends on the (a) dollar value (b) growth potential (c) newness and usefulness (d) none of the above.

_____ 13. Sanctions for Patent Act violations do not include (a) attorneys fees (b) fine or imprisonment (c) treble money damages (d) injunctions.

CASE PROBLEMS–SHORT ESSAY ANSWERS: Read each case problem carefully. When appropriate, answer by stating a Decision for the case and by explaining the rationale–Rule of Law–relied upon to support your decision.

1. Lanny Lantern comes up with a new design for battery-powered portable lamps. Searching for a name to attract and build sales as well as differentiate his product from that of competitors, Lanny coins the word "Portalantern." Lanny attempts to register this as a trademark. Will he be successful?

Decision: _____

_____

Rule of Law: _____

_____

2. A and B have been long-time employees of Toys Manufacturing Company. During their employment, they have acquired highly technical skills and knowledge. A competitor of Toys Company-Playthings, Inc.–offers A and B higher paying jobs if they leave Toys. Their employment contracts with Toys contain no clause prohibiting employment with a competitor. What, if anything, may Toys Manufacturing Co. do to prevent A and B from using the trade secrets of Toys when they go to work for Playthings, Inc.? Explain.

Decision: _____

_____

Rule of Law: _____

_____

3. Following years of expensive, painstaking research, Dr. Science has discovered a cure for the common cold: a strain of bacteria living in the nodules on the backs of Australian green toads. Excited over potential profits and benefits for humans, Dr. Science is asked whether he intends to patent his discovery. Is his reply, "You bet," legally sound? Explain.

Decision: _____

_____

Rule of Law: _____

_____

4. Elsie and Elmer Eskimo of Arctic Circle, Alaska, win $22 million in the Alaska lottery. They move south with their fortune to Guelph, North Dakota. Enjoying the warm climate and cultural wonders of their new home, the Eskimos co-author a book discussing the splendors of Guelph. They apply for and receive, but never register, a copyright for their publication. A few years later, another book, *Guelph, North Dakota: Paradise Found*, is released by Puffer Publishers. The Eskimos, believing the similarities between this book and their earlier work are more than coincidental, sue the authors of the new book for $1.5 million, alleging copyright infringement Who prevails and why?

Decision: _____

_____

Rule of Law: _____

_____

5. Home Products, Inc., markets their shaving cream under the name "Clean and Smooth." Over the past year, sales of the product have slipped substantially. To boost sales, Home launches a nationwide advertising campaign asserting that "Clean and Smooth" bears the American Association of Shaving Cream Producers (which does not exist) seal of hygienic purity. Cans of "Clean and Smooth" are marked with a circled "AASCP," the registered mark of the American Association of Silicone Chip Producers, to indicate such approval. C&S sales jump 200% within months after the first ads appear. Competitors of Home Products, concerned over declining shaving cream sales, seek your advice. What do you tell them?

Decision: _____

_____

Rule of Law: _____

_____

Chapter 41

ANTITRUST

SCOPE NOTE

America's economic philosophy is based on the belief that the public interest (availability and quality of products/services at fair prices, business innovation) is best served through free, fair, and open marketplace competition. Concentration of business power in the hands of a few, through combinations and monopolies, is seen as an unacceptable threat to the benefits of market competition. Chapter 41 examines the law of trade regulation which is intended to deter monopolistic practices and other anticompetitive activities amounting to unreasonable restraints on trade. The sources of antitrust laws, the types of activities prohibited, the role of Federal courts, administrative agencies, and state laws in promoting competitive practices in interstate commerce are discussed. The rights protected under federal/state laws and the remedies provided for unfair, anticompetitive business practices, are reviewed.

EDUCATIONAL OBJECTIVES

1. Evaluate the policy underlying laws proscribing "trusts" and "combinations" that threaten free and open competition.

2. Identify the types of business practices prohibited under Sections 1 and 2 of the Sherman Antitrust Act.

3. Define and develop the importance of the "rule of reason" test.

4. Differentiate the types of activities considered inherently anti-competitive under the Sherman Act.

5. Distinguish among the tests used to determine "monopolization" under the Sherman Act.

6. Know the types of acts prohibited under the Clayton Act–tying contracts; mergers; and exclusive dealings.

7. Explain how the Robinson-Patman Act strengthened government regulation of anti-competitive business practices.

8. Discuss the role of the FTC and the Justice Department in promoting fair, open, honest and free competition.

CHAPTER OUTLINE

I. Sherman Antitrust Act–prohibits contracts, combinations, conspiracies restraining trade; outlaws monopolies, attempts to monopolize
   A. Violations punished by prison (up to 3 years) and/or fines up to $350,000 for individuals, corporate officials up to $10,000,000
      1. Federal courts issue injunctions to restrain violations
      2. Civil suit for treble damages (three times actual loss) by injured parties
      3. Enforced by Department of Justice
      4. Jurisdiction applies to foreign companies
   B. Restraint of Trade Section–prohibits group restraints (conspiracy)
      1. Standards–courts invalidate only unreasonable restraints
         a. "Rule of reason test"–balance anticompetitive effects against procompetitive effects of restraint; U.S. Supreme Court declares certain restraints unreasonable, illegal *per se* (plaintiff need only show type of restraint occurred, presumably limiting competition, shifting burden of disproof on defendant)
      2. Horizontal restraint–collaboration among competitors at same level in distribution chain–(among manufacturers, retailers) considered illegal *per se*
      3. Vertical restraint–collaborating parties not directly competitive at same level of distribution (among manufacturer and wholesaler, or either and retailer); controlled by rule of reason
      4. Concerted action–unilateral conduct not prohibited; only concerted action (express agreement or circumstantial evidence); conscious parallelism (similar patterns of conduct among competitors) not itself a conspiracy
      5. Price fixing–purpose, effect to inhibit price competition; horizontal agreements illegal *per se*
         a. Retail price maintenance (vertical price fixing by wholesaler setting price at which purchaser-retailer must resell product) *per se* violation; covers any agreement to establish maximum/minimum prices
      6. Market allocation–competitors agree not to compete in specified markets (geographic area, type of customer or product, etc.)
         a. Horizontal agreements dividing markets–illegal *per se* (remaining firm in market controls price)
         b. Vertical territorial/customer restrictions–not illegal *per se;* judged by rule of reason; Justice Department uses "market structure screen" when applying rule of reason

7. Boycotts–seller's refusal to deal with particular buyer not violation since not a conspiracy, only unilateral action (manufacture refuses to sell to retailer selling below manufacturers suggested retail price)
   a. Group boycotts prohibited–concerted refusal to deal (parties agree not to deal with third party); some illegal *per se*, others subject to rule of reason

8. Tying arrangements–selling desired product (tying product–copier) conditioned upon purchasing second product (tied product–paper)
   a. Effect–limits buyer's freedom of choice, excludes competitors; seller exploits economic power in one market to expand into another *per se* illegal; seller without such economic power makes tying arrangements subject to rule of reason

C. Monopolies–Section 2; anticompetitive group/unilateral use of power limiting production, increasing prices, producing fewer goods; prohibited monopolies include attempts and conspiracies
   1. Monopolization–courts interpret Section 2 to require either unfair attainment of monopoly power or abusive use of power once attained; mere possession of market power not sufficient
      a. Monopoly power requirement–ability to control price, exclude competitors; issue of degree of market dominance constituting monopoly power
         (1) Market Share–fractional share of total relevant product, geographic markets; most common test of monopoly power; includes similar products, based on price, quality, adaptability in given territory (local, regional or national)
      b. Unfair conduct requirement–tests for determining, factors indicating
         (1) Passive vs. active acquisition of monopoly power
         (2) Conduct intended to exclude competition
         (3) Predatory practices (pricing, dealership controls, etc.)
   2. Attempts to monopolize–prohibited; requires specific intent to monopolize, dangerous probability of success
   3. Conspiracies to monopolize–combination in restraint of trade violating both Sections 1 and 2

II. 1914 Clayton Act–strengthens Sherman Act; allows federal civil actions by private parties, Justice Department, Federal Trade Commission to prevent violations (price discrimination, tying contracts, exclusive dealing, mergers)
   A. Tying Contracts/Exclusive Dealing–arrangements preventing purchasers from dealing with seller's competitors, substantially lessening competition; applies only to practices involving commodities; prohibits arrangements conditioning product sale/lease to not dealing with competitor's product
   B. Mergers–acquisition of competitor's stock/assets substantially lessening competition, tending to create a monopoly–horizontal, vertical, or conglomerate
      1. Horizontal–company acquires all, part of competitor's stock/assets
      2. Vertical–company acquires customers (forward) or suppliers (backward) stock/assets
      3. Conglomerate–acquisition not involving competitor, customer, or supplier
      4. Factors reviewed for legality of each merger–competition patterns, control of market

III. Robinson-Patman Act–amended Clayton Act; prohibits buyers from inducing, sellers from granting, price discrimination in interstate commerce of commodities of similar grade/quality; prohibited price discrimination substantially lessens competition, tends to create a monopoly; sellers prevented from granting discounts to buyers, unless same discounts offered to all other purchasers on proportionately equal terms; liability on both buyer, seller
   A. Permitted Price, Differential–proof of either seller's cost savings or good faith effort to meet competitor's lawful price
   B. Primary-Line Injury–injuries to sellers' competitors; plaintiff must show intent to harm competition (predatory pricing), actual resulting competitive harm
   C. Secondary-Line Injury–discounts to large buyers; harm to competition of favored customer; plaintiff must show substantial, sustained intra-market price differentials or show actual harm to competition
   D. Recognized Defenses–good faith, commercially reasonable practices
      1. Cost justification–seller saves cost by selling to particular buyer
      2. Meeting competition–seller lowers price to meet competition; seller acts reasonably in setting price.
      3. Changing market conditions–product demand, economic decline

IV. 1914 Federal Trade Commission Act–created Federal Trade Commission (FTC); prevent unfair methods of competition, unfair/deceptive business practices
   A. Commission–conducts investigations, hearings
   B. Cease and Desist Orders–effect of injunction; enforced by federal court
   C. Enforcement Options–affirmative disclosure, corrective advertising, granting licenses to patent users
   D. Prohibited Practices
      1. Unfairness–false advertising, shipping unordered goods, pressure sales tactics, promoting employee disloyalty
      2. Deception–misrepresenting quality, endorsement, savings, trademark/name use

TRUE-FALSE: Circle true or false.

T   F   1. Court decisions have had a major impact on defining what constitutes Sherman Act Section 1 violations since that Section is broadly worded.

T   F   2. For business practices to constitute prohibited monopolization attempts, both an intent to monopolize and a probability of success must be shown.

T   F   3. Violations of the Clayton Act are punished with criminal penalties.

T   F   4. A major objective of the Sherman Act is to promote free, open competition in the marketplace.

T   F   5. Price differentials are always Robinson-Patman violations regardless of whether they are based on cost savings or attempts to match competition prices.

T   F   6. Generally, monopolization by itself is sufficient to constitute a violation of the Sherman Act

T   F   7. Under terms of the antitrust settlement reached between Microsoft and the Department of Justice, Microsoft's competitors using Microsoft software in their computers may integrate non-Microsoft products and "desk shortcuts" into the computers.

T   F   8. A victim of a violation of the Sherman Antitrust Act is allowed to recover no more than twice the amount of actual loss suffered from the violation.

T   F   9. The U.S. Supreme Court has ruled that present/wholly owned subsidiary trade restraints are not Sherman Act violations.

T   F   10. Horticulture, labor and agricultural organizations are specifically subject to antitrust regulation by the Clayton Act.

T   F   11. The primary goal of antitrust law is to promote and protect free, fair and open competition in the marketplace.

T   F   12. Unilateral conduct by a single business can constitute an illegal restraint of trade under Section 1 of the Sherman Act.

KEY TERMS–MATCHING EXERCISE: Select the term that best completes each statement below.

1. Disparagement

2. Conglomerate merger

3. Exclusive dealing contracts

4. Boycott

5. Sherman Act

6. Market share

7. Monopoly power

8. Interlocking Directorate

9. Rule of reason

10. Horizontal

11. Vertical merger

12. Market allocations

13. Cease and desist order

14. Tying arrangements

15. Per se violations

16. Cost justification

17. National Cooperative Research Act

18. Robinson-Patman Act

19. Injunction

20. Retail price maintenance

_____ 1. Business arrangements that prevent buyers from doing business with competitors of a seller.

_____ 2. Ability of an enterprise to control prices or access to a marketplace.

_____ 3. Business arrangements considered automatic violations of antitrust laws.

_____ 4. Doctrine stating that only business arrangements that create unreasonable restraints of trade are violations of the Sherman Antitrust Act.

_____ 5. Business contracts that require a purchaser to buy more than one product from the seller.

_____ 6. Directives calling for an immediate halt to business practices and agreements that violate antitrust laws.

_____ 7. Refusal to do business with someone.

_____ 8. Antitrust violations involving restraint of trade agreements among competing retailers.

_____ 9. A test to determine whether an enterprise's control of a market is monopolistic based on product and geographic factors.

_____ 10. Illegal restraints of trade involving collaboration among competing enterprises to refrain from competition in specified markets.

_____ 11. Law passed by Congress to promote new technology research and development through joint ventures.

_____ 12. Manufacturers setting the prices at which retailers must sell products.

_____ 13. Defense to alleged Robinson-Patman violations based on documented cost differences among competing buyers.

_____ 14. A company purchasing one of its customers or suppliers.

_____ 15. Federal legislation outlawing practices that are monopolistic and restrain trade.

MULTIPLE CHOICE: Select the alternative that best completes each statement below.

_____ 1. Which of the following factors is not examined by courts to determine whether a horizontal merger violates the Clayton Act? (1) market share of each enterprise (b) extent of industry concentration and price competition (c) extent of market demand (d) gross capitalization value of the newly merged firm

_____ 2. FTC remedial options include (a) contribution (b) corrective advertising (c) receivership (d) all of the above.

_____ 3. Which of the following types of business transactions is a "per se" violation of Antitrust Statutes? (a) floating contracts (b) territorial allocation of markets (c) unilateral boycotts (d) none of the above

_____ 4. The Federal Trade Commission was established to (a) enforce state bankruptcy acts (b) draft a model antitrust code (c) supplement the Sherman and Clayton Antitrust Acts (d) enforce Fair Trade Statutes.

_____ 5. _____ refers to the area in which a firm sells its products or services. (a) geographic market (b) concentrated share (c) product market (d) none of the above.

_____ 6. Acquisition of the stock or assets of a competing company is referred to as a/n (a) vertical merger (b) conglomerate merger (c) horizontal merger (d) none of the above.

_____ 7. The FTC investigates (a) false or misleading advertising (b) stock swindles (c) fraudulent equitable receiverships (d) all of the above.

_____ 8. Which of the following acts prohibits price discrimination? (a) Lanham Act (b) Federal Trade Act (c) Robinson-Patman Act (d) Unfair Sales Act.

_____ 9. Restraints of trade among businesses at different distribution levels are labeled (a) triangular (b) vertical (c) multiple (d) equitable antitrust violations.

_____ 10. _____ injuries are Clayton Act Section 2 violations that cause harm to a seller's competitors. (a) tertiary (b) unconscionable (c) secondary line (d) primary line.

_____ 11. Factors assessed in determining geographic market share include (a) transportation costs (b) competitive product quality (c) marketplace efficiencies (d) all of the above.

_____ 12. Examples of "unfair conduct" under Section 2 of the Sherman Act include (a) technological advances (b) research and development efficiencies (c) activities intended to exclude competition (d) none of the above.

_____ 13. Antitrust law examines _____ to determine whether a merger violates antitrust. (a) absolute size of merged entry (b) size of merged firm relative to geographic and/or product market share (c) degree of unfair conduct (d) none of the above.

CASE PROBLEMS–SHORT ESSAY ANSWERS: Read each case problem carefully. When appropriate, answer by stating a Decision for the case and by explaining the rationale–Rule of Law–relied upon to support your decision.

1. Super Oil Company has contracts with its independent retail stations requiring them to purchase and sell only the Super Oil line of tires, batteries and auto accessories. Discuss the validity of this business arrangement.

   Decision: _____

   _____

   Rule of Law: _____

   _____

2. Whiskey, Inc., a liquor distributor, affixes a price tag to every bottle leaving its plant and requires all retailers handling its products to sell at the stated price. Discuss the significance of this business relationship.

   Decision: _____

   _____

   Rule of Law: _____

   _____

3. Home Furnishing, Inc., a retail furniture store, entered into an agreement with its supplier to sell Home Furnishing's inventory at prices below what the supplier was charging other retail furniture outlets in the same area. Learning of Home Furnishing's contract with the supplier, competitors argued that the agreement violated antitrust laws. Are they correct? Discuss.

   Decision: _____

   _____

   Rule of Law: _____

   _____

4. Pewtrid Paints, Inc., a manufacturer and retailer of paint products, is conducting a special advertising promotion offering one gallon of paint "free" with every two gallons purchased. The regular price of the paint is $9.99 a gallon. During this advertising campaign, Pewtrid raised its prices to $13.99 a gallon. Is this a violation of the FTC Act? Explain.

Decision: _____

_____

Rule of Law: _____

_____

5. Metropolis County Bar Association issued a minimum fees schedule to its member attorneys requiring all members to abide by the schedule or face "disciplinary" action. Does this action constitute a violation of the Sherman Act? Discuss.

Decision: _____

_____

Rule of Law: _____

_____

Chapter 42

CONSUMER PROTECTION

SCOPE NOTE

Over the past few decades, law has shown an increased concern for recognizing and protecting the rights of consumer purchasers. At state and federal levels, legislation, court decisions, and administrative rulings have assumed greater importance in equalizing the relationship between buyers and sellers in the consumer marketplace. Today's consumers are less at the mercy of *caveat emptor* (let the buyer beware) when they enter the marketplace. They have greater security in knowing that their contractual expectations will be satisfactorily met. Chapter 42 offers an overview of significant federal legislation designed to advance and protect the rights of purchasers at various stages and in certain types of consumer transactions. The policy underlying these laws is to recognize and give legal meaning to the various rights consumers assert under the "Consumer Bill of Rights": right to safety; right to information; right to recovery; right to fairness; and right to satisfactory fulfillment of contractual expectations. Chapter 42 examines the legal principles and policies of consumer protection in the context of credit transactions, real estate purchases, warranty coverage, safety, deceptive selling tactics and equality of bargaining positions.

EDUCATIONAL OBJECTIVES

1. Explain the policy underlying the emergence and growth of consumer protection laws.

2. Discuss the role of the Federal Trade Commission in controlling and preventing deceptive trade tactics and abusive, unfair warranty coverage practices.

3. Identify and discuss the purpose and authority of the Consumer Product Safety Commission.

4. Know the purpose and provisions of the Magnuson-Moss Warranty Act.

5. Explain the purpose and effects of the Equal Credit Opportunity Act, the Fair Credit Billing Act, the Fair Credit Reporting Act, the Fair Debt Collection Practices Act, the Credit Card Fraud Act, the Real Estate Settlement Procedures Act and Truth in Lending.

CHAPTER OUTLINE

I. State and Federal Consumer Protection Law–primarily legislative and administrative law
    A. State and Local Consumer Protection Agencies–focus on fraudulent/deceptive trade practices, fraudulent sales practices, helping consumers resolve complaints over defective goods, poor service
    B. Federal Trade Commission–1914; regulates unfair, deceptive trade practices; issues substantive rules, conducts investigations and hearings, issues cease and desist orders
        1. Standards–policy statements, guidelines based on cost/benefit analysis
            a. Unfairness–potential for exploitation
            b. Deception–misrepresentation, omission or practice likely to cause harm, mislead consumers acting reasonably
            c. Ad substantiation–advertisers must have reasonable basis for accuracy of claims at time they are made
        2. Remedies
            a. Affirmative disclosure–offender must provide certain information in advertisement to prevent deception
            b. Corrective advertising–disclosure that previous ads were deceptive
            c. Multiple product orders–requires deceptive advertiser to cease and desists making deceptive statements on all products
    C. Consumer Product Safety Commission–Consumer Product Safety Act (CPSA)–sets safety standards for consumer products, bans unsafe products, issues administrative "recall" orders for repair, replacement, refunds for hazardous defective products
    D. Other Federal Consumer Protection Agencies
        1. National Highway Traffic Safety Administration (NHTSA)–sets safety standards for motor vehicles; researches crash prevention and crashworthiness
        2. Food and Drug Administration (FDA)–sets standards for consumable products, requires premarket testing and approval of products to regulate adulterated, unsafe and misbranded food and medicine

II. Consumer Purchase Regulation–UCC primary law providing protection; common law, federal/state statutes also provide protection
    A. Federal Warranty Protection–1974–Magnuson-Moss Warranty Act; requires sellers of consumer products to give adequate warranty information; FTC enforced; applies to consumer products with written warranties
        1. Presale disclosures–prevent confusion/deception, enable purchasers to make informed product comparisons; warranty must fully, conspicuously, simply disclose terms and conditions

      2. Labeling requirements–written warranties divided into "limited"/"full"
         a. Full warranty–warrantor repairs, replaces defective product, or refunds purchase price if unrepairable; no limitation placed on duration of any implied warranty
         b. Limited warranty–any warranty not designated as full
      3. Limitations on disclaimers–written warranty may not disclaim any implied warranty; full warranty must not disclaim, modify, or limit any implied warranty; limited warranty may not disclaim or modify any implied warranty but may limit duration to that of written warranty

  B. State "Lemon Laws"–state legislation providing rights to new car purchasers similar to full warranties under Magnuson-Moss
      1. Lemon–defective car continues to have defects substantially impairing use, value, or safety after several attempts at repair
      2. Laws require manufacturer to repair defect, replace car or refund purchase price, if defect unrepairable

  C. Consumer Recission Rights–right to cancel contract; statutes allow consumer brief period (two or three business days) to rescind an otherwise binding credit obligation in home solicitation sales
      1. FTC trade regulation–door-to-door sales of goods/services more than $25; consumer cancellation right within three business days of signing contract
      2. Federal Consumer Credit Protection Act (FCCPA)–consumer three day cancellation right for credit obligation secured by a second mortgage on home
      3. Interstate Land Sales Full Disclosure Act–developer of unimproved land must file detailed statement of information about subdivisions with HUD before offering lots for sale/lease; must provide property report to prospective purchasers or lessees; seven day cancellation period when property report given; two year revocation period when no report given buyer

III. Consumer Credit Transactions–absent special regulation, consumer credit transactions governed by laws regulating commercial transactions
  A. Definitions–credit transaction involving goods, services, land acquired for personal, household, family purpose
  B. Federal Consumer Credit Protection Act (FCCPA)–requires disclosures of finance charges, credit extension charges, sets limits on garnishment proceedings
  C. Uniform Consumer Credit Code (UCCC)–integrates into single law all state regulation of consumer credit transactions
  D. Access to the Market–Equal Credit Opportunity Act prohibits businesses, regularly extending credit, from discriminating based on sex, marital status, race, color, religion, national origin, or age; enforced by FTC
  E. Disclosure Requirements–FCCPA Truth-in-Lending; supersedes state disclosure requirements; covers credit terms for consumer loans, credit sales under $25,000; requires finance charges, interest be stated as APR (annual percentage rate), calculated on a uniform basis; enforced by Federal Reserve Regulation Z

1. Fair Credit/Charge Card Disclosure Act–requires all credit/charge card applications, solicitations to disclose certain information
   a. Revolving open-ended credit–disclose time/method of finance charge computation, retention of security interest; applies to retail, bank credit cards
   b. Closed-ended credit–credit extension for specified period; periodic payments made in fixed amounts over fixed time agreed in advance
2. ARMs–disclosure rule for closed-ended loans, secured by debtor's principal residence, longer than a year, subject to interest rate changes
3. Home equity loans–Home Equity Loan Consumer Protection Act (HELCPA); lenders must provide disclosure statement, consumer pamphlet to prospective borrowers; applies to all open-end credit plans secured by consumer's principal dwelling
   a. Disclosure content–default triggers loss of home, contract terms, creditor acceleration option, debtor three day cancellation right
4. Billing errors–Fair Credit Billing Act–procedures for consumer to follow to complain about billing errors
5. Real Estate Settlement Procedures Act (RESPA)–information on nature, cost of settlement process related to home buying/refinancing; prohibits unnecessarily high settlement charges, kickbacks and referral fees; enforced by HUD

F. Contract Terms–standardized forms facilitate transferring creditor rights to third parties; state statutory ceilings (usury limits) on interest charges, no prepayment penalties;
   1. FTC rule–limits holder in due course rights for consumer credit contract commercial paper; similar rule for credit card issuers under Fair Credit Billing Act

G. Consumer Credit Card Fraud–covered by Credit Card Fraud Act; prohibits possessing/using unauthorized cards, counterfeiting credit cards; FCCPA credit card holder unauthorized use loss protection limit of $50 (no holder liability if proper notice given)

H. Fair Reportage–Fair Credit Reporting Act; applies to consumer credit reports used for securing employment, insurance, credit; prohibits inaccurate, obsolete information in consumer reports; requires written advance notice to consumers of report being made; consumer rights to request information in agency files, notification of disagreement with accuracy/completeness of information, require agency investigation and counter information

I. Creditors' Remedies–means of enforcing debt payment upon debtor's default; declare entire balance immediately due and payable (acceleration clause), sue on the debt, foreclose against collateral
   1. Wage assignments and garnishments–some states prohibit wage assignments; FCCPA, most state laws limit amount that may be deducted per pay period; FCCPA prohibits discharge of employee because of wage assignment/garnishment
   2. Security interest–creditor takes possession of collateral, retains as full satisfaction of debt or sells it, applies sale proceeds to debt on default; creditor sues for balance (deficiency judgment) if sale proceeds less than debt balance
   3. Debt collection practices–Fair Debt Collection Practices Act; eliminate commercial collection agency abusive, deceptive, unfair practices in collecting consumer debts; enforced by FTC; consumer's money damages recovery for collection agency violations

TRUE-FALSE: Circle true or false.

T   F   1. Lack of coordination and inconsistent consumer laws among the states create few problems and complications for interstate businesses.

T   F   2. Under Federal warranty law, written warranties may not disclaim implied warranty protection.

T   F   3. A Sears credit card, a Texaco credit card, and an American Express credit card are examples of open-ended credit accounts.

T   F   4. When a credit card is lost, the card issuer must be notified within 24 hours of the loss, otherwise the card owner will be liable for all purchases made by the finder.

T   F   5. The doctrine of caveat emptor is a long-standing, fundamental doctrine of the American free enterprise system that controls today's consumer marketplace.

T   F   6. The Warner-Lambert case illustrates the FTC's power to order corrective advertising.

T   F   7. The two basic elements of a credit transaction that must be disclosed to the borrower by the lender are loan repayment terms and the cost of the loan.

T   F   8 A secured creditor may repossess the goods sold from a defaulting debtor-purchaser and retain them as full satisfaction on the debt under all circumstances.

T   F   9. Federal warranty regulations require that written warranty protection be given to buyers in all consumer sales over $50 in value.

T   F   10. Under the FTC's ad substantiation policy, advertisers must have a reasonable basis for the claims made in the advertisement at the time they are made.

T   F   11. The FTC Act contains provisions that specifically define what constitutes unfair or deceptive practices.

T   F   12. The Home Equity Loan Consumer Protection Act includes second homes and vacation homes under its definition of principal dwelling.

KEY TERMS–MATCHING EXERCISE: Select the term that best completes each statement below.

---

1. Equal Credit Opportunity Act

2. Foreclosure

3. Waiver of abatement

4. Affirmative disclosure

5. Closed-ended

6. Rebate

7. Federal Trade Commission

8. Magnuson-Moss Act

9. Fair Debt Collection Practices Act

10. Cease and desist order

11. Hazardous Product Act

12. Consumer transaction

13. Fair Credit Billing Act

14. Consumer Product Safety Act

15. Interstate Land Sales Full Disclosure Act

16. Full

17. Truth in Lending

18. Fair Credit Reporting Act

19. Community Reinvestment Act

20. Limited

_____ 1. A single transaction issuance of non-revolving credit for a specific period of time.

_____ 2. A federal agency responsible for investigating unfair, deceptive fraudulent and misleading business practices.

_____ 3. Federal legislation designed to prevent deception and unfairness in consumer product warranties.

_____ 4. Federal legislation requiring that "statements of record" be filed in certain sales of unimproved land.

_____ 5. Federal legislation designed to end abusive, unfair debt enforcement tactics used by collection agencies.

_____ 6. A purchase of goods, services or credit for family, household or personal use.

_____ 7. A directive requiring businesses to halt deceptive or unfair practices.

_____ 8. Federal legislation enacted to protect purchasers of consumer goods from hazards associated with defective goods.

_____ 9. An FTC remedial device requiring advertisers to include in ad copy factual statements that reduce the likelihood of deception or misrepresentation.

_____ 10. Federal legislation prohibiting discriminatory extensions of credit.

_____ 11. Federal legislation designed to promote money expenditures in the geographic areas served by financial institutions.

_____ 12. Warranty granting purchaser rights of refund or replacement for unrepairable defects as well no-cost repair services.

_____ 13. Federal legislation requiring the disclosure of consumer credit costs

_____ 14. Federal legislation designed to eliminate various problems associated with credit billing errors.

_____ 15. Federal legislation designed to insure accuracy and updatedness of consumer credit information.

MULTIPLE CHOICE: Select the alternative that best completes each statement below.

_____ 1. The total charges payable to the creditor by the debtor in a consumer credit transaction is called a (a) carrying charge (b) lender's fee (c) finance charge (d) credit fee.

_____ 2. Purchasers of consumer credit who use their homes as collateral in the consumer transaction may effectively cancel the security interest (a) by telephone (b) in writing if done within three days after the transaction (c) only with the consent of the credit extender (d) none of the above.

_____ 3. The goals of Truth in Lending include: (a) promoting competition among credit extenders (b) facilitating comparison shopping for credit terms (c) increasing stability in the consumer credit marketplace (d) all of the above.

_____ 4. The cost of consumer credit must be expressed in an (a) annual percentage rate (b) appraisal fee ratio (c) allocated monthly formula (d) appreciated rate schedule.

_____ 5. Appeals from FTC orders are taken to (a) Federal District Court (b) U.S. Supreme Court (c) U.S. Court of Appeals (d) Federal Court of Claims.

_____ 6. Federal law provides for a three-day cooling-off period in (a) purchases of all major appliances (b) door-to-door sales over $25 in value (c) car sales over $6,000 (d) none of the above.

_____ 7. Federal warranty law requires that written warranties (a) be written in plain language (b) contain the description label "full" or "limited" (c) explain informal dispute settlement procedures (d) all of the above.

_____ 8. State legislation granting new car buyers refund or replacement rights for unrepairable defects is called (a) lemon (b) equitable allocation (c) lime aid (d) perpetuity laws.

_____ 9. Most FTC consumer protection actions are based on (a) unfairness (b) deception (c) negligence (d) fraud.

_____ 10. Information available to a consumer under the Fair Credit Reporting Act includes (a) the actual contents of a credit report file (b) the names of people from whom information was obtained (c) the source of the information (d) all of the above.

_____ 11. General nonfactual statements of opinion that the FTC does not consider unfair or deceptive are called (a) disclosures (b) puffery (c) warranties (d) disclaimers.

_____ 12. A Federal consumer protection agency with authority to regulate misbranded and adulterated products is the (a) National Safety Council (b) Wholesome Food Association (c) Safe Products Council (d) Food and Drug Administration.

_____ 13. The Real Estate Settlement Procedures Act (a) seeks to provide residential home purchasers accurate cost information regarding home purchases (b) grants home buyers a three day cooling off period to insure satisfaction with a home purchase (c) places a ceiling on mortgage interest rates (d) all of the above.

CASE PROBLEMS–SHORT ESSAY ANSWERS: Read each case problem carefully. When appropriate, answer by stating a Decision for the case and by explaining the rationale–Rule of Law–relied upon to support your decision.

1. Jackson was sent an unrequested credit card from Plakton Petroleum Corporation as part of a promotional campaign. The card was stolen from Jackson's mailbox. The thief made purchases of $250 with the card. When Plakton sends Jackson a monthly statement containing the $250 in charges, what amount will Jackson be responsible for? Explain.

   Decision: _____

   _____

   Rule of Law: _____

   _____

2. P bought $850 worth of furniture from S under an installment vendor credit contract. P is unable to make the fifth $85 monthly payment and enters a wage assignment agreement with S. S notifies P's employer E to apply a percentage of P's wages to the debt. E, greatly upset over the bookkeeping complications the wage assignment might cause, threatens to discharge P unless the debt to S is quickly paid off. Are E's actions legal?

   Decision: _____

   _____

   Rule of Law: _____

   _____

3. B purchased a new car from car dealer C. Under the terms of the credit agreement, B was to make 35 $160 monthly payments. A final monthly payment of $1,600 was called for to complete the purchase. If B falls on financial hard times and cannot make the final $1,600 payment, does B lose the car? Discuss.

Decision: _____

_____

Rule of Law: _____

_____

4. B purchases a lawnmower from S for $450. The written contract contains a clause stating that no warranties, express or implied, run with the sale. After two weeks of use, the mower breaks down. Has B any recourse through the Magnuson-Moss Act against S? Explain.

Decision: _____

_____

Rule of Law: _____

_____

5. New York married couple H and W receives a promotional flyer in the mail from Desert Land Sales Corp. of Arizona. The flyer advertises undeveloped one-acre sites as part of a 250-acre residential development in Suntown, Arizona. H and W, deciding the deal and its terms are quite appealing, sign for the purchase of one site. Other than the sales contract itself, H and W were given no other printed materials from Desert Land prior to or following their signing of the contract. Seven months after entering the agreement with Desert Land, H and W are laid off from work. Unable to make payment on their contract with Desert Land, they seek your advice. What will you tell them?

Decision: _____

_____

Rule of Law: _____

_____

Chapter 43

EMPLOYMENT LAW

SCOPE NOTE

Chapter 43 examines state and federal laws that regulate crucial aspects of employer-employee relations. Prior to the industrial revolution, most issues related to working conditions and employment practices were dealt with through contract and tort law. Following the industrial revolution, the personal relationship that characterized pre-industrial employer-employee relations was no longer an effective regulatory mechanism. The need arose for more formal intervention to resolve the problems of labor-management relations, job injuries, unemployment and other issues. This Chapter discusses those laws promoting worker safety, prohibiting discriminatory employment practices, protecting equal bargaining power between employer and employee, and providing worker economic protections.

EDUCATIONAL OBJECTIVES

1. Evaluate the policies underlying federal labor relations law.

2. Explain the scope and purpose of federal law regulating labor-management relations in the context of unionization and collective bargaining efforts.

3. Discuss the policy and scope of federal laws prohibiting discriminatory employment practices.

4. Outline state and federal laws dealing with worker safety issues, worker and unemployment compensation, job security and "civil" working conditions.

CHAPTER OUTLINE

I. Labor Law–statutory framework for management/labor negotiations over employment terms; promote labor-management cooperation

    A. Norris-LaGuardia Act–1932; prevents federal courts issuing injunctions in nonviolent labor disputes (any controversy concerning terms or conditions of employment or union representation); labor has freedom to form unions; prohibits "yellow dog" contracts (employees agree not to join a union)

    B. National Labor Relations Act (NLRA, Wagner Act)–1935; federal support for collective bargaining and unionization; employee right to be represented by union

        1. Prohibits employer unfair labor practices–interference with right to unionize, discrimination against union members, refusing to bargain in good faith

        2. Establishes National Labor Relations Board (NLRB)–remedy unfair labor practices, supervise elections, mediate disputes

    C. Labor-Management Relations Act (LMRA or Taft-Hartley Act)–1947; response to increased union membership, labor unrest

        1. Prohibits union unfair practices–coercing employees to join union, forcing employers to discharge nonunion employees, refusing to bargain in good faith, excessive union dues, featherbedding, engaging in secondary activities (boycotts, strikes, or picketing someone with no labor dispute against)

        2. Protects employer free speech–no employer unfair labor practice based on statement of opinion

        3. Prohibits closed shop–contract requiring employer to hire only union members; union shop contract permits employer to hire nonunion members but requires them to join union within specified period after being hired; state right-to-work law prohibits union shop contracts

        4. Reinstates civil injunctions in labor disputes if requested by NLRB to prevent an unfair labor practice

        5. Grants president power to obtain an injunction for eighty-day cooling-off period

    D. Labor-Management Reporting and Disclosure Act (Landrum-Griffin)–1959; eliminate corruption in labor unions; enacted union "bill of rights" to make unions more democratic

II. Employment Discrimination Law–federal statutes prohibiting discrimination based on race, sex, religion, national origin, age, and handicap; most states have similar laws

    A. Equal Pay Act–prohibits pay discrimination based on sex; equal wages for same work unless pay differential based on seniority, merit system, measuring earnings by quantity/quality of production, or other non-sex factor

        1. Remedies–back pay, liquidated damages, injunctions

        2. Enforced by Equal Employment Opportunity Commission (EEOC)

    B. 1964 Civil Rights Act–Title VII prohibits employment discrimination based on race, color, sex, religion, or national origin in hiring, firing, pay, promoting or training; applies to pregnant women; covers employers with fifteen or more employees; enforced by EEOC

1. Types of discrimination
   a. Disparate treatment–*prima facie* case of discrimination shown if plaintiff within protected class, applied for open position, was qualified for position, was denied job, and employer continued to try to fill position
   b. Present effects of past discrimination–employer conduct "neutral," nondiscriminatory on face but illegal if perpetuates past discriminatory practices
   c. Disparate impact–"neutral" rules illegal if adverse impact on protected class, not necessary to business
2. Defenses–*bona fide* seniority or merit system, professional ability test, *bona fide* occupational qualification (BFOQ)
3. Remedies–injunctions, affirmative action (active recruitment of a designated group of applicants) reinstatement of employees, award of back pay
4. Areas of controversy
   a. Reverse discrimination–affirmative action (directing employer to remedy race/sex underrepresentation in traditionally segregated job by considering race/gender when hiring or promoting) challenged as illegal reverse discrimination, subject to strict scrutiny test under 14th Amendment Equal Protection
   b. Sexual harassment–possible sexual discrimination violating Title VII; employer liable for sexual harassment committed by employee if knew or should have known of harassment; employee agent, supervisor over victim, makes employer liable even without knowledge, reason to know, of employee's misconduct
   c. Comparable worth–Equal Pay Act does not apply to similar but different jobs; no remedy for women whose jobs are systematically undervalued, underpaid; doctrine looks at relative values (training, experience, responsibility) of different jobs, measured through rating systems or job evaluations, maintaining no wage difference for similar jobs; not widely successful in courts

C. 1965 Executive Order–prohibits discrimination by federal contractors on basis of race, color, sex, religion, or national origin during federal contract period; requires affirmative action by federal contractors

D. Age Discrimination Act–1967; prohibits discrimination in hiring, firing, compensating or otherwise on basis of age; applies to private employers with twenty or more employees, to all governmental units; prohibits mandatory retirement of most employees based on age
   1. Statutory defense–*bona fide* occupational qualifications, *bona fide* seniority system, any other reasonable action
   2. Remedies–back pay, injunction, affirmative action, money damages

E. Disability Discrimination–1973 Rehabilitation Act–requires federal contractors/agencies to use affirmative action in hiring qualified people with disabilities; prohibits discrimination on basis of disability in federal programs, programs receiving federal funding
   1. Handicap–physical/mental impairment substantially affecting major life activities; history of major life activity impairment; alcohol, drug abuses not handicaps under the act

2. American Disabilities Act (ADA)–1990; prohibits employment discrimination based on disability (hiring, firing, pay, promotion, etc.)
   a. Duty of reasonable accommodation for disability unless safety, health, risk, undue hardship to employer, or job criteria/necessity
   b. Remedies–injunction, rehire, back pay, compensatory and punitive damages

III. Employee Protection–job related protections including limited right not to be unfairly dismissed, right to safe, healthy workplace, compensation for workplace injuries, financial security upon retirement or loss of employment
   A. Employee Termination at Will–common law doctrine that employment, unless for definite term, terminable at will by either party; employer may dismiss, employee may quit, for any reason without liability; recent limitations include judicial exceptions, federal/state statutes, contract terms
      1. Statutory limitations–Federal legislation protects certain employees from discriminatory discharge, from discharge for exercising statutory rights (whistleblower protection), from discharge without cause; some state statutes protect workers from discriminatory discharge for filing worker's compensation claims; many state statutes parallel federal legislation
      2. Judicial limitations–based on contract law, tort law, or public policy
         a. Contract theory–employer's promise of work for a reasonable period, implied promises of employment for a specific duration, existence of express or implied provisions of continued employment conditioned upon satisfactory work performance, assurances of nondismissal except for cause
         b. Tort obligations–based on intentional infliction of emotional distress, interference with employment relations
         c. Public policy cases–dismissal for refusing to violate a statute, exercising a statutory right, performing a statutory obligation, or reporting an alleged violation of a statute
   B. Occupational Safety and Health Act–1970; established Occupational Safety and Health Administration (OSHA); develop standards, conduct inspections, monitor compliance, and institute enforcement actions to promote workplace safety
      1. Employer duty–provide safe workplace ("free from recognized hazards causing or likely to cause death or serious physical harm"); employers may not discharge or discriminate against employees exercising rights under Act
      2. OSHA inspects workplaces–citations carrying civil, criminal liability for violations
   C. Employee Privacy–prohibit disclosure of confidential records
      1. Tort recovery–unreasonable intrusion into seclusion; unreasonable public disclosure of private facts; unreasonable publicity placing someone in false light; appropriation of person's name or likeness
      2. Federal/State drug testing laws–Supreme Court allows government random, universal drug testing where public health, safety or national security involved; selective testing where sufficient cause to believe employee has drug problem
      3. Private sector–employees have no protection from drug or alcohol tests without state statutory limitations

4. Union settings–subject to collective bargaining limitations
5. Federal Employee Polygraph Protection Act–prohibits private employers from requiring employees, prospective employees, to undergo lie detector test, inquiring about results of such a test, or using results of such a test or refusal to be tested as grounds for adverse employment decisions
    a. Exemptions allow testing–government employers, security firms, manufacturers of controlled substances, manufacturers investigating economic loss or injury

D. Workers' Compensation–state statutes provide economic relief to injured employees
    1. State boards–determine whether injured employee entitled to benefits, what amount, for how long
    2. Common law defenses abolished
    3. Compensation for injury arising out of, in course, of employment
    4. Civil actions against employer by employee prohibited; court jurisdiction to review decisions of compensation boards

E. Social Security–1935; originally limited to retirement and death benefits; now covers Old-Age and Survivors Insurance (OASI), Disability Insurance (DI), Hospitalization Insurance (Medicare), and Supplemental Security Income (SSI)
    1. Financed by employer/employee taxes
    2. Dependents (spouses and children) eligible for benefits

F. Federal Unemployment Insurance–1935; supplemented by Federal Unemployment Tax Act; employees do not pay tax; unemployment compensation based on state formula, for losing job; must actually seek similar replacement work; benefits denied for seasonal job loss, worker quits, good cause filing

G. Fair Labor Standards Act (FLSA)–regulates wages, hours, child labor outside agriculture
    1. Prohibits employing children under fourteen years except in farm work, newspaper delivery, child actors
    2. Age category/hazardous job restrictions up to 18 years of age
    3. Regulates minimum wage and overtime pay (time-and-a-half for over 40 hours/week)

H. Worker Adjustment and Retraining Notification Act (WARN)–sixty days advance notice of plant closing or mass layoff
    1. Plant closing–permanent or temporary shutdown of single site, units within a site, if shutdown results in fifty or more employees losing employment during a thirty-day period
    2. Mass layoff–loss of employment during a thirty-day period either for 500 employees or one-third (50 or more) of employees at a given site

I. Family and Medical Leave Act–1993; up to twelve weeks of leave during any twelve-month period for birth of child, adopting or gaining foster care of child, care of spouse, child, or parent with serious health condition
    1. Eligibility–employee has worked for employer at least twelve months or has worked at least 1,250 hours during twelve months preceding request
    2. Coverage–employers with fifty or more employees, all government agencies
    3. Leave–paid, unpaid, or combination

TRUE-FALSE: Circle true or false.

T   F   1. Workers taking leaves of absence due to family health crises or births/adoptions cannot be summarily fired for having taken such a leave.

T   F   2. In applying Equal Pay Act provisions to litigation, courts have interpreted "equal work" to mean identical work and not substantially equal work.

T   F   3. American citizens working abroad for U.S. owned companies are not protected by federal employment discrimination laws.

T   F   4. Under federal law, employers may use lie detector testing in investigating acts of employee sabotage against the business.

T   F   5. The 1991 Civil Rights Act limits recovery of compensatory and punitive damages to only cases of racial discrimination.

T   F   6. Federal legislation prohibiting discriminatory employment practices applies only to businesses with gross capitalization over $3,500,000.

T   F   7. Federal law prohibits mandatory retirement for employees based on their age.

T   F   8. Worker's Compensation Statutes eliminate traditional common law defenses in claims brought by injured employees.

T   F   9. The Fair Labor Standards Act prohibits employment of 14 to 18 year olds in non-farm hazardous job settings.

T   F   10. Workers in the private sector receive broad protection against workplace alcohol/drug testing program abuses under the comprehensive Federal Uniform Substance Abuse Testing Act.

T   F   11. Employers may be liable for sexual harassment committed by employees even if they did not know or should have known of the harassment incidents.

T   F   12. The Occupational Safety and Health Act specifically pre-empts state regulation of work setting safety issues leaving states with little regulatory authority.

KEY TERMS–MATCHING EXERCISE: Select the term that best completes each statement below.

1. Estoppel

2. Fair Labor Standards Act

3. Norris-LaGuardia

4. Labor dispute

5. Renunciation

6. Fellow Sevant Rule

7. Wagner Act

8. Worker Adjustment and Retraining Notification Act

9. Taft-Hartley Act

10. OSHA

11. NLRB

12. Reagan Act

13. Social Security

14. Fiduciary

15. Affirmative action

16. Yellow dog contract

17. Reverse discrimination

18. Employment at will

19. Comparable worth

20. Union shop

_____ 1. Controversies over employment terms and conditions or union representation.

_____ 2. Federal legislation intended to protect unionization and collective bargaining efforts of employees.

_____ 3. Federal agency responsible for enforcing employee rights under the Wagner Act.

_____ 4. Federal legislation designed to prevent various union unfair labor practices.

_____ 5. Employment programs focused on actively recruiting minority employees.

_____ 6. Federal legislation enacted to promote safe and healthy working conditions.

_____ 7. Federal legislation requiring 60 days advance notice of plant closing or extensive layoffs.

_____ 8. Congressional legislation establishing minimum hourly wage schedules.

_____ 9. Federal law providing retirement, death and disability benefits to workers.

_____ 10. Common law doctrine relieving employers of liability for work related injuries caused by the negligence of co-workers.

_____ 11. Employer/employee agreements prohibiting employees from joining or forming a union.

_____ 12. Work setting in which non-union members can be hired but must join the union representing other employees to continue on the job.

_____ 13. Description of employer affirmative action plans emphasizing racial or gender factors in hiring or promoting to achieve greater balance in formally secured jobs.

_____ 14. Concept stressing that wage scales among various jobs should be based on objectively grounded rating systems or performance assessments free of possible sex bias.

_____ 15. Common law doctrine allowing employers to hire employees at their own, generally unlimited, discretion.

MULTIPLE CHOICE: Select the alternative that best completes each statement below.

_____ 1. Present day statutory regulations of employment settings focus on (a) safety and health issues (b) discrimination (c) labor-management relations (d) all of the above.

_____ 2. Unfair labor practices by management include (a) mandatory dress codes (b) discrimination against non-union workers (c) refusal to bargain in good faith (d) all of the above.

_____ 3. Congressional legislation aimed at ending corrupt labor union practices was the (a) Landrum-Griffin Act (b) Fair Labor Standards Act (c) Norris-La Guardia Act (d) Fair Dealing Compliance Act.

_____ 4. Which of the following is an acceptable pay differential basis under the Equal Pay Act? (a) worker's sex (b) worker's age (c) worker's productivity level (d) none of the above

_____ 5. Valid defenses to claims filed under the Pregnancy Discrimination Act include (a) employer religious beliefs (b) productivity quotas (c) bona fide job qualification (d) all of the above.

_____ 6. Federal law allows for discriminatory employment practices based on (a) seniority (b) job qualifications (c) ability tests (d) all of the above.

_____ 7. The ADA allows screening out of disabled workers through job selection/qualification criteria and testing programs if (a) reasonable accommodation of a particular handicap is impossible (b) such discrimination conforms to standards set by the Uniform Job Discrimination Code (c) a majority of the workplace employees approve (d) all of the above.

_____ 8. Common law based injured employee actions were founded on a/n _____ theory of recovery (a) strict liability (b) nuisance (c) negligence (d) agency.

_____ 9. Federal law requires overtime payment when more than (a) eight hours is worked in a single day (b) 40 hours is worked in a single week (c) 25 hours is worked in a three-day period (d) none of the above.

_____ 10. Workers who _____ are not eligible to receive federal unemployment benefits (a) are not actively seeking suitable replacement work (b) lose seasonal work (c) are laid off following a business merger (d) all of the above.

_____ 11. _____ are state statutes prohibiting union shop agreements. (a) Closed Shop Acts (b) Fair Employment laws (c) Yellow Dog Contract laws (d) Right to Work laws.

_____ 12. Employers can fire employees for (a) trying to form a union (b) missed work days due to jury duty (c) reporting an OSHA violation (d) none of the above.

_____ 13. Union activity amounting to unfair labor practices includes (a) informational leafleting (b) enforcing union shop agreements (c) "feather bedding" (d) all of the above.

CASE PROBLEMS–SHORT ESSAY ANSWERS: Read each case problem carefully. When appropriate, answer by stating a Decision for the case and by explaining the rationale–Rule of Law–relied upon to support your decision.

1. Square Deal Lumber Yard employs male and female workers of all ages in various jobs. The male stock clerks at Square Deal learn that they receive less pay than female yard attendants. The stock clerks argue that this amounts to a violation of the Equal Pay Act. Are they correct? Explain.

   Decision: _____

   _____

   Rule of Law: _____

   _____

2. Aerospace Industries, Inc. puts out a hiring call for trained, experienced retrofitters. Chuck Campion, a 25-year-old certified retrofitter with four years work experience, applies for the job. He is turned down, the personnel department explaining that no one under 30 will be hired for the jobs. Chuck files a claim against the company arguing violation of federal age discrimination laws. Who wins the dispute and why?

   Decision: _____

   _____

   Rule of Law: _____

   _____

3. Fortisque Thistlemeyer, president and founder of Thistle Theatrical Productions, Inc., is embroiled in bitter contract negotiations with the union representing his employees. A bargaining impasse has been reached regarding overtime work on national holidays. The union threatens to strike if an accommodation cannot be reached. Fortisque, an outspoken, anti-union hard-liner, blasts the union as a collection of heartless, money-sucking, dishonest ingrates. The union files an unfair labor practices charge against him. Who prevails? Discuss.

Decision: _____

_____

Rule of Law: _____

_____

4. Charlene Carlisle, a storage drum loader at Petro Processors for the past four years, has just been fired. Her employment record is spotless. Petro unloads, stores and ships hazardous chemical wastes generated by chemical manufacturers. OSHA regulations require workers at Petro to be provided adequate protective goggles, masks, gloves, and outer garments to insure no health-endangering employee exposure to the toxins Petro handles. A truckload of dioxin-contaminated wastes arrives at Petro. The manager requests that it be unloaded but Charlene, unable to find a proper mask, refuses, citing health and safety hazards as her reason. The manager orders Charlene to unload the truck or "face the consequences." She refuses and is fired. She alleges violation of OSHA regulations and the company denies it. What outcome?

Decision: _____

_____

Rule of Law: _____

_____

5. Folsum Meatpacking, Inc. is entering its third month of a particularly bitter labor dispute. Its workers are beginning their second month of a strike. In an effort to induce the company to settle, the union, which also represents workers at other meatpacking houses in the area, tells those members not to handle any meat from shippers or ranchers who do business with Folsum. Folsum alleges that the union's activity is an unfair labor practice but the union asserts "just tough business tactics." Who is right?

Decision: _____

_____

Rule of Law: _____

_____

Chapter 44

SECURITIES REGULATION

SCOPE NOTE

In response to problems of fraud and inaccurate information in securities transactions, state (Blue Sky Laws) and federal regulations were passed to protect investors from losses caused by fraud and to promote public confidence in securities markets. Chapter 44 focuses on federal securities regulation, tracing the Federal government's involvement in controlling the securities marketplace from the early 1930s to the present. The rights/duties of people engaged in trading investment securities, under the 1933 Securities Act, which regulates issuing securities, and the 1934 Securities Exchange Act, that deals with securities trading, both administered by the Securities Exchange Commission, are focused on. Types and sanctions for violating securities law are also examined.

EDUCATIONAL OBJECTIVES

1. Identify the scope, purpose and major provisions of the 1933 Securities Act.

2. Outline the important procedural requirements under the 1933 Act.

3. Distinguish the various transactions and types of securities that are exempt from coverage under the 1933 Act.

4. Explain the nature and breadth of liability for violations of the 1933 Act.

5. Identify the scope, purpose and major provisions of the 1934 Securities Exchange Act.

6. Know federal regulations covering proxy solicitations and tender offers.

7. Discuss the extent of regulatory authority held by the SEC.

8. Know the purpose and significance of the Foreign Corrupt Practices Act of 1977.

CHAPTER OUTLINE

I. Securities Act of 1933–"Truth in Securities"; requires filing registration statement with SEC before public sale of any securities by issuers, non-issuers through interstate commerce; purpose to disclose accurate, adequate financial information; prospectus accompanies offer to sell containing important data from registration statement; antifraud provisions apply regardless whether registration required; civil/criminal liability imposed for violations

   A. Definition of Security–note, stock, bond, debenture, evidence of indebtedness, investment contract or interest, instrument, commonly known as a security

      1. Howey Test–investment in common venture, expectation of profit, gained from efforts of others

   B. Registration of Securities

      1. Disclosure requirements–description of properties, business, significant provisions of security, relationship to registrant's other capital securities, management financial statements certified by independent public accountants, compensation paid to senior executives/directors

        a. Effectiveness–information public immediately upon filing; unlawful to sell securities until date statement is effective; on filing securities may be offered orally, by summaries or "tombstone advertisement" or by preliminary prospectus ("red herring")

      2. Integrated disclosure–SEC system to reduce, eliminate filing duplication under 1933 and 34 Acts; corporations continuously reporting under 1934 Act for at least three years disclose less detailed information under 1933 Act and incorporate by reference information reported under 1934 Act; corporations filing under 1934 Act with $75 million voting stock minimum market value disclose less detail under 1933 Act and incorporate information by reference to 1934 Act report

      3. Shelf registrations–certain qualified issuers register securities for sale "off-shelf" on delayed or continuous basis; information in original registration must be accurate and current

   C. Exempt Securities–certain securities not covered by registration requirements

      1. Short-term commercial paper–instrument issued for working capital; with maturity less than nine months; no exemption if proceeds used for permanent purposes

      2. Other exempt securities–various securities not requiring registration; issued by domestic governments, domestic banks, savings and loan associations, non-profit charitable organizations, federally regulated common carriers, bankruptcy debtor under reorganization plan, insurance policies, annuities issued by state regulated insurance companies

   D. Exempt Transactions for Issuers–issuance of securities not subject to registration requirements: exemptions apply to transactions only in which securities are issued; resale requires registration unless resale qualifies as exempt transaction

      1. Limited offers–exemptions cover restricted securities; resales require registration unless resale transaction exempt

        a. Reasonable care rule–issuer must use reasonable care to assure against nonexempt, unregistered resales of restricted securities

    b. Private placements–transactions not involving any public offering; no dollar limit; advertising, solicitation not permitted; purchasers may be unlimited number of "accredited investors"; nonaccredited investors must be given specified material information; issuer's duty to guard against nonexempt, unregistered resales

    c. Limited offers not exceeding $5 million–offerings by noninvestment company issuers over twelve months; advertising, solicitation not permitted; purchasers are unlimited number of accredited investors; nonaccredited investors must be given specified material information; issuer duty to guard against nonexempt, unregistered resales

    d. Limited offers not exceeding $1 million–private, noninvestment company issuer's exemption of small issues not exceeding $1 million over twelve months; sales may be unlimited number of investors; does not require information be furnished them

    e. Limited offers solely to accredited investors–exemption for offers, sales solely to accredited investors not exceeding $5 million; advertising or public solicitation not permitted; unlimited number of accredited investors; no unaccredited investors may purchase; issuer duty to guard against nonexempt, unregistered resales

  2. Regulation A–exempts sales up to $5 million of securities in twelve-month period if issuer files offering statement with SEC regional office prior to sale; offering circular must be given purchaser; less detailed, less time-consuming filing; securities sold are resalable

  3. Intrastate issues–issuance to persons living in same state as resident issuer, primarily doing business there; local issues, local financing, by local person, local investments; no resales to nonresidents during selling period and nine months thereafter; precautions required against interstate distributions

E. Exempt Transactions for Non-Issuers–transaction exemption for any person other than an issuer, underwriter, or dealer as well as most transactions by dealers and brokers; exemptions do not extend to certain resales by non-issuers which require registration

  1. Rule 144–conditions met by affiliate (business ties to issuer) or person selling restricted securities which exempt registration

    a. Adequate current public information about issuer

    b. Seller must have owned securities for at least two years

    c. Only in limited amounts in unsolicited brokers transaction

    d. Notice of sale to SEC

  2. Rule 144A–registration exemption for resales of restricted securities (securities not in same class as securities listed on national securities exchange or nonfungible securities)

  3. Regulation–exemption for non-issuers of $1.5 million worth of securities sold in twelve-month period by non-affiliates

F. Liability–sanctions for violating 1933 Act include SEC administrative remedies, civil liability to investors, criminal penalties

  1. Unregistered sales–civil liability for selling unregistered security requiring registration, selling registered security without current prospectus, or offering sale before

filing; no defenses; purchaser recovers purchase price, or if no longer owner, monetary damages from seller

2. False registration statements–untrue statements, omitting material facts; broad range of liability; standing for anyone; who owned security without knowing untruth or omission
   a. Experts (CPA) liable for portion of registration prepared or certified
   b. Nonissuance defendants may assert due diligence defense–reasonable belief that no untrue statements, material omissions, in statement.

3. Antifraud provision–applies to all securities
   a. Liability for any person offering, selling security by prospectus or oral communication containing untrue statement, or omission of material fact; liability only to immediate innocent purchaser; seller has defense of no knowledge, could not have known of untrue statement or omission

4. Criminal sanctions–requires willful/violation; fine not more than $10,000, and/or imprisonment not more than five years

II. 1934 Securities Exchange Act–regulates secondary distribution (resale) of securities; promote fair orderly securities markets; sets rules for operation of markets; prohibits fraudulent/manipulative practices
   A. Disclosure–filing requirement for reporting companies: registrations, periodic reports, statements for proxy solicitations, statements for tender offers, compliance with Foreign Corrupt Practices Act, compensation to senior executives/directors
      1. Registration requirements–publicly held companies; onetime applying for entire class of securities
         a. Comprehensive, material information disclosure
      2. Periodic reporting requirements–annual periodic updates filed by issuer and officers, any person owning more than 10% of registered equity security, discloses ownership changes
      3. Regulation of proxy solicitations
         a. Writing signed by shareholder authorizing named person to vote shares at shareholder meeting
         b. Proxy statements–solicitation prohibited unless persons furnished with written proxy statement containing specified information
         c. Shareholder proposals–disclosure requirements when management makes a solicitation, opposes or proposes certain action
      4. Tender offers–general invitation to shareholders by company to purchase shares at specified price; reporting, disclosure requirements for tender offers and block acquisitions to provide public shareholders adequate, current, information to make informed decisions
         a. Disclosure requirements–applies where person or group offers to acquire more than 5% of a class of registered equity voting securities, issuer makes offer to repurchase own shares; statement filed with SEC contains material information; target company has ten days to respond to bidder's tender
         b. Required practices–offer remains open for at least twenty business days; shareholders may withdraw tenders; shares tendered must be purchased at same price

     c. Defensive tactics–management options responding to uninvited takeover bids

     d. State regulation–two-thirds of states have statutes regulating tender offers to protect target company from unwanted take over; state reviews offer's merits, adequacy of disclosure, imposes waiting periods before tender offer effective; have more detailed disclosure requirements than federal law

  5. Foreign Corrupt Practices Act–internal control requirements on companies with registered securities prohibiting bribing foreign governmental officials; accounting requirements assure accuracy of issuer's books; protect integrity of independent audits, promote reliability of financial information required under 1934 Act

B. Liability–violations of disclosure/antifraud requirements trigger civil liability to injured investors/issuers, and criminal penalties

  1. Misleading statements–civil liability for false, misleading statements regarding material facts in application, report, document, or registration; defense of acting in good faith, no knowledge of misstatement

  2. Short-swing profits–liability upon insiders (directors, officers, any person owning more than 10% of publicly voted stock) for profits from short-swing trading; corporation recovers profit gained by an insider selling stock within six months from the date of purchase or buying stock within six months after date of sale

  3. Antifraud provisions–prohibits using mails or other interstate commerce in buying/selling any security; covers any fraudulent act, practice, or course of business

     a. Requisites of antifraud rule–material misstatement, omission; relied upon; made with scienter (intentional, knowing conduct)

     b. Insider trading–antifraud provision applies to "insider" possessing material information not available to public; broad definition of insider (anyone with entrusted information from issuer–underwriters, accountants, lawyers, and "tippee"–persons receiving material, nonpublic information from insider)

  4. Insider trading liability–civil liability for profit gained, loss avoided

  5. Civil penalties for insider trading–SEC action in federal court against any insider or person controlling violator if controlling person knew, recklessly disregard knowledge, of likely violation

     a. Transaction requirement–through national securities exchange, broker or dealer

     b. Penalty not exceed three times profit gained, loss avoided

  6. Misleading proxy statements–materially false, misleading proxy statement; civil standing to shareholder suffering loss from purchasing, selling in reliance upon statement

  7. Fraudulent tender offers–false statement of material fact, omission, any deceptive, manipulative practice connected to tender offer

  8. Antibribery provision of FCPA–domestic concern, any officers, directors, employers, or agents, prohibited from offering, giving anything of value directly or indirectly to any foreign official, political party, or political official to influence act or decision, of person or party in official capacity; covers using influence to affect decision of foreign government to assist domestic concern in business activity

     a. Penalty–fines up to $2 million for companies, individuals up to $100,000, imprisonment up to five years

9. Criminal sanctions–for willful violations; fines up to $1 million, and/or imprisonment up to 10 years

TRUE-FALSE: Circle true or false.

T F 1. Federal laws have exclusive jurisdiction over regulating sales of securities.

T F 2. The SEC uses registration documents to evaluate the soundness and potential for profit of investment opportunities.

T F 3. New SEC registration and reporting regulations are designed to aid small businesses to compete more effectively in public financial markets.

T F 4. Liability for selling unregistered securities that are required to be registered under federal law is absolute, there being no defense for the violation.

T F 5. Anti-fraud provisions of the 1933 Securities Act apply only to intrastate sales of securities.

T F 6. Securities sales with a value not exceeding $5 million dollars may be made over any 12-month period and the sales require only that an offering statement be filed with the SEC.

T F 7. Once an issuer has filed registration documents, no additional filing is required to update the initial registration.

T F 8. A major objective of federal laws focused on preventing fraud in securities transactions is to promote and preserve public confidence in the securities market.

T F 9. The Foreign Corrupt Practices Act attempts to prevent bribery of foreign government officials by U.S. corporations.

T F 10. Under federal laws, the term "security" is limited in its definition to include only stocks and bonds.

T F 11. The primary goal of the Truth in Securities Act registration requirements is to reveal to potential investors material information that can assist them in assessing the worthiness of an investment opportunity.

T F 12. A security issue offered and sold only to purchasers residing in a single state by an issuer residing and doing business in the same state is exempt from registration requirements under the 1933 Act.

KEY TERMS–MATCHING EXERCISE: Select the term that best completes each statement below.

1. Short-term commercial paper

2. Da Ma Doctrine

3. Insider

4. Intrastate

5. Registration

6. Due diligence

7. Tender offer

8. Proxy

9. Private placements

10. Accredited investor

11. Exemption

12. Prospectus

13. Constructive disclosure

14. Reasonable diligence

15. Securities Act of 1933

16. Restricted

17. Integrated disclosure

18. Affiliate

19. Howey Test

20. Securities Exchange Commission

_____ 1. Federal legislation enacted to prevent fraud and promote accessible, truthful information in securities sales.

_____ 2. The act required of some securities sellers by which information is disclosed to potential investors.

_____ 3. Documents distributed to potential investors containing required disclosure information.

_____ 4. Notes, drafts or other working capital issuances with maturity dates of nine months or less.

_____ 5. One having knowledge of nonpublic, confidential and material information related to the value of a security.

_____ 6. A general invitation to all shareholders of a company to purchase their shares at a specified price.

_____ 7. A signed written statement, issued by a shareholder, granting authority to another to vote the signer's stock.

_____ 8. Defense available to non-issuers that an alleged violation of the 1933 Securities Act did not occur since they, in fact, reasonably believed that the registration statement contained no false information or material omissions.

_____ 9. Exempted security transactions by an issuer that do not involve a public offering.

_____ 10. Banks, insurance companies and investment firms purchasing securities sold under the private placement provisions of securities regulations.

_____ 11. Governmental agency primarily responsible for enforcing Federal securities laws.

_____ 12. Descriptor for the three-tiered registration system adopted to reduce duplication of effort in complying with requirements under the 1933 and 1934 Acts.

_____ 13. Securities sold under such registration transaction exemptions as private placements, accredited investor limited offer, or limited offers under $1 million.

_____ 14. One who controls, is controlled by, or is under common control with an issuer.

_____ 15. Standard used by the U.S. Supreme Court to determine whether a financial transaction falls within the Security Act's definition of a security.

MULTIPLE CHOICE: Select the alternative that best completes each statement below.

_____ 1. The anti-fraud sections of the Truth in Securities Act (a) apply to securities transactions in interstate commerce (b) impose only criminal sanctions for their violations (c) cover only securities sales that are exempt from registration (d) none of the above.

_____ 2. The date a registration statement becomes effective is _____ after filing. (a) 2 months (b) 2 weeks (c) 20 days (d) 1 month

_____ 3. Of the following, which is not information that must be disclosed on securities registration forms? (a) description of the business of the registrant (b) certified financial statements (c) management information (d) accounting procedures used by registrant.

_____ 4. Transactions exempted from registration under the 1933 Act include limited offers (a) solely to accredited investors (b) not exceeding $10 million (c) public displacements (d) all of the above.

_____ 5. Securities exempt from registration include those (a) from domestic banks (b) sold by domestic governments (c) involving short-term commitments (d) all of the above.

_____ 6. A/n _____ involves a financial transaction for profit, derived from the management efforts of others. (a) debt (b) lease (c) investment contract (d) gift

_____ 7. Enforcement options related to Federal securities laws include (a) criminal sanctions (b) administrative remedies (c) civil liability (d) all of the above.

_____ 8. A defense to an action based on untrue statements contained in a registration statement is (a) due diligence (b) innocent mistake (c) subjective honesty (d) capitalized equity.

_____ 9. Persons who receive nonpublic material investment information from insiders are referred to as (a) co-conspirators (b) accomplices (c) tippees (d) none of the above.

_____ 10. The Securities Exchange Act of 1934 applies primarily to (a) bankruptcy trust securities (b) secondary securities distributions (c) equitable receiverships (d) none of the above.

_____ 11. Tender offers must be kept open for at least (a) 2 weeks (b) 2 months (c) 30 days (d) 20 days.

_____ 12. _____ are state anti-fraud laws regulating security sales within a state's own borders. (a) grey sky laws (b) mini security acts (c) fair trading legislation (d) blue sky laws

_____ 13. Recent U.S. Supreme Court rulings have (a) upheld state anti-hostile-takeover laws (b) ruled that the Williams Act exclusively pre-empts state action (c) held golden parachute agreements unconstitutional (d) none of the above.

CASE PROBLEMS–SHORT ESSAY ANSWERS: Read each case problem carefully. When appropriate, answer by stating a Decision for the case and by explaining the rationale–Rule of Law–relied upon to support your decision.

1. Ajax, Inc., seeking to raise capital, issued $500,000 in securities during the past year. Regardless of whether this issue was subject to state laws, was it entirely exempt from Federal regulation? Discuss.

Decision: _____

_____

Rule of Law: _____

_____

2. Brown, president of Waylay, Inc., owns 25% of that corporation's stock, which is registered with the SEC. On October 25th, Brown purchases Waylay securities, which increases his share of ownership to 30%. The following January, Brown sells some of his Waylay shares reducing his ownership to 22%. What liability does Brown face for the profits from these transactions? Explain.

Decision: _____

_____

Rule of Law: _____

_____

3. World Food, Inc. is a non-profit organization distributing American crop surpluses to underdeveloped nations facing food shortages. To expand its operation, World Food issues $250,000 worth of securities. Must this issue be registered with the SEC?

Decision: _____

_____

Rule of Law: _____

_____

4. Explorations, Inc., to capitalize its development of a natural gas field, registers with the SEC to sell $3.5 million in securities. In its registration statement and prospectus, Explorations lists Sammy Maudlin and Edith Pringle, famous stars from the entertainment world, as members of its board of directors. Investor 1, reviewing Explorations' registration statement and prospectus, in which the working life of the gas field is stated to be at least 25 years, decides to purchase $20,000 of Explorations' stock issue. The venture eventually turns sour as Explorations discovers that the fields actually have a producing life of just over 10 years, too short a period to make the development profitable. Explorations abandons the project. Investor 1, remembering the statements made in the prospectus, sues for return of his investment alleging fraud. Named as defendants in the suit are Sammy and Edith, who claim no liability since they had no "hands-on" management responsibilities with Explorations. Is 1 entitled to a return of his $20,000 and are Maudlin and Pringle accountable for it? Discuss.

Decision: _____

_____

Rule of Law: _____

_____

5. XYZ Corporation, with assets totaling $8,500,000, needs additional capital to finance an expansion of its operations. The board of directors decides to promote an issue of $300,000 in equity securities to raise the necessary capital. At the time of this issue, XYZ has 430 shareholders owning this class of securities. Must XYZ register the securities it plans to sell if it anticipates trading them over the counter?

Decision: _____

_____

Rule of Law: _____

_____

Chapter 45

ACCOUNTANTS' LEGAL LIABILITY

SCOPE NOTE

Accountants face potential civil and criminal liability stemming from the work they perform for others. Chapter 45 examines common law and federal statutory bases for such liability. To whom are accountants liable; on what theory; what defenses may be asserted; what are the rights/duties flowing between accountants, clients and the general public. These are the major issues addressed in Chapter 45.

EDUCATIONAL OBJECTIVES

1. Explain explicit/implicit contractually based accountant liability.

2. Distinguish between tort (negligence or fraud) and criminal bases for accountant liability.

3. Discuss controversial issues related to client access to accountant working papers.

4. Develop the importance of client-accountant communication privileges.

5. Know accountant civil and criminal liability under Federal securities and tax laws.

CHAPTER OUTLINE

I. Common Law–state law; accountants' legal responsibility based on contract, tort & criminal law; accountants' rights include ownership of working papers, limited accountant-client privilege
   A. Contract Liability–bound to perform all duties stated in contract; accountant implicitly agrees to perform competently and professionally

1. Held to professional standards–Generally Accepted Accounting Standards (GAAS), Generally Accepted Accounting Principles (GAAP)
2. Agreement sets standards beyond GAAS, liability for breach of contract to client
3. Third party beneficiaries intended to benefit under accounting contract entitled to compensation for material breach
4. Substantially performing duties–compensation for completed work less damages caused by non-material breach

B. Tort Liability–to client, third parties for negligence or fraud; compensatory money damages
1. Negligence–failure to use care of reasonably competent accountant under circumstances
   a. Not liable for honest inaccuracies, judgment errors, (not insurer of report's accuracy)
   b. Privity of contract–liability extended only to client and third-party beneficiaries; majority of states, Restatements of Torts, adopt "foreseen users" test–liability to those accountant knew, should have known, would use the work; no liability to potential investors/general public unless "reasonably foreseeable users"
2. Fraud–broader liability; any person accountant should have reasonably foreseen would be injured by misrepresentation, who justifiably relied upon it
   a. Standard elements of fraud: knowingly made false representation of material fact; intention to deceive; justifiable reliance causes injury
   b. Compensatory and punitive damages

C. Criminal Liability–federal securities, tax law primary basis
1. State criminal liability–knowing, willful certification of false documents; alters or tampers with records; use of false financial reports; gives false testimony under oath, or forgery
2. Internal Revenue Code Liability–knowingly prepares false, fraudulent tax returns; willfully assisting, advising client, to prepare false return
3. Punishment–fine up to $100,000 ($500,000 for corporation) and/or three years imprisonment

D. Client Information–issues related to client information obtained during services: ownership of working papers; existence of accountant/client privilege
1. Working papers–accountant owner, need not give to client; accountant will not disclose contents without client consent or court order
2. Accountant-Client Privilege–issue relevant to tax disputes, criminal prosecution, civil litigation; privileged information not admissable evidence over objection of primary parties
   a. Common law/federal law–neither recognizes a privilege
   b. State law–some state statutes grant some form of privilege; usually in favor of client, few extend privilege to accountant
   c. Trade usage, customary practice–professionally unethical for accountants to disclose confidential communications from client, unless disclosure in accordance with AICPA or GAAS requirements, a court order, or client's request

II. Federal Securities Law–civil and criminal liability under provisions of the 1933 and 1934 Acts
   A. Securities Act of 1933–account civil liability under Section II covers false financial statements misleadingly prepared or certified for inclusion in a registration statement
      1. Liability to anyone who acquires the security without knowledge of untruth or omission
      2. No privity or proof of reliance on financial statements required
      3. Defense of due diligence–accountant, after reasonable investigation, reasonably believes, in fact believes, financial statements are true, complete and accurate; standard of reasonably prudent person managing own property
      4. Liability for negligence–conducting an audit or presenting information in financial statements
      5. Punishment–up to $10,000 in fines and/or 5 years imprisonment
   B. Securities Exchange Act of 1934–civil liability for false, misleading statements of material fact in application, report, document or registration filed with SEC
      1. Liability to any person who purchased or sold a security in reliance on statement
      2. Defense of acting in good faith–no knowledge of statement being false or misleading
      3. Liability–direct, indirect, participation in aiding/abetting others to violate the rule; oral or written participation in misstatements or omissions of material facts
      4. Liability to purchasers/sellers–based on relying on material, factual misstatement or omission connected to purchase/sale of securities
      5. Sceinter requirement–intentional, knowing conduct, or reckless disregard of truth
      6. Punishment–willful violations; up to $1 million fines &/or imprisonment up to ten years
      7. Auditor's requirements–reasonable procedures to find illegal, material acts, evaluate issuer's competitive business viability

TRUE–FALSE: Circle true or false.

T   F   1. Accountants provide financial information important in economic resource allocation decisions.

T   F   2. In the relationship with the client, an accountant is responsible for performing only to the level of competence explicitly provided for in the contract.

T   F   3. Accountants are generally not liable for insuring the absolute accuracy of their reports.

T   F   4. Most states employ the primary benefit test in deciding the extent of negligence-based accountant liability to third parties.

T   F   5. Accountant criminal liability is mainly based upon federal securities and tax laws.

T   F   6. Accountants are usually allowed to argue client-plaintiff contributory negligence in defending against malpractice claims.

T   F   7. The confidentiality of accountant-client communications is not a privilege recognized under either state or federal law.

T   F   8. To maintain a civil action against an accountant under Section 11 of the 1933 Security Exchange Act, the plaintiff must establish both privity and reliance.

T   F   9. Accountants are not civilly liable under Section 18 of the 1934 Securities Exchange Act if their actions are without knowledge of untrue statements and based on good-faith motivation.

T   F   10. Accountants are always liable for releasing information obtained from clients without their consent.

T   F   11. Accountant liability for services performed is based partly on federal securities laws.

T   F   12. The standard of competence applied when an accountant contractually agrees to conduct an audit to find embezzlement is Generally Accepted Auditing Standards.

KEY TERMS–MATCHING EXERCISE: Select the term that best completes each statement below.

---

1. Fraud	7. Privity	14. Substantial performance
2. Due diligence	8. Private interest	15. Scienter
3. Private Securities Litigation Reform Act	9. Third-party beneficiary	16. Willful violation
4. Privileged communication	10. Statute of limitations	17. Accountant
5. Interpretation	11. Material breach	18. Foreseen user
6. Trespass	12. Negligence	19. Estoppel
	13. Working papers	20. Judgment errors

_____ 1. Non-contractual party intended by the contracting parties to receive a direct, primary benefit under the contract.

_____ 2. Contractual non-performance that terminates an accountant's right to compensation.

_____ 3. Failure to use the care of a reasonably competent accountant.

_____ 4. Contractual doctrine limiting accountant liability to persons with whom a business relationship (clients) had been established.

_____ 5. Accountant's defense to civil liability under Section 11 of the 1933 Securities Exchange Act.

_____ 6. Intentional or knowingly wrongful conduct.

_____ 7. Federal legislation requiring auditors to establish procedures to detect material illegal acts and report those that are uncovered.

_____ 8. Accountant's records, including data-gathering process followed, information obtained, and conclusion drawn therefrom.

_____ 9. Confidential information that witnesses or others may rightfully refuse to release based on the nature of a relationship existing with the person providing the information.

_____ 10. False material statement of fact issued with deceitful intent.

_____ 11. Accountant misconduct that triggers criminal liability under federal securities law.

_____ 12. One who provides reliable financial information to assist the decision making of others.

_____ 13. Test for negligence-based, accountant-third-party liability applied to persons accountants know will use their work product.

_____ 14. Accountant behavior that triggers a right to compensation for services less damages for losses caused by less-than-complete performance.

_____ 15. Accountant misconduct triggering no liability so long as professional duties were performed with care.

MULTIPLE CHOICE: Select the alternative that best completes each statement below.

_____ 1. Which of the following is not a basis for accountant legal liability under state law? (a) criminal codes (b) tort law (c) constitutional clauses (d) contract law

_____ 2. The basis for tort liability applied to accountants in performing their professional services includes (a) negligence and fraud (b) strict liability and promissory estoppel (c) administrative construction and offsetting partition (d) all of the above.

_____ 3. Essential elements of a fraud-based cause of action do not include (a) justifiable reliance (b) false statement of fact (c) knowledge of falsity (d) undue influence.

_____ 4. Misconduct that is the basis for accountant criminal liability under state law includes (a) breach of fiduciary relationship (b) perjury (c) coercion (d) none of the above.

_____ 5. Criminal liability for accountants under federal tax laws includes (a) forgery (b) material alteration of accounting records (c) intentional assistance of a client to prepare false tax returns (d) all of the above.

_____ 6. Which of the following is not a test to determine an accountant's liability for negligence to third parties? (a) primary benefit (b) forseeable plaintiff (c) direct consequences (d) none of the above

_____ 7. Accountant liability for false financial information contained in registration statements filed under Section 11 of the 1933 Securities Exchange Act is based on (a) careless audit procedures (b) failure to register working papers (c) confidential meetings with clients (d) all of the above.

_____ 8. Accountants should not release confidential information drawn from client meetings unless (a) a conflict of interest exists (b) directed to do so by a court order (c) specifically provided for by enabling legislation (d) all of the above.

_____ 9. The test for accountant negligence under Section 11 of the 1933 Securities Exchange Act is (a) breach of a fiduciary duty (b) based on trustee duties of care (c) failure to act as prudent people would in managing their own property (d) none of the above.

_____ 10. Which of the following is not a valid requirement for an accountant-client contract? (a) fiduciary relationship (b) mutual agreement (c) capacity (d) consideration

_____ 11. _____ is accountant misconduct that triggers liability to anyone whom the accountant should have foreseen would have relied on the information and would be hurt through such reliance. (a) negligence (b) chemical dependence (c) perjury (d) fraud

_____ 12. An accountant cannot disclose information contained in working papers without (a) payment from the information seeker (b) first filing the papers with the Secretary of State in the client's state of residence (c) client consent or a court order (d) none of the above.

_____ 13. _____ is based upon an accountant's reasonable belief that financial statements accompanying a client's SEC registration statement contained accurate, true and complete information at the date the registration became effective. (a) GAAS defense (b) due diligence defense (c) statutory compliance defense (d) none of the above

CASE PROBLEMS–SHORT ESSAY ANSWERS: Read each case problem carefully. When appropriate, answer by stating a Decision for the case and by explaining the rationale–Rule of Law–relied upon to support your decision.

1. Client contracts with accountant to audit client's business and submit a final annual report by May 15th. Accountant, in accepting the terms of the agreement, assures client that no trouble will be encountered in meeting the completion date. Client is relieved to hear this and repeats the importance of having the audit completed by May 15th since annual reports must be distributed to stockholders by May 20th. During the audit, accountant experiences various unexpected misfortunes: employee illnesses; equipment failure; unavailable records; weather-related delays. By May 8th, accountant is less than half through with the audit and May 15th appears an unrealistic goal. What are the rights and liabilities of the parties if May 15th passes with no annual report completed? Explain.

   Decision: _____

   _____

   Rule of Law: _____

   _____

2. In conducting the above audit, accountant discovers various unexplainable discrepancies in client's records. Upon notifying client of this fact, accountant is assured that these are mere "entry oversights" that will "balance out when the audit is completed." Trusting client's word, accountant makes no further inquiries. Sometime later, accountant receives an anonymous tip that client and other company directors are siphoning funds from the company. Accountant does not pursue the matter, completes the audit and submits the final annual report pointing out the strong financial health of client's company. Relying upon the data, statements and conclusions in the report, various present stockholders in client's company increase their holdings. Shortly thereafter, the SEC files fraud, theft and swindling charges against client and the firm for embezzlement and falsely representing stock value. Client's company collapses, with most stockholders incurring heavy losses. Some stockholders sue accountant for compensatory and punitive damages in an attempt to recapture their losses. Who prevails and why?

   Decision: _____

   _____

   Rule of Law: _____

   _____

3. Pursuant to the SEC prosecution mentioned above, client subpoenas accountant working papers to examine for possible evidentiary benefit. Accountant refuses and client sues. Discuss who wins and why.

Decision: _____

_____

Rule of Law: _____

_____

4. Reread question 1. Assume that instead of a scheduled May 15th completion date that is crucial to client, May 15th is merely referred to as a convenient completion date. By May 16th, accountant has 80% of the final report completed and requires two additional days for finishing. What are the rights and liabilities of the parties at this point?

Decision: _____

_____

Rule of Law: _____

_____

5. In the federal government's prosecution of client mentioned in question 2, accountant is called to testify against client. Accountant refuses, alleging that an accountant-client privilege makes all communications between accountant and a client confidential. The judge threatens accountant with contempt unless the information is released. Who wins this dispute and why?

Decision: _____

_____

Rule of Law: _____

_____

Chapter 46

ENVIRONMENTAL LAW

SCOPE NOTE

Two major social developments which occurred during the Twentieth Century–urbanization and technology advances–had significant adverse effects on the environment. Waste pollution, depletion of natural resources and unregulated development of land created new problems and issues for the law. Traditional common law approaches, focusing on compensatory money damages, proved inadequate to effectively deal with environmental damage. Federal and state legislation and administrative regulations were enacted to more effectively respond to the issues of managing natural resources, controlling pollution and directing land use development. Chapter 46 examines the fundamental principles and procedures associated with common law's compensatory approach and the federal/state regulatory approach to preventing environmental damage and promoting natural resource conservation.

EDUCATIONAL OBJECTIVES

1. Identify and discuss the deficiencies of common law theories relied on in civil actions seeking to remedy environmental abuses.

2. Explain the difficulties associated with using common law remedies for environmental damage.

3. Discuss important federal legislation regulating environmental use and pollution control.

4. Outline the procedure for using and reviewing environmental impact statements.

5. Discuss efforts to deal with depletion of the ozone layer and global warming problems.

CHAPTER OUTLINE

I. Common Law Actions for Environmental Damage–private tort actions to redress environmental harm use nuisance, trespass, and strict liability doctrines
   A. Nuisance–applies to private and public disruptions
      1. Private–substantial/unreasonable interference with another's use/enjoyment of land; action for damages does not require proof conduct is unreasonable; action for an injunction requires proof of unreasonableness of conduct; does not require interference with possession.
      2. Public–interference with health, safety, or comfort of community; action brought by public representative (attorney general); few public nuisance actions brought against polluters for economic reasons
   B. Trespass to Land–action directly resulting in invasion, interference to exclusive possession of property
   C. Strict Liability–conduct carries unduly abnormal danger (ultrahazardous activity) in inappropriate location; plaintiff must show resulting damage
   D. Problems Common to Private Causes of Action–high costs of private litigation (legal fees); denial of injunctive relief due to equity defenses; public representatives unwilling to bring actions due to adverse economic impact (business losses); relief for aesthetic injury usually not available; question of causation where more than one polluting defendant; money damages leaves defendant still polluting; availability of sufficient evidence to sustain plaintiff's burden of proof

II. Federal Environment Regulation–response to inadequacy of private causes of action; statutes and administrative regulations to protect environment
   A. 1969 National Environmental Policy Act (NEPA)–environmental protection goal of federal policy; creates Environmental Quality Council (EQC); requires environmental impact statement (EIS) for federal action with significant environmental effect
      1. Council on Environmental Quality–part of President's Executive Office; makes recommendations on environmental matters, prepares annual reports on state of environment
      2. Environmental Impact Statements (EIS)–method for promoting federal environmental concerns
         a. Preparation procedure–proposed federal activity triggers "environmental assessment" (short analysis of need for an EIS); if EPA decides no EIS required, public so informed; if EIS required, draft made, distributed for comments, with final EIS adopted
         b. Scope–applies to range of projects (Federal action) having direct/indirect effect on environmental quality
         c. Content–unavoidable adverse environmental effects, reasonable alternatives, relationship between local short-term uses of environment and maintenance/enhancement of long-term productivity, irreversible/irretrievable resource commitments
         d. Nature of EIS requirement–primarily procedural; no requirement that federal agency mitigate adverse effects of proposed action

B. Clean Air Act–two regulatory schemes; states have primary responsibility for regulating present existing stationary sources/motor vehicles; federal regulations of new sources, new vehicles, and hazardous pollutants

1. Existing stationary sources/motor vehicles–federal government sets national air quality standards with state enforcement
   a. National ambient air quality standards–"primary" standards protect health; "secondary" standards protect public welfare
   b. State Implementation Plans (SIP)–states submit plans to EPA; public comments, EPA final approval
   c. Prevention of Significant Deterioration Areas (PSD)–prevent deterioration of air quality exceeding NAAQS levels; limited increases in air pollution allowed
   d. Nonattainment areas–special rules for areas not meeting applicable NAAQS; total emissions from existing stationary sources and proposed new/modified source must not exceed total emissions allowed from existing sources at time permit sought; obtaining permit requires reducing total emissions from all sources

2. New source standards–federal government establishes national standards for new stationary sources, hazardous air pollutants, and new vehicles
   a. Stationary sources–constructed or modified after publication of applicable regulations; standard more stringent than existing sources
   b. Vehicles–emission standards for new motor vehicles/engines; require reformulated fuels to reduce ozone, carbon monoxide pollution
   c. Hazardous air pollutants–establish national emission standards for hazardous/toxic pollutants carrying serious health threats
   d. Acid rain–end precipitation containing high levels of sulfuric or nitric acid; schedule requires significant reductions by 2000

C. Clean Water Act–applies to all U.S. navigable waters/tributaries, nonnavigable intrastate waters if misuse affects interstate commerce, and freshwater wetlands; goal to restore, maintain chemical, physical, and biological integrity of nation's waters; establishes different schemes for attaining quality levels; different programs for point and non-point pollution sources

1. Point sources–discernible, defined, discrete pollution discharge source; EPA establishes effluent limitations for categories
   a. Effluent limitations–required application of best practical control technology currently available by 1977 and application of best available technology economically achievable by 1983; different standards apply to publicly owned treatment works
   b. National Pollutant Discharge Elimination System (NPDES)–discharge permit required from EPA, the Army Corps of Engineers, or state agency
   c. 1977 Amendments–extend, modify deadlines; divide pollutants into categories: toxic, conventional, nonconventional with different deadlines, standards for each

2. Nonpoint source pollution–control difficulties; 1987 federal amendments require state identifying waters violating requirements and instituting "best management practices" to control nonpoint sources; EPA must approve state plans

3. New source performance standards–EPA establishes federal performance standards; requires best available demonstrated control technology; permits required to discharge of pollutants

D. Hazardous Substances–result from technological advances; statutes deal with different types of harm
    1. Federal Insecticide, Fungicide and Rodenticide Act (FIFRA)–pesticide registration with EPA before distribution; use permitted if "unreasonable adverse effects on environment" when used in accordance with commonly recognized practice, and pesticide complies with FIFRA labeling requirements
    2. Toxic Substance Control Act (TSCA)–EPA notification before using new chemical, new use of an existing chemical; requires testing of any existing or new substances if unreasonable health or environment risk might occur; substance banned if insufficient data on health or environment risk, testing necessary to develop such data, or substance poses unreasonable health or environment risk
    3. Resource Conservation and Recovery Act (RCRA)–comprehensive scheme for treating solid hazardous waste; states regulate nonhazardous waste; EPA regulates all phases of hazardous waste (EPA monitored manifest system); generator (producer/handler of hazardous waste) specifies quantity, composition, origin, routing, destination of hazardous waste on specified form; owner/operator of hazardous waste treatment, storage, disposal sites maintain records, comply with EPA system.
    4. Superfund–Comprehensive Environmental Response, Compensation and Liability Act; passed to cleanup abandoned, inactive hazardous waste sites; requires EPA establishing National Contingency Plan (NCP) for procedures, standards to respond to hazardous substance releases; EPA takes removal or remedial action; states, private parties also pursue such action

E. International Protection of Ozone Layer
    1. 1987 Montreal protocol on substances that deplete the ozone layer–signed by United States and twenty-three countries; signatories obligated to reduce production and consumption of chemicals depleting ozone layer; calls for elimination of chloroflurocarbons (CFCs) and halon by the year 2000; executive order eliminates these chemicals in United States by 1996
    2. 1997 Kyoto protocol–treaty to reduce greenhouse gases

TRUE/FALSE: Circle true or false.

T   F   1. When seeking an injunction based on a nuisance theory, the plaintiff must prove the unreasonableness of the defendant's conduct.

T   F   2. An action for trespass requires the plaintiff proving an interference with possession of land.

T   F   3. The National Environmental Policy Act focuses on preventing specific types of environmental damage caused by certain, targeted hazardous substances.

T   F   4. Under NEPA, "federal action" is broadly interpreted and applies to a variety of activities.

T   F   5. NEPA's requirements, since they are primarily substantive, require that the federal agency in question take positive steps to reduce the adverse environmental effects of the proposed federal action.

T   F   6. Under the Clean Air Act, states have primary responsibility for regulating new sources of air pollution including new vehicles and hazardous air pollutants.

T   F   7. Once the EPA issues new ambient air quality standards, states must submit implementation plans detailing how they will enforce and comply with the new standards.

T   F   8. Under amendments to the Clean Air Act seeking to prevent significant deterioration areas from expanding, the EPA allows increases in air pollution equal to the difference between current pollution levels and those established under the quality standards.

T   F   9. Air quality emission standards covering existing sources are more restrictive than those covering new sources.

T   F   10. The Clean Water Act applies only to coastal waters within fifty miles of America's coastlines and commercially navigable rivers within the United States.

T   F   11. During a cancellation process in accordance with FIFRA guidelines, pesticides under review can still be produced and sold for use.

T   F   12. The Resource Conservation and Recovery Act gives states primary responsibility for regulating all types of solid waste, both hazardous and nonhazardous.

KEY TERMS–MATCHING EXERCISE: Select the term that best completes each statement below.

1. Montreal Protocol

2. Environmental Quality Council

3. Nonattainment Area

4. Environmental Assessment

5. Strict Liability

6. Private nuisance

7. Bubble concept

8. Superfund

9. Nonpoint

10. Manifest System

11. Primary Standards

12. Kyoto Protocol

13. Clean Air Act

14. Implementation Plan

15. Environmental Support Statement

16. Effluent Limitation

17. Trespass

18. Environmental Protection Agency

19. Toxic Substance Control Act

20. Public nuisance

_____ 1. Federal legislation providing funds for cleaning up hazardous waste dump sites.

_____ 2. Air quality guidelines intended to protect public health.

_____ 3. Water quality control standard regulating the amount of pollution discharged into lakes and rivers.

_____ 4. Water pollution source caused by how land is used not originating from a single, specific discharge location.

_____ 5. Activity disrupting the health or safety of a community.

_____ 6. Proposed treaty for developed nations to reduce greenhouse gas emissions that contribute to global warming climatic changes.

_____ 7. Treaty limiting use of chemicals that deplete the ozone layer.

_____ 8. Advisory group recommending to the president environmental protection policy goals and initiatives.

_____ 9. State administered programs for enforcing and maintaining federal air quality standards.

_____ 10. EPA guidelines treating a facility emitting air pollution from several points as a single discharge source.

_____ 11. Location not in compliance with federal air quality guidelines.

_____ 12. Federal legislation regulating the production and use of hazardous chemicals.

_____ 13. Federally mandated record keeping tracking the production, storage and disposal of hazardous wastes.

_____ 14. Detailed assessment of how proposed federal action will affect the environment.

_____ 15. Common law tort theory of recovery based on abnormally dangerous activity.

MULTIPLE CHOICE: Select the alternative that best completes each statement below.

_____ 1. Drawbacks to using private, civil litigation to remedy and control environmental damage include (a) high costs of lawsuits (b) a losing defendant might not be deterred from continuing the activity (c) difficulty of proving causation (d) all of the above.

_____ 2. When the EPA decides proposed federal action requires an EIS, the process requiring the agency to consult other federal agencies and the general public to determine the breadth and issues addressed in the document is called _____ . (a) scraping (b) targeting (c) scoping (d) scanning

_____ 3. When deciding whether to issue an injunction in a private nuisance action, courts consider various factors including (a) gravity of harm (b) social value of the activity (c) public interest (d) all of the above.

_____ 4. An EIS must explain in detail _____ associated with proposed federal action. (a) irrevocable commitment of resources (b) unavoidable adverse environmental effects (c) alternatives to the proposed action (d) all of the above

_____ 5. _____ is the analytic process used by courts to decide whether an injunction is an appropriate response to a private nuisance claim. (a) equitable apportionment (b) balancing the equities (c) neutral analysis (d) none of the above

_____ 6. Under the Clean Air Act, the EPA may impose civil penalties of up to (a) $25,000 per violation (b) $25,000 per day of violation (c) $70,000 per violation (d) $70,000 per day of violation.

_____ 7. Under the National Pollution Discharge Elimination Program, persons discharging pollutants into U.S. waters from _____ must first receive a discharge permit. (a) point sources (b) nonpoint sources (c) agricultural runoff (d) all of the above

_____ 8. The RCRA's manifest system applies to _____ of hazardous wastes. (a) generators (b) stores and disposers (c) transporters (d) all of the above

_____ 9. _____ is a brief analysis by a federal agency proposing certain action to determine whether an EIS is required for the project. (a) environmental assessment (b) impact factor analysis (c) environmental priority statement (d) goals allocation proposal

_____ 10. Under the Clean Water Act, a "discernible, confined and discrete conveyance" discharging pollutants is called a _____ source. (a) nonpoint (b) nonattainment (c) point (d) target

_____ 11. FIRA regulations grant EPA authority to permit distribution and use of registered pesticides if (a) they pose no risk of adverse environmental effects (b) products meet state labeling requirements (c) their composition meets manufacturer performance claims (d) all of the above.

_____ 12. CERCLA funds to cover hazardous waste clean-up costs come from taxes on (a) businesses with over $20 million in annual income (b) all chemical manufactures (c) the petroleum industry (d) sales of chemicals used for consumer purposes.

_____ 13. TSCA gives the EPA authority to require testing of substances if (a) manufacturing or distributing them may present unreasonable risks of injury to health or the environment (b) there is not sufficient data on the effects of the substance on health and the environment (c) testing is necessary to develop data on the effects of the substance on health and the environment (d) all of the above.

CASE PROBLEMS–SHORT ESSAY ANSWERS: Read each case problem carefully. When appropriate, answer by stating a decision for the case and by explaining the rationale–Rule of Law–relied upon to support your decision.

1. Ajax Petro Industries Inc. produces agricultural pesticides, marketing their line of chemical products in America and abroad. To what extent are Ajax's operations subject to FIFRA regulations?

   Decision: _____

   _____

   Rule of Law: _____

   _____

2. Executive Home Builders Inc. purchases a tract of farmland for a residential development site. Before completing their purchase, Executive examines the ownership history of the land and finds it had been used exclusively for agricultural purposes since the 1890s. Executive hires Water Quality Consultants Inc. to test whether the ground water is suitable for residential wells and finds wide spread contamination from agricultural chemical wastes. Executive reports the findings to the EPA, which orders a clean-up of the site and bills Executive for the costs. Executive refuses to pay, arguing that since they neither participated in nor knew of the waste dumping, they should not face any liability. Who wins this dispute and why?

   Decision: _____

   _____

Rule of Law: _____

_____

3. Travis Trucking Inc. ships hazardous waste from the manufacturer to federally licensed disposal sites. To what extent does the RCRA manifest systems apply to Travis' operations?

Decision: _____

_____

Rule of Law: _____

_____

4. Petro Industries, Inc. produces a range of chemical products for manufacturing and agricultural use. One of its products, Zalene, properly registered under TSCA, is used widely as a leather preservative and sealant. Recent company health records reveal a sudden increase in skin problems and headaches reported by employees handling Zalene. Stores selling Zalene-treated products report customers complaining of similar problems. What action can be taken in response to these reports?

Decision: _____

_____

Rule of Law: _____

_____

5. Re-read question #2. What recourse under CERCLA might Executive Inc. have against the former owners of the land for money damages compensating them for lost property value attributable to the environmental damage?

Decision: _____

_____

Rule of Law: _____

_____

Chapter 47

INTERNATIONAL BUSINESS LAW

SCOPE NOTE

Today's marketplace is increasingly global in nature. Transnational business–commercial activity conducted across national boundaries–is commonplace. The flow of goods, services, technology, credit and information in an international marketplace requires understanding legal principles and processes beyond that of the U.S. alone. Since single authority of international law exists, problems arise over which nation's laws apply to interpreting and enforcing multinational business agreements. Knowledge of international legal systems, doctrines and procedures associated with worldwide trade and commerce is important. Chapter 47 examines that area of law dealing with multinational business activities. The controlling principles, purposes, organizations and business relationships relating to international law are discussed in the context of the contemporary reality of a global economy.

EDUCATIONAL OBJECTIVES

1. Understand the importance of the sources and institutions of international law.

2. Explain the authority and functions of the International Court of Justice and Regional Trade Communities.

3. Discuss the role of treaties in multinational business relations–GATT and NAFTA.

4. Know the significance of jurisdiction over foreign government action by differentiating the doctrines of Sovereign Immunity and Act of State.

5. Delineate the risks of and protection against governments taking over foreign investment property.

6. Outline crucial aspects, complications and problems associated with multinational commercial activity in the context of (a) trade relations; (b) labor force; (c) investment financing and payments; (d) contract negotiations; and (e) American antitrust laws.

7. Identify and distinguish among the various forms of transnational enterprises including (a) direct export sales; (b) foreign agents; (c) distributorships; (d) licensing agreements; (e) joint ventures; and (f) wholly owned subsidiaries.

CHAPTER OUTLINE

I. International Legal Environment–covers conduct/relations of nations, international organizations, and persons; not enforceable since international courts lack compulsory jurisdiction to resolve disputes, enforce rulings; courts of nations enforce international law to same extent as domestic law if nation has adopted international law as its own law
    A. International Court of Justice–United Nations 15 judge judicial branch; all judges from different nations; nations, not private parties, have standing to bring actions; jurisdiction only when nations agree to be bound by decision; no official means to enforce decisions
    B. Regional Trade Communities–organizations, conferences, treaties focus on business/trade regulation
        1. European Economic Union (formerly Common Market)–formed in 1957 (Treaty of Rome), to remove trade barriers, unify economic policies
        2. Other regional trade communities: Central American Market (CACM), Caribbean Common Market (CARICOM), Association of South East Asian Nations (ASEAN), Andean Common Market (ANDEAN), and Economic Community of West African States (ECOWAS)
    C. International Treaties–agreements between independent nations; U.S. Constitution provides all valid treaties are "law of the land" with legal force of federal statute
        1. General Agreement on Tariffs and Trade (GATT)–multinational trade treaty; now called World Trade Organization; facilitates flow of trade by limiting trade barriers (import quotas, custom duties, export regulations, subsidies, import fees, etc.); most favored nation provision requires signatories to treat one another as favorably as they treat other countries
        2. North Atlantic Free Trade Agreement (NAFTA)–1994; free trade area among United States, Canada, Mexico

II. Jurisdiction Over Actions of Foreign Governments–limits on power, nations to exercise jurisdiction over foreign nation or to take property of foreign citizens
    A. Sovereign Immunity–nation's absolute, total authority over what happens within own territory; immunity of foreign sovereign from courts of host country
        1. Foreign Sovereign Immunities Act–establishes when immunity given foreign nations; nation not immune from jurisdiction of U.S. or state courts if action based on foreign nation's commercial activity in U.S., commercial activity carried on out outside U.S. having direct effect in U.S.
    B. Act of State Doctrine–nation's courts do not question validity of actions of foreign governments within own borders; nations respect independence of other sovereign nations

1. Exceptions to act of state doctrines–waiver of right to raise the defense; commercial activities of foreign nation

C. Taking Foreign Investment Property–expropriation, nationalization when government seizes foreign-owned property, assets for public purpose, pays owner just compensation; confiscation when no payment (or an inadequate payment) given for seized property, or property sized for nonpublic purpose; U.S. firms insured against risk through private insurer or Overseas Private Investment Corporation (OPIC)

III. Transacting Business Abroad–selling goods, information, services, investing capital or arranging for movement of labor; legal controls imposed on flow of trade, labor, capital across national borders

A. Flow of Trade–devices used by nations to protect domestic businesses
   1. Tariff–tax on goods entering a country; raise price of imported goods, causing consumers to purchase less expensive, domestic goods
   2. Nontariff barriers–import quotas, import bans, overly restrictive safety or manufacturing standards, complicated customs procedures, subsidies to local industry
   3. Export controls–control flow of goods out of country for various policy reasons (national defense, foreign policy, protect scarce resources)

B. Flow of Labor–passports to enter; visas permit entrances for specific purpose; specified length of stay

C. Flow of Capital–International Monetary Fund (IMF) facilitates expansion, balanced growth of international trade, assists eliminating foreign exchange restrictions; banks also facilitate flow of capital, trade

D. International Contracts–issues of language, customs, legal systems, currency differences; contract should designate language, currency, what law will govern, which nation's courts will resolve disputes, including arbitration; *force majeure* clause apportions liabilities/responsibilities of parties in event of unforeseeable occurrence
   1. CISG–United States, forty other countries, ratified U.N. Convention of Contracts for the International Sale of Goods; governs contracts for international sales of goods between parties located in ratifying nations
   2. Letters of credit–promise by buyer's bank to pay seller when certain conditions met; buyer enters second contract with local bank (issuer), calling for bank to pay agreed price upon presentation of documents; commitment by buyer's bank is irrevocable letter of credit; correspondent paying bank in seller's country makes payment to seller

E. Antitrust Laws–Sherman Act provides broad, extraterritorial reach of U.S. antitrust laws; amendments limit application to unfair methods of competition having direct, substantial, foreseeable effect on U.S. commerce

F. Securities Regulation–U.S. securities laws apply to securities issued in America; antifraud provisions apply where either *conduct* or *effect* in U.S. from violation

G. Protection of Intellectual Property–U.S. laws do not apply in foreign countries; owner of intellectual property right protected under laws of country in question; U. S. belongs to multinational treaties designed to protect intellectual property

H. Foreign Corrupt Practices Act (FCPA)–prohibits domestic firms from bribing foreign governmental or political officials; violations result in fines for individuals up to $100,00 (corporations up to $2 million) and/or imprisonment up to five years
    1. International Antibribery/Fair Competition Act–updates FCPA

IV. Forms of Multinational Enterprises–business engaging in transactions involving movement of goods, information, money, people, or services across nations; considerations regarding form of multinational business enterprise include financing, tax consequences, legal restrictions, degree of control over the business sought by enterprise
    A. Direct Export Sales–seller contracts directly with buyer in other country; simplest, least involved
    B. Foreign Agents–agency relationships desired by companies wanting limited involvement in international market
    C. Distributorships–distributor takes title to merchandise; susceptible to antitrust violations
    D. Licensing–sale of intellectual property right; foreign firm pays royalties for using right
        1. Franchising–form of licensing; owner grants permission to foreign business to use intellectual property under specified conditions
    E. Joint Ventures–independent businesses from different countries coordinate efforts for common result; share profits/liabilities according to contract; companies assigned responsibility
    F. Wholly Owned Subsidiaries–advantage of retaining authority, control over all phases of operation

TRUE-FALSE: Circle true or false.

T   F   1. Generally speaking, expropriations are considered violations of international law while confiscations are not.

T   F   2. Under contemporary policies, the sovereign immunity doctrine applies only to public acts.

T   F   3. GATT favors import quotas as the preferred method to protect domestic businesses.

T   F   4. Foreign enterprises issuing securities for sale in America must comply with U.S. security regulation laws.

T   F   5. American citizens working for U.S. businesses in foreign countries are not protected by U.S. employment discriminate laws.

T   F   6. Judges sitting on the International Court of Justice are elected by the U.N. General Assembly and Security Council.

T   F   7. A significant advantage associated with the wholly owned subsidiary approach to conducting transnational business is the retention of control and authority this approach affords overall aspects of the commercial activity undertaken.

T F 8. Using direct export sales as a method of conducting international business carries the most risk of committing antitrust violations.

T F 9. In most cases, American companies conducting business abroad are fully protected by American intellectual property laws.

T F 10. International law, in contrast to domestic law, is generally not readily enforceable.

T F 11. The Foreign Sovereign Immunities Act allows for jurisdiction of U.S. courts over foreign commercial activity.

T F 12. In cases of transnational commercial activity carried out through agency relationships, the agent typically acquires title to the goods bought and sold.

KEY TERMS–MATCHING EXERCISE: Select the term that best completes each statement below.

1. Customs certificate
2. Joint venture
3. Favored nation status
4. European Union
5. Distributorship
6. Sovereign immunity
7. Passport
8. European Economic Community

9. Treaty
10. Tariff
11. General Agreement on Trade & Tariffs
12. Letter of credit
13. Acts of State Doctrine
14. Expropriation
15. NAFTA

16. International Court of Justice
17. Confiscation
18. International law
19. Licensing
20. Foreign Corrupt Practices Act

_____ 1. Doctrine protecting foreign countries from application of host country laws.

_____ 2. Multinational agreement intended to remove trade barriers between countries and enhance international trade relations.

_____ 3. Agreement between countries to accomplish common, desirable goals.

_____ 4. Judicial branch of the United Nations.

_____ 5. Law relating to activities, relations between countries.

_____ 6. Policy limiting extent of host country judicial intervention in internal foreign government actions.

_____ 7. Government seizure of foreign-owned property for a public purpose accompanied by just compensation.

_____ 8. Government tax on imports or exports to protect domestic business.

_____ 9. Treaty establishing a free trade zone among Canada, the U.S. and Mexico.

_____ 10. Individual companies from different countries coordinating commercial activity to achieve a common goal.

_____ 11. Sale of intellectual property rights to foreign companies for use in foreign markets.

_____ 12. Congressional act prohibiting American enterprises from bribing foreign officials for economic political gain.

_____ 13. Commitment from purchaser's bank to pay seller of goods or services upon happening of specified conditions.

_____ 14. Document from customs officials clearing goods for export.

_____ 15. Agreement among European nations to promote common economic policy and eliminate trade barriers.

MULTIPLE CHOICE: Select the alternative that best completes each statement below.

_____ 1. Nontariff barriers used by countries to protect and promote domestic industries include (a) export controls (b) import quotas (c) streamlined customs procedures (d) all of the above.

_____ 2. _____ occurs when governments take control over foreign owned property without returning just compensation or for a nonpublic purpose. (a) expropriation (b) equitable cloture (c) confiscation (d) liquidation

_____ 3. Under U.S. law, the Act of State doctrine does not apply to (a) waivers of the defense (b) property claims based on alleged improper confiscation by a third nation (c) business conducted by a foreign government (d) all of the above.

_____ 4. Public activities undertaken by governments to which the Sovereign Immunity doctrine applies are (a) restrictions on natural resource use (b) military equipment purchases (c) buying stock in an American corporation (d) none of the above.

_____ 5. The effectiveness of the International Court of Justice is limited since (a) its decisions are enforceable only through criminal sanctions (b) jurisdiction is limited to disputes between private parties (c) it has authority only over parties who voluntarily submit to its jurisdiction and agree to abide by its ruling (d) no provisions are made for exercising advisory jurisdiction.

_____ 6. Under a/n _____ form of multinational business relationship, the foreign business representative acquires ownership in the goods received. (a) agency (b) distributorship (c) wholly owned subsidiary (d) licensing

_____ 7. _____ is a type of licensing arrangement tied to specific limitations. (a) franchising (b) partitioning (c) joint partnership (d) none of the above

_____ 8. The _____ was created in part to help reduce foreign currency exchange limitations that hinder the development of international trade. (a) United Nations Bank (b) International Trade. Bank (c) World Financial Federation (d) International Monetary Fund

_____ 9. Problems unique to transnational business agreements include (a) contract negotiations (b) mutually acceptable terms of agreement (c) language and currency differences (d) all of the above.

_____ 10. Factors influencing which type of business organization should be chosen to undertake multinational business transactions include (a) limitations imposed by a host country (b) financing considerations (c) taxation issues (d) all of the above.

_____ 11. A contractual clause defining the rights of parties to a multinational business transaction upon the occurrence of an unforeseeable natural disaster or political crisis is called a/n _____ clause. (a) liquidated risk (b) force majeure (c) assumption of risk (d) equitable apportionment

_____ 12. The type of business relationship readily suited to limited involvement in an international market is (a) agency (b) joint venture (c) distributorship (d) wholly owned subsidiary.

_____ 13. American courts have applied the _____ or _____ test in deciding whether American securities laws apply to foreign transactions. (a) geographic area/total capitalization (b) compulsory ratio/prorated income flow (c) conduct/effect (d) none of the above

CASE PROBLEMS–SHORT ESSAY ANSWERS: Read each case problem carefully. When appropriate, answer by stating a Decision for the case and by explaining the rationale–Rule of Law–relied upon to support your decision.

1. Glewbenstein, a tiny country between France and Spain, is home to the Glewbenstein tree, whose sap is renown for its natural adhesive qualities. The Ministry of Science for Glewbenstein, in conjunction with the Economic Development Ministry, undertakes an extensive research program to determine the feasibility of developing industrial-strength adhesive products from the sap. The experimental results prove quite promising. Lacking extensive capital reserves, production capacity or management expertise within the country, the Ministry for Economic Development seeks foreign investors and businesses to develop a Glewbenstein glue industry. Several parties express an interest and it appears a deal will soon be struck. Glewbenstein officials, concerned that the company that emerges from the agreement remain under Glewbenstinian control, come to you for help in achieving that goal. What advice do you give them?

    Decision: _____

    _____

    Rule of Law: _____

    _____

2. Mediterranean Moods, Inc., a Spanish cosmetics and perfume company, and Splendid Scents of York, Pennsylvania, are competitors in the international perfume market. Desiring to protect their respective market shares, the two companies enter a reciprocal import/export restriction contract, agreeing to eliminate all direct competition between them in their home countries. What is the legal status of that agreement under American law?

    Decision: _____

    _____

    Rule of Law: _____

    _____

3. Monaco Enterprises, Inc., a gambling education program owned and operated by the government of Monaco, guarantees that program enrollees, using the expertise gained through the course, will become "instant winners." The $350, three-day seminar attracts many customers during its American tour. Grumblings from program graduates are soon heard, however, expressing general dissatisfaction over the level of skill and strategy presented in the course, arguing that it amounts to no more than a basic introductory, how-to course on typical gambling games. Many commence civil actions against Monaco Enterprises, Inc., in various state courts, seeking restitution of their enrollment fees based on false advertising and breach of an express warranty of "instant winners." The Monaco

government moves to dismiss these lawsuits on grounds of sovereign immunity. Is the defense likely to prevail on this argument?

Decision: _____

_____

Rule of Law: _____

_____

4. Re-read question # 1. Assume that a French bank and an Italian industrialist are interested in undertaking such an enterprise. They, along with representatives from the Glewbenstein Ministry of Economic Development, commence contract negotiations. Realizing the need for an international law business expert, the parties seek your advice regarding contract form and content to provide for complications and problems associated with multinational commercial ventures. What do you tell them?

Decision: _____

_____

Rule of Law: _____

_____

5. Re-read question #2. Could the parties seek an advisory opinion regarding the legality of their agreement from the International Court of Justice? Explain.

Decision: _____

_____

Rule of Law: _____

_____

Chapter 48

CYBERLAW

SCOPE NOTE

Over the past decade, as advances in communications technology and business practices grew rapidly, legal issues and problems relating to clarity and certainty of business transactions as well as opportunities for fraud and theft emerged. Chapter 48 examines the various legal, regulatory issues surrounding the relationship between business e-commerce, Internet communication and the law in several areas most affected by the rapid developments in communications technology: defamation; intellectual property; contract and sales law; privacy; securities regulation; and cybercrime.

EDUCATIONAL OBJECTIVES

1. Discuss the interrelationship of defamation law, e-commerce and Internet practices.

2. Identify areas of intellectual property law directly related to and affected by Internet and e-commerce practices.

3. Explain specific areas of contract and sales law having special relevance to developments in e-commerce and the Internet.

4. Know the types of privacy intrusion problems associated with e-commerce and Internet use and the legal doctrines available for protection.

5. Discuss the nature of abuses involving Internet-based securities transactions and attempts to control them under federal securities laws.

6. Explain the nature of online crime and the law's response to cybercrime.

CHAPTER OUTLINE

I. Defamation–unprivileged false statement damaging another's reputation.
  A. Elements for recovery: false, defamatory statement about another; publication; intentionally or recklessly communicated; resulting harm
  B. Types: oral/spoken (slander); written, printed, Internet (libel)
  C. 1996 Communications Decency Act: Internet service providers immune from defamation liability for publishing information provided by another

II. Intellectual Property Protection–federal laws giving exclusive ownership rights to creators, expressors of original ideas; type of protection varies with type of idea, medium of expression
  A. Copyrights: exclusive ownership rights to authors of original works–use, reproduce, sell works; applies to computer programs
    1. No Electronic Theft Act–criminalizes willful infringement (pirating) of copyrighted material; absence of personal profit motive no defense
    2. Digital Millennium Copyright Act–criminalizes circumventing, developing/distributing technology to circumvent, programs designed to prevent unauthorized access to copyrighted material
    3. Digital Theft Deterrence and Copyright Damages Improvement Act–raises statutory damages minimums
    4. Types of infringement–postings; e-mailings; hyperlinking; framing
    5. Defenses to infringement–fair use doctrine (research, teaching, news reporting, criticism, comment) depends on purpose, intent of use (non-commercial, no personal financial gain), type, amount, portion of use, and effect (market value, value of copyrighted material) of use
  B. Trademarks: Federal Trademark (Lanham) Act covers trademarks (identifies, distinguishes goods), service marks (identifies, distinguishes services), certification marks (goods, services meet certain specifications), collective marks (membership in trade organization)
    1. Required elements–distinctive (clear origin identification), not immoral or deceptive
    2. Infringement–unauthorized use of identical/similar mark likely to cause confusion, mistake or deception
      a. Cybersquatting prohibited under Cybersquatting Consumer Protection Act: bad faith, profit motivated pirating (public benefit, charitable purpose defense)
      b. Metatagging–using another's metatags and representing them as one's own may be infringement
  C. Patents: unrenewable federal exclusive ownership protection for inventors (self use, etc.) for designated term
    1. Utility patents–cover products, process, machine, composition; 20 year duration
    2. Requirements–useful, novel, not obvious
    3. Applies to Internet related programs
    4. Unrestricted public use at expiration of protection term–enters public domain

   D. Trade Secrets: commercially valuable, secret, confidential information
       1. State law governs–misappropriation triggers civil remedies
       2. Economic Espionage Act–federal law prohibits theft (unloading/downloading another's protected trade secrets)

III. Contracts/Sales Law–state common law and U.C.C. Article 2
   A. E-Commerce General Pattern: usually follows Article 2, sales of goods law
   B. Areas of Confusion: when do enforceable contracts exist
       1. Shrinkwrap license
       2. Click wrap license
   C. Uniform Computer Information Transaction Act: rules for computer information (create, modify, transfer, license) agreements; covers transfer and access contracts
   D. Electronic Records: Uniform Electronic Transaction Act; state law validating electronic (e-mail, online) contracts; covers signatures, machine based transactions
   E. Electronic Signatures/Global National Commerce Act: federal law validating personal property sale, lease, licensing, exchange, or service and real property sale, lease or exchange; assures validity of Internet and e-mail agreements regardless of statute of frauds
   F. Covenants Not to Compete: contract prohibits employees from working for competitor of former employer (similar trade, profession or business)
       1. Validity requirements–purpose to protect property interest; reasonable limitations (geographic area, time period, activity, hardship created)
       2. Valid in e-commerce employment

IV. Internet and Privacy Law
   A. Protecting Personal Identifiable Information on Internet: U.S. Constitution protects personal privacy rights against government intrusion, not against intrusion by private parties
       1. Protection against privacy intrusion by private parties–common or statutory law
           a. Tort law–protection against behavior of private individuals; invasion of privacy claim
           b. Types of privacy invasion–appropriating name or likeness; intrusion on seclusion; publicly disclosing private facts; publicly putting another in false light
           c. Individual has few protections against online intrusion; FTC recommendations for establishing privacy protection covering consumer focused web sites
       2. Protecting Children–Children Online Privacy Protection Act gives children under 13 and their parents privacy rights regarding Internet transactions–web sites collecting, storing, distributing personal information
           a. COPPA requirements–post notice of information sought; purpose of information; disclosure practices; obtain verifiable parental consent
   B. Freedom From Government Intrusion: consitutional protection
   C. Freedom from Employment Intrusion: no constitutional protection; based on employment/union contract terms
       1. Employee e-mail usage–employer accesses employee messages when employee using workplace e-mail system; private non-employer e-mail system not employer accessible

V. Securities Regulation Law and Internet Transaction
   A. Security Defined: any stock, bond, note, interest certificate or investment contract
      1. Federal regulation of interstate securities transactions–1933 & 1934 SEC Acts
   B. Regulation of Securities Issuance: 1933 SEC Act
      1. Registration requirement for interstate sales unless exemptions apply
      2. Disclosure of accurate, material information required for public offering unless exempted
      3. Anti-fraud provisions
   C. Regulation of Secondary (Resale) Transactions: 1934 SEC Act
      1. Security registration required for regulated, publicly held companies
      2. Reporting requirements
      3. Anti-fraud provisions
   D. Electronic Media: SEC permitted online information delivery if notice, access and proof similar to paper delivery exists
   E. EDGAR: SEC computerized collecting, validation, indexing, acceptance and distribution of required reports
   F. Permitted Internet Securities Activities
      1. 1933 Act Registered Public Offerings–Internet disclosure of required documents acceptable if electronic delivery notice, access, and proof similar to paper delivery exists
        a. Investor consent required for web site electronic disclosure
      2. Regulation A–unregistered issuance of up to $5 million of securities in a 12 month period requires SEC regional office filing, accessible prospectus
      3. Private Offerings of Securities–Regulation D–no general, public solicitation; exempt from 1933 Act registration; securities repurchaseable by qualified accredited investors
        a. Internet sales prohibited without screening procedure (password protected web site page) assuring access only by qualified, accredited participants
   G. Internet and Fraudulent Use: Internet securities sales and increased fraud
      1. Recovering defrauded money difficult
      2. Examples of online securities fraud–selling worthless, overvalued ("pump and dump") stock; price manipulation
      3. SEC's education, surveillance, prosecution response

VI. Cybercrime: "instrument" crime committed by computer usage (gambling, pornography, money laundering, intellectual property infringement, gambling); "target" crime committed against a computer (theft, destruction of proprietary interest, vandalism, service denial, defacing, etc)
   A. Computer Fraud and Abuse Act: criminalizes certain interstate computer usage: unauthorized access or damage; fraudulent access, distributing confidential passwords; extortion, threats based on computer damage
   B. Other federal/state anti fraud laws applied to Internet use

TRUE–FALSE: Circle True or False

T   F   1. Most Internet related defamation cases are dealt with as slander.

T   F   2. Federal copyright law gives protection to computer programs.

T   F   3. When employee Elmore sends a defamatory message about fellow employee Elmer only to Elmer at work, no publication has occurred.

T   F   4. A violation of the No Electronic Theft Act occurs even if the person pirating another's copyrighted work has no intention to personally profit from the infringement.

T   F   5. Mickey Mouse's sperm count is not information subject to trade secret protection.

T   F   6. Internet related processes are not given patent protection since they rarely if ever meet the general requirements for receiving a patent.

T   F   7. Congressional efforts to regulate Internet pornography marketed to children have been ruled unconstitutional by the U.S. Supreme Court.

T   F   8. The U.S. Constitution does not protect the privacy of people from being interfered with by the acts of other individuals.

T   F   9. The Federal Trade Commission has primary authority to issue and enforce federal security regulations.

T   F   10. Using computers as an instrument of crime includes money laundering and copyright infringement.

T   F   11. When Ajax Inc. posts online notice of a private offering of its stock in a password protected page on its web site, which can be opened only by members who meet qualifications as accredited investors, it has complied with Regulation D covering private stock offerings.

T   F   12. E-commerce has created few if any problems or complications in complying with state sales tax laws.

KEY TERMS–MATCHING EXERCISE: Select the term that best completes each statement below.

---

1. Service mark
2. Non-compete agreement
3. Cyberlaw
4. Carnivore
5. Slander
6. Trade secret
7. Communications Decency Act

8. Cybercrime
9. Metatags
10. Domain name
11. Hyperlinking
12. Securities Act of 1934
13. Securities Act of 1933
14. Trageted marketing

15. Pump and dump
16. Defamation
17. Fair use
18. Uniform Electronic Transactions Act
19. Keying
20. Collective mark

____ 1. False, unprivileged statement to a third person damaging another's reputation.

____ 2. Act of Congress giving immunity from liability to Internet service providers for publishing information originating from another.

____ 3. Doctrine allowing use of another's copyrighted work for legitimate teaching, research, news reporting or artistic criticism purposes.

____ 4. Designated title of a web site's electronic address.

____ 5. Distinctive symbol indicating the product manufacturer's membership in a trade association.

____ 6. Employer's contract with employees prohibiting them from obtaining future employment with a competitor of the employer.

____ 7. Argument presented by Internet sites justifying compiling personal information on customers to create a demographic profile.

____ 8. E-mail scanning software program used by the FBI to search the Internet use for evidence of criminal activity.

____ 9. Using a computer to steal another's property or to conduct illegal gambling.

____ 10. Entering false or misleading information online to raise a stock's value for the purpose of increasing personal profits on the stock's sale.

____ 11. Area of law dealing with legal and regulatory issues surrounding the growth of the Internet and contemporary business practices.

_____ 12. Federal law regulating the interstate sales of securities.

_____ 13. Words used by web site owners to describe the contents of their sites.

_____ 14. Commercially valuable confidential information not available to public knowledge.

_____ 15. Uniform state law enacted to overcome Statute of Frauds enforceability issues surrounding e-commerce contracts.

MUTLIPLE CHOICE: Select the alternative that best completes each statement below.

_____ 1. _____ is not required for a false statement to be either libel or slander. (a) knowledge of falsity (b) publication (c) allegation of immoral behavior (d) unprivileged communication

_____ 2. Protection under federal law giving exclusive ownership rights to authors of original works is a (a) trade name (b) copyright (c) patent (d) collective mark.

_____ 3. In determining whether the fair use doctrine applies in a case, courts review the (a) amount and portion of copyrighted material used (b) degree of harm sustained by a copyright owner resulting from unauthorized use (c) nature and purpose of unauthorized use (d) all of the above.

_____ 4. Registering the name of a web site electronic address containing trademarks owned by others with the intent to sell the web site name to the trademark owner is called (a) formsetting (b) hyperlinking (c) cybersquatting (d) none of the above.

_____ 5. Patents apply to _____ inventions. (a) novel (b) useful (c) non-obvious (d) all of the above

_____ 6. Factors evaluated in determining the reasonableness and enforceability of agreements not to compete include (a) geographic area and length of time covered (b) respective market share and profitability of the parties (c) number of persons employed by the parties (d) all of the above.

_____ 7. _____ is federal law that prohibits creating or distributing technology designed to circumvent technological protection against the unauthorized access of copyrighted materials. (a) No Electronic Theft Act (b) Digital Millennium Copyright Act (c) Uniform Computer Transaction Act (d) Uniform Electronic Transfer Act

_____ 8. The FTC has recommended that online services _____ before they can collect and/or sell personal identification information on their customers. (a) take reasonable security measures against unauthorized access or use (b) allow customer access to the information (c) give customers notice of the practice (d) all of the above

_____ 9. _____ is not a federally recognized trade symbol. (a) metamark (b) service mark (c) collective mark (d) none of the above

____ 10. Before companies can direct online services to children, federal law requires the businesses to first _____ and _____ . (a) post a $1.5 million security bond/obtain an FCC operator's license (b) verify compliance with the FTC best business judgment standard/receive approval from the Department of Justice (c) notify customers of their business/receive parental consent (d) none of the above

____ 11. Deliberately flooding an Internet service provider with junk e-mail to "lock-up" the service is an example of a/n (a) instrument (b) target (c) metatagged (d) hyperlinked type of computer crime.

____ 12. The Internet has (a) expanded the pool of potential investors (b) reduced the opportunities for fraud in investing (c) decreased the scope of federal securities law (d) all of the above.

____ 13. Under federal securities law, electronic media includes (a) phone messages (b) e-mail (c) videotapes (d) all of the above.

CASE PROBLEMS–SHORT ESSAY ANSWERS: Read each case problem carefully. When appropriate, answer by stating a Decision for the case and by explaining the rationale–Rule of Law–relied upon to support your decision.

1. Clyde Hatfield and Elmer McCoy, aerospace engineers at Aviatec International, a defense contractor, dislike one another intensely. Their bitter dispute-ridden work association recently erupted into open hostility. Clyde sends messages from his home computer to the e-mail work addresses of colleagues falsely accusing Elmer of selling secret, classified Aviatec weapons system information to North Korea. Aviatec is quickly abuzz over whether Elmer is a spy and traitor. Livid with rage, Elmer threatens a lawsuit. Who, based on what theory of recovery, may be liable for the office gossip? Explain.

Decision: _____

_____

Rule of Law: _____

_____

2. Betty makes scone dough for Best Bakery's famous, feathery, light, flaky scones. The dough is made from a four-generations old secret Best family recipe. Betty, who takes pride in her work, is suddenly shifted to cookie cutting. Feeling slighted by what she considers a demotion, Betty e-mails the scone recipe to her quilting club members to get even with the Bests. Advise the Best family about their best course of action.

Decision: _____

_____

Rule of Law: _____

_____

3   Winston Winer, owner of the financially strapped Winey Enterprises, registers "WinNow.com" for his company's web site. Hoping to raise enough money to save the nearly insolvent Winey Company from possible creditor forced bankruptcy, Mr. Winer makes an online offering to the general public of Winey stock. In the Internet solicitation, Winston falsely lists Winey's net earnings for the previous fiscal year at $75 million on $125 million in sales. Several thousand investors who purchase Winey stock under the offering are saddened and infuriated to learn of Winston declaring personal and company bankruptcy and wonder what recourse they might have. Advise them.

Decision: _____

_____

Rule of Law: _____

_____

4. Under his web site BarrTen.com, Barry sells tennis equipment, instructional materials, and game strategy and advice. Customers desiring to do business with Barry are notified that all transactions are conducted electronically, a mandatory condition for making purchases off BarrTen. Pete, needing to improve his level of play, orders $1,785 of products for delivery to his home. The parties complete all necessary documents online and the goods are shipped. Three days after accepting delivery, Pete e-mails Barry of his intent not to pay for the goods asserting the Statute of Frauds as his defense. Is he correct in his assertion? Why or why not?

Decision: _____

_____

Rule of Law: _____

_____

5. Re-read Question #1. If Aviatec searched Clyde's e-mail postings through its own e-mail system, would they be liable for invading his privacy? Explain.

Decision: _____

_____

Rule of Law: _____

_____

REGULATION OF BUSINESS RESEARCH QUESTIONS: Drawing upon information contained in the text, as well as outside sources, discuss the following questions.

1. Two controversial areas of employment law are AIDS and drug-testing of employees. What legal issues surround such testing programs? Explain the rationale underlying employer and employee perspectives on these tests. How does Federal law deal with such testing programs? How do your state laws deal with this controversy?

2. Over the past several meetings among WTO leading member nations, civil demonstrators have called for WTO members to pay greater attention to humanitarian concerns in its trade policies with un- or underdeveloped nations. Demonstrations have focused on such issues as environmental degradation and pollution, livable wage scales, child and slave labor controls, IMF lending guidelines, and healthy/safe working conditions. What role, if any, can/should American law play in shaping WTO policy on these concerns? Explain.

Chapter 49

INTRODUCTION TO PROPERTY AND PROPERTY INSURANCE

SCOPE NOTE

Property rights, along with life and liberty, are among the most highly valued elements of our legal identities. English and American law view property rights as a fundamental component of a society governed by a system of laws. In the following chapters, we discuss the general principles and basic concepts of the American system of property law. What is property? What are the various categories of property interests? What limitations are placed on property ownership rights/duties? How does one acquire ownership to property? These and other concerns are the focus of attention in the upcoming materials.

Chapter 49 concludes by examining the basic principles and terminology of property insurance law-the nature and function of insurance, as well as the regulation of the conduct and the contract of the insurance parties. The types of property interests that can be insured against loss are focused upon.

EDUCATIONAL OBJECTIVES

1. Explain what is meant by the term "property."

2. Distinguish between the basic categories of property.

3. Know the rights/responsibilities of property ownership.

4. Understand the ways of acquiring title to personal property.

5. Describe the principles governing the law of fixtures.

6. Define insurance and discuss the role it plays in our lives.

7. Identify how the insurance industry is regulated.

8. Explain the characteristics of the various types of insurance companies.

9. Differentiate among the various types of property insurance.

10. Outline the requirements for and the steps involved in creating a valid, enforceable insurance contract.

11. Know the significance of the Insurable Interest doctrine in property insurance coverage.

12. Contrast waiver, estoppel, representations and warranties as they affect forfeiture and avoidance of an insurance contract.

13. Explain the rules controlling party performance and termination of an insurance contract.

CHAPTER OUTLINE

I. Kinds of Property–property classified based on nature/character of existence; classifications not mutually exclusive
   A. Tangible/Intangible–physical objects (chair, farm, pet) or protected interest in non-physical thing (stock certificate, patent, copyright, etc.)
   B. Real/Personal–land, all interests related to (non-movable); all property not real property (movable); transfer of real property requires formalities; personal property transferred simply, informally
   C. Fixtures–personal property firmly attached to, part of real property
      1. Determination depends on
         a. Intention of parties expressed in agreement
         b. No agreement–physical relationship of item to land or building, intention of person attaching item; purpose served by item; interest of person attaching item; degree of physical attachment (removal without damage)
      2. Trade fixture doctrine–item used in connection with tenant's trade; tenant removes trade fixture if can be done without material injury

II. Incidents of Property Ownership–significance of distinctions between real/personal property
   A. Proper Transfer of Title
   B. Taxation

III. Transferring Title to Personal Property–relatively easy; little formality; codified in U.C.C. Articles 2, 3 and 8–sales of goods, commercial paper, investment securities
   A. Sale–transfer for consideration (price); title passes when parties intend
   B. Gift–transfer without consideration (basic distinction to sale); promise to make a gift not binding
      1. Requirements–elements for valid gift

      a. Delivery–manual/physical transfer of item or constructive delivery (something symbolic representing control over an item not suitable for manual delivery–safe deposit key for contents)

      b. Intent–donor intends present gift

      c. Acceptance–by donee; actual or implied

  2. Classification

      a. *Inter vivos*–irrevocable made during lifetime

      b. *Causa mortis*–made in contemplation of imminent death; conditional and revocable

C. Will or Descent–transfer by inheritance, with/without a will

D. Accession–right of owner to any value increase by natural or artificial means

E. Confusion–intermixing of goods of different owners; separate property of all if no longer identifiable except as part of mass of like goods (fungibles); results from accident, mistake, willful act, or agreement; if goods apportionable, each owner has proportionate share of whole mass; willful/wrongful act causing confusion triggers loss of entire interest for wrongdoer who cannot prove proportionate share

F. Taking Possession

  1. Abandoned property–intentionally disposed of by owner; finder gains title

  2. Lost property–unintentionally left by owner; finder entitled to except to true owner; lost property in ground gives landowner superior claim over finder

  3. Mislaid property–intentionally placed by owner but forgotten; owner of premises, not finder, has first claim

  4. State statutes–vest title to lost property in finder when prescribed search, notice for owner, followed and no owner asserts claim

IV. Concurrent Ownership–property owned by two or more persons together; co-tenants hold undivided interests in entire indivisible whole

A. Forms–joint tenancy; tenancy in common; tenancy by entireties; community property; condominium; cooperative

V. Insurance

A. Nature of Insurance–distributes risk of loss among members (insured) through company (insurer); contractual undertaking by insurer to pay money to insured upon happening of event beyond control of contracting parties; McCarran-Ferguson Act gives states regulatory authority

B. Fire/Property Insurance–protection against loss resulting from fire, lightning, explosion, earthquake, water, wind, rain, collision, riot; coverage enlarged through "endorsement" or "rider"

C. Types of Fire–policies cover damage from "hostile" (outside normal area) fires, not "friendly" fires (contained in intended, usual area)

D. Co-insurance Clauses–sharing risk between insurer/insured; property insured for less than full, stated value; recovery based on formula: face value of policy or fair market value of property × co-insurance % × loss

E. Other Insurance Clauses–recovery liability distributed pro ratally among various insurers

F. Types of Policies

    1. Valued policy–marine policy; payment of value specifically agreed upon by insured/insurer at time policy entered

    2. Open policy–non-marine policy; no agreement of specific value of property; insurer pays fair market value of property immediately prior to loss

VI. Name of Insurance Agreements–contract law applies; policies generally standardized

  A. Offer/Acceptance–applicant makes offer; contract created when offer accepted by insurer (agent of); binders make agreement enforceable until completion of formal contract

  B. Insurable Interest–relationship between person and person/property insured; happening of possible, specific, damage-causing event results in direct loss/injury to insured; protects against risk of loss, not for gain or profit

  C. Premiums–amount paid, in installments, for insurance policy; rates must be reasonable, not unfairly discriminatory

  D. Defenses of Insurer–justifies non-payment

    1. Material misrepresentation–innocent/wrongful; relied on by insurer; inducement to enter contract substantially false when made; insured's knowledge of falseness

      a. Triggers rescission–insurer must return all premiums paid

      b. Incontestability clause–insurer prevented from voiding policy after specified time; prevents stale defenses by insurers

      c. Immaterial misrepresentation–not ground for avoidance

    2. Breach of warranty–conditions precedent or subsequent existing before contract effective or insurer's promise to pay enforceable; failure of condition relieves insurer from obligation to pay

    3. Concealment–failure of applicant to disclose material facts not known by insurer; normally fraudulent, material

  E. Waiver–intentional relinquishment of a known right

  F. Estoppel–prevention from asserting position inconsistent with own behavior based on conduct justifiably relied on by another

  G. Termination–due performance terminates insurer's obligation (insurer pays sum due), contract discharged; cancellation by mutual consent requires insurer to return unearned portion of premiums; rescission requires insurer to return all premiums paid

TRUE-FALSE: Circle true or false.

T   F   1. Generally, "property" means those legally protected rights or interests a person holds in physical things and objects.

T   F   2. Insurance policies are controlled by contract law principles.

T   F   3. The recipient of a gift is referred to as the donor.

T   F   4. Finders of abandoned property acquire title to the property.

T   F   5. When identical goods of two different owners are accidentally intermixed, all loss falls on the person who caused the "confusion."

T   F   6. To rescind an insurance contract for nonfraudulent misrepresentation, all premiums paid by the insured must be returned by the insurer.

T   F   7. An owner of land on which lost property is discovered through excavation generally has a superior claim to what is found over the finder.

T   F   8. Gratuitous promises to make gifts are usually not enforceable.

T   F   9. When a tenant builds a brick fireplace attached to the living room wall of a leased house, the fireplace can usually be removed by the tenant upon the expiration of the lease.

T   F   10. Transferring title to personal property is generally less formalized and ritualized than real property title transfers.

T   F   11. A representation by an applicant for insurance is generally not a part of the insurance contract.

T   F   12. Generally, intention of parties expressed in an agreement is the controlling factor determining whether an article of personal property is a fixture.

KEY TERMS–MATCHING EXERCISE: Select the term that best completes each statement below.

1. Accession	8. Co-tenants	15. Friendly
2. Estoppel	9. Real	16. Constructive
3. Attachment	10. Deed	17. Personal liberty
4. Fixture	11. Tangible	18. Movability
5. Binder	12. Intangible	19. Premium
6. Conveyance	13. Donor	20. Concealment
7. Gift	14. Personal property	

_____ 1. Act transforming personal property into real property.

_____ 2. Transfer of property without an exchange for return value.

_____ 3. Category of property that includes land and all items thereon.

_____ 4. Property that cannot be reduced to physical possession.

_____ 5. Personal property that is attached to land or a building.

_____ 6. Document used by an agent that makes the insurance coverage effective immediately.

_____ 7. Two or more people who hold title to real or personal property concurrently.

_____ 8. Property that can be reduced to physical possession.

_____ 9. Doctrine giving an owner of property all that is added to or produced from the property.

_____ 10. Kind of fire not covered by fire insurance policies.

_____ 11. A principal characteristic of personal property.

_____ 12. Type of delivery where the subject of a gift is incapable of actual delivery and is accomplished by delivering a symbol of ownership.

_____ 13. The failure of an applicant for insurance to disclose material facts that the insurer does not know.

_____ 14. Legally protected interest–right–not falling within the definition of property.

_____ 15. Consideration given in exchange for insurance coverage.

MULTIPLE CHOICE: Select the alternative that best completes each statement below.

_____ 1. A method used to increase coverage of a fire insurance policy to include benefits not provided in the standard policy is a/an (a) binder (b) endorsement (c) waiver (d) none of the above.

_____ 2. A/n _____ gift is one that is conditional and made in contemplation of the donor's impending death. (a) inter vivos; (b) equitable (c) in perpetuity (d) causa mortis

_____ 3. When A gives B the key to A's safe deposit box at Friendly Full Service Bank, telling B that the contents of the box are now B's, A has delivered the safe deposit box to B (a) constructively (b) actually (c) equitably (d) allocatedly.

_____ 4. Requirements for a valid gift include (a) donor's payment (b) revocability by a trustee (c) acceptance by the donee (d) all of the above.

_____ 5. An $8,000 fire insurance policy covers a $10,000 building, and there is an 80% co-insurance clause. If there is total destruction, the insured's recovery is (a) $8,000 (b) $2,000 (c) $10,000 (d) $6,400.

_____ 6. The insurable interest for property insurance must exist at the time the (a) property loss occurs (b) policy is taken out (c) property is purchased (d) none of the above.

_____ 7. Defenses an insurance company can assert to an insurance contract include (a) breach of warranty (b) concealment (c) misrepresentation (d) all of the above.

_____ 8. Personal property is a fixture if it (a) has become part of land (b) cannot be removed without material injury (c) is intended to be a fixture by parties (d) all of the above.

_____ 9. "Trade fixtures" are removable by a tenant (a) provided no material injury will result to the building or land (b) at any time (c) only before the lease has expired (d) only with the consent of the landlord.

_____ 10. Conflicts over who has superior rights to claim a fixture as theirs commonly arise between (a) Federal and State officials (b) intestate and testate heirs (c) landlords and tenants (d) bailors and bailees.

_____ 11. Major concepts underlying America's system of property include (a) emphasis on public ownership (b) constitutional protections of ownership (c) roots in French civil law (d) all of the above.

_____ 12. Examples of intangible property include (a) patent rights (b) commercial paper (c) mortgages (d) all of the above.

_____ 13. Where found property is classified _____, the owner of the premises where the property was found prevails over the finder. (a) mislaid (b) abandoned (c) lost (d) none of the above

CASE PROBLEMS–SHORT ESSAY ANSWERS: Read each case problem carefully. When appropriate, answer by stating a Decision for the case and by explaining the rationale–Rule of Law–relied upon to support your decision.

1. Susan receives a phone call from her physician informing her that she has only a few months to live due to advanced cancer. Shocked but clear of mind, Susan calls her sister Janet and tells her the bad news. Susan tells Jan that she wants her to have all her jewelry, located in a safe deposit box at a local bank, since she will no longer have any use for it after her death. Susan gives Jan the key to the box and tells her to get the jewelry since "it's now yours." Jan goes down to the bank and gets the jewelry. A few days later, Susan's doctor calls and informs her that the previous message regarding cancer was in error and that in fact she is in excellent health. The doctor apologizes for the mistake and Susan assures Dr. Noname that she is "ok". Susan quickly shares the good news with Jan who is overjoyed. But when Susan requests that her jewelry be returned, Jan balks saying "a gift is a gift and I don't have to

give anything back to you. Try and get the jewelry back, you welcher." Who has superior rights to the jewelry and why?

Decision: _____

_____

Rule of Law: _____

_____

2. Generous Gene, desiring to share material wealth with others less fortunate, issues three $250,000 money orders to strangers Sam, Sean and Sallie and delivers them. Gene hears nothing from the three for six months. In the seventh month, Gene receives Sam's returned money order, which had never been deposited, with a note from Sam saying he had taken a vow of poverty and must refuse Gene's generosity. Gene's budget and accounting schedules will be substantially unsettled if the money is refused by Sam. Gene sues Sam to force him to take it. Who prevails and why?

Decision: _____

_____

Rule of Law: _____

_____

3. While eating lunch at Smith's restaurant, Brown finds a ring on the floor. Brown gives the ring to Smith to hold in case the true owner returns. When the true owner cannot be found, Brown demands the return of the ring. Smith refuses and Brown sues Smith for the ring. Who prevails?

Decision: _____

_____

Rule of Law: _____

_____

4. Audrey has a $30,000 face value policy on her $50,000 house. A devastating fire totally destroys the house. Does Audrey recover for her loss? How much? Explain.

Decision: _____

_____

Rule of Law: _____

_____

5. Homeowners H and W sell their home to purchasers M and F. The purchase agreement makes no mention of what appliances are to be sold along with the sale of the house. H and W believe that no appliances will be sold while M and F believe that most of the household appliances will be sold along with the house. Acting on their belief, H and W remove a stereo home entertainment center bricked into the fireplace wall of the family room, a combination stove/oven built into the center of the kitchen, and a lighted, 100 gallon aquarium mounted in the wall of the sunken living room. Finding these items absent when they take possession, M and F demand their return but H and W refuse. Who has superior claim to these missing items?

Decision: _____

_____

Rule of Law: _____

_____

Chapter 50

BAILMENTS AND DOCUMENTS OF TITLE

SCOPE NOTE

Transferring possession of goods (without title) is a common everyday occurrence. "May I borrow a cup of sugar" illustrates the pervasive influence bailments has in our private and public lives. This chapter focuses upon the rights and obligations between parties to a bailment–situations where one has transferred possession of personal property but not title to another. Chapter 50 examines the general types of bailments recognized by law, how bailments are created and the rules of liability applied to the various types of bailment. Also discussed in the chapter are two special cases of bailments: freight transporters and lodging operators. What are the legal dynamics surrounding hotelkeeper/guest relationships, as well as owners and storers/carriers of goods? The chapter closes with an examination of the types, functions and transferability of documents of title, instruments used to transfer ownership of goods when the actual transfer of the goods is cumbersome and inconvenient.

EDUCATIONAL OBJECTIVES

1. Define and discuss the importance of bailments.

2. Identify characteristics of a bailment that distinguish it from other property transactions.

3. Differentiate the rights/duties of parties associated with the various types of bailments.

4. Distinguish among common possessory liens on personal property.

5. Identify the type of and rationale for a hotelkeeper's protective duty to guests and their property.

6. Discuss the differences between common law and statutory definitions of hotelkeeper liability.

7. Explain definitional and liability differences between private and common carriers of goods.

8. Outline the breadth of and defenses to common carrier liability for freight damage during transit as well as warehousers liability for stored goods.

9. Discuss the role played by title documents in sales transactions.

10. Identify the two most common documents of title used in sales of goods and the rights/duties of parties under those documents.

11. Discuss the significance of negotiability and the rights/duties of the parties related to the process of "due negotiation."

CHAPTER OUTLINE

I. Nature of Bailments–temporary transfer of possession, not title, of personal property from bailor (transferor) to bailee (recipient); with or without compensation
  A. Classification of Bailments
    1. Bailor's sole benefit–gratuitous possession of personal property; gratuitous services by bailee (repairs, storage, transportation)
    2. Bailee's sole benefit–gratuitous loan of personal property for bailee's use
    3. Mutual benefit of both parties–commercial bailments (goods delivered for storage, transport, repair)
  B. Essential Elements of a Bailment
    1. Delivery of possession to bailee–power to exercise physical control of property
      a. Parking lot cases: lease (right to use space) if driver locks car, keeps keys; bailment (attendant exercises control over car) if keys are left
    2. Personal property–tangible or intangible
    3. Possession for determinable time–bailee duty to return exact, identical property; returning property of equal value/money transfers title (sale)
    4. Restoration of possession to the bailor–at end of bailment; fungible goods requires bailee to return goods of same quality/quantity
      a. Conversion–money damages liability for bailee mistakenly/intentionally misdelivering property to someone not the bailor
  C. Rights and Duties of Bailor/Bailee
    1. Bailee's duty to exercise due care–not allow himself or others to damage, destroy property
      a. Degree of care–based on nature of bailment, character of property
        (1) Commercial bailment–mutual benefit of parties–bailee must exercise reasonable care (prudent person under same circumstances)
        (2) Bailment for sole benefit of bailor–use less than reasonable care
        (3) Bailment for sole benefit of bailee–use more than reasonable care
      b. Property lost, damaged, destroyed while in bailee's possession–bailee's burden to prove exercised proper degree of care (disprove presumption of negligence)

2. Bailee's absolute liability to return property–duty to return undamaged property to proper person; bailee liable for improper use resulting in damage

3. Bailee's right to limit liability–common carriers, public warehousers, innkeepers may not limit liability for breach of duties excepts as provided by statute; other bailees may vary duties/liabilities by contract with bailor; liability limitations must be properly brought to bailor's attention before property bailed

4. Bailee's right to compensation–for services/work to property; possessory lien on goods to secure payment

5. Bailor's duties
   a. Sole benefit of bailee–bailor warrants no knowledge of any defects in bailed property
   b. All other instances–bailor duty to warn bailee of all defects knows of, should have discovered, on reasonable inspection

D. Special Types of Bailments–extraordinary bailee (innkeepers, common carrier) absolutely liable for safety of bailed property regardless of cause of loss (absolute liability); liable for any loss/injury to goods regardless of degree of care exercised

1. Pledge–bailment to secure performance of obligation (payment); debtor gives possession to creditor (secured party) to secure debt or other performance

2. Warehousing–bailee receives goods to be stored for compensation; subject to state/federal regulation

3. Safe deposit boxes–mutual benefit bailment with bank; bailee liable only for negligence

4. Carriers of goods
   a. Types–common carrier (offers services to general public); private/contract carrier (limits services to specific customer, not offered to general public)
   b. Parties–consignor (delivers goods to carrier); consignee (to whom goods delivered)
   c. Bill of lading–contains terms of transportation contract
   d. Common carrier–duty to accept goods it normally transports; strict liability approaching insurer for condition/delivery of goods
   e. Private carrier–absolute duty to deliver goods to proper person; accepts goods only by contract

5. Innkeepers–old common law strict liability for stored goods substantially changed by case/statutory law

II. Documents of Title–written instrument evidencing right to receive, hold, dispose of goods covered by document
   A. Validity Requirements–issued by, addressed to bailee; cover identified goods in bailee's possession
   B. Nature of–symbol of ownership of goods described; ownership of documents equivalent to ownership, control of goods
   C. Controlling Law–U.C.C. Article 7
   D. Types of Documents of Title
      1. Warehouse receipts–issued by person whose business is storing goods
         a. Warehouser's duty of reasonable care, liability for breach

      b. Warehouser's duty of proper delivery (per terms of document), liability for breach

      c. Liability limitation by contract

      d. Warehouser's lien on goods enabling public/private sale, after notice, to apply net proceeds to unpaid charges

  2. Bills of lading–document issued by carrier on receipt of goods for transportation

      a. Function–receipt for goods; evidence of contract of carriage; document of title

      b. Carrier's duty of proper delivery

      c. Common carriers–extraordinary bailees subject to greater degree of liability

      d. Liability limitation by contract

      e. Carrier's lien–on goods in possession for charges, expenses necessary for preserving goods

E. Negotiability of Documents of Title–warehouse receipt, bill of lading, other document of title, negotiable if terms deliver goods to bearer or to order of named person; nonnegotiable documents transferred by assignment only

  1. Due negotiation–good faith purchaser of negotiable document takes, without notice of adverse claim/defense, pays value in regular course of business or financing not in settlement or payment of money obligation

      a. Effect–creates new rights in holder; defects/defenses available against transferor not available against new holder

      b. Rights of holder–title to identified goods; rights under agency law or estoppel; obligation of issuer to hold/deliver goods according to contract terms

  2. Rights acquired absent due negotiation–applies to nonnegotiable document, negotiable document transferred without due negotiation; transferee has transferor's rights, defeatable by transferor's creditors other claimants

  3. Warranties–transferor for value warrants document genuine, no knowledge of any impairment of validity or worth, rightful negotiation/transfer

  4. Ineffective documents of title–thief, finder may not deliver goods to warehouser/carrier in return for negotiable document of title; cannot defeat rights of true owner

  5. Lost/Missing documents–claimant applies to court for order requiring carrier/warehouser to deliver goods or issue substitute document; bailee's liability for delivery of goods without court order

TRUE-FALSE: Circle true or false.

T   F   1. A negotiable bill of lading provides for the delivery of goods to the bearer or to the order of the named person.

T   F   2. Carriers have a lien for unpaid charges that may be enforced by public or private sale of the goods shipped.

T   F   3. Warehousemen are statutorily prohibited from limiting their liability through contractual provisions.

T   F   4. In bailments of fungible goods, the bailee is under a duty to return the identical goods that were bailed.

T   F   5. A bailment presumes separation of ownership and possession between different people.

T   F   6. When bailed goods are destroyed, the law presumes that the bailor negligently caused the damage.

T   F   7. An owner of a document of title has ownership of the goods covered only if accompanied by actual, physical possession of the goods.

T   F   8. Both private and common carriers have an absolute duty to deliver goods to the correct person.

T   F   9. A warehouseman has no separate, enforceable right against goods to secure and enforce payment for services.

T   F   10. Extraordinary bailees are generally insurers of the safety of the goods bailed.

T   F   11. The carrier of goods subject to a bearer or order title document has no further liability under the shipping contract once the goods are delivered at the destination point, regardless of whether the carrier obtains possession of the document.

T   F   12. Naming in a negotiable title document the person to receive notice upon the arrival of goods does not limit the document's negotiability.

KEY TERMS–MATCHING EXERCISE: Select the term that best completes each statement below.

1. Extraordinary	8. Possession	15. Negotiation
2. Warehouser	9. Common	16. Non-negotiable
3. Bailee	10. Custody	17. Good faith purchaser
4. Consignee	11. Bailment	18. Document of title
5. Lease	12. Pledge	19. Negotiable
6. Bill of lading	13. Private carrier	20. Through bills
7. Abandoned	14. Common carrier	

_____ 1. Person to whom goods are to be delivered by a carrier.

_____ 2. Relationship created when a person parks a car in a parking lot, pays a charge, receives a ticket, locks the car and takes the keys.

_____ 3. Person to whom property is transferred under a bailment.

_____ 4. Title document issued by a carrier or transporter of goods.

_____ 5. Bailment for the purpose of securing payment on a debt.

_____ 6. Transaction in which possession of personal property is delivered without a transfer of title.

_____ 7. Bailee who receives compensation for storing goods.

_____ 8. Transporter of goods offering services and facilities to the public indifferently and not in a casual or individual manner.

_____ 9. One carrying another's goods only on isolated occasions, serving a limited number of customers under single, long-term contract.

_____ 10. Method of transferring rights to title documents under which the transferee can acquire rights greater than the assignor.

_____ 11. Document of title made out to "bearee" or "order" of a named person.

_____ 12. Document of title under which delivery of goods, without surrender of the document, completely discharges the carrier or warehouser from further contractual liability.

_____ 13. Bills of lading that specify connecting carriers.

_____ 14. One taking an interest in goods sold to enforce a lien free of any rights of the persons against whom the lien was valid.

_____ 15. Written document representing ownership in goods.

MULTIPLE CHOICE: Select the alternative that best completes each statement below.

_____ 1. Transferors for value of documents of title warrant (a) the genuineness of the document (b) the rightfulness of the transfer (c) no knowledge of any fact impairing the validity or worth of the document (d) all of the above.

_____ 2. A bailment in which the bailee must exercise greater care than a reasonably prudent person is a bailment for the benefit of the (a) bailee (b) bailor (c) bailor and bailee (d) third person.

_____ 3. A non-negotiable document of title is transferable only by (a) negotiation (b) the process of laches (c) assignment (d) ratification.

_____ 4. Property subject to bailment includes (a) promissory notes (b) corporate bonds (c) treasury bonds (d) all of the above.

_____ 5. Unauthorized use of the bailed goods by the bailee is considered (a) misappropriation (b) trespass (c) assumption of risk (d) immaterial if the possession is lawful.

_____ 6. A document of title issued by a carrier who promises to deliver goods to the named consignee is a (a) straight bill of lading (b) destination receipt (c) delivery order (d) sub-bill.

_____ 7. A bailment is not automatically terminated by (a) mutual consent (b) breach of the agreement by the bailor (c) destruction of the goods (d) accomplishment of the purpose of the bailment.

_____ 8. The liability a private carrier owes to the goods transported is that of a/an (a) insurer (b) bailee (c) reasonable person (d) fiduciary.

_____ 9. Essential elements to a bailment include (a) transfers of real property (b) parties are buyer and seller (c) conveyance of title but not possession (d) none of the above.

_____ 10. When a document of title is lost, the claimant of the goods (a) may seek an issuance of a substitute document from the courts (b) must find the document or surrender right to delivery (c) has lost all delivery rights (d) can use the doctrine of detrimental reliance to gain possession of the goods.

_____ 11. Code requirements for "due negotiation" of title documents include all of the following except (a) purchase for value (b) in good faith (c) as settlement or payment of debt (d) none of the above.

_____ 12. Duly negotiating documents of title (a) cuts off defenses and claims valid against the transferor (b) creates new rights in the holder (c) facilitates credit extensions based on such documents (d) all of the above.

_____ 13. Persons who cut off transferee rights under transfer of a non-negotiable title document include (a) bailee creditors (b) transferor creditors (c) any good faith purchaser for value (d) all of the above.

CASE PROBLEMS–SHORT ESSAY ANSWERS: Read each case problem carefully. When appropriate, answer by stating a Decision for the case and by explaining the rationale–Rule of Law–relied upon to support your decision.

1. Thief T bails goods stolen from owner O with carrier C and, in return, receives a negotiable bill of lading. The bill, transferred several times, is eventually duly negotiated to H. H and original owner O both claim the goods. Who wins and why?

Decision: _____

_____

Rule of Law: _____

_____

2. Cheesemaker C sues warehouseman W for damage done to C's stored cheese, asserting W's negligence as the cause. The warehouse receipt C received from W provided: "All stored property is at the owner's risk of loss or damage from riot, fire, water, deterioration, leakage, frost, the goods being perishable or otherwise inherently defective." W failed to keep a proper temperature in the storage rooms and the cheese became moldy. W argues that the warehouse receipt exempts any liability for the damage to the cheese. Who prevails? Discuss.

Decision: _____

_____

Rule of Law: _____

_____

3. A hires B to deliver a stove to a certain address. B accidentally delivers it to the wrong house, which B cannot later locate. Is B liable for this loss? Discuss.

Decision: _____

_____

Rule of Law: _____

_____

4. Harriet's Honey of Helena, Montana sells forty cases of honey to Sam's Sweetshop of Sioux City, Iowa. Harriet contracts with Tracy Transportation, a local trucking firm, to ship the order. Not having direct service to Sioux City, Tracy issues and forwards a bill of lading to Sam's order providing for final delivery of the honey at Sam's shop from Terry's Trucking of Tremont, Iowa. The cases of honey arrive at Terry's terminal without incident and are loaded onto one of Terry's trucks. On route to Sam's shop, the truck blows a tire, hitting a guard rail with total loss to all goods on board. Terry notifies Sam of the accident and Sam contacts Tracy requesting coverage for the loss. Tracy seeks your advice, which is . . .

Decision: _____

_____

Rule of Law: _____

_____

5. Ms. Guest spends a night at Innkeeper Hotel. Guest has with her a $2,500 Swiss watch. Innkeeper has a hotel safe for protecting customer valuables. No notice of its availability is posted at the registration desk or in any of the individual guest rooms. When Guest registers, Innkeeper fails to mention the safe. Sometime during the night, following Guest's check-in, a thief enters her room and steals the watch. Who bears the loss of the watch and why?

Decision: _____

_____

Rule of Law: _____

_____

Chapter 51

INTERESTS IN REAL PROPERTY

SCOPE NOTE

The legal doctrines relating to the ownership, use and transfer of interests in land are discussed in Chapters 51 and 52. This is an extremely technical and complicated area of law due partly to the fact that the origins for our system of real property law are found in the highly formalized, intricate structure of feudal land-tenure that dominated English law during the 13th and 14th centuries. Chapter 51 introduces the study of real property law by discussing the types of ownership interests in real property. The terms and doctrines associated with freehold interests in land are examined. The chapter continues by contrasting ownership of land held by one person (ownership "in severalty") to ownership shared by several people (ownership in tenancy). Possessory interests in real property (reducible to control and occupancy) are distinguished from nonpossessory interests (incapable of control and occupancy). The essential doctrines associated with forms of concurrent (multiple) ownership are developed. Also examined are the legal principles that control the legal relationship of co-owners (co-tenants) of real property. The chapter closes with a discussion of the types of interests one may hold in another's land and the nature of the reciprocal rights/duties among the parties to such a legal relationship.

EDUCATIONAL OBJECTIVES

1. Define real property and differentiate freehold from non-freehold interests in land.

2. Identify, outline the essential characteristics of recognized fee–simple estates and explain the means of creating them.

3. Describe the unique characteristics of, the methods for creating, and the purposes served by a life estate.

4. Explain the types and purposes of future interests associated with qualified or conditional estates.

5. Contrast vested with contingent future interests and how they are affected by the rule against perpetuities.

6. Distinguish the various classes of leasehold estates and how they are created.

7. Discuss the methods used and the consequences of parties to a leasehold transferring their respective interests to other individuals.

8. Outline the rights/duties of the parties to a rental agreement and how they are influenced by such factors as condition of the premises, presence of government regulation and acts of the parties.

9. Contrast common forms of concurrent ownership in terms of their definitional characteristics, method of creation and purposes served.

10. Compare the types of easements and discuss how they are created.

11. Differentiate between profits à prendre and licenses.

CHAPTER OUTLINE

I. Freehold Estates–ownership for indefinite time (fee estate) or life (life estate)
   A. Fee Estates–right to immediate possession for indefinite period; right to transfer by deed or will
      1. Fee simple estate–absolute ownership; freely transferable, inheritable; no limitations
      2. Qualified/base fee estate–conditional fee simple (subject to restrictions)
   B. Life Estates–created by acts of parties or operation of law
      1. Conventional life estates–created by parties; ownership for life of a designated person
         a. Remainder–ownership in third person takes effect when prior life estate terminates
         b. Life tenant may make reasonable use of property
         c. Waste–act or omission permanently damaging, unreasonably changing value of property
         d. Reversion held by grantor/heirs
   C. Future Interests–property interests without right to immediate possession
      1. Reversions–grantor's right to property upon termination of another estate
      2. Possibility of reverter–conditional reversionary interest; property may return to grantor or successor in interest when event limiting fee simple occurs (conditional fee simple); ends estate
      3. Remainders–estate in property taking effect on termination of prior estate, created by same instrument, held by person not grantor or successors
         a. Vested remainder–unconditional, fixed, present interest

       b. Contingent remainder–conditional upon event in addition to termination of preceding estate

II. Leasehold Estates–right to possess real property; contract based; landlord grants tenant exclusive right to use/possess land for definite time; landlord retains reversionary interest; tenant's rent payment duty

    A. Creation/Duration–must be written for term from one to three years
       1. Definite term–automatically expires at end of term; estate for years; no notice to terminate required
       2. Periodic tenancy–indefinite duration for successive periods unless terminated by notice
       3. Tenancy at will–lease terminable at any time
       4. Tenancy at sufferance–possession of real property without valid lease

    B. Transfer of Interests–both tenant's and landlord's interest freely transferable; contract/statute may prohibit
       1. Transfers by landlord–landlord may transfer either or both reversion/rent interest
       2. Transfers by tenant–lease usually requires landlord's consent
          a. Assignment–tenant transfers all interest in leasehold; retains no reversionary rights; assignee takes over tenant's position
          b. Sublease–transfer by tenant of less than all tenant's rights; tenant retains reversion in leasehold

    C. Tenant's Obligations–leasehold estate carries implied duty to pay reasonable rent; lease provides tenant breach terminates lease, triggers landlord's repossession; tenant no duty to make repairs unless lease requires; tenant duty not to substantially damage premises
       1. Destruction of premises–common law rule that tenant leasing land and building must pay rent if building destroyed by fire/other event substantially modified by state statute
       2. Eviction–removal from premises; triggered by tenant breaching lease; landlord evicts tenant, lease terminated
          a. Wrongful eviction–terminates tenant's obligations; landlord liable for breach of tenant's quiet enjoyment
       3. Abandonment–landlord reentering, reletting terminates tenant's rent obligation

    D. Landlord's Obligations–Fair Housing Act prohibits landlord discriminating against tenant based on race, color, religion, national origin, family status
       1. Quiet enjoyment–landlord duty to provide tenant with quiet/peace (right of tenant not to have physical possession interfered with by landlord)
          a. Doctrine of constructive eviction–landlord breaching lease causing substantial/lasting injury to tenant's enjoyment; tenant may abandon, terminate lease (ends rent duty)
       2. Fitness for use–common law that landlord has no obligation to maintain premises in livable condition, fit for any purpose, changed by state statute, court rulings imposing implied warranty of habitability (fit for occupation, ordinary purposes) for residential leases; zoning health regulations apply

3. Repair–common law rule unless specific provision in lease or statutory duty, landlord has no duty to repair/restore premises; landlord duty to maintain, repair, keep safe, common areas

4. Landlord's liability for injury caused by third parties–landlord liable for injuries suffered by tenants, others, resulting from foreseeable criminal conduct of third parties; duty "to take minimal precautions to protect against reasonably foreseeable criminal acts of third persons"

III. Concurrent Ownership–two or more persons hold title together (co-tenants); undivided interests
   A. Tenancy in Common–estate of inheritance; no right of survivorship
      1. Partition–physical division of property; changes undivided interests into separate ones owned individually
   B. Joint Tenancy–right of survivorship (death of joint tenant triggers title transfer to surviving co-owners)
      1. Severance–joint tenancy becomes tenancy in common by conveying/mortgaging interest to third party
      2. Four unities–common law requires similarity of time, title, interest, and possession; failure of any of first three unities destroys joint tenancy, creates tenancy in common
   C. Tenancy by Entireties–joint tenancy between husband/wife; neither may convene interest during life, destroy right of survivorship
   D. Community Property–Arizona, California, Idaho, Louisiana, Nevada, New Mexico, Puerto Rico, Texas, Washington, and Wisconsin; one-half ownership of property acquired by efforts of husband/wife during marriage (marital asset); property belonging separately to either spouse (non-marital asset) acquired before marriage, during marriage by gift/inheritance
   E. Condominiums–purchaser acquires separate ownership to individual unit, becomes tenant in common for other facilities
   F. Cooperatives–leasing units to shareholders as tenants, who acquire right to use/occupy their units

IV. Nonpossessory Interests–holder entitled to use, take something from land; interest does not give right to possess land
   A. Easements–limited right to use land in specific manner created by acts of parties, operation of law
      1. Dominant parcel–one whose owner has rights in other's land
      2. Servient parcel–land subject to easement (use by another)
      3. Types of easements
         a. Appurtenant–rights/duties pertain to land itself, not individuals who created them; easement stays with land when transferred
         b. In gross–personal to individuals who created/received benefit from; an irrevocable personal right to use; ends when land transferred unless expressly retained
      4. Creation
         a. Express grant/reservation–agreement of parties
         b. By implication–owner of adjacent properties establishes apparent, permanent use (easement), conveys one property without mentioning interest; law implies

grant of easement by necessity to give taker access to property across transferor's land

  c. By dedication–landowner transfers to public
  d. By prescription–open, continuous, obvious, known use of another's land adverse to rightful owner
 B. Profits à Prende–right to remove products from another's land; arises by prescription, act of parties; Statute of Frauds applies
 C. Licenses–permission to use another's land creating no property interest in property; subject to revocation by owner at any time; protection against trespass action

TRUE-FALSE: Circle true or false.

T   F   1. A fee simple estate is of indefinite duration and could therefore last forever.

T   F   2. By statute in most states today, joint tenancy can be created by a conveyance "to A and B and their heirs."

T   F   3. "To A and his heirs" is the only language that can effectively create a fee simple estate today.

T   F   4. At common law, landlords had no obligation to keep rented residential premises in a habitable/tenantable condition.

T   F   5. Survivorship refers to the interest of a joint tenant passing to his heirs at his death.

T   F   6. Landlords are not held strictly/absolutely liable for harm caused by the criminal conduct of other persons.

T   F   7. A license, like an easement, creates an interest in real property.

T   F   8. Where a tenant has expressly agreed to pay rent in the rental agreement, an assignment of the lease to another person does not free the first tenant from further rent payment obligation.

T   F   9. Most courts hold that when a tenant wrongfully abandons rented premises and the landlord re-rents the premises to another, the abandoning tenant's obligation to pay rent ceases.

T   F   10. Divorce automatically terminates a tenancy by the entireties.

T   F   11. When a lease does not mention time for rent payment, rent is due and payable at the end of the rental term.

T   F   12. Under a contingent remainder, the remainderman has rights to immediate possession upon termination of the preceding estate.

KEY TERMS–MATCHING EXERCISE: Select the term that best completes each statement below.

1. Periodic tenancy	8. Constructive eviction	15. Community property
2. Life estate	9. Reversion	16. Tenant
3. Appurtenant	10. Assignment	17. Tenancy at sufferance
4. Waste	11. Profit à prendre	18. Dower
5. Remainder	12. Dominant estate	19. Tenancy at will
6. Partition	13. Contingent	20. Curtesy
7. Vested	14. Possibility of reverter	

_____ 1. Future interest held by one not the grantor or the grantor's heirs.

_____ 2. Failure to care properly for property that is held for only a limited time.

_____ 3. Easements that create rights and duties pertaining to the land itself and not personal to the parties that created them.

_____ 4. Interest retained by a grantor or his heirs when no disposition is made of the balance of a life estate.

_____ 5. Type of co-ownership recognized in some states creating a one-half undivided interest between spouses in property acquired during marriage.

_____ 6. Parcel of land that is benefited by an easement.

_____ 7. Doctrine that allows a tenant to abandon rented premises and terminate a lease when a landlord has failed to meet the terms of the lease.

_____ 8. Right to harvest crops from another's land.

_____ 9. Act of changing undivided interests in land into separate and divided interests.

_____ 10. Future interest that has as its only condition to possession the termination of the preceding estate.

_____ 11. Tenant's transfer of the entire lease hold interest.

_____ 12. Tenant's holding land after expiration of a lease.

_____ 13. Someone who has temporary use and possession of another's land.

_____ 14. Holding land for an indefinite period subject to termination by either party to the agreement.

_____ 15. Lease lasting an indefinite time for successive periods until ended by proper notice.

MULTIPLE CHOICE: Select the alternative that best completes each statement below.

_____ 1. When a tenant under an eight-year lease transfers the premises to another person for a five-year period, the transfer is called a/n (a) conditional apportionment (b) assignment (c) sublease (d) equitable allocation.

_____ 2. A tenancy in common may be created by (a) operation of law (b) an ineffective attempt to create a joint tenancy (c) more than one instrument (d) all of the above.

_____ 3. An easement arises by _____ through the open, continuous, hostile, uninterrupted and adverse use of another's land. (a) dedication (b) necessity (c) prescription (d) reservation

_____ 4. A gross easement is (a) personal to the parties that created it (b) similar in purpose to a zoning restriction (c) nothing more than a negative covenant (d) much like a constructive trust.

_____ 5. When a landlord breaches a warranty of habitability, a tenant (a) is still bound to the lease (b) may not avoid liability for further rent (c) can sue for damages (d) is precluded from withholding rent.

_____ 6. The type of co-ownership by which a buyer acquires separate title to a purchased unit while also becoming a tenant in common vis-a-vis the common facilities of which the unit is a part is called a (a) condominium (b) cooperative (c) tenancy by estoppel (d) unified severalty.

_____ 7. Creation of concurrent ownership by the same instrument is an absolute requirement of (a) community property (b) tenancy at will (c) tenancy in common (d) joint tenancy.

_____ 8. Among the four "unities" that exist, the only one required of a tenancy in common is the unity of (a) possession (b) time (c) title (d) interest.

_____ 9. A rental agreement covering a definite period of time (a) expires automatically at the end of the stated rental term (b) terminates only upon one of the parties giving notice (c) is automatically renewed if no termination notice is given (d) none of the above.

_____ 10. Under common law, a tenant must repair (a) damage caused by ordinary wear and tear (b) extraordinary damage even though caused without fault (c) damages that are caused by fault (d) all of the above.

_____ 11. _____ is an indirect form of co-ownership that gives shareholders leasehold rights to individual units. (a) tenancy by entireties (b) cooperative (c) tenant by estoppel (d) condominium

_____ 12. _____ prohibits landlords from discriminating against renters on the grounds of race, sex, religion, nationality, family status, or handicap. (a) no laws (b) the Uniform Housing code (c) the Fair Housing law (d) none of the above

_____ 13. Landlord's obligation not to disrupt the tenant's possession and use of the premises is known as the covenant of (a) repair (b) habitability (c) no disposition (d) quiet enjoyment.

CASE PROBLEMS–SHORT ESSAY ANSWERS: Read each case problem carefully. When appropriate, answer by stating a Decision for the case and by explaining the rationale–Rule of Law–relied upon to support your decision.

1. A, B and C are joint-tenant owners of Greenacre. C conveys an interest in the land to D. Following this action, A dies. What form or forms and percentage of concurrent ownership exist between the surviving parties? Explain.

   Decision: _____

   _____

   Rule of Law: _____

   _____

2. A conveys land "to B so long as the property is used for church purposes." B sells the property to C, who builds a liquor store on the property. A and B are dead. A's heirs, B's heirs and C claim the property. Who prevails? Discuss.

   Decision: _____

   _____

   Rule of Law: _____

   _____

3. Fran rents an apartment from Mary for $325 a month under a six-month written lease. After paying rent for two months, Fran loses her job and stops paying rent. Mary quickly evicts her, angrily commenting "You'll pay for this." Fran responds sharply, "Just try and get any money, you old skinflint." What future payment liability, if any, might Fran face? Explain.

   Decision: _____

   _____

Rule of Law: _____

_____

4. A has a right to cross neighbor B's land. When B sells the land to C, may C stop A from crossing the land? Explain.

Decision: _____

_____

Rule of Law: _____

_____

5. A conveys, by deed, an undivided one-half interest in Blackacre to B and wills the other one-half interest in the same land to C, stating in both documents that C and B are to hold as "joint tenants." A dies. Are B and C joint-tenant owners of Blackacre? Explain.

Decision: _____

_____

Rule of Law: _____

_____

Chapter 52

TRANSFER AND CONTROL OF REAL PROPERTY

SCOPE NOTES

Title to real property may be transferred in many ways. Ownership may pass to government (through tax default, escheat, dedication or eminent domain) or out from government (through grants and tax sales). Events (marriage, natural forces) may trigger passage of title. Acts by the present owner (sale, gift) or inaction by the present owner (adverse possession, mortgage foreclosure proceedings) may pass title. In Chapter 52, the legal principles controlling methods of acquiring title to real property are discussed in the context of purchase agreements, security interests in land (mortgages) and adverse possession.

As a general rule, owners of real property enjoy the benefits of title according to their own wishes with little outside interference. Under various circumstances, however, public (government regulation) and private (contractual controls) restrictions are placed on the manner and degree to which one may enjoy the incidents of owning real property. To protect and promote the general welfare of society, as well as to carry out the intent of contractual provisions, restrictions determine how one may exercise title interests in land. Chapter 52 also focuses on the conflicting interests between enjoyment of the incidents of title and promoting the general welfare of society through public and private controls on ownership.

EDUCATIONAL OBJECTIVES

1. Outline the major steps involved in purchasing real property.

2. Explain formation requirements for valid land sales contracts.

3. Define and discuss the significance of marketable title.

4. Discuss the importance of deeds and distinguish among the various types of deeds.

5. List execution requirements for a valid deed.

6. Describe the importance of delivery and recording deeds in terms of their effectiveness.

7. Define and explain the significance of adverse possession.

8. Discuss the purpose and execution requirements of mortgages.

9. Identify the rights/duties of parties to a mortgage and how their legal relationship is affected by transfers of the mortgage interest.

10. Outline various issues and problems related to discharge, foreclosure and redemption of mortgages.

11. Define and discuss the importance of eminent domain.

12. Specify how the public use, just compensation and due process doctrines relate to eminent domain.

13. Describe the purposes served by zoning ordinances.

14. Distinguish among the various ways of avoiding zoning limitations.

15. List the types and ways of creating private controls over land.

16. Discuss how restrictive covenants are interpreted and how they are terminated,

CHAPTER OUTLINE

I. Transfer of Real Property–commonly by contract for sale or gift with delivery of deed; less common method by adverse possession
    A. Contract of Sale–general contract law, Fair Housing Act (Title VIII of the Civil Rights Act) governs
        1. Formation–written buyer/seller agreement, under Statute of Frauds, signed by party to be charged
        2. Marketable title–seller's implied duty to transfer marketable title (free from encumbrances, defects in chain of title, events depriving seller of title)
            a. Title search–reveals defect not specifically excepted in contract
        3. Implied warranty of habitability–old common law rule *caveat emptor* (buyer beware) placed quality risk of loss on buyer (duty to inspect); seller liable only for misrepresentations, express warranties; most states abandoned rule for sales by residential builders (builder-seller impliedly warrants newly constructed homes free from hidden defects)
    B. Deeds–formal document transferring interest in land
        1. Types of deeds

        a. Warranty–grantor (donor/seller) promises grantee (donee/buyer) valid title; grantor duty to reimburse grantee for loss due to grantor's defective title; promises include title, against encumbrances, quiet enjoyment, warranty

        b. Special warranty–title not impaired, encumbered, made defective, by act/omission of grantor alone; does not warrant title re acts/omissions of others

        c. Quitclaim–grantor transfers whatever interest held; used for releases of interests

  2. Formal requirements

        a. Description–clear, certain, permits identification of property, quantity/quality of estate conveyed

        b. Covenants–title, against encumbrances, quiet enjoyment, warranties

        c. Others–signature of grantor; seal, acknowledgment before notary public

  3. Delivery of deeds–required for transfer of title

        a. Types–manual/physical transfer; delivery to third party (escrow agent) holding until contract conditions met

  4. Recording–generally not necessary to pass title to grantee

        a. Function–protect grantee from subsequent good faith purchaser for value cutting off interest

        b. Procedure–delivery of executed, acknowledged deed to recorder's office in county where property located

        c. Notice states–unrecorded deed invalid against subsequent purchaser without notice

        d. Notice-race states–unrecorded deed invalid against subsequent purchaser without notice who records first

        e. Race states–unrecorded deed invalid against any deed recorded before it

II. Secured Transactions–debt (obligation to pay money); creditor interest in land securing payment

  A. Using Real Estate as Security–subject to statutes, common laws regarding mortgages and trust deeds

  B. Parties–mortgagor/debtor; mortgagee/creditor

  C. Form of Mortgages

    1. Definition–interest in land created by written document, provides security for payment of debt; instrument creating mortgage must meet formality requirements

    2. Requirements–writing, adequate description of property; executed, delivered deed; deed of trust nearly identical to mortgage (property not conveyed to creditor, but to third person as trustee for benefit of creditor)

  D. Rights/Duties of Parties–depends on whether lien or title jurisdiction

    1. Lien theory–most states; mortgagor retains title, entitled to possession

    2. Title theory–few states; mortgagee holds title until debt paid

    3. Redemption–debtor removes mortgage by payment of debt

  E. Transfer of Interests Under Mortgage–original mortgage interests transferable depending on agreement of assignment parties; rules protect interests of original parties to mortgage but not transfer parties

    1. Purchaser "assumes" mortgage–purchaser personally obligated to pay debt; mortgagee can hold mortgagor to payment duty

    2. Purchase "subject to mortgage"–purchaser not personally obligated to pay debt; mortgagor payment duty

    3. Mortgagee's right to assign mortgage without mortgagor's consent

    4. Recording assignment–protects against subsequent persons acquiring property without knowledge of assignment

  F. Foreclosure–sale of mortgaged property upon default to satisfy debt

    1. Mortgagee deficiency judgment–unsatisfied balance of debt enforced out of other mortgagor's assets

III. Adverse Possession–acquisition of title by open, continuous, hostile occupancy for prescribed statutory period; act of dominion by true owner (trespass action) stops period running; period must start anew from that time

IV. Public and Private Controls–state's police power controls use of private property for community benefit; no duty to pay owner for loss, damage sustained by police power exercising regulatory control (pollution from asphalt plant)

  A. Zoning–public control over private land use; based on police power of state (public health, safety, morals, welfare); not taking but regulating property use

    1. Enabling acts/zoning ordinances–power to zone delegated to authorities by enabling statutes granting various regulatory powers to municipalities

    2. Variance–allowing use differing from that provided in zoning ordinance to avoid undue hardship

    3. Nonconforming uses–zoning ordinance cannot immediately end lawful use existing before enactment; use permitted to continue for reasonable time

    4. Judicial review–zoning process traditionally legislative; judicial review on grounds that ordinance is invalid, applied unreasonably, ordinance is confiscation, taking of property

    5. Subdivision master plans–state legislation enabling local authorities to require municipality approval of land subdivisions; statutes provide penalties for failure to secure approval where required by local ordinance

  B. Eminent Domain–power to take (for just compensation) private property for public use

    1. Public use–interpreted as "public advantage"; power delegatable to railroads, public utilities

    2. Just compensation–owners of property receive fair market value of property at time of taking

    3. Power expands as society becomes more complex

  C. Private Restrictions on Land Use–real property owners impose restrictive covenants on land use contained in conveyance document

    1. Requirements for running covenants–restrictive covenants may bind not only original parties to conveyance but also remote parties subsequently acquiring property (covenant runs with land)

    2. Restrictive covenants in subdivisions–limit use of property to residential purposes, restrict area of lot on which structure built, provide special type of architecture

3. Termination of restrictive covenants–by terms of original agreement, changed circumstances making enforcement inequitable/oppressive, court ruling or statute
4. Validity of restrictive covenants–enforced by injunction to restrain violation
    a. Discriminatory covenants (race, age, ethnic origin, marital status, sex, etc.)–prohibited by Fair Housing Act, court rulings

TRUE-FALSE: Circle true or false.

T F 1. Most States follow the common law rule that after the land sales contract is made, risk of loss to the real property passes to the seller.

T F 2. A quitclaim deed could convey as much interest in land as a warranty deed.

T F 3. A warranty deed does not transfer an after-acquired title.

T F 4. The contract for the sale of land impliedly requires that the seller convey a marketable title to the buyer.

T F 5. Recording a deed is always necessary for title to pass from the grantor to the grantee.

T F 6. A mortgagor may generally assign the mortgage to a third person without having to receive the mortgagee's consent unless the mortgage agreement provides otherwise.

T F 7. The police power of government may be employed to regulate property use as well as to take property.

T F 8. The power of eminent domain may not be delegated to private enterprise.

T F 9. Compensation for property taken under eminent domain is determined on the basis of market value of the property condemned.

T F 10. The usual method for enforcing restrictive covenants is a suit for money damages.

T F 11. In real estate secured transactions, the creditor is the mortgagee and the debtor the mortgagor.

T F 12. The single-family, private-ownership exemption to the Fair Housing Act regulation of selling/renting residential property does not apply to racial-color-based discrimination.

KEY TERMS–MATCHING EXERCISE: Select the term that best completes each statement below.

---

1. After-acquired title	8. Due process	15. Allocation
2. Variance	9. Deficiency judgment	16. Foreclosure
3. Eminent domain	10. Conveyance	17. Title theory
4. Warranty deed	11. Enabling laws	18. Police power
5. Quitclaim deed	12. Trust deed	19. Confiscation
6. Adverse possession	13. Allonge	20. Redemption
7. Title insurance	14. Restrictive covenant	

_____ 1. Method for freeing property from zoning restrictions in cases of "particular hardship."

_____ 2. Statutory basis of authority for city zoning powers.

_____ 3. Constitutional principle protecting the interests of private property owners from unreasonable exercises of eminent domain powers.

_____ 4. Property ownership protection against losses stemming from title defects, liens, and encumbrances.

_____ 5. Private limitations placed upon how land may be used.

_____ 6. Method of transferring title to land involuntarily.

_____ 7. Deed under which grantor assumes all liability for any title defects.

_____ 8. Document in a secured real estate transaction conveying property to a third person to hold for the benefit of the creditor.

_____ 9. Power to convert private property to public use.

_____ 10. Action taken by the mortgagee against the mortgagor to recover any balance still owing on the debt when foreclosure proceedings are insufficient to satisfy the full debt owing.

_____ 11. Common law doctrine giving ownership rights and possession to the mortgagee in secured real estate transactions.

_____ 12. Mortgagor's right to remove a mortgage lien by paying off the debt in full.

_____ 13. Mortgagee's debt satisfaction rights following mortgagor's default.

_____ 14. Regulatory action resulting in property owner's being deprived of any and all beneficial use of their land.

_____ 15. Regulatory authority of government to protect public health, safety and morals.

MULTIPLE CHOICE: Select the alternative that best completes each statement below.

_____ 1. Private property may be taken by the government if (a) private use is to be made of the property (b) the owner is reimbursed the purchase price paid for the property (c) due process has been followed in condemnation proceedings (d) an equitable trust is established in the owner's name.

_____ 2. For restrictive covenants to run with the land, they must (a) in most states be in writing (b) directly affect the land's use or value (c) cover legally enforceable conditions or promises (d) all of the above.

_____ 3. Promises that the grantor makes in the deed regarding the quality of the interest conveyed do not include a covenant (a) of quiet enjoyment (b) of reasonably fair market value (c) against encumbrances (d) none of the above.

_____ 4. Which of the following is not necessary for the valid transfer of land (a) delivery of the deed (b) grantor's intention to make a transfer (c) title search (d) grantor's issuing a deed.

_____ 5. Of the following, which is not an absolute requirement for adverse possession to ripen into title (a) open and continuous possession (b) constructive possession (c) possession for a required statutory time period (d) possession without owner's consent.

_____ 6. A marketable title is free from (a) all encumbrances except mortgages (b) all encumbrances except easements (c) zoning restrictions (d) title defects appearing in the chain of title available through land records.

_____ 7. Compensation for condemned property is given to (a) holders of contingent remainders (b) owners of the property taken (c) wife for her dower interest in her living husband's land (d) none of the above.

_____ 8. A purchaser of mortgaged real property is not personally liable for the mortgage debt unless the (a) mortgage note is pledged (b) property is taken "subject to" the mortgage (c) mortgage is "expressly assumed" by the purchaser (d) notice is given to the assignor.

_____ 9. The primary tool for public regulation of private land use is a (a) zoning ordinance (b) restrictive statute (c) court decision (d) condemnation proceeding.

_____ 10. Which of the following is not an example of restrictive covenant? (a) covenant that limits the use of property to residential purposes (b) restriction specifying the minimum cost of each house that is built in a given area (c) covenant against encumbrances (d) covenant prohibiting the sale of intoxicating beverages.

_____ 11. In a lien-theory state the (a) mortgagee has title (b) mortgagor has possession and title (c) mortgagee has possession (d) none of the above.

_____ 12. _____ was the common law doctrine that freed the land seller of liability for defects in the property that were discoverable by the land buyer making a thorough inspection prior to completing the sale. (a) laches (b) equitable discharge (c) delectus personae (d) *caveat emptor*

_____ 13. Secured real estate transactions are governed by (a) state statute and common law (b) the U.C.C. (c) federal real estate laws (d) none of the above.

CASE PROBLEMS–SHORT ESSAY ANSWERS: Read each case problem carefully. When appropriate, answer by stating a Decision for the case and by explaining the rationale–Rule of Law–relied upon to support your decision.

1. A restrictive covenant banning the sale of cigarettes within the village of Bloomfield has been in existence for fifty years. For the past ten years, two tobacco shops and three pharmacies have been selling cigarettes in the village. When Frank Cooper decides to sell cigarettes from vending machines in his general store in Bloomfield, will he be prohibited by the covenant? Explain.

Decision: _____

_____

Rule of Law: _____

_____

2. Wing and Wang Chan, husband and wife, are recent arrivees from China. Desiring to settle quickly, they hire a real estate agent and start looking for a home. They find a "priced-right" dream house and submit a purchase offer. Their bid is refused and upon further inquiry they learn that no homes in the area may be sold to persons of Asian descent according to the dictates of the original deed from the first owner of the tract development. Dismayed, the Chans seek your advice. What can you tell them?

Decision: _____

_____

Rule of Law: _____

_____

3. A has been operating a junkyard within the city limits of Springfield for the past 35 years. The Springfield City Council passes a zoning ordinance forbidding the presence of junk yards within the city limits. The city demands that A shut down his junkyard immediately and A refuses. The city then sues A. Who wins and why?

Decision: _____

_____

Rule of Law: _____

_____

4. L owns an undeveloped 2 acre lot in a run-down area of mixed residential and light commercial use. The city adopts an urban renewal plan for the area that provides for the location of a park on L's site. State and Federal officials have not yet approved the plan, nor has funding or a developer been located. As part of its plan, the city states that landowners who build on lots scheduled for condemnation will not be compensated for the loss of those buildings when condemnation proceedings commence. L believes the city's plan is unfair and asks for advice. What advice will you give?

Decision: _____

_____

Rule of Law: _____

_____

5. Railroad Company R.R. wants to increase the width of its roadbeds that abut A's land. R.R. approaches A, requesting to purchase land from A. A refuses to sell the land arguing that widened roadbeds are not necessary. The railroad company fears loss of business if its tracks are not widened. Can the company force A to give up the land? Explain.

Decision: _____

_____

Rule of Law: _____

_____

Chapter 53

TRUSTS AND DECEDENTS' ESTATES

SCOPE NOTE

At various times during our financial lives, we might find it necessary and worthwhile to transfer control of property we own to another person to manage for our own benefit or for the benefit of a third party. Such arrangements are called trusts. Under what circumstances are trusts useful devices? What formalities are associated with the creation of a trust? What is the nature of the legal relationship between the parties to a trust? Chapter 53 focuses upon these and other matters in its discussion of the law of trusts, its vocabulary, and essential doctrines. Chapter 53 also provides a general overview of the law of testate and intestate succession and how property passes following the death of its owner. Attention is placed on the benefits/costs of dying without a will. Also discussed is the process of property distribution following death.

EDUCATIONAL OBJECTIVES

1. Explain the nature and purpose of trusts.

2. Discuss the requirements for establishing a valid, enforceable trust.

3. Identify the parties to a trust and outline their individual and mutual rights and duties.

4. Describe how the existence of a trust may come to an end.

5. Differentiate the various types and classes of trusts.

6. Differentiate testate and intestate succession.

7. Explain the nature and purpose of a will.

8. Identify the requirements for drafting a valid will.

9. List the types and respective characteristics of recognized wills.

10. Discuss the events and acts associated with altering/revoking a will.

11. Understand under what circumstances an apparently valid testamentary instrument will not be enforced.

12. Know the rights of beneficiaries and the spouse of the decedent under a will,

13. Define and identify the problems associated with abatement and ademption.

14. Explain the purpose and role of the Uniform Probate Code.

15. Discuss how and to whom property passes when its owner dies without a valid, enforceable will.

16. Outline the probate duties of a personal representative.

17. Describe the tax consequences of death.

CHAPTER OUTLINE

I. Trusts–transfer of property to a party for another's benefit for any legal purpose; involves settlor, trustee, beneficiary, and trust corpus
   A. Types of Trusts–express or implied
      1. Express trusts–an oral or written trust established by voluntary action; no particular words necessary so long as intent is clear; statute of frauds requires a writing for land trusts
         a. Testamentary trust–a trust used in wills that becomes effective after the settlor's death
         b. Inter vivos trust–a living trust established during the settlor's lifetime
         c. Charitable trusts–any trust that has for its purpose the benefit of the public
         d. Spendthrift trusts–a provision in a trust instrument under which the trust estate is removed from the beneficiary's control and from liability for her individual debts
         e. Totten trusts–is a bank (savings) account opened by the settlor of the trust and payable to the beneficiary on death of the settlor
      2. Implied trusts–court imposed upon property because of acts of the parties
         a. Constructive trusts–are imposed upon property by the equity court to rectify misconduct or to prevent unjust enrichment arising from fraud, undue influence
         b. Resulting trusts–serve to carry out the true intent of the parties in cases where the intent was inadequately expressed; exists independently of contract
   B. Creation of Trusts–by agreement, will, or judicial decree; no consideration required
      1. Settlor–the person who creates the trust; requires contractual capacity
      2. Trust corpus–trust property, must be definite and specific real or personal property
      3. Trustee–an individual or institution that is legally capable of holding title to and dealing with property; holds legal title; lack of does not eliminate trust; can be court appointed

a. Duties of the trustee–three primary duties: carry out provisions; act with care, loyalty; acts as fiduciary

b. Powers of the trustee–determined by the settlor and state statutes; prudent investor rule

c. Allocation of principal and income–trusts often specify how the trust property or funds shall be allocated between present and future beneficiary; receipt allocation and expense charging; ordinary expense charged to present beneficiary; extraordinary charged to future beneficiary

4. Beneficiary–there are very few restrictions on who (or what) may be a recipient of trust property; creditor access to interest; hold equitable interest

C. Termination of a Trust–as a general rule a trust is irrevocable unless the power of revocation is reserved by the settlor; instrument states end date; merger doctrine gives title to beneficiary holding legal and equitable title

II. Decedents' Estates–assets (estate) pass at death under a will (estate) or by statute to next of kin (intestate); escheat to state where no will and no heirs

A. Will–the legal document that determines to whom the assets of a decedent will be distributed after death; written; follows statutory formalities; revocable

1. Mental capacity–competence to execute a will

a. Testamentary power and capacity–the power to make a will is granted by the State; capacity refers to limits placed upon particular persons because of mental deficiencies; ability to know nature, extent of estate, who are heirs, and know disposition plan

b. Conduct invalidating a will–includes duress, undue influence, fraud, and mistake; not testator's intent

2. Formal requirements of a will–demonstrate capacity and intent

a. Writing–a basic requirement of a valid will; may be informal

b. Signature–a will must be signed by the testator; usually at end

c. Attestation–a will must be attested (certified) by witnesses, usually two or three as required by statute; usually a witness cannot be a beneficiary

3. Revocation of a will–by act of will maker or operation of law for changed circumstance

a. Destruction or alteration–tearing or burning will revoke the will and in some states, erasure or obliteration may; required intent; interlineation ineffective

b. Subsequent will–the execution of a second will does not itself revoke an earlier will; irreconcilable inconsistency revokes earlier will

c. Operation of law–common law and the UPC differ on the effect marriage and divorce have on a will; after born/omitted child issues

4. Effectiveness of testamentary provisions

a. Renunciation by the surviving spouse–the right to renounce the decedent spouse's will is set by statute; guaranteed minimal interest in estate

b. Abatement and ademption of a bequest–both have serious implications for beneficiaries of a will; abatement revokes gifts due to increased debt; ademption revokes wills by destruction of asset

5. Special types of wills
   a. Nuncupative wills–oral wills; requires life-threatening crisis
   b. Holographic wills–a completely handwritten will by testor
   c. Soldiers' and Sailors' wills–may be valid but cannot pass title to real estate; combat, access crisis relaxes formalities
   d. Conditional wills–a will that takes effect only on the happening of a specific condition
   e. Joint and mutual or reciprocal wills–are types of wills involving two or more persons
   f. Living wills–a document by which an individual states that she does not wish to receive extraordinary medical treatment in order to preserve her life
6. Codicil–is an addition or revision of a will; must meet normal will requirements

B. Intestate Succession–state statutory rules of descent control how non-gift, non-will property passes at death
   1. Inheritance priority–based on degree of family relationship to decedent; surviving spouse, children, and grandchildren prevail over more distant family relatives
   2. Per stirpes–predeceased heir's interest shared equally by own heirs
   3. Per capita–members of a class of heirs share equally

C. Administration of Estates–the statutory rules and procedures that control management and distribution of decedent's estate–probate: collect assets, pay debts, and distribute remainder
   1. Locate and submit will if it exists
   2. Appointment of administrator if no will or executor
   3. Fiduciary duties–file inventory of assets/debts
   4. Asset protection and debt payment priority

TRUE-FALSE: Circle true or false.

T   F   1. A will does not have to be recorded to be valid.

T   F   2. Because a will takes effect only upon death, it is revocable during the will maker's life.

T   F   3. The beneficiary's interest under a spendthrift trust is beyond the reach of creditors.

T   F   4. The settlor's death generally does not terminate a trust.

T   F   5. A second will automatically revokes the first will.

T   F   6. A resulting trust is often used to rectify fraud or to prevent unjust enrichment.

T   F   7. Stepchildren inherit from an intestate decedent to the same extent as natural children (heirs).

T   F   8. Consideration is a necessary requirement to create an enforceable trust.

T   F   9. Trusts are generally revocable during the settlor's life.

T   F   10. Anyone legally capable to handle rights/duties of property ownership may be a trustee.

T   F   11. Rules controlling intestate succession are the same across the states.

T   F   12. An inheritance tax is imposed by the Federal government on the privilege of an heir or beneficiary to receive property from the decedent's estate.

KEY TERMS–MATCHING EXERCISE: Select the term that best completes each statement below.

1. Totten trust	8. Escheat	15. Revocation
2. Probate	9. Holographic	16. Executor
3. Attestation	10. Per capita	17. Ademption
4. Trust res	11. Spendthrift clause	18. Renunciation
5. Per stirpes	12. Charitable trust	19. Abatement
6. Express trust	13. Codicil	20. Administrator
7. Resulting trust	14. Nuncupative	

_____ 1. A written or oral agreement in which property is transferred to a trustee for the benefit of another.

_____ 2. The act of witnessing a will.

_____ 3. The legal effect of the testator intentionally destroying a will.

_____ 4. A trust provision prohibiting the beneficiary from impairing the trust rights by an assignment of the rights.

_____ 5. A trust created when a settlor opens a bank account.

_____ 6. Property that is the subject matter of the trust.

_____ 7. An oral will.

_____ 8. A trust established for public benefit.

_____ 9. Lineal descendants of a predeceased heir inheriting that heir's inheritance interest in the estate of another.

_____ 10. The procedure for managing the decedent's estate.

_____ 11. The person named in a will to manage the administration of the decedent's estate.

_____ 12. A document that revises an existing will.

_____ 13. The statutory right of surviving spouse to elect an intestate succession statutory share of a decedent's estate in place of the share left the spouse under the will.

_____ 14. A handwritten will.

_____ 15. A prioritized reduction of gifts by category following the reduced estate value after the execution of a will.

MULTIPLE CHOICE: Select the alternative that best completes each statement below.

_____ 1. Although no particular words are necessary to create a trust, one element that must be present is the (a) formal writing (b) intent to create a trust (c) designation of a trustee (d) all of the above.

_____ 2. The subject matter of a trust must be (a) definite and certain property (b) real property (c) intangible (d) all of the above.

_____ 3. To incorporate by reference the terms of a written document into a will, the document must be (a) attached to the will (b) existing when the will is executed (c) notarized (d) all of the above.

_____ 4. If a person has obtained money by duress, the person will be treated as a trustee over a(n) (a) constructive trust (b) resulting trust (c) express trust (d) precatory trust.

_____ 5. The trustee must (a) carry out the trust's purposes (b) use prudence and care in the administration of the trust (c) be loyal to the beneficiary (d) all of the above.

_____ 6. _____ is not a necessity for a valid will. (a) power (b) capacity (c) intent (d) intelligence

_____ 7. A valid codicil must be (a) in writing (b) signed by the testator (c) witnessed (d) all of the above.

_____ 8. An estate tax is imposed upon the (a) assets owned at death (b) executor (c) recipient of the estate (d) attorney.

_____ 9. A nuncupative will generally must (a) be handwritten (b) be made when no attorney is available (c) be made during the testator's last illness (d) dispose of real property only.

_____ 10. Which of the following persons cannot be disinherited? a surviving (a) parent (b) child (c) spouse (d) none of the above can be disinherited

_____ 11. A will may be revoked by (a) tearing or burning the will (b) operation of law (c) a subsequent will that is inconsistent with the original will (d) all of the above.

_____ 12. Under the UPC, _____ automatically revokes a previously executed will. (a) marriage (b) divorce (c) an heir accidentally causing the testator's death (d) all of the above

_____ 13. _____ is the type of trust that is incorporated into a will and takes effect only on the settlor's death. (a) living (b) totten (c) testamentary (d) resulting

CASE PROBLEMS–SHORT ESSAY ANSWERS: Read each case problem carefully. When appropriate, answer by stating a Decision for the case and by explaining the rationale–Rule of Law–relied upon to support your decision.

1. A sets up a spendthrift trust for her son, B. C is a creditor of B to whom B owes $800 for a motorcycle. Under what circumstances can C obtain payment?

   Decision: _____

   _____

   Rule of Law: _____

   _____

2. A appoints B trustee of a trust for the benefit of C and D. B dies. C and D petition the court to have the trust terminated. What result?

   Decision: _____

   _____

   Rule of Law: _____

   _____

3. Ted dictated a will to his nurse. It was typed, signed, and attested. In it, he divided his entire estate among his wife and children. Ted dies. Eight months later, a son is born to Ted's widow. Does the new child share in the estate? Explain.

   Decision: _____

   _____

   Rule of Law: _____

4. When Tom wrote his will, his estate was worth $35,000. Tom's will left $1,000 to A, $500 to B, and the balance to C. At the time of his death, Tom's estate was worth $1,500 after estate debts had been paid. What does C receive? Explain.

Decision: _____

_____

Rule of Law: _____

_____

5. Abby's will left her business, a pizza parlor, to her nephew, Harry. One year before her death, Abby sold the pizza parlor for $50,000. Is Harry entitled to the $50,000 in lieu of the pizza parlor? Explain.

Decision: _____

_____

Rule of Law: _____

_____

PROPERTY RESEARCH QUESTIONS: Drawing upon information contained in the text, as well as outside sources, discuss the following questions.

1. Research your State's laws on intestate succession. If you were to die without a will, how and to whom would your property pass? Is that how you would want it distributed? Draft a will distributing your property in the manner (what, how and to whom) you desire. Is it the same as the plan of distribution under your State's intestate succession laws? Explain.

2. Assume you want to purchase a house. Trace the steps and complete drafting and processing the documents necessary for buying the home.

UNIFORM CPA EXAMINATION: INFORMATION ON BUSINESS LAW

To practice their profession, public accountants must meet various competence standards established by state accounting boards intended to assure minimal knowledge and skill levels. All states require candidates to demonstrate this proficiency by passing the Uniform Certified Public Accountant Examination, administered by the American Institute of Certified Public Accountants (AICPA). This two and one-half day test is given the first Wednesday and Thursday in May and November of each year and consists of four separate sections: accounting practice I and II; accounting theory; auditing; and business law.

The business law section of the CPA Examination lasts approximately three and one-half hours and consists of multiple choice and case analysis essay questions designed to test candidate knowledge over a broad range of business law rules, principles and doctrines. These questions are similar in form to those in this Study Guide.

The breadth of business law knowledge required to pass the CPA Examination is reflected in the guidelines adopted by the AICPA Board of Examiners:

"The Business Law section tests the candidates' knowledge of the legal implications of business transactions, particularly as they relate to accounting and auditing situations, including accountant legal liability. Many of the subjects in this section are normally covered in standard textbooks on business law, auditing, taxation, and accounting. However, some subjects either are not included in such texts or are not covered in adequate depth. Important recent developments with which candidates are expected to be familiar may not yet be reflected in some texts. Candidates are expected to recognize the existence of legal implications and the applicable basic legal principles, and they are usually asked to indicate the probable result of the application of such basic principles . . ."

"The Business Law section is chiefly conceptual in nature and broad in scope. It is not intended to test competence to practice law nor expertise in legal matters, but to determine that the candidates' knowledge is sufficient to enable them to recognize relevant legal issues, recognize the legal implications of business situations, apply the underlying principles of law to accounting and auditing situations, and know when to seek legal counsel, or recommend that it be sought, when appropriate."

"This section deals with federal and widely adopted uniform laws. Where there is no federal or appropriate uniform law on a subject, the questions are intended principally to test candidates' knowledge of the majority rules. Federal tax elements (income, estate or gift) are only covered where appropriate in the overall context of a question."

Students planning to take the examinations should obtain copies of *Information for CPA Candidates* issued by AICPA. Copies are available from:

> AICPA Order Department
> P.O. Box #1003
> New York, NY 10108–1003
> (800) 334-6961

FUTURE CPA EXAMINATION DATES:

2003   May 7, 8; November 5, 6
2004   May 5, 6; November 3, 4
2005   May 4, 5; November 2, 3

Business Law–Content Specification Outline

I.   Professional and Legal Responsibilities (15%)
    A. Code of Professional Conduct
    B. Proficiency, Independence, and Due Care
    C. Other Professional Service Responsibilities
    D. Regulatory Board Disciplinary Systems
    E. Common Law Liability to Clients and Third Persons
    F. Federal Statutory Liability
       1. Securities Acts
       2. Internal Revenue Code
    G. Workpapers, Privileged Communication, and Confidentiality
    H. Public Sector Business and Industry CPA Responsibilities

II.   Business Organizations (20%)
    A. Agency
       1. Formation, Operation and Termination
       2. Duties of Agents and Principals
       3. Authority and Liabilities of Agents and Principals
    B. Partnerships and Joint Ventures
       1. Formation, Operation and Termination
       2. Liabilities and Authority of Partners and Joint Owners
    C. Corporations
       1. Formation and Operation
       2. Stockholders, Directors, and Officers
       3. Financial Structure, Capital, and Distributions
       4. Reorganization and Dissolution

D. Estates and Trusts
1. Formation, Operation and Termination
2. Allocation between Principal and Income
3. Fiduciary Responsibilities
4. Distributions and Termination

III. Contracts (10%)
A. Formation
B. Performance
C. Assignments
D. Discharge, Breach, and Remedies

IV. Debtor-Creditor Relationships (10%)
A. Rights, Duties, and Liabilities of Debtors and Creditors
B. Rights, Duties, and Liabilities of Guarantors
C. Bankruptcy

V. Government Regulation of Business (15%)
A. Regulation of Employment
B. Federal Securities Acts
C. Environmental Regulation

VI. Uniform Commercial Code (20%)
A. Negotiable Instruments
B. Sales
C. Secured Transactions
D. Documents of Title

VII. Property (10%)
A. Real Property
B. Personal Property, Bailments and Computer Technology
C. Fire Insurance

CROSS REFERENCES TABLE
Business Law Topics Appearing on CPA Examinations
Text and Study Guide Chapters

TOPIC, ESTIMATED AICPA EMPHASIS & GROUP CHAPTERS IN STUDY GUIDE:

ACCOUNTANTS AND THE LAW (15%)   45

BUSINESS ORGANIZATIONS (20%)
A.	Agency	19 and 20
B.	Partnerships and Joint Ventures	31–33
C.	Corporations	34–37
D.	Estates and Trusts	53

CONTRACTS (10%)
A.	Introduction to Contracts	9
B.	Mutual Assent	10
C.	Invalidating Assent	11
D.	Consideration	12
E.	Illegal Bargains	13
F.	Capacity	14
G.	Statute of Frauds	15
H.	Parol Evidence Rule	15
I.	Third Party Rights	16
J.	Performance, Breach and Discharge	17
K.	Remedies	18

DEBTOR-CREDITOR RELATIONSHIPS (10%)
A.	Secured Transactions	38
B.	Suretyship	38
C.	Bankruptcy	39

GOVERNMENT REGULATION OF BUSINESS (15%)
A.	Employment Law	43
B.	Federal Securities Acts	44
C.	Anti-trust	41
D.	Unfair Competition	40–42

UNIFORM COMMERCIAL CODE (20%)
A.	Commercial Paper	26–30
B.	Documents of Title	50
C.	Sales	21–25

PROPERTY (10%)
A.	Real and Personal Property	49–52
B.	Mortgages	52
C.	Fire and Casualty Insurance	49
D.	Computer Technology	48

ANSWERS TO CHAPTER 1–Introduction to Law

TRUE-FALSE

1.	T	4.	T	7.	F	10.	T
2.	T	5.	F	8.	T	11.	F
3.	F	6.	T	9.	F	12.	T

KEY TERMS–MATCHING

1.	4	5.	14	9.	3	13.	2
2.	6	6.	7	10.	5	14.	18
3.	9	7.	13	11.	20	15.	19
4.	15	8.	10	12.	8		

MULTIPLE CHOICE

1.	d	5.	d	9.	b	13.	d
2.	d	6.	c	10.	d		
3.	a	7.	d	11.	a		
4.	c	8.	d	12.	b		

CASE PROBLEMS–ESSAY ANSWERS

1. This landmark U.S. Supreme Court decision would be found in the following two source books: first, in Volume 347 of the United States Supreme Court Reports at page 686, and second, in Volume 74 of the Supreme Court Reporter at page 686. This is an example of a case citation.

2. No. This is a trial in equity and equity courts do not allow jury trials.

3. No. This state has not proven beyond a reasonable doubt that Horn caused the fire and they are charged with the burden of proof.

4. Anita's civil lawsuit would be an "action at law" since the remedy obtained was a money judgment. Yes, the right to a jury trial applies only to actions at law not to suits in equity.

5. No. Society may condemn John's failure to attempt a rescue as morally wrong, but the law generally imposes no legal duty on him to act.

ANSWERS TO CHAPTER 2–Business Ethics and the Social Responsibility of Business

TRUE-FALSE

1. T	4. F	7. T	10. F
2. F	5. F	8 T	11. F
3. F	6. T	9. T	12. F

KEY TERMS–MATCHING

1. 3	5. 15	9. 20	13. 9
2. 6	6. 12	10. 7	14. 2
3. 10	7. 13	11. 18	15. 16
4. 1	8. 11	12. 19	

MULTIPLE CHOICE

1. d	5. b	9. d	13. d
2. d	6. c	10. d	
3. d	7. d	11. c	
4. a	8. d	12. b	

CASE PROBLEMS–ESSAY ANSWERS

1. To say "whatever is legal is also moral" is too simplistic and is inaccurate. Some acts that are legal are immoral. See examples in text.

2. Ethical fundamentalists are individuals who look to a central authority to guide them in ethical decision making: Jerry Falwell, the Bible; Ayatollah Khomeini, the Koran. Criticisms: 1) The Bible and Koran do not always agree. No one yet has managed to demonstrate convincingly which authority is the "correct one." 2) The Bible cannot serve as an example of a central authority, as its proponents cannot agree on what its verses mean.

3. The theory our criminal laws apply is deontology. Deontologists judge a murderer depending on the mental processes and motives that led him to commit the crime.

4. Lawrence Kohlberg's three stages of moral development are the preconventional level, the conventional level, and the postconventional level. See his explanations and conclusions in text.

5. Corporations, like other members of society, must contribute to its betterment. They owe a moral debt to society to help make improvements, including pollution control, safe products, quality education, cures for illness, and freedom from crime. Corporations can help in each of these areas.

ANSWERS TO CHAPTER 3–Legal Process

TRUE-FALSE

1. F	4. F	7. T	10. T
2. T	5. T	8. F	11. T
3. T	6. T	9. T	12. F

KEY TERMS–MATCHING

1. 6	5. 10	9. 2	13. 3
2. 5	6. 11	10. 13	14. 17
3. 14	7. 8	11. 12	15. 9
4. 15	8. 4	12. 20	

MULTIPLE CHOICE

1. d	5. a	9. d	13. d
2. a	6. c	10. d	
3. c	7. d	11. d	
4. d	8. b	12. c	

CASE PROBLEMS–ESSAY ANSWERS

1. Remand means the original decision by the State district court is reversed by the Supreme Court. The case will now be retried in the original trial court, i.e., the district court.

2. Arbitration. Arbitration makes possible a speedy resolution to the labor/management problem and is binding.

3. No. Generally, State court decisions are not binding upon another State's courts.

4. Yes. If Malcolm is a citizen of Colorado, the Federal district court would have jurisdiction because (a) Malcolm could sue for over $75,000, and (b) "diversity of citizenship" exists, i.e., the parties are citizens of different states.

5. No. A decision of a Federal circuit court is not binding upon other circuit courts.

ANSWERS TO CHAPTER 4–Constitutional Law

TRUE-FALSE

1. T	4. T	7. F	10. F
2. F	5. F	8. F	11. T
3. F	6. F	9. T	12. F

KEY TERMS–MATCHING

1. 3	5. 7	9. 1	13. 17
2. 6	6. 9	10. 10	14. 19
3. 12	7. 11	11. 4	15. 14
4. 13	8. 15	12. 20	

MULTIPLE CHOICE

1. c	5. d	9. c	13. d
2. d	6. b	10. d	
3. a	7. c	11. a	
4. b	8. d	12. b	

CASE PROBLEMS–ESSAY ANSWERS

1. President Nixon contended that the separation of powers doctrine precluded the judicial branch of the government from reviewing the executive branch, i.e., the President's claim of executive privilege. The Supreme Court rejected this claim and ruled that the judicial, not the executive branch, interprets and decides what is the law.

2. Datsun. The commerce clause and the import-export clause of the Constitution immunize from state taxation goods that have entered the stream of commerce, whether they are interstate or foreign and whether they are imports or exports.

3. Our Constitution divides the government into three distinct and independent branches: executive, legislative and judicial. The purpose of the doctrine is to avoid excessive power in any branch of government.

4. The Tenth Amendment. This amendment states, "the powers not delegated to the United States by the Constitution, nor prohibited by it to the States, are reserved to the States respectively, or to the people."

5. The U.S. Supreme Court applies the strict scrutiny test whenever governmental action affects fundamental rights or involves suspect classifications, which include those made on the basis of race or national origin. Thus, the Court ruled in the *Brown* case that segregated public schools violated the equal protection guarantee.

ANSWERS TO CHAPTER 5–Administrative Law

TRUE-FALSE

1. T	4. T	7. T	10. F
2. F	5. F	8. T	11. T
3. F	6. F	9. T	12. F

KEY TERMS–MATCHING

1. 3	5. 7	9. 1	13. 17
2. 6	6. 9	10. 10	14. 19
3. 12	7. 11	11. 4	15. 14
4. 13	8. 15	12. 20	

MULTIPLE CHOICE

1. c	5. d	9. c	13. d
2. d	6. b	10. d	
3. a	7. c	11. a	
4. b	8. d	12. b	

CASE PROBLEMS–ESSAY ANSWERS

1. No. Juries are never used in administrative hearings.

2. Administrative Procedure Act of 1946. The Act sets basic procedures all agencies must observe, but agencies are free to fashion their own procedural rules beyond the APA minimum.

3. The three are the U.S. Constitution, the enabling Statute, and the APA. The regulation cannot violate the Constitution, the agency must not exceed the authority granted by the Statute, and it must follow the rule making procedures of the APA.

4. The substantial evidence test means if a reasonable person might reach the same conclusion as the agency, then the court will uphold the rule.

5. The arbitrary and capricious test. It requires only that the agency had a rational basis for reaching its decision.

ANSWERS TO CHAPTER 6–Criminal Law

TRUE-FALSE

1. F	4. F	7. T	10. F
2. T	5. F	8. T	11. T
3. T	6. T	9. T	12. F

KEY TERMS–MATCHING

1. 6	5. 1	9. 8	13. 2
2. 5	6. 9	10. 4	14. 18
3. 12	7. 11	11. 20	15. 19
4. 13	8. 15	12. 17	

MULTIPLE CHOICE

1. d	5. b	9. c	13. c
2. d	6. b	10. d	
3. c	7. c	11. c	
4. a	8. d	12. d	

CASE PROBLEMS–ESSAY ANSWERS

1. Entrapment. Melvin was induced to commit the crime by Allen, the F.B.I. agent.

2. Carol loses. The U.S. Supreme Court has ruled that the use of a six-member jury in a criminal case does not violate the Constitution.

3. Indictment. A grand jury, on the basis of probable cause, could vote a "true bill" and indict (charge) her with the commission of the crime.

4. No. Criminal intent without an overt act is not a crime.

5. The Supreme Court held that depriving the defendant, Gideon, of the assistance of a lawyer in a felony trial is a denial of due process. The Sixth and Fourteenth Amendments allow the accused the right to obtain the assistance of an attorney.

ANSWERS TO CHAPTER 7–Intentional Torts

TRUE-FALSE

1. T	4. F	7. F	10. T
2. F	5. F	8. F	11. T
3. F	6. T	9. F	12. T

KEY TERMS–MATCHING

1. 7	5. 9	9. 13	13. 17
2. 1	6. 11	10. 5	14. 16
3. 4	7. 6	11. 20	15. 2
4. 8	8. 12	12. 19	

MULTIPLE CHOICE

1. d	5. b	9. d	13. d
2. a	6. c	10. c	
3. d	7. d	11. c	
4. d	8. a	12. d	

CASE PROBLEMS–ESSAY ANSWERS

1. Yes. The tort of battery has occurred consisting of intentional contact causing serious injury.

2. Potentially, B could be guilty of battery. However, if B reasonably believed A was about to inflict death or serious bodily harm to B, then B is privileged to use even deadly force in self-defense.

3. Yes. The "publication" requirement of defamation (in this case, specifically, libel) and the unreasonable publicity requirement of invasion of privacy have both been met.

4. The tort is slander. Slander is the oral publication of a defamatory statement which is not true and which injures a person's reputation.

5. B wins. A is liable for the tort of emotional distress.

ANSWERS TO CHAPTER 8–Negligence and Strict Liability

TRUE-FALSE

1. T	4. T	7. T	10. F
2. T	5. F	8. F	11. F
3. F	6. F	9. T	12. T

KEY TERMS–MATCHING

1. 6	5. 1	9. 8	13. 3
2. 13	6. 14	10. 5	14. 10
3. 11	7. 2	11. 7	15. 9
4. 4	8. 20	12. 19	

MULTIPLE CHOICE

1. a	5. c	9. d	13. a
2. d	6. a	10. c	
3. d	7. b	11. d	
4. b	8. c	12. d	

CASE PROBLEMS–ESSAY ANSWERS

1. Sarah wins. Joelene was flying the plane negligently and is liable to Sarah for this tort, i.e., negligence.

2. Yes. As the person responsible for Kathy's care, Mark would have a duty to act and would be liable for not taking action.

3. No. Abner's act of leaving Baker unconscious in the middle of the street could "normally result" in additional injury to Baker. It is also foreseeable that Baker would be struck by a car, and Abner has a duty of affirmative action when there is a danger of further harm to the unconscious person. At the very least, Abner should have carried or dragged Baker out of the street.

4. $45,000. The amount of the judgment award is determined by multiplying the percentage of the defendant's negligence times the amount of damage, e.g., 90% times $50,000, which is $45,000.

5. This is an example of strict liability because this activity is so unreasonably dangerous to the public that absolute liability is imposed regardless of fault.

ANSWERS TO CHAPTER 9–Introduction to Contracts

TRUE-FALSE

1. T	4. F	7. F	10. T
2. T	5. T	8. F	11. T
3. F	6. F	9. T	12. F

KEY TERMS–MATCHING

1. 15	5. 3	9. 9	13. 20
2. 5	6. 7	10. 2	14. 4
3. 12	7. 8	11. 18	15. 19
4. 1	8. 6	12. 16	

MULTIPLE CHOICE

1. a	5. c	9. c	13. c
2. d	6. d	10. c	
3. d	7. b	11. a	
4. b	8. d	12. b	

CASE PROBLEMS–ESSAY ANSWERS

1. An implied contract is created. Sara requested and accepted Mary's services, and Sara's estate must pay Mary a reasonable amount for the services.

2. Yes. The moment Julie purchased the microscope a unilateral contract existed.

3. Yes. It is clearly understood from the statements of both parties that they were making and exchanging mutual promises. The parties need not use the actual word "promise" to create a bilateral contract.

4. A false statement that is material to the contract agreed upon by the parties is fraud. Fraud makes the contract voidable to the defrauded party, Joyce.

5. Yes. This is an example of a quasi contract, or an implied in law contract.

ANSWERS TO CHAPTER 10–Mutual Assent

TRUE-FALSE

1. T	4. T	7. F	10. T
2. T	5. T	8. F	11. T
3. F	6. T	9. T	12. T

KEY TERMS–MATCHING

1. 15	5. 10	9. 9	13. 20
2. 11	6. 1	10. 4	14. 6
3. 14	7. 12	11. 16	15. 18
4. 2	8. 3	12. 19	

MULTIPLE CHOICE

1. d	5. d	9. b	13. c
2. d	6. d	10. a	
3. a	7. b	11. d	
4. d	8. d	12. d	

CASE PROBLEMS–ESSAY ANSWERS

1. Sam wins. The U.C.C. and the Restatement would require that Jerome accept by telegram, as requested by Sam, in order for Sam to be bound.

2. B wins. Today such unsolicited items, e.g., the candy, would be considered a gift.

3. A wins. The option is a binding promise not to revoke for one year and is enforceable against B's executor.

4. No. Statements made under circumstances of emotional stress are not offers since they lack contractual intent.

5. No. This is an example of the parties engaging in preliminary negotiations. B's letter is the actual offer, not the acceptance of the offer

ANSWERS TO CHAPTER 11–Conduct Invalidating Assent

TRUE-FALSE

1. T	4. F	7. F	10. F
2. T	5. T	8. T	11. T
3. F	6. F	9. T	12. T

KEY TERMS–MATCHING

1. 5	5. 12	9. 9	13. 6
2. 7	6. 8	10. 13	14. 10
3. 1	7. 2	11. 14	15. 19
4. 3	8. 15	12. 11	

MULTIPLE CHOICE

1.	c	5.	a	9.	d	13.	d
2.	a	6.	d	10.	d		
3.	b	7.	b	11.	d		
4.	a	8.	b	12.	d		

CASE PROBLEMS–ESSAY ANSWERS

1. Yes. One may have a duty of disclosure because of prior representations innocently made but which are later discovered to be untrue before making a contract. Abner's lack of disclosure is fraud.

2. No. This is an example of duress.

3. Yes. One who assents to a writing is presumed to know its contents and cannot escape being bound to its terms by contending he did not read them. Generally, a party is held to what he signs.

4. No to both questions. A prediction is normally not a factual statement and does not form the basis for fraud.

5. No. If the subject matter of the contract (potatoes) is destroyed without fault of either party, then if the loss is total, the contract is voidable by the adversely affected party (buyer) unless he bears the risk of the mistake.

ANSWERS TO CHAPTER 12–Consideration

TRUE-FALSE

1.	T	4.	F	7.	T	10.	T
2.	T	5.	T	8.	F	11.	T
3.	F	6.	T	9.	F	12.	F

KEY TERMS–MATCHING

1. 13	5. 7	9. 6	13. 16
2. 2	6. 4	10. 10	14. 14
3. 3	7. 5	11. 1	15. 18
4. 12	8. 11	12. 20	

MULTIPLE CHOICE

1. d	5. c	9. c	13. c
2. a	6. c	10. d	
3. b	7. c	11. d	
4. d	8. d	12. d	

CASE PROBLEMS–ESSAY ANSWERS

1. The fund had already substantially relied on the pledge, and normally courts will uphold these charitable subscriptions.

2. Ray wins. Because Samantha knew the check was tendered as full payment of a disputed debt, and because she cashed it, she would probably be unable to collect the remainder.

3. The U.C.C. would hold that a good faith agreement modifying a contract for the sale of goods needs no new considerations to be binding.

4. No. Past consideration is no consideration. Bill's promise to pay is for a past transaction.

5. Courts will usually hold that William's forbearance is a legal detriment and the uncle must pay the $10,000.

ANSWERS TO CHAPTER 13–Illegal Bargains

TRUE-FALSE

1. F	4. F	7. F	10. F
2. T	5. T	8. T	11. F
3. F	6. T	9. F	12. T

KEY TERMS–MATCHING

1. 9	5. 8	9. 5	13. 3
2. 10	6. 12	10. 15	14. 19
3. 7	7. 2	11. 11	15. 1
4. 6	8. 14	12. 16	

MULTIPLE CHOICE

1. b	5. c	9. d	13. c
2. c	6. d	10. a	
3. a	7. d	11. c	
4. c	8. c	12. d	

CASE PROBLEMS–ESSAY ANSWERS

1. No. The maximum rate of interest in state Z is 8% or $80 per year on a $1,000 loan. A and B agreed to $72 interest and thus no usury.

2. Barbara wins. The statute was for revenue purposes only and not for protection of the public.

3. No. Where one person has a superior bargaining position which enables that person to impose an exculpatory clause upon another person as part of their contract, the courts tend to nullify the clause.

4. C loses. The issue is whether or not the restraint is reasonable. Since a barber shop is localized business, a restraint that prohibits a barber business anywhere in the county for a period of five years is unreasonable.

5. B loses. Since the contract is a violation of a criminal statute, it will be held unenforceable.

ANSWERS TO CHAPTER 14–Contractual Capacity

TRUE-FALSE

1. F	4. T	7. F	10. F
2. F	5. F	8. T	11. F
3. T	6. F	9. F	12. F

KEY TERMS–MATCHING

1. 10	5. 1	9. 9	13. 11
2. 8	6. 2	10. 7	14. 20
3. 15	7. 3	11. 5	15. 16
4. 12	8. 4	12. 19	

MULTIPLE CHOICE

1. d	5. b	9. d	13. d
2. a	6. d	10. b	
3. b	7. b	11. d	
4. d	8. d	12. c	

CASE PROBLEMS–ESSAY ANSWERS

1. The majority view is that even though a minor (Mary) misrepresents her age, she may nevertheless disaffirm the contract.

2. Contracts entered into by persons judged incompetent and who are under a guardianship appointed by a court order are void and have no legal effect.

3. No. A minor may disaffirm a contract for the sale of personal property within a reasonable time after reaching majority age. Continued use after reaching majority age is an implied ratification.

4. A wins. An intoxicated person who is unable to comprehend the nature and consequences of a contract can avoid the contract.

5. A minor is not liable for anything, including necessaries, unless they are actually furnished to the minor or used by the minor. Also, the minor is not liable if the minor is already supplied or is being supplied with the items (necessaries) by someone else, such as the minor's parents.

ANSWERS TO CHAPTER 15–Contracts in Writing

TRUE-FALSE

1. T	4. T	7. T	10. F
2. T	5. T	8. T	11. T
3. T	6. F	9. T	12. T

KEY TERMS–MATCHING

1. 9	5. 2	9. 4	13. 19
2. 11	6. 15	10. 1	14. 5
3. 12	7. 3	11. 20	15. 17
4. 7	8. 13	12. 10	

MULTIPLE CHOICE

1. b	5. d	9. a	13. d
2. c	6. a	10. d	
3. d	7. d	11. b	
4. c	8. b	12. b	

CASE PROBLEMS–ESSAY ANSWERS

1. No. The parol evidence rule does not apply whenever parties to an existing contract subsequently agree to cancel it.

2. No. Neither the Statute of Frauds nor the U.C.C. would allow this memo to bind the parties since the subject matter and quantity are not clear.

3. No. This is a contract for the sale of an interest in land and thus it is unenforceable. However, A may recover damages for the work done and damages would be the appropriate remedy.

4. A loses. The Code states that oral contracts for goods specifically manufactured for the buyer and which are not suitable for resale in the ordinary course of business are enforceable. This contract is not within the Statute of Frauds.

5. Allen loses. The party to be charged, i.e., Bernard, has not signed the letter.

ANSWERS TO CHAPTER 16–Third Parties to Contracts

TRUE-FALSE

1. T	4. F	7. T	10. T
2. F	5. T	8. F	11. T
3. F	6. F	9. T	12. T

KEY TERMS–MATCHING

1. 11	5. 12	9. 2	13. 17
2. 6	6. 9	10. 4	14. 3
3. 13	7. 14	11. 8	15. 18
4. 15	8. 10	12. 19	

MULTIPLE CHOICE

1. d	5. d	9. b	13. d
2. d	6. c	10. d	
3. d	7. a	11. b	
4. b	8. a	12. c	

CASE PROBLEMS–ESSAY ANSWERS

1. Y wins. Y is a donee beneficiary and may recover; it does not matter that Y was unaware of the policy.

2. B wins. Because C is only an incidental beneficiary, C has no rights under the contract and cannot sue.

3. Company X wins. Since the risk assumed by the appliance company was with A, the assignment to B would be an entirely different risk to the company, and they need not take it.

4. X wins. Because E made a contract with X for a personal service, E does not have the right to delegate the duty to another.

5. The majority view says Y wins because Y was prior in time. A minority view would give the wages to T because T gave first notice.

ANSWERS TO CHAPTER 17–Performance, Breach, and Discharge

TRUE-FALSE

1. T	4. F	7. F	10. F
2. T	5. F	8. F	11. T
3. F	6. T	9. T	12. T

KEY TERMS–MATCHING

1. 7	5. 15	9. 4	13. 5
2. 9	6. 1	10. 8	14. 14
3. 11	7. 2	11. 16	15. 20
4. 13	8. 3	12. 18	

MULTIPLE CHOICE

1. a	5. d	9. b	13. c
2. b	6. d	10. a	
3. d	7. c	11. b	
4. c	8. a	12. c	

CASE PROBLEMS–ESSAY ANSWERS

1. Decision for A because this situation presents an impossibility for which neither party was responsible. This is the frustration of purpose doctrine.

2. Yes. The contract is discharged by an accord and satisfaction.

3. Yes. By novation, Z has become the new debtor and is liable for the debt.

4. Y wins. This is an example of mutual rescission.

5. B wins. The law will imply concurrent conditions whereby A and B have a duty to perform the acts of delivery and payment at the same time.

ANSWERS TO CHAPTER 18–Remedies

TRUE-FALSE

1. T	4. F	7. F	10. T
2. F	5. F	8. F	11. T
3. F	6. F	9. T	12. F

KEY TERMS–MATCHING

1. 4	5. 13	9. 6	13. 16
2. 9	6. 14	10. 10	14. 2
3. 11	7. 3	11. 20	15. 18
4. 15	8. 12	12. 17	

MULTIPLE CHOICE

1. b	5. a	9. c	13. a
2. c	6. b	10. d	
3. a	7. c	11. d	
4. b	8. b	12. d	

CASE PROBLEMS–ESSAY ANSWERS

1. You might sue for lost profits, but under the reasoning of *Hadley v. Baxendale*, you would have to have told Ace of your need specifically to render them liable.

2. Possibly. Although punitive damages are not generally recoverable for breach of contract, if the conduct constituting the breach is also a tort (fraud), punitive damages may be obtained.

3. Probably not, because the courts would look at this as a penalty rather than a valid liquidated damage clause since the $2,000 would not bear a reasonable relationship to the amount of probable loss.

4. For all the lawnmowers A built after the repudiation, B would probably not be liable, because A could have mitigated the damages by not continuing to build.

5. Yes. B can ask for the remedy of specific performance from A because the car is unique.

ANSWERS TO CHAPTER 19–Relationship of Principal and Agent

TRUE-FALSE

1. T	4. T	7. T	10. F
2. F	5. F	8. T	11. F
3. T	6. T	9. F	12. T

KEY TERMS–MATCHING

1. 7	5. 15	9. 12	13. 19
2. 6	6. 10	10. 5	14. 17
3. 9	7. 13	11. 20	15. 18
4. 1	8. 3	12. 16	

MULTIPLE CHOICE

1. c	5. b	9. b	13. a
2. a	6. d	10. c	
3. b	7. d	11. d	
4. a	8. a	12. c	

CASE PROBLEMS–ESSAY ANSWERS

1. No. This would be considered a contract for personal services, and A cannot delegate them. This case is beyond the scope of agency purposes.

2. Yes, because A has breached the fiduciary duty to P. Agents who are employed to buy may not buy from themselves.

3. No. An agent has a duty not to make any secret profit while dealing for the principal.

4. No. The authority of the agent to perform a specific act is terminated when the act is performed. A could not sell the second painting without new authority from P.

5. When war occurs, which puts a principal and an agent in the position of hostile enemies from countries at war, the agency relationship is terminated due to supervening illegality. Thus, D no longer has authority to represent T since their agency contract has been terminated through operation of law.

ANSWERS TO CHAPTER 20–Relationship with Third Parties

TRUE-FALSE

1. T	4. T	7. T	10. T
2. F	5. T	8. F	11. F
3. F	6. F	9. F	12. T

KEY TERMS MATCHING

1. 14	5. 2	9. 4	13. 16
2. 7	6. 11	10. 5	14. 20
3. 9	7. 8	11. 1	15. 17
4. 15	8. 13	12. 19	

MULTIPLE CHOICE

1. b	5. a	9. a	13. b
2. a	6. d	10. c	
3. c	7. b	11. b	
4. d	8. d	12. a	

CASE PROBLEMS–ESSAY ANSWERS

1. Probably not. A pattern of conduct has been established, based on A's five year purchases, where C has continuously done business with P. C may assume, having no knowledge otherwise, that the established purchase pattern will continue. The apparent authority of A to act, coupled with C's lack of knowledge that A is not so authorized, gives C a right of recourse against P.

2. Yes. Agents are liable for their own wrongful and negligent acts, whether or not the principal is also liable.

3 No. An agent who makes a contract with a third person on behalf of a disclosed principal has no right of action against the third person for breach of contract.

4. No. A third person can proceed to trial against both the principal and agent but if, before the entry of judgment, the third person elects to obtain a judgment against the principal alone and does obtain a judgment, the third person could not seek another judgment from the

agent. An election to obtain judgment against one party irrevocably binds the third person to that choice.

5. Normally a principal is not liable for the torts of an independent contractor unless they arise from breach of non-delegable duties that are imposed by law. Usually, dangerous activity falls within non-delegatable duties. Since the duty to act safely is imposed by law, and dynamiting is a dangerous activity, P is most likely liable for X's dynamiting. T can sue P.

ANSWERS TO CHAPTER 21–Introduction to Sales

TRUE-FALSE

1. T	4. T	7. F	10. F
2. F	5. T	8. T	11. T
3. F	6. F	9. T	12. F

KEY TERMS–MATCHING

1. 4	5. 15	9. 13	13. 19
2. 7	6. 10	10. 6	14. 17
3. 11	7. 8	11. 1	15. 18
4. 9	8. 2	12. 16	

MULTIPLE CHOICE

1. c	5. d	9. d	13. b
2. d	6. b	10. a	
3. b	7. a	11. c	
4. d	8. b	12. d	

CASE PROBLEMS–ESSAY ANSWERS

1. Yes. Under U.C.C. 2-205, a merchant's written offer containing a statement that it will remain open for a specified period is irrevocable during the stated time.

2. No. The U.C.C. holds output and quantity contracts valid. An objective standard, based on the good faith of the parties, drawing upon prior agreements, course dealings and usages of trade, is used to supply the missing term.

3. Yes. The unequal bargaining positions of the parties to the contract and the $800 purchase price for an item with a $180 fair market retail value render the agreement "unconscionable." Under section 2-302 of the U.C.C., courts have the authority to deny or limit enforcement of such unfair, harsh and indecent contracts.

4. A contract exists and Penny's additional terms are not a rejection or counteroffer. Under U.C.C. 2-207, Penny's acceptance, definitely and seasonably made, is effective. Since both parties are merchants, her additional terms will become part of the contract because the offer was not expressly limited to its terms and the additional terms probably do not materially alter the terms of the offer unless Yummy objects to them in writing within a reasonable time.

5. Wally loses. The Code states that oral contracts for goods specially manufactured for the buyer, which are not suitable for resale in the ordinary course of business, are enforceable. This contract is not within the Statute of Frauds.

ANSWERS TO CHAPTER 22–Performance

TRUE-FALSE

1. T	4. T	7. T	10. T
2. F	5. F	8. F	11. F
3. F	6. T	9. F	12. T

KEY TERMS–MATCHING

1. 7	5. 12	9. 10	13. 19
2. 3	6. 5	10. 11	14. 17
3. 6	7. 9	11. 20	15. 18
4. 15	8. 1	12. 16	

MULTIPLE CHOICE

1. a	5. c	9. d	13. c
2. d	6. b	10. b	
3. d	7. a	11. d	
4. b	8. c	12. a	

CASE PROBLEMS–ESSAY ANSWERS

1. Probably not. Assuming that the masks were specified and identified to the contract when it was made, their total loss during the flood, before risk of loss passed to B, avoided the contract.

2. For B. Although this is a breach of an installment contract with commercial units and therefore gives rise to a cause of action, S may not treat the one-day delayed payment as a material breach striking at the heart of the contract. The one-day delay is not justification to cancel the entire contract.

3. B probably wins. For H.H. to effectively revoke her acceptance, the defect in the non-conforming rifle must substantially impair its value. Arguably, the scratches and nicks do not detract from the usefulness or performance capacity of the rifle and are therefore not substantial value impairments. However, since the test for value impairment is subjective–personal to the buyer–H.H. could argue that she intended to use the gun as a showcase collector's piece, as well as for hunting, and the blemishes, foreclosing the showcase capacity, are substantial value impairments.

4. Decision for S. A merchant buyer, who has possession of rightfully rejected goods, must make reasonable efforts to resell the goods, if they are perishable, even if the seller gives the buyer no instructions. Failure to comply with the Code makes merchant buyer B liable for losses stemming from holding the perishable bananas and not selling them on seller's account.

5. S probably wins. Ordinarily, impossibility of performance (in this case, the trade embargo) does not excuse performance on the contract. But where the parties understood when they entered their contract that performance would depend upon a certain event or condition (availability of Australian widgees), the non-occurrence or termination of that presupposed basic condition (trade embargo on Australian goods) will excuse duties of performance.

ANSWERS TO CHAPTER 23–Transfer of Title and Risk of Loss

TRUE-FALSE

1. T	4. F	7. F	10. T
2. F	5. T	8. T	11. T
3. T	6. T	9. F	12. F

KEY TERMS–MATCHING

1. 8	5. 5	9. 14	13. 16
2. 9	6. 12	10. 1	14. 19
3. 7	7. 3	11. 20	15. 18
4. 11	8. 13	12. 17	

MULTIPLE CHOICE

1. c	5. d	9. b	13. d
2. c	6. a	10. b	
3. d	7. a	11. a	
4. b	8. c	12. c	

CASE PROBLEMS–ESSAY ANSWERS

1. It depends. Under old U.C.C. Article 6, failing to comply with the Article's requirements made the purchaser's goods subject to unpaid creditors' claims. Thus, B's creditors could proceed against the goods in A's possession. Under revised Article 6, however, the buyer's failure to comply with Article 6 requirements does not affect title to the goods but makes the buyer liable for noncompliance damages to the seller's creditors. Thus, B's creditors would have no recourse against the goods in A's possession.

2. A buyer who has rightfully exercised revocation of acceptance for nonconforming goods may hold the seller accountable for any insurance coverage deficiency following damage or destruction to the goods. Thus, Mary's insurance covers $7,000 of her loss and Ajax must reimburse her for the $3,000 difference.

3. A has lost title to the coat and has no rights against C. By "entrusting" the fur coat to merchant dealer B, A has given the latter power to transfer all of her rights to a buyer in the ordinary course of business, which C was. A's only recourse is money damages against B.

4. Buyer suffers the loss. When goods held by a bailee are sold to another and the goods are covered by a negotiable title document, risk of loss passes to the buyer on the latter's receipt of the document. Since grain owner delivered the title document to buyer, buyer suffers the loss.

5. Francine may recover the $1,280 from Mary since, as a merchant seller, the risk of loss remained on her as the goods had yet to be received by Francine.

ANSWERS TO CHAPTER 24–Product Liability: Warranties and Strict Liability in Tort

TRUE-FALSE

1. T	4. F	7. F	10. T
2. F	5. F	8. T	11. F
3. T	6. T	9. F	12. T

KEY TERMS–MATCHING

1. 8	5. 6	9. 15	13. 16
2. 12	6. 10	10. 3	14. 5
3. 7	7. 14	11. 4	15. 20
4. 9	8. 2	12. 18	

MULTIPLE CHOICE

1. a	5. a	9. c	13. b
2. c	6. c	10. d	
3. a	7. b	11. d	
4. b	8. d	12. a	

CASE PROBLEMS–ESSAY ANSWERS

1. No. Strict liability in tort does not apply to an occasional seller not in the business of selling the defective product.

2. B may revoke acceptance and seek damages from S based upon a breach of the implied warranty of merchantability. The car is obviously not fit for ordinary driving purposes.

3. A manufacturer has a duty to warn of potential hazards or foreseeable dangers arising out of the normal or probable use of a product. Where a consumer has misused a product, the manufacturer has no duty to warn about dangers therefrom and faces no liability. For the manufacturer.

4. It depends. Assuming that the rods were warranted, the seller must be notified of any breach within a reasonable time after a defect is or should have been discovered. If B fails to notify S, no damages are recoverable. If B does seasonably notify S, damages are $300: the

difference between the value of the goods as accepted and the value they would have had had they been conforming to the contract.

5. C loses. Since the inedible ingredient in question, the bone, was both natural to the food consumed and its presence could have been reasonably expected, C will have to bear her own loss, based on either the natural substance or the reasonable expectation test.

ANSWERS TO CHAPTER 25–Remedies

TRUE-FALSE

1. T	4. F	7. T	10. F
2. T	5. T	8. F	11. T
3. F	6. F	9. F	12. T

KEY TERMS–MATCHING

1. 1	5. 6	9. 12	13. 16
2. 13	6. 7	10. 4	14. 19
3. 2	7. 9	11. 20	15. 18
4. 5	8. 10	12. 17	

MULTIPLE CHOICE

1. b	5. b	9. c	13. c
2. d	6. a	10. b	
3. c	7. a	11. d	
4. c	8. c	12. b	

CASE PROBLEMS–ESSAY ANSWERS

1. Since the seller is usually never accountable to the buyer for any profit made on a resale of the goods, B recovers nothing.

2. Since the difference between the cost of the goods purchased by B's "cover" and the contract price resulted in a $1,000 "better deal" for B, all that B might recover are incidental or consequential damages, less expenses saved as a result of S's breach.

3. B should exercise a right of recovery against S for the identified goods in which B holds a special property interest. The Code gives a buyer the right to recover goods from an

insolvent seller when the seller becomes insolvent within 10 days of the first installment payment on the sales contract. To perfect this special interest in the goods, B must tender the remaining $7,500 to S.

4. B may store the nails for the seller's account, reship them to the seller or resell them for the seller's account. By disposing of them, B is neither converting them nor accepting them. B would be liable to the seller for any excess over his security interest in the goods.

5. Because the painting in this case is unique, a court of equity will issue a decree of specific performance requiring delivery of the painting from C to A rather than an award of money damages.

ANSWERS TO CHAPTER 26–Form and Content

TRUE-FALSE

1.	T	4.	F	7.	T	10.	T
2.	F	5.	T	8.	T	11.	T
3.	T	6.	F	9.	F	12.	F

KEY TERMS–MATCHING

1.	5	5.	4	9.	3	13.	19
2.	2	6.	8	10.	1	14.	16
3.	14	7.	11	11.	9	15.	18
4.	12	8.	15	12.	17		

MULTIPLE CHOICE

1.	b	5.	b	9.	c	13.	a
2.	d	6.	d	10.	a		
3.	d	7.	d	11.	b		
4.	b	8.	a	12.	b		

CASE PROBLEMS–ESSAY ANSWERS

1. S wins. Where words and figures on an instrument are in conflict, the words, unless unclear themselves, are controlling. B must come up with the $810 difference.

2. None. Provisions in commercial paper granting the obligor the option to extend the maturity date for a definite time period do not affect negotiability.

3. Yes. Auxiliary clauses of this nature do not affect the sum certain due on the instrument. The note is therefore negotiable.

4. Yes. Any symbol is sufficient as a signature so long as the person signing has adopted it and intends it to be their authentic signature.

5. No. A bare indebtedness acknowledgement, such as an "I.O.U.," is not a negotiable instrument carrying with it an obligation of payment to its holder. M has made no promise of payment at all.

ANSWERS TO CHAPTER 27–Transfer

TRUE-FALSE

1. T	4. F	7. T	10. F
2. F	5. T	8. F	11. T
3. T	6. F	9. T	12. F

KEY TERMS–MATCHING

1. 4	5. 15	9. 12	13. 16
2. 14	6. 13	10. 7	14. 6
3. 5	7. 10	11. 18	15. 19
4. 1	8. 2	12. 20	

MULTIPLE CHOICE

1. d	5. c	9. b	13. d
2. c	6. b	10. a	
3. d	7. d	11. a	
4. a	8. b	12. b	

CASE PROBLEMS–ESSAY ANSWERS

1. For Z, the U.C.C. makes these types of indorsement unenforceable. A conditional indorsement limiting the indorsee's payment rights to the occurrence of a specific event does not affect the indorsee's right to enforce payment.

2. No. Under the Fictitious Payee Rule, assuming the bank used ordinary care in paying the $600, it is not liable to Fran since Frank's signature is effective against Fran who bears the risk of loss of her dishonest employees.

3. Only if X's signature appeared on the note. Since the bearer paper became order paper through P's special indorsement, any further negotiation of the note would require X's indorsement. M may rightfully refuse payment to F if the note does not contain X's signature.

4. Yes. Anyone who possesses bearer paper is a holder entitled to payment.

5. To protect the interest in the instrument, B can convert the blank indorsement to a special indorsement by writing over A's signature any restriction not contrary to the type of indorsement. Thus, B may write "Pay to the order of B" to protect the interest.

ANSWERS TO CHAPTER 28–Holder in Due Course

TRUE-FALSE

1. T	4. F	7. T	10. T
2. T	5. T	8. F	11. F
3. F	6. F	9. T	12. F

KEY TERMS–MATCHING

1. 4	5. 6	9. 1	13. 18
2. 2	6. 13	10. 12	14. 17
3. 7	7. 10	11. 19	15. 9
4. 3	8. 11	12. 16	

MULTIPLE CHOICE

1.	d	5.	d	9.	d	13.	c
2.	a	6.	b	10.	c		
3.	d	7.	c	11.	a		
4.	a	8.	b	12.	b		

CASE PROBLEMS–ESSAY ANSWERS

1. H is holder of the full $1,000 face value of the note. A holder is not required to pay the full face amount to give value, but only the amount agreed upon with the transferor.

2. No. One not a holder in due course cannot cleanse paper by transferring the paper to and re-acquiring it from a holder in due course. P cannot use the Shelter Rule to profit from wrongdoing.

3. S's alteration is not a fraudulent one that would operate to discharge M on the instrument. Changing figures to comply with the controlling written number merely brings them into compliance with the original written terms.

4. Probably not. Under the Code, notice must be received in a timely manner sufficient to provide a reasonable opportunity to act on it. Such is not the case here.

5. No. Based on an FTC regulation, effective May 1976, holders of commercial paper issued in connection with consumer credit transactions acquire the paper subject to all claims, defenses and demands, including fraud and defective goods, which the consumer debtor could have asserted against the payee on the instrument.

ANSWERS TO CHAPTER 29–Liabilities of Parties

TRUE-FALSE

1.	T	4.	F	7.	F	10.	T
2.	T	5.	T	8.	T	11.	T
3.	F	6.	T	9.	F	12.	F

KEY TERMS–MATCHING

1. 4	5. 9	9. 13	13. 1
2. 11	6. 7	10. 12	14. 20
3. 14	7. 2	11. 18	15. 17
4. 8	8. 6	12. 16	

MULTIPLE CHOICE

1. c	5. c	9. b	13. a
2. d	6. a	10. d	
3. b	7. c	11. c	
4. b	8. a	12. b	

CASE PROBLEMS–ESSAY ANSWERS

1. M can collect on the instrument from the drawer, A, to the original tenor of $500. The drawer faces secondary liability on the instrument when the drawee fails to make proper payment.

2. A's willingness and ability to pay at the specified place, i.e., the bank, is the equivalent of tender of payment. A is liable for the face amount and interest accrued at the time payment was due, but not for additional interest thereafter or for subsequent costs and attorney's fees.

3. H can hold B liable for breaching the transferor's warranties of enforcement, entitlement and the authenticity of all signatures.

4. Assuming H is not aware of P's involvement, M is liable. By having failed to identify P, P is not obligated on the instrument to H, and M is solely bound to make payment.

5. H loses. Presenters of instruments warrant that no material alteration has occurred. H has breached this warranty and is liable for the difference.

ANSWERS TO CHAPTER 30–Bank Deposits, Collections, and Fund Transfers

TRUE-FALSE

1. T	4. F	7. T	10. T
2. F	5. F	8. F	11. F
3. T	6. T	9. F	12. T

KEY TERMS–MATCHING

1. 1	5. 14	9. 2	13. 18
2. 3	6. 15	10. 6	14. 16
3. 13	7. 8	11. 17	15. 19
4. 7	8. 11	12. 20	

MULTIPLE CHOICE

1. a	5. b	9. d	13. b
2. d	6. c	10. a	
3. c	7. b	11. d	
4. c	8. a	12. c	

CASE PROBLEMS–ESSAY ANSWERS

1. C wins. A payor bank receiving an item properly payable from a customer's account that lacks sufficient funds to cover the designated amount may pay the item, charge the account, and seek reimbursement from the customer for both the overdraft created by the item and any service charges connected with its handling.

2. Cathy will be liable for only $50 of the withdrawals if she notifies her bank of the card's disappearance within two days after she knows of its absence. After two days, she will be liable for the full amount of Frank's withdrawals up to a maximum of $500 if she notifies the bank within 60 days of the card's absence.

3. H may bring an action for payment against B because a stop payment order does not automatically relieve the drawer of liability to the holder. Since H is a holder in due course of a negotiable instrument arising from a non-consumer transaction, the personal defense of failure of consideration may not be used by B to avoid payment to H.

4. Under the U.C.C., a bank may fix a time at or after 2:00 p.m. as a cut-off hour for handling items and making appropriate entries on its books. This rule permits the bank to extend the banking day until a later hour without starting the running time for the midnight deadline. An item, having been received after the cut-off time, is deemed to be received at the opening of business on the next banking day. In this case, the next banking day is Monday and the midnight deadline is thus on Tuesday. Here, the bank did not act until Wednesday. Therefore it did not act seasonably.

5. P wins. The payor bank's authority to honor checks drawn by its customers is not affected by the incompetence of a customer at the time collection is undertaken and payment made when the bank is, in fact, not aware of the adjudication of incompetence. The bank may make payment without incurring any liability.

ANSWERS TO CHAPTER 31–Formation and Dissolutions of General Partnerships

TRUE-FALSE

1. F	4. F	7. F	10. T
2. T	5. T	8. F	11. F
3. F	6. F	9. F	12. F

KEY TERMS–MATCHING

1. 13	5. 7	9. 3	13. 18
2. 12	6. 10	10. 2	14. 5
3. 1	7. 14	11. 20	15. 9
4. 4	8. 8	12. 16	

MULTIPLE CHOICE

1. a	5. a	9. d	13. b
2. d	6. a	10. d	
3. a	7. b	11. d	
4. a	8. d	12. c	

CASE PROBLEMS–ESSAY ANSWERS

1. Yes. They have an agreement to share the profits and continue to manage the business. This constitutes a partnership.

2. Yes. If Z's departure is a dissociation, then the partnership continues unaffected and X and Y can buy Z's interest and release Z from debts through novation. If the partnership agreement contains a continuation agreement, and Z's departure is a dissolution, X and Y continue the business, and Z may be discharged from liabilities through a novation.

3. No. An adjudicated incompetent person's contracts, including a partnership agreement, are void. A lacks the capacity to enter a partnership.

4. Yes. A partner can apply for dissolution by court order since partner A is guilty of conduct prejudicial to the business and has willfully breached the partnership agreement.

5. X wins. Even though C retired with the consent of the other partners, who agreed to assume full liability for all old partnership debts, C is still liable to creditors whose claims arose prior to dissolution. C's recourse would be to seek indemnification from A and B for their failure to live up to the agreement.

ANSWERS TO CHAPTER 32–Operation of General Partnerships

TRUE-FALSE

1.	T	4.	F	7.	F	10.	T
2.	T	5.	T	8.	F	11.	T
3.	F	6.	T	9.	F	12.	T

KEY TERMS–MATCHING

1.	8	5.	4	9.	11	13.	7
2.	1	6.	9	10.	6	14.	10
3.	2	7.	15	11.	20	15.	19
4.	3	8.	14	12.	17		

MULTIPLE CHOICE

1.	a	5.	d	9.	c	13.	c
2.	d	6.	a	10.	d		
3.	d	7.	d	11.	d		
4.	c	8.	b	12.	b		

CASE PROBLEMS–ESSAY ANSWERS

1. B and C win. P does not become a partner and is not entitled to participate in the management of the partnership. No person can become a member of a partnership without consent of all of the partners.

2. Q wins. Unanimous agreement among all the partners is required when a matter involves changing the terms of the partnership agreement.

3. A loses. The Uniform Partnership Act provides that, unless otherwise agreed, no partner is entitled to compensation for acting in the partnership business.

4. No. Elizabeth need not account for her executor fees where it cannot be shown that her service in this other capacity impaired her fiduciary duty to the partnership (the law firm).

5   No. A partner may not sue the partnership for damages, but if the partner is denied the right to participate in the management of the partnership, then the partner may sue in equity for an accounting.

ANSWERS TO CHAPTER 33–Limited Partnerships and Limited Liability Companies

TRUE-FALSE

1. F	4. T	7. F	10. F
2. F	5. F	8. T	11. T
3. T	6. T	9. T	12. T

KEY TERMS–MATCHING

1. 5	5. 10	9. 7	13. 12
2. 8	6. 13	10. 15	14. 17
3. 6	7. 1	11. 20	15. 19
4. 9	8. 2	12. 4	

MULTIPLE CHOICE

1. d	5. d	9. b	13. d
2. d	6. b	10. c	
3. c	7. d	11. c	
4. d	8. a	12. c	

CASE PROBLEMS–ESSAY ANSWERS

1. No. Absent a provision in the partnership agreement, a limited partner has limited personal liability and does not share in the losses of the partnership beyond her capital contribution.

2. C can sue both A and B. A limited partner whose name is used as part of the partnership name renders the limited partner liable as a general partner to any creditor who did not know of the limited partnership. In addition, since the words "limited partnership" must be in the partnership name, B is also liable for this reason.

3. No. The bankruptcy of a limited partner does not dissolve the limited partnership.

4. Yes. If all partners, general and limited, agree in writing, the new general partner may be added. This is necessary only if the partnership agreement fails to deal with the issue.

5. The certificate shall contain the name of the limited partnership, the location of the business office, the name and address of the business agent, the name and address of each general partner, the latest date upon which the limited partnership is to dissolve, and any other matters the general partners decide to include in the certificate.

ANSWERS TO CHAPTER 34–Nature, Formation, and Powers

TRUE-FALSE

1. T	4. F	7. T	10. F
2. T	5. F	8. T	11. F
3. T	6. T	9. F	12. T

KEY TERMS–MATCHING

1. 3	5. 8	9. 9	13. 1
2. 2	6. 7	10. 11	14. 19
3. 5	7. 14	11. 17	15. 16
4. 6	8. 12	12. 18	

MULTIPLE CHOICE

1. c	5. a	9. d	13. d
2. a	6. c	10. c	
3. d	7. b	11. d	
4. c	8. d	12. d	

CASE PROBLEMS–ESSAY ANSWERS

1. Yes. If the business is operated as a corporation, the business' debts can be satisfied only from assets of the corporation. C's personal assets would be protected.

2. Possibly. A corporation may be liable for crimes committed by its agents or employees and punished for the violation by a fine.

3. Contracts made by a promoter for a corporation not yet formed are binding only on the promoter. The corporation becomes liable if it ratifies the contract after the corporation is formed, but the promoter usually also remains liable.

4. No. A promoter has a fiduciary duty to the initial shareholders and the corporation and cannot retain secret profits resulting from this relationship.

5. No. The case illustrates the formation of a de facto corporation. The corporation would be liable to the customer. A, B, and C would not be personally liable. Only the State can challenge the existence of a de facto corporation. Under the Revised Act, liability is imposed on persons who purport to act as a corporation only if they know there is no proper incorporation. A, B, and C did not know and are not personally liable.

ANSWERS TO CHAPTER 35–Financial Structure

TRUE-FALSE

1.	F	4.	F	7.	F	10.	T
2.	T	5.	F	8.	F	11.	T
3.	F	6.	F	9.	T	12.	F

KEY TERMS–MATCHING

1.	7	5.	8	9.	10	13.	17
2.	6	6.	5	10.	14	14.	18
3.	2	7.	12	11.	20	15.	19
4.	4	8.	9	12.	16		

MULTIPLE CHOICE

1. d	5. d	9. c	13. d
2. d	6. a	10. d	
3. b	7. d	11. c	
4. b	8. d	12. a	

CASE PROBLEMS–ESSAY ANSWERS

1. No. The majority position states that in the absence of fraud, the judgment of the board of directors as to the value of the consideration received for shares shall be conclusive.

2. Yes. If provided for in the articles of incorporation, a corporation does have the power of redemption. To protect creditors, however, most states have statutory restrictions upon redemption that may overrule the articles of incorporation (charter), and the Revised Act does not permit redemption if the corporation would be unable to pay its debts as they become due in the usual course of its business.

3. Yes. A corporation becomes the debtor of its shareholders when a cash dividend is properly declared. Once declared, a dividend cannot be rescinded without the shareholders' consent.

4. No. A buyer (transferee) who acquires these shares in good faith and without knowledge or notice that the full value of the shares has not been paid is not personally liable to the corporation for the unpaid balance of the shares.

5. A will own 1,500 shares and her relative interest in the corporation will be unchanged.

ANSWERS TO CHAPTER 36–Management Structure

TRUE-FALSE

1. T	4. T	7. T	10. F
2. T	5. T	8. T	11. T
3. F	6. F	9. F	12. F

KEY TERMS–MATCHING

1. 15	5. 11	9. 2	13. 7
2. 4	6. 12	10. 14	14. 18
3. 8	7. 9	11. 16	15. 5
4. 10	8. 6	12. 20	

MULTIPLE CHOICE

1. a	5. b	9. d	13. d
2. d	6. c	10. a	
3. d	7. a	11. d	
4. d	8. d	12. d	

CASE PROBLEMS–ESSAY ANSWERS

1. Because the vote is cumulative, X has 30 votes. X may give all 30 votes to one director or apportion the 30 votes between two or among all three of the candidates.

2. No. Because of an officer's fiduciary duty and the "corporate opportunity" doctrine, A must make full disclosure of the opportunity to the corporation before A purchases the land.

3. No. Unless all the directors signed a consent in writing to vote without a meeting, they do not have the power to bind the corporation when acting individually.

4. X wins. Absent fraud or intentional misconduct, a court will not hold X liable for damages for an honest mistake if X is using good faith judgment which later proves to be financially unsound.

5. X is liable. Either directors or officers may be held liable for not fulfilling their duty of diligence to the corporation.

ANSWERS TO CHAPTER 37–Fundamental Changes

TRUE-FALSE

1. F	4. T	7. F	10. F
2. F	5. F	8. T	11. F
3. T	6. F	9. T	12. T

KEY TERMS–MATCHING

1. 3	5. 9	9. 12	13. 1
2. 2	6. 6	10. 13	14. 11
3. 15	7. 7	11. 20	15. 17
4. 4	8. 8	12. 16	

MULTIPLE CHOICE

1. d	5. d	9. d	13. b
2. d	6. d	10. d	
3. d	7. d	11. d	
4. d	8. b	12. b	

CASE PROBLEMS–ESSAY ANSWERS

1. Upon dissolution, the assets of the corporation are liquidated and used first to pay creditors and the expenses of liquidation. A will be paid ahead of all the shareholders.

2. No. The Revised Act requires a written demand for the money on a form provided by the corporation within a time period set by the corporation. Unless Abby makes the demand within that time period, she is not entitled to payment for her shares.

3. No. Only the dissenting shareholders of the subsidiary corporation have the right to obtain payment for their shares from the parent corporation.

4. Merger, consolidation, the purchase of the assets of one corporation by the other, or dissolution of one corporation are all possible remedies.

5. Yes. When one corporation becomes the parent over another, no change is made in the legal existence of either, i.e., the separate existence of both corporations is not affected by the exchange.

ANSWERS TO CHAPTER 38–Secured Transactions in Personal Property and Suretyship

TRUE-FALSE

1. F	4. T	7. T	10. T
2. T	5. F	8. F	11. F
3. F	6. T	9. T	12. F

KEY TERMS–MATCHING

1. 5	5. 1	9. 12	13. 15
2. 7	6. 13	10. 3	14. 20
3. 9	7. 8	11. 19	15. 18
4. 10	8. 2	12. 16	

MULTIPLE CHOICE

1. c	5. c	9. d	13. c
2. b	6. a	10. a	
3. d	7. b	11. d	
4. b	8. c	12. a	

CASE PROBLEMS–ESSAY ANSWERS

1. S wins. Under a conditional sales contract, the seller retains "title" in the goods as a security until they are fully paid for. When the buyer defaults on the contract, the seller may usually recover the goods.

2. L has incorrectly identified the collateral. The books are likely equipment under the U.C.C.'s broad definition of this term.

3. Unless the agreement between debtor and creditor provides otherwise, the secured creditor has rights to sale proceeds upon transfer of the collateral. Assuming the agreement between L and B did not speak to this issue, B may assert a claim against the $1,000.

4. L has priority since that security interest was perfected first and C could have found out about it by checking the recorded financing statement.

5. Assuming that following default B did not sign a written waiver of any rights, S's actions are improper since B has paid at least 60% of the original $2,500 debt. S must therefore sell the repossessed unit within 90 days after repossession and reimburse B for any amount of the sale proceeds that exceed the debt balance, plus expenses associated with repossession and resale.

ANSWERS TO CHAPTER 39–Bankruptcy

TRUE-FALSE

1. F	4. T	7. F	10. T
2. T	5. F	8. T	11. T
3. F	6. F	9. T	12. F

KEY TERMS–MATCHING

1. 12	5. 5	9. 15	13. 19
2. 3	6. 1	10. 8	14. 17
3. 4	7. 2	11. 20	15. 18
4. 11	8. 7	12. 16	

MULTIPLE CHOICE

1. c	5. d	9. b	13. d
2. b	6. c	10. c	
3. b	7. a	11. b	
4. a	8. d	12. a	

CASE PROBLEMS–ESSAY ANSWERS

1. No. Student loans are non-dischargeable debts for five years after they become due.

2. No. Since the agreement was made after D's discharge, it is unenforceable under the Bankruptcy law.

3. Creditors 1, 2. and 3 hold some degree of priority claims. The portion of their debts given priority status must be fully satisfied before any general unsecured creditors receive payment. Accordingly, Creditor 1 receives $10,000, Creditor 2 $2,000, and Creditor 3 $6,000, totaling $18,000 of priority claims satisfied. This leaves $27,000 to apply to the remaining

$36,000 in unsecured debt: $7,000 to Creditor 1; $6,000 to Creditor 2; $12,000 to Creditor 4; and $11,000 to Creditor 5. Creditor 6 will not share in debtor's estate since it failed to list its claim with the court. The $27,000 will be divided pro rataly among Creditors 1, 2, 4, and 5. Each will receive 75% (27,000/36,000 or 3/4) return on the debt owed them: Creditor 1 receives $5,200; Creditor 2 receives $4,500; Creditor 4 receives $8,250; and Creditor 5 receives $9,000.

4. Dingle's transfers constitute a fraudulent conveyance. It can result in Doodles being denied discharge as well as the trustee avoiding the transfers and bringing the boat and car back into Doodle's estate.

5. The transfer is legal since before it can be a voidable preference, Paddywack must be insolvent or the transfers must make him insolvent. Here, Paddywack is solvent (assets exceeding liabilities).

ANSWERS TO CHAPTER 40–Protection of Intellectual Property

TRUE-FALSE

1. T	4. F	7. T	10. F
2. T	5. T	8. F	11. T
3. F	6. F	9. T	12. F

KEY TERMS–MATCHING

1. 14	5. 2	9. 6	13. 18
2. 1	6. 7	10. 3	14. 19
3. 15	7. 4	11. 17	15. 16
4. 9	8. 10	12. 20	

MULTIPLE CHOICE

1. b	5. a	9. b	13. b
2. d	6. c	10. a	
3. c	7. c	11. d	
4. b	8. a	12. c	

CASE PROBLEMS–ESSAY ANSWERS

1. Probably not. Since "Lantern" describes the function, purpose and characteristics of Larry's lamps, he cannot tie up the word for exclusive application to his lamps.

2. Toys Mfg., Inc. may restrain A and B, through an injunction, from using the special knowledge and skills they developed while employed at Toys that constitute trade secrets for the benefit of Playthings. If Toys were not allowed to so protect its trade secrets, Playthings would gain an unfair competitive advantage at Toys' expense.

3. Probably not. Natural substances are not patentable. Discovering the usefulness of an already existing and known bacteria does not meet the requirements of a human-made or modified invention. Only if Doctor Science's efforts amount to genetically engineering the bacteria could it be patentable.

4. The Puffers. By failing to register their copyright, the Eskimos are foreclosed from bringing an infringement action against the Puffers.

5. Home Products has violated the Lanham Act by intentionally and knowingly using a counterfeit mark. Accordingly, H. P. faces fines upwards of $1 million and all "Clean and Smooth" cans marked with the AASCP insignia may be confiscated and destroyed.

ANSWERS TO CHAPTER 41–Antitrust

TRUE-FALSE

1. T	4. T	7. T	10. F
2. T	5. F	8. F	11. T
3. F	6. F	9. T	12. F

KEY TERMS–MATCHING

1. 3	5. 14	9. 6	13. 16
2. 7	6. 13	10. 12	14. 11
3. 15	7. 4	11. 17	15. 5
4. 9	8. 10	12. 20	

MULTIPLE CHOICE

1. d	5. a	9. b	13. b
2. b	6. c	10. d	
3. d	7. a	11. a	
4. c	8. c	12. c	

CASE PROBLEMS–ESSAY ANSWERS

1. This is an example of an exclusive supply contract that might be a violation of antitrust statutes (Section 3 of the Clayton Act) if it results in a considerable reduction of competition or has the effect of establishing a monopoly.

2. This is an example of retail price maintenance (vertical price fixing). This practice was once legal under state Fair Trade Acts but is now a per se violation of the Sherman Antitrust Act when interstate commerce is affected.

3. Probably. Since the contract between Home Furnishings and the distributor calls for lower prices than competitors of Home Furnishings pay, this could amount to the type of price discrimination prohibited by Section 2 of the Robinson-Patman Act. For the price differentials not to be violations, they would have to be justified on the basis of legitimate business reasons.

4. Yes. Since Pewtrid raised the price on the paint to be purchased, and the sales price for the three gallons of paint was more than the usual retail price for two gallons, the ad campaign was deceptive by referring to the third gallon as "free."

5. Yes. Since the practice of law is professional commerce, and lawyers are sellers of professional services, agreements between these sellers to establish minimum prices at which their services are sold is prohibited under the Act.

ANSWERS TO CHAPTER 42–Consumer Protection

TRUE-FALSE

1. F	4. F	7. F	10. T
2. T	5. F	8. F	11. F
3. T	6. T	9. F	12. T

KEY TERMS–MATCHING

1. 5	5. 9	9. 4	13. 17
2. 7	6. 12	10. 1	14. 13
3. 8	7. 10	11. 19	15. 18
4. 15	8. 14	12. 16	

MULTIPLE CHOICE

1. c	5. c	9. b	13. a
2. b	6. b	10. c	
3. d	7. d	11. b	
4. a	8. a	12. d	

CASE PROBLEMS–ESSAY ANSWERS

1. Jackson is not liable for any of the $250. Since the card was neither requested nor accepted, the entire loss for its unauthorized use falls on Plakton Petroleum as provided for under the FCCPA.

2. According to provisions in the FCCPA, an employer may not fire employees simply because creditors of employees have exercised a right of wage assignment or garnishment against them. In this case, E's threat of discharge is improper and illegal.

3. The final $1,600 payment is called a balloon payment. In such cases, a debtor unable to meet the amount is not automatically in default with the possibility of losing the goods. In some states, balloon payment clauses are void and prohibited. In others, B may refinance the $1,600 on the same terms as the prior payment of $5,600 without any penalty.

4. The Magnuson-Moss Act applies only where written warranties accompany the sale of goods or services. The Act does not require that such warranties be given. Since, in this case, no warranty was given by S, B has no rights under Magnuson-Moss.

5. Under the Federal Interstate Land Sales Full Disclosure Act, purchasers of land through an interstate promotional campaign must be provided a "statement of record" or property report prior to entering a contract of sale with the Teal property seller. When sellers fail to provide such a statement, buyers may cancel their contracts with the seller any time within two years after the contract was signed. Since in this case H and W were never given a report from S, you should advise them to exercise their revocation rights as allowed under the ILSFDA.

ANSWERS TO CHAPTER 43–Employment Law

TRUE-FALSE

1. T	4. T	7. T	10. F
2. F	5. F	8. T	11. T
3. F	6. F	9. T	12. F

KEY TERMS–MATCHING

1. 4	5. 15	9. 13	13. 17
2. 7	6. 10	10. 6	14. 19
3. 11	7. 8	11. 16	15. 18
4. 9	8. 2	12. 20	

MULTIPLE CHOICE

1. d	5. c	9. b	13. c
2. c	6. b	10. a	
3. a	7. a	11. d	
4. c	8. c	12. d	

CASE PROBLEMS–ESSAY ANSWERS

1. Probably not. Since stock clerks and yard attendants are most likely different with different responsibilities, they may have different salary scales without violating the Equal Pay Act.

2. Aerospace wins. Federal age discrimination laws apply only to persons at least 40 years old.

3. Fortisque wins if his opinions carry no direct reprisal or threat of coercion against his workers. This falls under the employer free speech section of the Taft-Hartley Act.

4. Charlene wins. OSHA forbids discharge of employment based on employees exercising their rights under the Act.

5. Folsum wins. The union's action is a prohibited secondary boycott under the terms of Taft-Hartley and amounts to a union unfair labor practice.

ANSWERS TO CHAPTER 44–Securities Regulation

TRUE-FALSE

1. F	4. T	7. F	10. F
2. F	5. F	8. T	11. T
3. T	6. T	9. T	12. T

KEY TERMS–MATCHING

1. 15	5. 3	9. 9	13. 16
2. 5	6. 7	10. 10	14. 18
3. 12	7. 8	11. 20	15. 19
4. 1	8. 6	12. 17	

MULTIPLE CHOICE

1. a	5. d	9. c	13. a
2. c	6. c	10. b	
3. d	7. d	11. d	
4. a	8. a	12. d	

CASE PROBLEMS–ESSAY ANSWERS

1. No. Under Regulation A, although Ajax is exempt for registration purposes, it still must file a notification and an offering circular with the SEC.

2. Since this transaction meets the definition of "short-swing" trading by "insiders," Brown is liable for the profits to the corporation and its shareholders.

3. No. Under Section 3 of the 1933 Securities Act, securities marketing by non-profit organizations are exempt from registration requirements.

4. Yes. Since an untrue statement was made by Explorations in its registration statements, I is entitled to a return of his investment plus interest. Because Sammy and Edith were named as directors in the registration, they are liable to I unless they can apply the defense of due diligence to their case.

5. No. Since XYZ's assets are less than $10 million and the class of equity securities shareholders is less than 500, it does not have to register these securities.

ANSWERS TO CHAPTER 45–Accountant's Legal Liability

TRUE-FALSE

1. T	4. F	7. F	10. F
2. F	5. T	8. F	11. T
3. T	6. F	9. T	12. F

KEY TERMS–MATCHING

1. 9	5. 2	9. 4	13. 18
2. 11	6. 15	10. 1	14. 14
3. 12	7. 3	11. 16	15. 20
4. 7	8. 13	12. 17	

MULTIPLE CHOICE

1. c	5. c	9. c	13. b
2. a	6. c	10. a	
3. d	7. a	11. d	
4. b	8. b	12. c	

CASE PROBLEMS–ESSAY ANSWERS

1. Since accountant explicitly agreed to furnish a final report by May 15th and time was of the essence, failure to meet this deadline constitutes a material breach, which discharges clients payment obligation.

2. Accountant's failure to follow up on the discrepancies may constitute negligence, opening liability to the parties as "foreseeable plaintiffs" for compensatory damages. But since no fraud was involved on accountant's part, no basis for punitive damages exists.

3. Accountant wins. As owner of the working papers, accountant is not obligated to give them over to client.

4. Accountant has substantially performed on the contract. As such, contractually agreed upon compensation is due from client, reduced by damages caused by accountant's delay.

5. Prosecutor wins. Accountant must testify since federal law does not recognize an accountant/client privilege.

ANSWERS TO CHAPTER 46–Environmental Law

TRUE-FALSE

1. T	4. T	7. T	10. F
2. T	5. F	8. T	11. T
3. F	6. F	9. F	12. F

KEY TERMS–MATCHING

1. 8	5. 20	9. 14	13. 10
2. 11	6. 12	10. 7	14. 15
3. 16	7. 1	11. 3	15. 5
4. 9	8. 2	12. 19	

MULTIPLE CHOICE

1. d	5. b	9. a	13. d
2. c	6. b	10. c	
3. d	7. a	11. c	
4. d	8. d	12. c	

CASE PROBLEMS–ESSAY ANSWERS

1. Ajax domestic sales are subject to FIFRA regulations but its foreign sales–exports–are generally excluded from the Act's coverage except for the labeling requirement–"This product is not registered for use in the U.S.A."

2. If Executive meets the qualifications of an "innocent landowner" under recent CERCLA Amendments, it will not be liable for the clean-up costs.

3. RCRA regulations require shippers of hazardous waste to keep comprehensive records of the type, quantity, generator, route and disposal site of hazardous waste transported.

4. The EPA can obtain a seizure order through federal court if it can prove zalene poses an imminent hazard–unreasonable risk of serious, widespread health injury–to the public.

5. Probably none. The Superfund Act provides federal money for waste clean-ups undertaken by federal and state authorities and does not provide liability in private lawsuits for damages for environmental harm.

ANSWERS TO CHAPTER 47–International Business Law

TRUE-FALSE

1. F	4. T	7. T	10. T
2. T	5. F	8. F	11. T
3. F	6. T	9. F	12. F

KEY TERMS–MATCHING

1. 6	5. 18	9. 15	13. 12
2. 11	6. 13	10. 2	14. 1
3. 9	7. 14	11. 19	15. 4
4. 16	8. 10	12. 20	

MULTIPLE CHOICE

1. b	5. c	9. c	13. c
2. c	6. b	10. d	
3. d	7. a	11. b	
4. a	8. d	12. a	

CASE PROBLEMS–ESSAY ANSWERS

1. Tell Glewbenstein officials to enact laws preventing foreign investors and businesses from owning more than 49% of the glue company formed. Also, the laws should state that Glewbensteinians comprise a majority of the workers and management in the company.

2. Since Section 1 of the Sherman Act allows application of U.S. antitrust laws to foreign businesses, the agreement in question is probably illegal trade restraint in violation of this Act and therefore void.

3. Probably not. Today, only public, not commercial, acts of a foreign government are immune from a host country's laws and courts. Marketing the gambling seminar submits the Monaco government to U.S. jurisdiction over disputes arising out of conducting the business.

4. Since international commercial activity carries complications arising from language, customs, legal system and currency differences, advise the parties to include in their contract the following clauses: controlling language; choice of legal system; definition of important

terms; acceptable medium and method of payment; unforeseeable event risk-of-loss apportionment.

5. Only an official United Nations agency may seek advisory jurisdiction from I.C.J. Advisory opinions cannot be sought by individuals or governments.

ANSWERS TO CHAPTER 48–CyberLaw

TRUE-FALSE

1. F	4. F	7. T	10. T
2. T	5. T	8. T	11. T
3. F	6. F	9. F	12. F

KEY TERMS–MATCHING

1. 16	5. 20	9. 8	13. 9
2. 7	6. 2	10. 15	14. 6
3. 17	7. 14	11. 3	15. 18
4. 10	8. 4	12. 13	

MULTIPLE CHOICE

1. c	5. d	9. a	13. d
2. b	6. a	10. c	
3. d	7. b	11. b	
4. c	8. d	12. a	

CASE PROBLEMS–ESSAY ANSWERS

1. Clyde is liable to Elmer for libel–the defamatory e-mail message. If Aviatec fails to quickly remove the false statement from its workplace e-forum, it also might be liable. Aviatec might be considered a party to publication and vicariously liable to Elmer since the message was transmitted through its e-mail system.

2. Betty is civilly liable for violating the trade secret protection of the Best's family recipe by transmitting it to others. She is also criminally liable for violating the anti-theft provisions of the Economic Espionage Act.

3. Winston faces civil and criminal liability for violating the solicitation regulations and anti-theft provisions of the 1933 Securities Act.

4. Assuming that "Barr Ten" complies with the notice and consent provisions of the Uniform Electronic Transactions Act and the Electronic Signatures in Global and National Commerce Act, Pete is wrong. Under these laws, the Statutes of Frauds writing requirements cannot be used to invalidate otherwise enforceable e-commerce contracts.

5. No. Aviatec may properly review the personal messages its employees send one another over its workplace e-forum regardless of the messages' points of origin without invading employee privacy.

ANSWERS TO CHAPTER 49–Introduction to Property and Property Insurance

TRUE-FALSE

1. T	4. T	7. T	10. T
2. T	5. F	8. T	11. F
3. F	6. F	9. F	12. T

KEY TERMS–MATCHING

1. 3	5. 4	9. 1	13. 20
2. 7	6. 5	10. 15	14. 17
3. 9	7. 8	11. 18	15. 19
4. 12	8. 11	12. 16	

MULTIPLE CHOICE

1. b	5. b	9. a	13. a
2. d	6. a	10. c	
3. a	7. d	11. b	
4. c	8. d	12. d	

CASE PROBLEMS–ESSAY ANSWERS

1. For Susan's causa mortis gift to be valid, she must die as expected without revoking the gift beforehand. Since neither condition has occurred, the jewelry remains Susan's and Jan must return it.

2. Sam probably must keep the money. The law generally presumes that donees accept gifts when the property does not impose a burden on them and they are benefited from it. Since Sam remained silent for six months after receiving the money order, he is presumed to have accepted it.

3. Since the ring was on the floor when it was discovered, it would probably be considered lost and not misplaced. Therefore, Brown, the finder, would have superior rights to the ring vis-a-vis Smith. Brown wins.

4. Audrey recovers $30,000. She is under-insured under her "valued" policy, which calls for the insurer to pay the value specified in the policy and not the actual value at the time of loss.

5. M and F probably have superior rights to the items in question. The goods are most likely fixtures since they have been so firmly attached to the home as to lose their identity as personal property and have become part of the home. In addition, they most likely cannot be removed without material damage. Therefore, they were sold with the house to M and F.

ANSWERS TO CHAPTER 50–Bailments and Documents of Title

TRUE-FALSE

1. T	4. F	7. F	10. T
2. T	5. T	8. T	11. F
3. F	6. F	9. F	12. T

KEY TERMS–MATCHING

1. 4	5. 12	9. 13	13. 20
2. 5	6. 11	10. 15	14. 17
3. 3	7. 2	11. 19	15. 18
4. 6	8. 14	12. 16	

MULTIPLE CHOICE

1. d	5. b	9. d	13. b
2. a	6. a	10. a	
3. c	7. b	11. c	
4. d	8. b	12. d	

CASE PROBLEMS–ESSAY ANSWERS

1. The owner. The holder of a negotiable bill issued to a thief following bailment of stolen goods acquires no right to the goods as against the true owner, regardless of intervening due negotiation. A thief who delivers goods to a carrier and receives a negotiable document cannot extinguish the true owner's title.

2. C wins. U.C.C. 7-204(l) holds W's obligation to C as that of a reasonably careful warehouseman. In this case, reasonable care would have avoided the damage to the cheese. Although W may limit by contract the extent of liability by setting a damages maximum, the duty of reasonable care cannot be completely waived.

3. Yes. B, as the bailee for hire, has an absolute duty to deliver the goods to the right person. The innocent misdelivery is a conversion of the goods and B is not excused from liability.

4. Tracy, as the originating carrier receiving the cases of honey from Shipper Helen, issuing a through bill of lading naming same as taker, is liable to Sam for the loss. Tracy, however, has reimbursement rights against Terry.

5. Innkeeper suffers the loss. By Statute, innkeepers may avoid their common law strict liability for the belongings of their guests by providing a safe for guest use and posting notice of its existence. Here, however, no notice was given Guest of Innkeeper's safe. Innkeeper is therefore the insurer of Guest's watch under common law.

ANSWERS TO CHAPTER 51–Interests in Real Property

TRUE-FALSE

1. T	4. T	7. F	10. T
2. F	5. F	8. T	11. T
3. F	6. T	9. T	12. F

KEY TERMS–MATCHING

1. 5	5. 15	9. 6	13. 16
2. 4	6. 12	10. 7	14. 19
3. 3	7. 8	11. 10	15. 1
4. 9	8. 11	12. 17	

MULTIPLE CHOICE

1. c	5. c	9. a	13. d
2. d	6. a	10. c	
3. c	7. d	11. b	
4. a	8. a	12. c	

CASE PROBLEMS–ESSAY ANSWERS

1. Initially, A, B and C each have a one-third undivided interest in the land. Upon C conveying a one-third interest to D, D becomes a tenant in common with A and B, who remain joint-tenant owners of Greenacre for their two-thirds interest. When A dies, B acquires A's undivided one-third interest by right of survivorship and, as a result, holds a two-thirds interest as a tenant in common with D, who has an undivided one-third interest.

2. A's heirs. The qualification, which limited the fee estate in the land, runs against all subsequent owners. When the property no longer is used for the specific purpose mentioned, it automatically reverts to the grantor or the grantor's heirs through "possibility of reverter."

3. Mary's evicting Fran terminates the lease and ends any further rent obligation on Fran's part. Unless the lease contains a "survival clause" specifically providing for such liability, Fran is not liable for damages based on the difference between her monthly rent and what a replacement renter might pay.

4. It depends. If A's land is the dominant parcel of an appurtenant easement, then it is not necessary to refer specifically to that easement in the deed from B to C in order to give A the ongoing use of the easement over C's land. But if A's easement is in gross, then it must be mentioned in the deed from B to C, otherwise it is extinguished.

5. No. Since B and C acquire their interests by different instruments, which take effect at different times, the unities of time and title are lacking from the "four unities" required for joint tenancy. B and C are therefore tenants in common.

ANSWERS TO CHAPTER 52–Transfer and Control of Real Property

TRUE-FALSE

1. F	4. T	7. F	10. F
2. T	5. F	8. F	11. T
3. F	6. T	9. T	12. T

KEY TERMS–MATCHING

1. 2	5. 14	9. 3	13. 16
2. 11	6. 6	10. 9	14. 19
3. 8	7. 4	11. 17	15. 18
4. 7	8. 12	12. 20	

MULTIPLE CHOICE

1. c	5. b	9. a	13. a
2. d	6. d	10. c	
3. b	7. b	11. b	
4. c	8. c	12. d	

CASE PROBLEMS–ESSAY ANSWERS

1. Due to the two tobacco shops and three pharmacists selling cigarettes in violation of the dictates of the restrictive covenant, Frank can persuasively argue that the character of the area has changed and that the covenant has been abandoned. There would thus be no justification for enforcing the covenant against him.

2. Racially based restrictive covenants are invalid and unenforceable under both the Fair Housing Act and the 1947 U.S. Supreme Court decision in *Shelly vs. Kramer*. Advise the Chans to resubmit the bid and if they are turned down again for the same reason, bring action against the sellers to invalidate the restriction.

3. A prevails. Zoning ordinances may not be used to immediately end a lawful use of property existing prior to the passage of the ordinance. A will be permitted to operate the junkyard for a reasonable time.

4. Zoning ordinances that result in a "taking" of property without compensation are invalid. If the effect of a zoning restriction is to render nearly any beneficial use of property

impossible, then the ordinance is an invalid confiscation. The city is not certain whether its urban renewal plan will ever go into effect. During the interim, L is essentially barred from pursuing beneficial development of the site, given the plan's building compensation restriction. L should therefore argue that this part of the plan amounts to a confiscation and seek to invalidate it.

5. Possibly. The power of eminent domain can be delegated to R.R. if the increased width of the tracks would result in improved service to the public and therefore constitute promoting a "public purpose."

ANSWERS TO CHAPTER 53–Trusts and Decedents' Estates

TRUE-FALSE

1. T	4. T	7. F	10. T
2. T	5. F	8. F	11. F
3. T	6. F	9. F	12. F

KEY TERMS–MATCHING

1. 6	5. 1	9. 5	13. 18
2. 3	6. 4	10. 2	14. 9
3. 15	7. 14	11. 16	15. 19
4. 11	8. 12	12. 13	

MULTIPLE CHOICE

1. b	5. d	9. c	13. c
2. a	6. d	10. c	
3. b	7. d	11. d	
4. a	8. c	12. b	

CASE PROBLEMS–ESSAY ANSWERS

1. If properly created, creditors of a beneficiary of a spendthrift trust cannot attach the trust fund or its income but must wait until the income is received by the beneficiary to obtain payment.

2. The death of the trustee does not terminate the trust. Nor will the court terminate the trust simply because all beneficiaries ask for it. The court will decide according to the trust purposes of the settlor.

3. Yes. The birth of a child after execution of a will may revoke the will at least as far as that child is concerned.

4. Nothing. This is an example of abatement. Specific gifts must be satisfied first.

5. No. This is an example of ademption; the will provision is impossible to perform.